Christian Initiation
and
Baptism in the Holy Spirit

Evidence from the First Eight Centuries

Second, Revised Edition

A Michael Glazier Book

THE LITURGICAL PRESS
Collegeville, Minnesota

To Leo Cardinal Suenens

who led the Catholic charismatic renewal

into the heart of the church

A Michael Glazier Book published by The Liturgical Press.

Design by Frank Kacmarcik.

Library of Congress Cataloging-in-Publication Data

McDonnell, Kilian.
    Christian initiation and baptism in the Holy Spirit : evidence from the first eight centuries / Kilian McDonnell and George T. Montague.
    p. cm.
    "A Michael Glazier book."
    Includes bibliographical references and index.
    ISBN 0-8146-5009-0
    1. Baptism in the Holy Spirit—History of doctrines—Early church, ca. 30–600. 2. Baptism in the Holy Spirit—History of doctrines—Middle Ages, ca. 600–1500. 3. Initiation rites—Religious aspects—Christianity—History of doctrines—Early church, ca. 30–600. 4. Initiation rites—Religious aspects—Christianity—History of doctrines—Middle Ages, 600–1500. I. Montague, George T. II. Title.
    BT123.M145   1990   90-49536
    234'.12'09015—dc20   CIP

Précis

Christian Initiation and Baptism in the Holy Spirit (Collegeville: The Liturgical Press, A Michael Glazier Book, 1991) by Kilian McDonnell and George Montague

Up to now the explanations of baptism in the Holy Spirit were based on New Testament texts, whose interpretation was disputed. Now eleven post-biblical texts have been identified demonstrating how the early Christian authors understood baptism in the Holy Spirit. The evidence makes clear that the imparting of charisms, including the prophetic charisms, belong to the celebration (baptism, confirmation, Eucharist) by which new believers were made part of the Christian community and therefore Christians.

George Montague re-examines the New Testament texts and finds that the gift of the Spirit, including the charisms, was integral to Christian initiation. In the Synoptics the baptism of Jesus is the paradigm for this Spirit-imparting grace of initiation. In Luke-Acts the prophetic dimension of the Spirit predominates, but, despite opinions to the contrary, it is not possible to separate the gift of the Spirit from integral initiation. Paul too understands the Holy Spirit to be given in Baptism and charismatic expression to be a normal, though certainly not the only, effect of the sacrament. The aim of this charismatic grace is ministry for the building up of the community. In the Johannine literature, the Spirit appears primarily as the Spirit of life. But the Spirit also gives insight and understanding into revealed truth and reveals the future (either as forecasting or as interpreting the events), a function of the gift of prophecy. And Jesus' disciples will do greater works than he did, a statement that surely includes the charisms. All of this is made possible by the new birth of water and the Spirit, hence it is an endowment received from the moment of Christian initiation.

Kilian McDonnell examines the post-biblical texts. These texts testify to the historical span, geographical extension, and linguistic differentiation of theologies, liturgies, and cultures, which place the charisms within, or in reference to, initiation. They are Tertullian (during his Catholic years in a treatise in which Johannes Quasten says there is not a trace of his later Montanism) in North Africa at Carthage (c. 198), Origen at

Alexandria (c. 234), Hilary in Gaul at Poitiers (c. 350), Cyril in Palestine at Jerusalem (c. 364), Basil in Cappadocia at Caesarea (366 and 374–75), Gregory Nazianzus at Constantinople (380), in Syria Philoxenus at Mabbug (end of the 5th and beginning of the 6th centuries), John the Solitary at Apamea (430–50), Theodoret at Cyrrhus (c. 444), and Joseph Hazzaya (beginning of the 8th century) at Qardu (in contemporary Iraq). John Chrysostom (c. 392–93) and Severus at Antioch (end of the 6th and beginning of the 7th centuries) recall that in the apostolic paradigm, the charisms, including the prophetic, were imparted during Christian initiation. Almost the whole of the Mediterranean seaboard bears witness, representing Latin, Greek, and Syriac cultures.

In brief, these authors demonstrate that the experience of baptism in the Holy Spirit is integral to Christian intiation. Therefore it belongs not to private piety but to public liturgy. If baptism in the Holy Spirit is integral to those sacraments, which are constitutive of the church, then baptism in the Spirit is normative.

Some of the witnesses are not minor characters. Tertullian, quite apart from his later association with Montanism, is perhaps the greatest theologian of the West during the first millennium, Augustine excepted. Origen is a towering figure. Hilary, Cyril, Basil, and Gregory are all Doctors of the Church, a title given to those who have a weightier role in identifying the faith and experience of the church. Philoxenus is a major figure in the Syrian church.

This scholarly, nontechnical presentation was the basis of the Heart of the Church Consultation, which met from May 6–11, 1990, at Techny, Illinois. Ten theologians and three pastors discussed the meaning of this research for the life of the church. The consultation issued a thirty-page popular pastoral document which presents the essentials of the biblical texts and those from the early church, indicating how they impact the life of the local church. The document is *Fanning the Flame: What Does Baptism in the Holy Spirit Have to Do with Christian Initiation?* (eds. Kilian McDonnell and George Montague; Collegeville: The Liturgical Press, A Michael Glazier Book, 1991). At the beginning of the document are printed two letters of encouragement from Bishops Samuel Jacobs and Joseph McKinney.

Contents

Abbreviations vii

Introduction xi

PART ONE:
The New Testament Evidence

1 Fire and Power: Spirit-Baptism in Q and Mark 3

2 Works of Mercy and Righteousness:
Spirit-Baptism in Matthew 15

3 Pentecostal Fire: Spirit-Baptism in Luke-Acts 23

4 Spiritual Body and Spiritual Rock:
Spirit-Baptism in the Pauline Tradition and Hebrews 42

5 The Witness of Rome—1 Peter:
Baptismal Grace Is Saving and Charismatic 56

6 Living Water: Spirit-Baptism in John 66

7 Charism and Community: Spirit-Baptism and the
Building of the Church 73

8 Conclusions: Spirit-Baptism in the New Testament 86

PART TWO:
The Early Post-Biblical Evidence

Introduction 93

9 Tertullian: African/Enthusiast/Rigorist 104

10 Tertullian:
Montanism and Reluctant Withdrawal of Communion 116

11 Origen: "Baptism Is the Principle
and Source of the Divine Charisms" 133

12 Origen: "No River Is Good Except the Jordan" 144

13 Hilary of Poitiers: The Poet Bishop as Bridge 155

14 Hilary of Poitiers: The River of God and Intense Joy 172

15 Cyril of Jerusalem:
Apostolic Memories in the Very Theater of Salvation 191

16 Cyril of Jerusalem:
The Geography and History of the Spirit 207

17 Cyril of Jerusalem:
From Outside the Mystery to Inside 219

18 Cyril of Jerusalem: "We Can Also See and Feel"—
The Transformation of Jerusalem 233

19 Apostolic Constitutions: Standardizing the Charisms 252

20 John Chrysostom: From Jordan to Calvary 259

21 John Chrysostom:
Then and Now—A Study in Zeal and Apathy 282

22 Philoxenus: "Our Baptism is the Holy Spirit" 299

23 Philoxenus and the Syrians: The Monasticized Charisms 321

24 Conclusion: Spirit-Baptism and Initiation
in the Early Post-Biblical Tradition 339

25 General Conclusions:
Where We Were and Where We Are 350

General Index 383

Index of Biblical References 389

Abbreviations

1QH *Hôdāyôt* (*Thanksgiving Hymns* from Qumran Cave 1)
1QS *Serek hayyaḥad* (*Community Rule, Manual of Discipline,*
from Qumran Cave 1)

AB Anchor Bible
AC *Apostolic Constitutions*
AH *Against Heresies*
AnBoll Analecta Bollandiana
Apoc Bar Syriac Apocalypse of Baruch
ATR *Anglican Theological Review*
AV Authorized (King James) Version

b.Hag. (*b.* = *Babylonian Talmud*), *Hagiga*

CAO *Cyrilli Hierosolymarum Archiepiscopi Opera Quae Supersunt*
Omnia, 2 vols.; eds. W. K. Reischl, J. Rupp (Munich:
Keck, 1848–1850)
CChr Corpus Christianorum
CL *Catechetical Lectures*
CPJ *Commentary on the Prologue of John*
CPJE *Commentary on the Prologue of John in English*
CSCO Corpus Scriptorum Christianorum Orientalium
CSEL Corpus Scriptorum Ecclesiasticorum Latinorum

DB   *The Discourses of Philoxenus*
DBSup   *Dictionnaire de la Bible, Supplément*
DTC   *Dictionnaire de Théologie Catholique*

EH   *Ecclesiastical History*
ExpTim   *Expository Times*

FCML   Fragments of the Commentaries of Matthew and Luke
FL   Fragments of Luke
FM   Fragments of Matthew

GNO   *Gregorii Nysseni Opera*, 8 vols.; ed. W. Jaeger (Leiden: Brill, 1960–1972)

HeyJ   *Heythrop Journal*
HMS   *History of the Monks in Syria*
HSMS   *Homiliae Selectae Mar-Jacob, Sarugensis*

JBL   *Journal of Biblical Literature*
JEH   *Journal of Ecclesiastical History*
JES   *Journal of Ecumenical Studies*
JTS   *Journal of Theological Studies*
Jub.   *Jubilees*

LTK   *Lexikon für Theologie und Kirche*
LP   *Letter to Patricius*

Mansi   *Sacrorum Conciliorum Nova et Amplissima Collectio*
MBC   *Montfaucon Baptismal Catecheses*
MC   *Mystagogical Catecheses*

NAB   New American Bible
NABR   New American Bible, Revised New Testament
NAS   New American Standard Version
NCE   *New Catholic Encyclopedia*
NEB   New English Bible
NICNT   New International Commentary on the New Testament
NIV   New International Version

NJBC New Jerome Biblical Commentary
NovT *Novum Testamentum*
NovTSup Supplement to *Novum Testamentum*
NRT *La Nouvelle Revue Théologique*
NTS *New Testament Studies*

OB *On Baptism*
OCP *Orientalia Christiana Periodica*
OrSyr *L'Orient Syrien*

PG Patrologia Graeca
PH *Prescription Against the Heretics*
PKBC A. Papadopoulos-Kerameus, *Varia Graeca Sacra* (St. Petersburg: University of St. Petersburg, 1909) xx–xxv and 154–183.
PL Patrologia Latina
PO Patrologia Orientalis
PWK Pauly-Wissowa, *Real-Encyclopädie der classischen Altertumswissenschaft*

RB *Revue Biblique*
RCIA Rite for the Christian Initiation of Adults
RevScRel *Revue des Sciences Religieuses*
RHE *Revue d'Histoire Ecclésiastique*
RSR *Recherches de Science Religieuse*
RSV Revised Standard Version

SBC *Huit Catéchèses Baptismales*, ed. A. Wenger (Paris, 1970); Sources Chrétiennes 50bis.
SC Sources Chrétiennes
SE *Studia Evangelica*
Sib. Or. Sibylline Oracles
SNTS MS Society for New Testament Studies Monograph Series
ST *Studia Theologica*

TDNT *Theological Dictionary of the New Testament*
TRE *Theologische Realenzyklopädie*

TS   Theological Studies
TZ   Theologische Zeitschrift

VCaro   Verbum Caro
VC   Vigiliae Christianae

ZThK   Zeitschrift für Theologie und Kirche

Introduction

The results of a *Christianity Today*-Gallup poll published in 1980 indicated that 19 percent of the total population of the United States were Pentecostals or Charismatics. Broken down by denominations, the poll reported as charismatics 18 percent of the Roman Catholics and 22 percent of all Protestants. Among the latter, 20 percent of the Baptists, 18 percent of the Methodists, 20 percent of the Lutherans, and 16 percent of the Presbyterians were charismatics.[1] An international survey published in 1988 claimed that aside from the 176 million Classical and Independent Pentecostals, 123 million Protestant and Catholic Christians have in the last three decades experienced what is commonly referred to as the "baptism in the Holy Spirit."[2] Catholics active in the charismatic renewal in 1988 numbered slightly over 10 million while "post-charismatic Catholics" (those irregular, or less active, or annually active, or formerly active, or engaged elsewhere in church ministry) numbered

[1] K. S. Kantzer, "The Charismatics Among Us," *Christianity Today*, February 22, 1980, 25–29.

[2] Though other terms are occasionally used, such as "release of the Spirit," "renewal in the Spirit," "effusion (outpouring) of the Spirit," or even "being born again," we shall in this study use the most commonly accepted expression, "baptism in the Holy Spirit."

over 53 million.[3] The same study claims that as many as 54,000 persons a day are being touched by the experience, leading to an annual increment of 19 million.[4] Even should these figures prove to be inflated, the spread of the charismatic movement, particularly in the third world, and its success at evangelization, is a major challenge to the wider church, especially those churches or communions with a strong sacramental emphasis.

This book is not, however, a study of Pentecostalism or the charismatic movement. It is rather a research into that early Christian literature which Classical Pentecostals, charismatics, and sacramentalists as well claim in some sense to be theirs. In this we hope the study will be of service both to Classical Pentecostals and charismatics on the one hand, and sacramental theologians and liturgists on the other.

In our study of the New Testament the "baptism in the Holy Spirit" refers (as we hope to demonstrate) to the integral event of Christian initiation. But the contemporary experience called the "baptism in the Spirit" often is not a first conversion but a new departure in one's Christian life; it involves an openness to and a seeking of one or more of the charisms. It is the latter point that sets this experience apart from other conversion or "new departure" experiences. Is the experience the same thing that the New Testament understands by being "baptized in the Holy Spirit"?

Since the expression is used in both senses, the reader will have to determine from the context whether we are speaking about the New Testament event or about the contemporary experience. Because the awakening today often occurs years after sacramental baptism, a plethora of attempts have been undertaken to explain the experience in terms of New Testament evidence—as a second moment or blessing (the neo-Pentecostal

[3] Pastoral experience seems to confirm the claim of this study, that the number of persons touched by the "baptism in the Holy Spirit" far exceeds the number who regularly attend prayer meetings. Many who experienced a genuine renewal of their spiritual life have found other expressions of it either in support groups or in ministry.

[4] *Dictionary of Pentecostal and Charismatic Movements*, ed. S. M. Burgess and G. B. McGee; assoc. ed. Patrick Alexander (Zondervan, 1988); reprinted in *International Bulletin of Missionary Research*, July 1988. A more conservative figure of 60 million is given by H. I. Lederle, *Treasures Old and*

position), as a development of the grace of baptism (the "sacramental" interpretation more common among the mainline churches), or as a "new departure" unrelated to the sacrament. The Catholic tradition of confirmation is a further complicating factor. The variety of interpretations, recently surveyed and documented in a thorough study by H. I. Lederle, indicates that there is no clear agreement on the interpretation of the New Testament evidence.[5] Within the rites of initiation itself, the roles of water-baptism, laying on of hands, prayer, and anointing still divide the exegetes. As for the early post-biblical period, as far as we know there has been no in-depth study of the relationship of the charisms to the rites of initiation in the first centuries.

The questions we pose here fall into two categories. First, what do the biblical texts understand to constitute integral Christian initiation? Is there a broader biblical basis for the baptism in the Holy Spirit than the usual texts from the book of Acts? Do the texts have anything to say about the relation of baptism in the Spirit to Christian initiation? Secondly, does the life of the early post-biblical church, in particular its celebration of Christian initiation, throw any light on the baptism in the Holy Spirit?

In Part I George Montague investigates the Scriptural evidence; in Part II Kilian McDonnell researches the pertinent writings of Tertullian, Hilary of Poitiers, Cyril of Jerusalem, Basil of Caesarea, Gregory Nazianzus, John Chrysostom, John of Apamea, Philoxenus, Theodoret, Severus, and Joseph Hazzaya. No claim is made that all of the relevant texts up to the eighth

New: Interpretations of "Spirit-Baptism" in the Charismatic Renewal Movement (Peabody, Mass.: Hendrickson, 1988) xi. For a history of the development of Pentecostalism and the charismatic movement see W. J. Hollenweger, The Pentecostals (Minneapolis: Augsburg, 1972); E. D. O'Connor, The Pentecostal Movement in the Catholic Church (Notre Dame: Ave Maria, 1971); K. and D. Ranaghan, Catholic Pentecostals Today (South Bend: Charismatic Renewal Services, 1983); M. Harper, As at the Beginning: The Twentieth Century Pentecostal Revival (Plainfield, N.J.: Logos, 1971); V. Synan, In the Latter Days: The Outpouring of the Holy Spirit in the Twentieth Century (Ann Arbor: Servant, 1984).

[5] Lederle, Treasures: see note 1.

century have been identified. A commonly written final chapter proposes our conclusions.

Our special thanks go to scholars and experts we consulted in the process of this study: Knute Anderson, O.S.B., Allan Bouley, O.S.B., Sebastian Brock, Raniero Cantalamessa, O.F.M. Cap., Harold Cohen, S.J., Emmanuel Cutrone, Robert Eno, S.S., Patrick G. Henry, William Kurz, S.J., Boniface Luykx, Francis Martin, Joseph Milner, Cecil M. Robeck, Jr., Dolores Schuh, C.H.M., Columba Stewart, O.S.B., Francis Sullivan, S.J., William Tabbernee, and Edward Yarnold, who made invaluable comments on our work. Special thanks to Frank Kacmarcik for his care in the design of the book. Also to the staff of Marynook House of the Lord, Galesville, Wisconsin, and Holy Spirit Monastery, Steubenville, Ohio, for the hospitality they provided for meetings of the authors.

Kilian McDonnell, O.S.B.
George T. Montague, S.M.

A Word on the Second Edition

Further research has led to this second, revised edition. Important new evidence has now been incorporated from the First Letter of Peter and from Origen. A number of additional entries have been made throughout, and our major conclusions have been significantly strengthened.

Part One:

The New Testament Evidence

Chapter One

Fire and Power: Spirit-Baptism in Q and Mark

For our question the most logical point of entry into the New Testament is the very term "baptism in the Holy Spirit."[1]

[1] Major studies that deal with the exegesis of the texts are: F. D. Bruner, *A Theology of the Holy Spirit: The Pentecostal Experience and the New Testament Witness* (Grand Rapids: Eerdmans, 1970) with bibliography; J. D. G. Dunn, *Baptism in the Holy Spirit* (Naperville, Ill.: Allenson, 1970); *Jesus and the Spirit* (Philadelphia: Westminster, 1975) with bibliography; C. K. Barrett, *The Holy Spirit and the Gospel Tradition* (New York: Macmillan, 1947); G. W. H. Lampe, *The Seal of the Spirit: A Study in the Doctrine of Baptism and Confirmation in the New Testament and the Fathers* (London: Longmans, Green, 1951); H. Gunkel, *The Influence of the Holy Spirit* (Philadelphia: Fortress, 1979; German orig. 1888); E. Schweizer, *The Holy Spirit* (Philadelphia: Fortress, 1980); R. Schnackenburg, *Baptism in the Thought of St. Paul* (New York: Herder & Herder, 1964); M. Quesnel, *Baptisés dans l'Esprit* (Paris: Cerf, 1985) with extensive bibliography; H. Ervin, *Conversion-Initiation and the Baptism in the Holy Spirit* (Peabody, Mass.: Hendrickson, 1984); C. F. D. Moule, *The Holy Spirit* (Grand Rapids: Eerdmans, 1978); P. Schoonenberg, "Le Baptême d'Esprit-Saint," *Concilium* 18 (1976) 71–96; H. D. Hunter, *Spirit-Baptism: A Pentecostal Alternative* (Lanham, Md.: University Press, 1983); F. Martin, *Baptism in the Holy Spirit: A Biblical Foundation* (Steubenville, Ohio: Franciscan University Press, 1986)—revised English version of "Le baptême dans l'Esprit, tradition du Nouveau Testament et vie de l'Eglise," *NRT* 106 (1984) 23–58; Y. Congar, *I Believe in the Holy Spirit* II (New York: Seabury, 1983) 189–201.

While the noun *baptism* does not appear in the New Testament phrase, the verb "baptize" with the Spirit as complement appears eight times.[2] Of these, four are the promise of John the Baptist that the one coming after him will baptize in (the) Holy Spirit (Mark 1:8; Matt 3:11; Luke 3:16; John 1:33). The fact that this saying appears at the beginning of all four gospels argues for its belonging to one of the earliest strata of the gospel tradition. It comes in two forms. In Mark and John, the coming one "will baptize in (the) Holy Spirit," while the Q tradition represented by Matthew and Luke says that he "will baptize with Holy Spirit *and fire*."[3] Which of these versions is nearer to the original saying of the Baptist? And, assuming that the Baptist did indeed announce another coming after him, what specific role did this saying assign to him?

In Q: The Meaning of "Fire"

The Q source fortunately provides its own interpretation of the fire image. It signifies judgment: "His winnowing fork is in his hand, and he will clear his threshing floor and gather his wheat into the granary, but the chaff he will burn with unquenchable *fire* (Matt 3:12; Luke 3:17). Several factors argue for the Q version, "with Holy Spirit and fire," meaning the wind or spirit of searing judgment, being nearer to the original saying of the Baptist:

(1) The association of *fire* and *judgment* was used by the prophets in their preaching (Amos 7:4; Mal 3:2, 19) and was greatly exploited by the apocalyptists of later Judaism.[4] The Qumran community, to which the Baptist was probably ex-

---

[2] I include among the eight the trinitarian formula of Matthew 28:19 and Paul's "In one Spirit we were all baptized into one body" (1 Cor 12:13) but not his reference to being "washed . . . in the Spirit of our God" (1 Cor 3:11) nor to being "baptized . . . in the cloud and in the sea" (1 Cor 10:2), quite clearly allusions to "baptism in the Spirit."

[3] "Q," standing for the German *Quelle* ("source"), indicates that source largely of sayings of Jesus not found in Mark, from which both Matthew and Luke (independently) drew.

[4] 1 *Enoch* 100:9; 102:1; *Sib. Or.* 3:543; 4:176-78; 5:274, 377; 2 *Apoc. Bar.* 48:39, 43.

posed, spoke of "destruction in the fires of darkness" (1QS IV.13). (2) The association of *spirit* and *judgment* is also a prophetic theme (Isa 4:4; 27:8; Jer 4:11-12). (3) *Spirit* and *fire* are joined in Isaiah 33:11 ("My spirit shall consume you like fire," NAB); and *spirit*, *fire* and *judgment* are joined in Isaiah 4:4: "a spirit of judgment and a spirit of fire." (4) The absence of "fire" from Mark and John can be explained by the fact that neither evangelist presents the Baptist as an announcer of judgment. It is more plausible that they would have omitted "fire" from a text or a tradition which they found difficult to reconcile with the actual ministry of Jesus than that Q would have added it, with the additional harsh words about judgment, to a text that said nothing about judgment.[5] The "fire" of Q does not present a problem for Matthew and Luke because Q also deals with the fact that Jesus did not actually fit the Baptist's portrayal. It does so in the inquiry by John's disciples as to whether Jesus was the one the Baptist foretold or should they expect someone else (Matt 11:2-6; Luke 7:18-23). Thus the redefinition of Jesus' role is explicitly dealt with and, implicitly, a reinterpretation of the fire image.

Most commentators, then, hold that the "Holy Spirit" foretold by John the Baptist was, in the Baptist's mind, the kind of spirit of purification and judgment foretold by Isaiah 4:4 and described in the Qumran literature thus:

"God in his mysterious insight and glorious wisdom has assigned an end to the existence of injustice, and at the appointed time of the visitation he will destroy it forever. Then truth will appear in the world forever, for it has defiled itself in the ways of wickedness during the reign of injustice until the time decreed for judgment. Then God will purify by his truth all the deeds of man and will refine for himself the frame of man, removing all spirit of injustice from within his flesh, and purifying him by *the spirit of holiness* from every wicked action. And he will sprinkle upon him the spirit of truth like waters for

[5] So J. D. G. Dunn, "The Birth of a Metaphor—Baptized in Spirit," *ExpTim* 89 (1978) 135-36. We are not discussing here whether Mark or John knew of Q but whether the tradition that preceded both Mark and Q spoke of "fire."

purification (to remove) all the abominations of falsehood (in which) he has defiled himself."[6]

John's baptism was a ritual of repentance and preparation for this coming of God; the baptismal waters of the Jordan, received with the proper dispositions, were the way to avoid being consumed by the coming fire of God's judgment.[7] That John should link the future event with a "coming one" is not surprising in the light of Malachi 3:1-2, which speaks of the coming "messenger of the covenant" who will be like the refiner's fire.

Mark: Anointing with Power

If Mark introduces Jesus as the one who baptizes with the Holy Spirit, what does this mean, and how does Jesus do it? How, in other words, does Mark understand Jesus to fulfill the prophecy of the Baptist? The evangelist, as we have noted, is not interested in the Baptist's preaching of judgment nor in Jesus' Spirit-baptism as fire. The Baptist is simply a herald of Jesus. But this Jesus is the "more powerful one" (Mark 1:7), and the association of the Spirit with power gives us our first clue to Mark's understanding of Jesus' Spirit-filled mission. The Holy Spirit comes upon Jesus at his baptism by John, visibly at least to Jesus, in the form of a dove (1:9-11), symbol of the be-

[6] 1QS IV 18-21, trans. M. A. Knibb, *The Qumran Community* (Cambridge University Press). *See also* 1 QH 16:1-12. On the spirit in the community of Qumran, *see* G. T. Montague, *The Holy Spirit, Growth of a Biblical Tradition* (New York: Paulist, 1976) 116-24.

[7] Did Jesus himself and/or his disciples during the public ministry baptize, and if so, what kind of baptism was it? John 3:22-26 indicates that Jesus baptized, and the text has much to commend its historicity, since the report does not fit the evangelist's theological interests, and later on (4:2) someone, probably a redactor, felt obliged to say that only the disciples baptized. Since, according to the evangelist himself, the Spirit was not given until Jesus was glorified (7:39), the baptism was probably similar to that of the Baptist, and it seems that Jesus ceased to baptize when he left Judea, the arena of John's ministry, for Galilee. *See* R. E. Brown, *The Gospel according to John* AB 29 (Garden City: Doubleday, 1966) 155, 164; J. A. Fitzmyer, *Luke the Theologian: Aspects of His Teaching* (Mahwah, N.J.: Paulist, 1989) 95.

ginning of a new age and new creation.[8] Concomitantly, the heavenly voice proclaims him as God's son. Therefore the baptism in the Holy Spirit is first of all something Jesus receives, though Mark is careful to note that it is not at the moment of the baptism by John, but rather after Jesus' coming up from the water that the Spirit is manifested (a sequence Matthew and Luke will reinforce). The rending of the heavens and the heavenly voice highlight the giving of the Spirit to Jesus as a sovereign intervention of God, not as an automatic effect of John's baptism. To the extent that Mark sees Jesus' baptism as the foundational model for Christian baptism, it is evident that two moments can be distinguished, that is, immersion into the water and the gift of the Spirit. Yet these two moments are inseparable and integral to Christian initiation, all the more so since the water rite recalls not John's baptism but that of Jesus.

After the baptism, the Spirit first drives Jesus into the desert to encounter Satan, where he relives successfully Israel's forty-years' testing. Thus in this early view Jesus is subject to the Spirit.

It is not sufficient, however, to say that the Baptist's prophecy that Jesus would baptize with the Holy Spirit was fulfilled when the Spirit was manifested at Jesus' baptism. The verb *he will baptize* is not passive but active. The Spirit is not merely something Jesus receives but something by which he acts upon others or communicates to them. Thus we must look beyond the baptism to Jesus' public ministry. Though the word *baptism* reappears only in Mark 10:38-39, his empowerment by the Spirit is implicit in the *exousia* (power, authority) by which he functions. Already in John's prophecy, Jesus' baptizing in the Holy Spirit is explicitly identified with his being "the more powerful

---

[8] Although a number of scholars suggest that the dove is meant to evoke the dove of spring-time in Canticles 2:12, identified in the Targum as the "voice of the Holy Spirit of salvation," the more likely identification is with Genesis 1:2, where the spirit of God is described as a bird hovering over the waters ("like a dove" according to Ben Zoma, *b. Hag* 15a) and/or with Genesis 8:8-12, where the dove is the herald of the new world after the flood. Swete, Taylor, Grundman, Gnilka, Lane, J. Ernst. *See further* L. E. Keck, "The Spirit and the Dove," *NTS* 17 (1970) 41–67; H. Greeven, *TDNT* 6:63-72; A. Feuillet, "Le Symbolisme de la colombe dans les récits évangeliques du baptême," *RSR* 46 (1958) 524–44.

one'' (*ischuroteros*, 1:7-8). His power and authority are manifested in his "new teaching" (1:22), in his healings (1:32-34) and forgiveness of sins (2:10), but particularly in his exorcisms.

It is in the exorcisms that the role of the Holy Spirit in this empowerment becomes explicit. Mark relates four specific cases of exorcism: the demoniac in the synagogue (1:22-28), the "legion" in the possessed man of Gerasa (5:1-20), the Canaanite woman's daughter (7:24-30), and the "epileptic" boy (9:14-29). In addition he makes the general report: "Unclean spirits would catch sight of him, fling themselves down at his feet, and shout, 'You are the Son of God!' '' (Mark 3:11). The exorcisms are, in Mark's view, a revelation of the Spirit that came upon Jesus at his baptism. This appears most clearly in the dispute with the scribes who accuse Jesus of being possessed by Beelzebul and of casting out demons by the prince of demons. In his response Jesus claims to be the stronger man foretold by the Baptist, who binds the vaunted strong-man, Satan, and he protests that the spirit by which he casts out Satan is the Holy Spirit (3:22-30).

This struggle with Satan is so important a motif for Mark that he models other scenes of the ministry on the temptation account and the exorcisms. Thus the traps laid by his enemies are *temptations:*

"The Pharisees came forward and began to argue with him, seeking from him a sign from heaven *to test him.* (Mark 8:11—*perizein*, the same word used in 1:13 for Jesus' paradigmatic encounter with Satan.)

"The Pharisees approached and asked, 'Is it lawful for a husband to divorce his wife?' They were testing him. (Mark 10:2: again the same word.)

"They sent some Pharisees and Herodians to him to ensnare him in his speech. . . . 'Is it lawful to pay the census tax to Caesar or not? Should we pay or should we not pay?' Knowing their hypocrisy he said to them, 'Why are you *testing* me?' '' (Mark 12:15: again the same word.)

Even the resistance of his own disciples is described as Jesus' meeting the Satan of the desert all over again:

"At this he turned around and, looking at his disciples, *rebuked*

Peter [the same Greek word used for rebuking Satan in 1:25; 3:12; 9:25] and said, 'Get behind me, Satan. You are thinking not as God does, but as human beings do' '' (Mark 8:32-33).

Hence, the healings and especially the exorcisms (which belong to the earliest stratum of the gospel tradition) in Mark function as confirming signs of Jesus' identity as revealed in the baptism: he is the Son of God (1:1; 3:11; 5:7) upon whom the Spirit rests. This appears then to be Mark's understanding of Jesus as baptizer in the Holy Spirit—a charismatic ministry of healing and a binding of Satan in all his manifestations, whether through evil spirits or the resistance of his enemies and even of his own disciples.[9]

Does Mark expect this ministry to continue in the church? Since we may assume that his interest in writing his gospel was nor archival but rather to portray the foundations for what is actually going on in his community, Jesus' commissioning his apostles (disciples?[10]) to preach and deliver from evil spirits (3:14-15) has a paradigmatic value. It is immediately after this constitution of the *twelve* that occurs the dispute about the Spirit by which *Jesus* operates. This can hardly be accidental. On the one hand, ministry in the Christian community is authorized and empowered by the authority and the Spirit of Jesus. On the other hand, all ministry of the Spirit after Jesus is to be done only *in his name*.[11]

Thus Mark sees Jesus' own baptism in the Holy Spirit not only as a proclamation of divine sonship but also as an anointing with divine power, which Jesus exercises through healings and exorcisms, whether performed by himself personally or through the disciples.[12]

[9] *See* J. M. Robinson, *The Problem of History in Mark* (Naperville, Ill.: Allenson, 1957) 33–53.

[10] The words "whom he named apostles" of 3:14 are missing from some important manuscripts, leading some scholars to hold they are an interpolation from Luke 6:13. But they are present in Sinaiticus, Vaticanus, and other important manuscripts, so that the balance of probabilities lies in favor or their authenticity.

[11] That they did so can be inferred from 9:38, where the disciples forbid *others* to cast out devils in the name of Jesus.

[12] Jesus' "baptism in the Spirit could well be taken as typical of all later

The Baptism of the Passion

There is, however, a subtle shift in Mark's understanding of the meaning of Jesus' baptism, and it occurs in the latter part of the gospel which deals with the scandal of the cross.[13] To the request of James and John to sit at the right and left of Jesus in his kingdom, Jesus replies: "You do not know what you are asking. Can you drink the cup that I drink or be *baptized* with the *baptism* with which I am *baptized*? . . . The cup that I drink, you will drink, and with the *baptism* with which I am *baptized*, you will be baptized" (10:38-39). The cup is clearly an allusion to the passion, which Jesus in the agony calls his cup (Mark 14:36). That he should also call his passion a baptism is unusual.

Why should this term be chosen? The majority of commentators hold that the language is metaphorical for the bath of suffering into which Jesus will be immersed.[14] Some in addition hold that John's practice of baptism influenced the choice of the image, inasmuch as it was a ritual dramatizing of God's judgment upon sin.[15] The most obvious interpretation, however, is that Jesus is alluding not to John's baptism in general but to the event of his own baptism by John, which Jesus now understands to have been a ritual preparation for his surrender to the

Spirit-baptisms—the means by which God brings each to follow in Jesus' footsteps. . . . Jesus' anointing with the Spirit was what equipped him for his messianic ministry of healing and teaching (Acts 10:38)." Dunn, *Baptism*, 32. This holds true whatever the position one takes concerning the relation of the Spirit to water-baptism, whether this be Jesus' baptism by John or subsequent Christian baptism.

[13] It is more in keeping with Mark's intentional plot-development to understand him as introducing the passion motif here as a new (or previously hidden) dimension of the baptism of Jesus, than to interpret the baptism of 1:9-11 as already indicating Jesus' desire to sacrifice himself for sinful humanity. So Feuillet, "La coupe de la baptême de la passion," *RB* 74 (1967) 376, against Cullmann, Hunter, Fuller, Grundmann, Cranfield.

[14] This was prepared for by the Old Testament passages in which the imagery of submersion was used for being overwhelmed by suffering and disaster (Pss 42:7-8, 69:2-3, 15; Job 9:31; 22:11; Isa 43:2; Jonah 2:3-6) and the occasional use of *baptizein* in some of the Greek versions of these passages. Cf. W. L. Lane, *The Gospel according to Mark* (Grand Rapids: Eerdmans, 1974) 380. Cranfield, Ernst, Gnilka, Swete, Taylor, and others maintain the metaphorical sense on the basis of passages such as those cited.

[15] Lane, *Mark*, 380–81; Feuillet, "La coupe," 381.

judgment of God in his expiatory death.[16] If so, then what was unique about Jesus' baptism—namely, the descent of the Spirit—must also be in the background of the "baptism" metaphor here.[17]

Consequently, this passage is meant by Mark to be an important reinterpretation of Jesus' baptism in the Spirit. In keeping with Mark's shift to the surprise of the passion in this section, beginning at 8:31, Jesus' Spirit-baptism is not only an empowering to heal and exorcise the evil spirits; it is an anointing also to become the Servant who gives his life as a ransom for many (the climactic line of the cup-baptism pericope, 10:45). Though the gift of the Spirit is not expressly associated with Jesus' salvific death, as, for example in John 19:30, the metaphor "baptism," echoing as it does Jesus' own baptism, certainly raises the question of the relation of Jesus' death to the imparting of the Spirit manifested in the baptism. At any rate, Mark intends his community, faced with the threat of martyrdom, to hear both dimensions of the Spirit-impelled life: the ministry of power but also the ministry of fidelity unto death.

Sacramental Allusion?

There are commentators who would even see a sacramental allusion in both cup and baptism—at least in verse 39, which speaks of the disciples' share in both—the cup being an allusion to the eucharist, the baptism to the Christian sacrament of initiation.[18] The sacramental interpretation is difficult to prove, be-

[16] So W. F. Flemington, *The New Testament Doctrine of Baptism* (London: SPCK, 1948) 31-32; G. W. H. Lampe, *Seal*, 39; and Feuillet, "La coupe," 376, who holds that Jesus' baptism by John was an act of solidarity with sinful humanity, thus preparing an expiatorial understanding of 10:38.

[17] J. G. D. Dunn, "The Birth of a Metaphor—Baptized in Spirit," 134-38, shows how the Q tradition understands Jesus' being "baptized with the Holy Spirit and *fire*" to be fulfilled in his passion. In Luke 12:49-50 Jesus does associate the image of fire with that of baptism, referring to his passion, thus suggesting that the Holy Spirit can only be given by Jesus' passing through death. Though the fire imagery is missing from Mark, the same idea underlies Jesus' allusion to his baptism here in 10:38.

[18] Best, Borman, Feuillet, S. E. Johnson. Others listed by Feuillet, "La coupe," 386: Bacon, Lohmeyer, Rawlinson, Schelkle, Bartsch, Taylor, Lampe, Richardson, Carrington, Oepke.

cause the metaphors make perfect sense in the light of their
Old Testament precedents and Jesus' use of the cup metaphor
later for his passion (14:36). It is not necessary, of course, to assume that verse 39 refers to the actual martyrdom of James and
John, since apostolic suffering alone would suffice to share in
the cup and baptism of Jesus. But does that rule out a
sacramental allusion here? Possibly not. There is some plausibility in the suggestion that the "baptism" metaphor is an intrusion into the Markan text, for in the parallel passage in
Matthew 20:23 the baptism metaphor is missing. Was it missing
in the version of Mark known to Matthew? Or did Matthew intentionally omit it?

The reasons advanced for Matthew's omitting the metaphor
are varied: that he wished to eliminate an obscure metaphor,[19]
or that he intended to reserve "baptism" for the sacramental,
not a metaphorical, sense; or that he knew that John, unlike
James (cf. Acts 12:2) did not undergo a martyr's death.[20] But the
latter argument would apply equally to the cup, and therefore it
is not entirely clear why Matthew would use one metaphor and
discard the other. If such an intrusion of the baptism metaphor
into Mark were the case, it could only be from the practice of
Christian baptism, with the awesome sense (understandable in
Mark's day) that to accept baptism "is to take a step which
might lead to martyrdom; let would-be converts count the cost!"[21]

Though the case is not strong for a Christian sacramental
dimension here, it would, if proved, only confirm the direction
Mark laid out in his understanding of Jesus' baptism in the
Spirit: it is an anointing for martyrdom.

The Markan Conclusion: The Signs that Follow

The conclusion of Mark 16:9-20 has been generally regarded as a

[19] Feuillet, "La coupe," 368.

[20] J. P. Meier, *Matthew* (Wilmington: Glazier, 1980) 228.

[21] D. E. Nineham, *The Gospel of St. Mark* (New York: Seabury, 1963) 284.
Paul in Romans 6:3 speaks of being baptized into the death of Christ.
Some authors hold that Mark is influenced by this tradition here, but
Feuillet, "La coupe," 389-90, thinks the influence may have been in the
opposite direction, namely, that a saying of Jesus about his death being a
baptism influenced Paul in Romans 6:3.

later addition, compiled from other gospel accounts, particularly Luke. W. Farmer has argued for the inclusion of these verses, "though the order of probability claimed for these findings is not high."[22] And E. Linnemann has argued for the Markan authenticity of part of the conclusion.[23] But neither proposal has met with acceptance. The conclusion may well date from the second century. Critical expositors of Mark discount it in their reconstructions of Markan theology. Inasmuch as the church considers this text inspired scripture, even the biblical theologian must take into account the significance of this short pericope in assessing the teaching of the New Testament. The author not only reports the mission given by the risen Jesus to his disciples, but he underscores the charismatic nature of it, adding that they will speak in "new tongues":

"These signs will accompany those who believe: in my name they will drive out demons, they will speak new languages. They will pick up serpents with their hands, and if they drink any deadly thing, it will not harm them. They will lay hands on the sick, and they will recover" (Mark 16:17-18).

Since Jesus cast out demons by the power of the Holy Spirit (3:29), when the disciples do so *in his name*, they are implicitly, as we have seen, doing it *by his Spirit*. There is no mention of the prospect of martyrdom in the conclusion, as there was in the body of the gospel. But the Markan conclusion makes it clear that believing in Jesus, which implies baptism (16:16), is sufficient to share in the charismatic power of Jesus. It is not said that *every* believer receives *all* these powers, but neither are they reserved to a special class. Although in the body of the gospel the disciples, named apostles, receive power to cast out demons in a special conveyance of authority by Jesus (3:14), no such special appointment is envisaged here. There is a clear promise, and therefore an expectation, of charismatic activity flowing from the very nature of discipleship. Thus on the one hand the Markan conclusion does not do violence to the gospel, since charismatic power is given in both, but on the other hand

[22] W. R. Farmer, *The Last Twelve Verses of Mark* (Cambridge University, 1974) 109.

[23] "Die (wiedergefundene) Markusschluss," *ZThK* 66 (1969) 255–87.

it does make clear that such empowerment is meant for all disciples and not just for the original twelve.

What is unclear here is whether the author of the conclusion regarded the charismatic power to be an effect of faith or baptism or both. The least that can be said is that the charismatic activity appears to follow upon initiation rather than upon some second stage or "blessing" of the believer's life—a view clearly reflected by Hilary of Poitiers in the fourth century.[24] In this view, the "baptism in the Holy Spirit" for the Christian is identical with initiatory baptism or at least with the initiatory stage of the Christian life.

In Mark, then, as completed by the inspired non-Markan conclusion, the baptism in the Holy Spirit is: (1) something that Jesus himself first experiences. It is (a) a proclamation of him as Son of God and his anointing as Servant for the ransom of many; (b) an empowering of Jesus with charismatic power to heal and deliver from evil spirits; (c) a ministry Jesus exercises through healings and exorcisms—his own and those of the disciples in his name—and ultimately through his redemptive suffering and death. This is how Mark understands Jesus during his ministry to "baptize in the Holy Spirit."

(2) For the disciples after the resurrection, their initiation into the faith is a participation in Jesus' "baptism in the Holy Spirit" in that it is an empowering to continue Jesus' charismatic ministry. At the time of Mark's redaction, the evangelist quite likely understood the Baptist's prophecy that Jesus would baptize in the Holy Spirit to be fulfilled not only in Jesus' ministry and saving death but also in Christian baptism and the charismatic ministry it initiated. In any case, charismatic manifestation was expected as a normal effect of initiation. But inasmuch as Jesus' baptism is also one of suffering unto the cross (10:38-39), which Jesus demanded each disciple to carry after him (8:34), the empowering is not merely charismatic. It is also the power to follow Jesus to the cross.

[24] Hilary of Poitiers, *Psalm* 64:14-15, CSEL 22:245-46. Kilian McDonnell will study this text in detail in Part Two.

Chapter Two

Works of Mercy and Righteousness: Spirit-Baptism in Matthew

The Surprise of John the Baptist

As was obvious in our discussion of Mark, the meaning each evangelist sees in the Baptist's prophecy "he will baptize with (the) Holy Spirit (and fire)" depends on the role he gives the saying in the framework of his entire gospel. Matthew here is dependent upon Q, not only for the words "and fire" but for a longer development of the theme of judgment in 3:7-10, 12. Matthew finds this Q material congenial to his frequent theme of righteousness and judgment, which is more often directed to members of the community than it is to outsiders.[1] In light of this subsequent development, we may assume that "Holy Spirit" here is heavily freighted with the notion of purification, that is, an ethical holiness.

But we would be mistaken if we understood Jesus in his ministry to be the eschatological judge John foretold. Matthew keeps Q's *and fire* because the Q tradition permits Matthew, like Luke, to reinterpret Jesus' mission in the encounter with John.

---

[1] *See* G. Barth, "Expectation of the Judgment and Exhortation to Do the Will of God" in G. Bornkamm, G. Barth, H. J. Held, *Tradition and Interpretation in Matthew* (Philadelphia: Westminster, 1963) 58–62.

Matthew alone hints at this already when Jesus thwarts John's expectations by presenting himself as a penitent (3:13-15). But it becomes clearest at 11:2-6, when John sends his disciples to ask Jesus whether he is the one who was to come "or shall we look for another?" In response Jesus points to his charismatic ministry of healing and ministry to the poor. *This*, not the fire of judgment, shows in what sense Jesus baptizes with the Holy Spirit.[2] The Holy Spirit on Jesus means a charismatic, humanly-oriented ministry.[3]

The Spirit upon Jesus

Even more so than Mark, Matthew presents Jesus as *the* one endowed with the Holy Spirit. In a text proper to Matthew (12:15-21), Jesus is said to have healed all who followed him, ordering them not to make him known, and this, Matthew says, was to fulfill the prophecy of Isaiah: "Behold my servant whom I have chosen, my beloved with whom my soul is well pleased. *I will put my Spirit upon him.* . . . He will not wrangle or cry aloud, nor will any one hear his voice in the streets . . . " (Isa 42:1-2) The text from Isaiah serves a double function here. On the one hand, it supports Jesus' imposition of silence on his beneficiaries; on the other, it underlines his charismatic activity as evidence that he is endowed with the Spirit of God.

This text prepares the reader, in a way that Mark and Luke do not, for the next section about the spirit by which Jesus expels demons (12:22-30) and the blasphemy against the Holy Spirit (12:31-32). In his response to the Pharisees' Beelzebul accusation, Matthew uses a Q saying which equates Jesus' Spirit-empowered ministry with the coming of the kingdom: "If it is by the Spirit of God that I cast out demons, then the kingdom of God has come upon you" (Matt 12:28). Whereas Luke has

[2] It is remarkable that, while the three Isaian texts to which Jesus alludes in his answer include both judgment and blessing (35:3-6; 29:18-21; 61:1-2), Jesus avoids the judgment phrases and evokes only those having to do with blessing. Cf. Dunn, "Birth of a Metaphor," 136.

[3] Those in the charismatic renewal, who have sometimes merited the accusation that they pay little attention to social concerns, would do well to note how important this dimension of charismatic expression is to Jesus.

"the finger of God," probably the original reading of Q, Matthew has the *Spirit of God*.[4]

Matthew, too, like Luke, introduces the Holy Spirit at the very conception of Jesus. Some neo-Pentecostals see this as correlated to the moment of Christian regeneration, while Jesus' baptism as empowerment for ministry correlates with the "baptism in the Holy Spirit."[5] But there is no New Testament evidence whatever that any of the evangelists or early Christian tradition viewed Jesus' conception by the Holy Spirit as a paradigm for Christian baptism.

The Prophetic Gifts
Though Matthew is even clearer than Mark in attributing Jesus' charismatic activity to the Holy Spirit, he is also concerned to tether those who claim charismatic gifts like prophecy, to the ethical base of the Spirit:

"On that day many will say to me, 'Lord, Lord, did we not prophesy in your name, and cast out demons in your name, and do many mighty works in your name?' And then will I declare to them, 'I never knew you; depart from me, you evil-doers' " (7:22-23).

Notice, too, in the following passage, the paralleling of "righteous man" to "prophet":

"Whoever receives a prophet because he is a prophet will receive a prophet's reward, and whoever receives a righteous man because he is righteous will receive a righteous man's reward" (10:41).

This is not the paralleling of two different ministries in the community; rather the implication is that the authentic prophet must be a righteous person.

---

[4] It is improbable that Luke, to whom the Holy Spirit is so important, would have found "Spirit of God" in Q and changed it to the more primitive "finger of God." Matthew's change from "finger" to "Spirit" can easily be explained by his desire to lead into the saying about blasphemy, which Luke has in a different context (12:10). For a further discussion *see* R. H. Gundry, *Matthew: A Commentary on His Literary and Theological Art* (Grand Rapids: Eerdmans, 1982) 235.

[5] Lederle, *Treasures*, 57.

Matthew's concern with the evil effects of false prophecy appears in Jesus' eschatological discourse, where the effect of false prophecy and its ensuing lawlessness is to cool the charity "of the many" (24:11-12).

It would be a mistake to conclude from this that Matthew is anti-charismatic.[6] "Prophet" is a category for understanding Christian discipleship. In the ninth beatitude, Jesus blesses his persecuted disciples because they fulfill the role of the "prophets who were before you" (Mt 5:12). And authentic prophets were held in honor in his community (10:41; 23:34). There is even a high probability that a number of the sayings transmitted in Matthew as those of Jesus are, in fact, later actualizations, expansions, or interpretations by Christian prophets of the original words of Jesus.[7] And in the introduction to the missionary discourse, which Matthew reads as a program for the church of his day, Jesus commissions his disciples to "heal the sick, raise the dead, cleanse lepers, cast out demons" (10:1, 8). His concern is not to suppress charismatic activity but rather to root all of it in Jesus and to regulate it according to Jesus' teaching. Matthew omits Mark's benign treatment of the

[6] The charismatic nature of Matthew's community is well demonstrated by E. Schweizer, "Observance of the Law and Charismatic Activity in Matthew," NTS 16 (1969-70), 213-30.

[7] The prophets in Matthew's community habitually speak *in the name of Jesus* (Matt 7:22). This probably means that they delivered at least some of their messages in the "I" form. Though Bultmann's thesis that this procedure had little concern for rooting the message in the words of Jesus during his ministry has been largely rejected, it is widely accepted today that the Christian prophets applied, expanded, and interpreted words of the historical Jesus for their communities, after the manner of the Jewish *pesher* or commentary on an earlier text. *See* E. Cothenet, "Prophétisme" in *DBSup 8*, 1285-87; E. E. Ellis, *The Gospel of Luke* (Grand Rapids: Eerdmans, 1974) 173, 191; and especially J. I. H. McDonald, *Kerygma and Didache. The Articulation and Structure of the Earliest Christian Message*, SNTS MS 37 (Cambridge: University Press, 1980) *passim*, esp. 37-38, 159, n. 253; M. E. Boring, *The Continuing Voice of Jesus: Christian Prophecy and the Gospel Tradition* (Louisville: Westminster/John Knox, 1991). As far as Matthew is concerned, this principle is invoked in a recent study of the "You are Peter" saying in Matthew 16:18 by G. Claudel: "A Christian prophet gives a word of comfort, actualizing in part the name *kepha* given by Jesus to his disciple." *La Confession de Pierre: Trajectoire d'une péricope évangélique* (Paris: Gabalda, 1988), 370.

strange exorcist (Mark 9:38-40) and revises Mark's conciliatory "He who is not against us is for us" to read, "He who is not with me is against me, and he who does not gather with me scatters" (Matt 12:30).

Baptism in the Holy Spirit?

In none of the above is there an explicit reference to Christian baptism. The only explicit reference to the ecclesial sacrament is in the great commission at the end of the gospel, where the "trinitarian" formula, "in the name of the Father and of the Son and of the Holy Spirit" (28:19), reflects a liturgical tradition different from the practice of baptizing in the name of Jesus witnessed extensively in Acts (2:38; 8:12, 16; 10:45; 19:5). It has been generally assumed that the Acts tradition is earlier (see 1 Cor 1:13, 15), but already in Paul there are several trinitarian formulas, especially 2 Corinthians 13:13, and one at least that refers to Christian initiation (1 Cor 6:11). So it is quite possible that Luke, for his own theological purposes, simplified a trinitarian formula, perhaps to underline the contrast of the Spirit-baptism in Jesus' name with that of John the Baptist, a gospel theme Luke repeats in Acts (Luke 3:16; Acts 1:5). In any case the most plausible reason for the trinitarian formula in Matthew appears to be that the evangelist, and perhaps the tradition before him, saw Christian baptism as a participation in Jesus' own experience in the Jordan, in which the Father and the Spirit figured prominently.[8]

The Matthean relationship between Jesus' baptism and the formula of 28:19 becomes evident when we examine the way in which Matthew edits Mark's account of Jesus' baptism. While Mark has "he saw the heavens opened and the Spirit descending upon him" (1:10), Matthew has "he saw the Spirit *of God* descending upon him" (3:16). By adding "of God" to "the Spirit" instead of his usually preferred expression "*Holy* Spirit" (1:18, 20; 3:11; 12:32; 28:19), Matthew signals a trinitarian emphasis that will correlate with the Christian baptism proclaimed in 28:19. Matthew uses the same expression "Spirit of God" in 12:28, probably with the same intent.

[8] R. H. Gundry, *Matthew*, 52.

Another very significant change: Whereas Mark and Luke have the Spirit "descending upon him like a dove" (Mark 1:10; "in bodily form" Luke 3:22), Matthew, known for his frequent contractions and rare expansions, adds the phrase "and *coming upon him*" (3:16). The result is a paralleling of the Spirit's mission upon Jesus with Jesus' own mission as the *coming one* (3:11 where Matthew alone has the same participle *coming*). What enables Jesus to be the "coming one" is the "coming" of the Spirit upon him. However much the traditions later show Jesus as source of the Spirit for the church, the synoptic tradition is unanimous in showing Jesus, after his baptism, as himself obedient to the movement of the Holy Spirit (Mark 1:10; Matt 4:1; Luke 4:1).

"[Matthew] wants to establish continuity between Jesus' baptism and later Christian baptism 'in the name of the Father and of the Son and of the Holy Spirit' (28:19). Such continuity gives the story more exemplary force. . . . The Spirit's descent on Jesus makes him an example of baptism in the Spirit as well as of baptism in water."[9]

The significance of this relationship is easily overlooked. At no time in Matthew's Gospel does Jesus specifically convey the Holy Spirit to his disciples (as, for example in John 20:22 or in the pattern of Luke-Acts). Yet the disciples are empowered fully by Jesus' Spirit because through baptism *they participate in Jesus' own inaugural empowerment by the Holy Spirit*. Christian baptism *is* Jesus' own baptism. No other empowerment is needed.

It follows from this that all that was contained in Jesus' own anointing by the Spirit in the Jordan is acquired by the church in its celebration of baptism. And that would surely include the kind of prophetic and charismatic gifts that were clearly operative in Matthew's community. Yet the emphasis in the great commission falls rather upon the observance of all that Jesus taught ("baptizing them . . . , teaching them to observe all I have commanded you" 28:19), hence of his high ethic, the righteousness that surpasses that of the scribes and the Pharisees

---

[9] Ibid.

(5:20).[10] It is an eschatological ethic that may seem impossible to observe, but its demands are balanced by the promise of Jesus' continuing presence, which is empowerment enough.

Is this empowerment to live Jesus' ethic, like the empowerment of the charisms, an effect of Jesus' presence alone, or is it also a gift of the Spirit? In Matthew there is no hint of a separate Pentecostal experience, just as there is no description of an ascension which would prepare it. The reason appears to be that Matthew, unlike Luke, considers the resurrection-glorification of Jesus to be his entering, not heaven, but the church as an abiding presence. He is the promised Immanuel (1:23) whose final word to the church is: "I am with you all days, even to the consummation of the world" (28:20). That means, though, that the Spirit which the Father places upon Jesus (3:17; 12:18) rests also upon the church which is one with him. The church has the Spirit, then, not because Jesus left the Spirit as his replacement until he returns (the view of Luke and John), or because at some moment during his ministry or after the resurrection he specifically conveyed the Spirit to the church, but rather because, remaining with the church, Jesus baptizes with the Spirit through sharing his own baptism with the disciples of all ages. Jesus does not *give* the Spirit to the church but rather *receives* it *for* the church.[11] Whence the intimate and necessary identification of Christian baptism with his. And this is a further way in which he shows himself to be the

[10] It is noteworthy that in the challenge to the sons of Zebedee (20:22-23) Matthew drops the metaphor of baptism, retaining only that of the cup. This could be merely another of Matthew's simplifications of Mark. But it is more likely that Matthew feels he has already depicted Jesus' baptism as a surrender to the Father's will (3:15), thus modeling in another way the ethical consequences of Christian baptism (28:19). As Jesus surrendered to the Father's will in being baptized, so must Christians accept the Father's will expressed in Jesus' teaching when they are baptized. Instead of using "baptism" metaphorically as part of a lesson given to the two brothers about readiness for martyrdom, Matthew uses it for the sacramental initiation of all the baptized by which they surrender to God's plan of righteousness in their daily lives.

[11] Similarly in the great commission scene Jesus does not give his authority to the disciples (as he did in 10:1). "All authority" is given to Jesus and it is that same authority (rather than a delegated authority) which the disciples will exercise.

new Israel, summing up the best of the old Israel and embodying the fullness of the new.

In Matthew, then, the "baptism in the Holy Spirit" is (1) something that Jesus himself experiences in the Jordan, where he is proclaimed Son and Servant; (2) an empowerment for a ministry of preaching, healing, and works of compassion; (3) an ecclesial event in the sacrament of baptism, which introduces the neophyte into the mystery of Jesus' own baptism with its trinitarian relationships and, by implication, its empowerment for living the new righteousness and for ministry.

Chapter Three

Pentecostal Fire: Spirit-Baptism in Luke-Acts

Pentecostals and neo-Pentecostals, as well as Catholic theologians seeking a biblical basis for confirmation, find their greatest support in Luke-Acts, and with reason, for no other New Testament author gives so much attention to the Holy Spirit. While the term "Holy Spirit" occurs only four or five times in Mark and Matthew, it appears thirteen times in Luke and forty-one times in Acts. And it is to Acts that we owe the specific promise that the disciples "will be baptized in the Holy Spirit" (1:5).

Jesus' "Baptism in the Holy Spirit"

To begin with the gospel, Luke, following Q, carries the Baptist's promise that the one coming after him will baptize with the Holy Spirit and fire (3:16). And while Luke also has the explanatory verses on judgment, and the reinterpretation of Jesus' mission in terms of mercy and healing in 7:18-23, he is unique in relaying the promise of the baptism in the Holy Spirit on the lips of Jesus himself (Acts 1:5) and in reporting the tongues of fire at Pentecost. There can be no doubt that Luke sees the Pentecost phenomenon as the ultimate fulfillment of the Baptist's prophecy. The "fire" of Luke 3:16 becomes the fire of Acts 2:3.

But there is a unique note also about Jesus' baptism by John in the Jordan. The Spirit descends upon Jesus not at his coming up from the water (Mark, Matthew) but expressly "after Jesus had been baptized and was praying" (Luke 3:21). Could this be a Lukan retrojection of the procedure for Christian baptism—water rite followed by prayer for the outpouring of the Holy Spirit?[1] This is possible, and it is the sequence we find in Tertullian, as Kilian McDonnell will demonstrate later in this study. But given the uncertainty of the evidence in Acts as to the actual procedure of the initiation rites (as we shall see), this proposal can only remain a conjecture. It is more likely that this is Luke's way of distancing John's baptism from any suggestion of instrumentality in conveying the Spirit to Jesus,[2] a point made again in Acts 1:5 with respect to the community ("John baptized with water, but in a few days you will be baptized with the Holy Spirit"); or it may be simply the first of Luke's connections of the Spirit with the prayer of Jesus, or both. It would in any case be most hazardous to suggest, on the basis of this text, a separation of the coming of the Holy Spirit from the moment of Christian baptism, for that baptism is in the name of Jesus and thus different from John's (Acts 2:38; 10:48; 8:16; 19:5).[3] Even so, Christian baptism was surely accompanied by prayer (cf. Acts 22:16), so that it would be difficult to isolate the

[1] So F. Bovon, *Luke the Theologian* (Allison Park, Penn.: Pickwick, 1987) 235.

[2] Luke does not say John baptized Jesus. In fact, he places Jesus' baptism immediately *after* the report of John's imprisonment. Is he trying to suggest that Jesus was not in fact baptized by John but only participated in a general baptist movement, being baptized by a disciple of John? Or is this simply an editorial technique of anticipating John's later imprisonment and martyrdom? In any case Luke's description of Jesus' baptism diminishes the role of John to give greater prominence to what happened to Jesus on this occasion.

[3] Dunn mistakenly assumes that the Christian water-rite was simply a taking over of John's baptismal rite: "Christian water-baptism takes the place of John's water-baptism as symbol of and contrast with Christ's Spirit-baptism," *Baptism,* 20. If that were so, it is not apparent why the first Christians would not simply have repeated John's baptism "for the forgiveness of sins," whereas in fact they radically changed the rite by baptizing in the name of Jesus. Paul's baptism of the Ephesian disciples who had been baptized by John confirms this point (Acts 19:1-6).

coming of the Spirit to one element of the initiation rite. "Prayer and baptism should not be played off at each other's expense."[4] If we can overcome an anxiety to get a clear sequential picture of the early rites and take Jesus' Jordan experience as a whole, then surely for Luke it serves as a model for Christian initiation, which involved baptism and the gift of the Holy Spirit (Acts 2:38).

More than any of the gospels, however, Luke portrays Jesus' public ministry of healing and deliverance as empowered by the Holy Spirit, stemming from the Spirit's anointing at his baptism. In Acts 10:38, Luke notes "how God anointed him with the Holy Spirit and with power," a reference to Jesus' baptism[5] which empowered him to perform healings and exorcisms. With the exception of two cures which fall in the "great omission" (the largest part which Luke omits from Mark—Mark 6:45 to 8:26), Luke takes over all of the healings of Mark, adding three of his own: the woman with a "spirit of infirmity" (13:10-17), the man with dropsy (14:1-6), and the ten lepers (17:11-19). In the inaugural scene in the Nazareth synagogue, Jesus puts his entire ministry under the seal of the Spirit:

"The Spirit of the Lord is upon me, because he has anointed me to bring glad tidings to the poor. He has sent me to proclaim liberty to captives and recovery of sight to the blind, to let the oppressed go free, and to proclaim a year acceptable to the Lord." (Luke 4:18-19).

It is obvious here that Jesus, who will later send the Holy Spirit upon the community (Luke 24:49; Acts 2:33), himself receives the Spirit at his baptism, or at the very least a new manifestation of the Spirit upon him since his conception,[6] and that this Spirit

---

[4] Bruner, *A Theology of the Holy Spirit*, 171, n. 16.

[5] J. A. Fitzmyer, *The Gospel According to Luke I-IX*, AB 28 (Garden City: Doubleday, 1981) 482. Dunn, *Baptism*, 32. Peter's statement in Acts gives Jesus' baptism a messianic twist not evident in the gospel account of the event. Fitzmyer, *Luke the Theologian*, 105.

[6] According to Acts 2:33, it is upon his ascension to the Father that Jesus receives the Spirit. This may indeed be the most primitive understanding, the baptism later being seen as a proleptic anointing with the Spirit, and the final stage of the tradition being the presence of the Holy Spirit from the moment of Jesus' conception. *See* R. E. Brown, *The Birth of the Messiah* (Garden City: Doubleday, 1977) 29-32, 313.

endows him with prophetic and healing charisms for his ministry. For Luke the baptism of Jesus is a paradigm of the baptism
of the community at Pentecost. Clearly, therefore, the prophetic
charisms are an essential part of the endowment of both baptisms.

Lest the activity of the Spirit be limited to the prophetic
charisms, however, it should be noted in Luke 4:18-19, that
along with works of healing, the Spirit's anointing is also
manifested in Jesus' mission to the poor and the oppressed.
The Spirit works in Jesus in other ways too. The Spirit leads
Jesus into the desert to confront Satan (4:1-2), brings him to
Galilee to begin his ministry (4:14) and inspires Jesus' prayer:
"At that moment Jesus rejoiced in the Holy Spirit and said, 'I
praise you, O Father, Lord of heaven and earth . . . ' " (10:21).
Jesus appears here as subject to the Spirit and empowered by
the Spirit.

It is in Luke above all that the image of *fire* is connected with
the baptismal passion, and through it to the fire of the Baptist's
prophecy: "I came to cast fire upon the earth, and would that
it were already kindled! I have a baptism to be baptized with;
and how I am constrained until it is accomplished!" (12:49-50).
The fire of the Holy Spirit which Jesus will cast upon the earth
is made possible by his first taking upon himself the fire
of judgment.[7]

Since the prophetic, charismatic Spirit given to Jesus in his
baptism and manifest in his ministry is given to the community
on Pentecost, the "baptism in the Holy Spirit" for the community is necessarily an empowerment with prophetic and charismatic gifts. To this development we now turn.

Christian "Baptism in the Holy Spirit"

A. IN THE FOUNDATIONAL PENTECOST EVENT OF ACTS 2
Luke is the only one who records, on the lips of Jesus, the
repetition of John's promise of the baptism of the Spirit: "John
baptized with water, but before many days you shall be baptized with the Holy Spirit" (Acts 1:5). The text counterposes the
baptism in/with the Holy Spirit and the water-baptism of John.
This opposition plus the fact that the Pentecost event in Acts 2

[7] Feuillet, "La Coupe," 379–81; Martin, *Baptism,* 32.

is in no way connected with water-baptism, has led some to locate the baptism in the Spirit in a second moment or second blessing separated in time from Christian baptism. This is the classical Pentecostal position and that of many neo-Pentecostals as well.[8]

J. D. G. Dunn goes further in denying to Christian water-baptism any efficacy in conveying the Spirit, which alone makes one a Christian.[9] M. Quesnel, following W. Wilkens and J. Kremer, holds, on grammatical grounds, that Luke's opposition to water-baptism/Spirit-baptism is not exclusive, as in Mark and Matthew, but inclusive, i.e., not with water only but with the Holy Spirit as well.[10] Though the grammatical argument is not strong, there are other reasons sufficient to invalidate the disjunction of water-baptism and the gift of the Spirit, at least for the post-pentecostal church. Not only was the Pentecost event a unique founding moment of the church, but the water-baptism by John, which many, if not all, of the disciples had received, was not Christian baptism. It may well be that for the primitive disciples water-baptism was not repeated because the Pentecost event supplied what was lacking in John's water-baptism; but this in no way authorizes the conclusion that

[8] As early as 1915 the Assemblies of God rejected the identification of re-birth and the baptism of the Spirit as false doctrine. Cf. Hollenweger, *The Pentecostals*, 332. Classical Pentecostals grant some activity of the Spirit in the first moment and some would even say that all Christians have the Holy Spirit, but they distinguish regeneration from the "filling" by the Spirit, the latter being an empowering for service. R. M. Riggs, *The Spirit Himself* (Springfield, Mo.: Gospel Publishing House, 1949) 47–48. *See* the survey of Classical Pentecostal and neo-Pentecostals authors in Lederle, *Treasures*, 1–103.

[9] Christian water-baptism "is not a channel of grace, and neither the gift of the Spirit nor any of the spiritual blessings which he brings may be inferred from or ascribed to it." Dunn, *Baptism*, 228; cf. also 100, 219, 227.

[10] Mark uses *baptizein* with the dative in both cases (*hydati . . . pneumati hagiô*); Matthew uses the preposition with the dative for both (*en hydati . . . en pneumati hagiô*); whereas Luke has the dative for the first and the preposition for the second (*hydati . . . en pneumati hagiô*), suggesting an intentional breaking down of the sharp distinction between the water through which (instrumental dative) baptism was given and the Spirit with which they will be filled. W. Wilkens, "Wassertaufe und Geistempfang bei Lukas," *TZ* 23 (1967) 31–32; J. Kremer, *Pfingstbericht und Pfingstgeschehen* (Stuttgart: KBW Verlag, 1973) 184–85; Quesnel, *Baptisés*, 39.

Christian baptism thereafter was of "water only," to be followed by a Pentecost experience essentially unrelated to the
water-baptism. It is crucial to remember that Christian baptism
was modeled not on John's baptism, as Dunn invariably maintains[11] and S. Brown holds for Luke-Acts,[12] but on the unique
baptism of Jesus. While John was the minister of that baptism,
the uniqueness of the event was proclaimed by divine intervention and the gift of the Spirit anointing Jesus with power. It is
of course a fact that the early church was a bit embarrassed at
Jesus' having received baptism from John. Yet it felt compelled
to pass on the tradition (a good argument for its historicity).
The concern to distance Jesus from any suggestion of subordination to John was eventually allayed by the realization that the
gift of the Spirit upon Jesus, though occasioned by John's baptism, was not mediated by it. On the contrary, the Spirit not
only anointed Jesus but in some way effected a sanctifying of
the baptismal water through him. Far from the water sanctifying Jesus, Jesus sanctified the water for all subsequent baptisms
in his name. Such a conclusion was drawn quite early in the
tradition. John 3:5 could speak of being born of *water* and the
Spirit (see next chapter). In a statement that may well reflect
earlier liturgical practice, Ignatius states that Jesus by his baptism and passion sanctified the waters (*Eph* 18:2), the underlying
idea being probably that he conquered the dragon of the
abyss.[13] Even clearer is Tertullian: "The nature of the waters,
having received holiness from the Holy, itself conceived power
to make holy. . . . All waters, when God is invoked, acquire
the sacred significance of conveying sanctity: for at once the
Spirit comes down from heaven and stays upon the waters,
sanctifying them from within himself."[14] Such conclusions apparently were the result of reflecting on how a water ritual
similar to John's, which did not convey the Holy Spirit, could

[11] Dunn, *Baptism*, 18–19.

[12] S. Brown, "Water-Baptism and Spirit-Baptism in Luke-Acts," *ATR*,
59/2 (1977) 135–51.

[13] W. R. Schoedel, *Ignatius of Antioch: A Commentary on the Letters of Ignatius of Antioch* (Philadelphia: Fortress, 1985) 85–86.

[14] *On Baptism*, 4. Translation by E. Evans, *Tertullian's Homily on Baptism*
(London: SPCK, 1964) 11.

be part of an initiation rite that did. The problem does not present itself in Luke's treatment of the primordial Pentecostal
event, but it is a legitimate question in the subsequent Christian
initiation rites he describes, in which water-baptism is invariably an integral part.

As for the Pentecostal "baptism in the Spirit" in Acts 2, it
goes without saying that the presence of the Spirit was
manifested through the charisms of tongues and prophecy, for
such is precisely the interpretation Peter gives the event
(2:14-18).

B. IN SUBSEQUENT CHRISTIAN BAPTISM

In Luke-Acts, Jesus gives no command to the apostles to baptize others, such as we find in Matthew 28:19 and (implicitly) in
Mark 16:16. A clue to this omission may be found in Luke's
preference for the passive voice of the verb *baptizein*, which, like
the "divine passive" generally, proclaims the action of God
rather than the work of the human baptizer. Nevertheless, the
church obviously baptized. To see what baptism and the gift of
the Holy Spirit meant for those who had not had the foundational experience of the first disciples, we turn to other texts in
Acts, and first of all to the conclusion of Peter's Pentecost sermon in 2:37-39:

"Now when they heard this, they were cut to the heart, and
they asked Peter and the other apostles, 'What are we to do,
my brothers?' Peter said to them, 'Repent and be baptized,
every one of you, in the name of Jesus Christ for the forgiveness of your sins; and you will receive the gift of the Holy
Spirit. For the promise is made to you and your children and to
all those far off. . . .' "

Peter is answering the people's question by showing them how
they can experience what the apostles have experienced (the
"promise" of verse 39 echoes the "promise of the Father" of
Luke 24:49 and Acts 1:4, which is the Pentecost event). But
there are significant differences between the structure of initiation envisaged by this text and the inaugural experience of the
one hundred and twenty disciples. Instead of water-baptism being contrasted with the gift of the Holy Spirit, as it was for

those who had received the baptism of John (Acts 1:5), here water-baptism *in the name of Jesus* is coordinated with the gift of the Holy Spirit. Though prayer and the laying on of hands is not necessarily excluded by the text, there is certainly no time-lapse envisaged between the initial baptismal rite and the gift of the Spirit. Christian initiation involves baptism *and* the gift of the Holy Spirit. This text justifies concluding that in Luke's view Christian baptism, understood integrally, *is* the baptism in the Holy Spirit.[15] Peter's hearers do not have to *wait*, as the apostles did, for the coming of the Spirit after water-baptism:

"Rather than telling his inquirers to await the Holy Spirit in a second Pentecost event . . . , Peter offers Christian baptism. Rather than telling the candidates to 'wait,' as the Lord had instructed him, Peter offers baptism. After Pentecost the command to 'wait' in connection with the Holy Spirit is not repeated in the New Testament. And the apostolic wait in Jerusalem applied only to that unusual period in the apostles' career between the ascension of Jesus and his gift of the Spirit to the church at Pentecost. Subsequent Christians do not need to wait in Jerusalem for the promise of the Father."[16]

Luke here is not concerned with the external manifestations of the Pentecost event (wind, sound, tongues of fire) any more than with the specifics of the initiation ritual. But it would be legitimate to infer that the gift of the Spirit implies a charismatic dimension. It is the same promise of the Father, which Jesus in Luke 24:49 identifies with *power* and the disciples on Pentecost manifest through tongues and prophecy, which drew the crowds in the first place. And this dimension is confirmed by other descriptions of the coming of the Spirit in Acts, as we shall see.

[15] "To be baptized in his name involves the reception of the same baptism of fulfillment, the Spirit-baptism to which John had looked forward. Baptism is thus a re-presentation of Christ's own baptism, and it necessarily carries with it the gift of the Spirit for those who repent and acknowledge him as Messiah. So much is implied in Acts 2:38." G. W. H. Lampe, "The Holy Spirit in the Writings of St. Luke," in *Studies in the Gospels*, ed. D. E. Nineham (Oxford: Blackwell, 1955) 197–98.

[16] Bruner, *A Theology of the Holy Spirit*, 168.

Acts 4:23-31: *The "Little Pentecost"*

This passage is an important balance to the sacramental text of
2:38. It portrays a second coming of the Holy Spirit, not immediately in a sacramental context but in answer to prayer. Already in the gospel, the Lukan Jesus promises that the Holy
Spirit will be given to those who ask for the gift (Luke 11:13).
Significantly here, the community prays for the gifts of healing,
signs, and wonders to be worked in the name of Jesus. The
shaking of the house is intended as an echo of the first Pentecost, as is the expression "they were all filled with the Holy
Spirit" (2:4).This is important data to incorporate into our conclusions about the modern phenomenon of the later coming of
the Holy Spirit upon Christians already baptized.

Acts 8:9-19: *The Samaritans*

The anomalous situation of the mission to Samaria, where those
baptized in the name of the Lord Jesus later were prayed over
by the apostles Peter and John for the Holy Spirit has provided
Classical Pentecostals with justification of a subsequent "baptism in the Holy Spirit" and Catholics with a basis for the
sacrament of confirmation.[17] Embarrassed by this departure
from the apparent unity of the two effects elsewhere recorded
in Acts, some commentators say that here the coming of the

[17] Classical Pentecostals or neo-Pentecostals: R. M. Riggs, *The Spirit Himself* (Springfield, Mo.: Gospel Publishing House, 1949) 52; D. Basham, *A
Handbook on Holy Spirit Baptism* (Reading, Berkshire: Gateway Outreach,
1969) 15-17. The first witness of a ritual of confirmation involving the imposition of the hand and anointing with oil appears with Hippolytus of Rome
in the third century (*The Apostolic Tradition*, 22, trans. G. Dix [London:
SPCK, 1968] 38). Official usage of this text in support of confirmation restricted to the ministry of bishops goes back at least to Pope Innocent I. Cf.
K. McDonnell, *The Baptism in the Holy Spirit as an Ecumenical Problem* (Notre
Dame: Charismatic Renewal Services, 1972) 42. The Council of Florence
(1439) cited Acts 8:14-17 in connection with confirmation. Denzinger, *Enchiri-
dion Symbolorum*, 1317-18. A lengthy Catholic study of this text in support of
confirmation was made by N. Adler, *Taufe und Handauflegung: Eine
exegetisch-theologische Untersuchung von Apg., 8:14-17* (N. T. Abhandlungen
XIX, 3: Münster: Aschendorffsche Verlagsbuchhandlung, 1951) and was followed by B. Neunheuser, *Baptism and Confirmation*, trans. J. J. Hughes
(New York: Herder & Herder, 1964) 47-48.

Spirit is only an outward manifestation of the Spirit already received earlier,[18] or that the text refers to a second coming of the Spirit[19]—in flat contradiction of 8:15-19. It is obvious that Luke's intention is to say that the Holy Spirit had not come upon these men in or after their baptism, and that it was precisely to remedy the situation that Peter and John were sent from Jerusalem.

M. Quesnel, in a doctoral thesis presented in 1984 at the Institut Catholique in Paris, and published in substance in 1985, has tried to break new ground here.[20] His redaction-critical study touches both this text and the troublesome one in which Paul deals with the dozen Ephesians who received John's baptism and knew nothing of the Holy Spirit (Acts 19:1-7). Luke, he maintains, is trying to integrate two different traditions about Christian initiation, one of gentile Christian and Pauline origin, represented by the baptism of the Samaritans and the Ephesians (and also Paul's own baptism and Philip's baptism of the Ethiopian, 8:26-40), and the other of Jewish-Christian origin represented by Acts 2:38-39 and 10:44-48 (baptism of Cornelius). The key to the distinction lies in the different terminology. Acts 2:38 and 10:48 speak of being baptized *"in* the name of Jesus Christ" *(en/epi tô onomati Iesoû Christoû),* while the other two texts both use the expression *"into* the name of the Lord Jesus" *(eis to onoma toû kyrioû Iesoû).* Most commentators, assuming that *eis* (meaning "into" in classical Greek) is in the popular koine Greek of Paul's day frequently equivalent to *en* ("in," which is equivalent to *epi)* have assumed that Luke was speaking of identical understandings of baptism in all four texts. But Quesnel goes to great lengths to show that such is not the case here, that "in the name of Jesus Christ" represents a Jewish-Christian understanding and "into the name of the Lord Jesus"

---

[18] J. E. L. Oulton, "The Holy Spirit, Baptism, and Laying on of Hands in Acts," *ExpTim* 66 (1954–55) 238–39. G. R. Beasley-Murray, *Baptism in the New Testament* (Grand Rapids: Eerdmans, 1962) 119, argues from the joy experienced in Samaria at the ministry of Philip (Acts 8:8) that the Samaritans indeed had received the Spirit at that time. But the rejoicing is at the miracles and before there is any mention of the Samaritans being baptized, unlike the eunuch's joy in 8:39, which immediately follows his baptism.

[19] Riggs, *The Spirit Himself,* 52; P. T. Camelot, "Confirmation," *NCE* IV, 145.

[20] *See* above, chapter 1, note 1.

a Pauline, gentile-Christian understanding of baptism. The expression "into the name" is unique, without parallels in the LXX and the apocrypha, and with no corresponding semitic original.[21] It is, however, demonstrably Pauline, taken from the commercial language of the Hellenistic world and used with "Lord," a more current title for Jesus among Gentile Christians.

On the basis of this difference, Quesnel maintains there was a difference in rites and in the understanding of the effects of these rites. Both involved water-baptism, but the Jewish-Christian rite ("in the name of Jesus Christ") involved conversion and repentance and the conveying of the Spirit without the laying on of hands.[22] The gentile-Christian rite ("into the name of the Lord Jesus"), on the other hand, was not tied to repentance or the remission of sins. In it the laying on of hands, not the preceding water-baptism, was understood to be the conveyor of the Spirit.[23] The Pauline/gentile procedure was followed in the baptisms of Saul (9:17-18), the Samaritans (8:9-19), the Ethiopian (8:26-40), and the Ephesians (19:1-7), and in them the Holy Spirit was conveyed only with the laying on of hands.

The merit of Quesnel's study lies primarily in the light he throws on the two different expressions for Christian baptism and the high probability of diversity in early Christian initiation rites. But his reconstructions on the basis of this insight are difficult to sustain. Since Philip must have used the same procedure with the Ethiopian as with the Samaritans, Quesnel must conclude that the Ethiopian did not receive the Holy Spirit (pp. 61, 195), an argument from silence further weakened by indications of the Ethiopian's rejoicing, a Lukan mark of the Spirit.[24] That the Pauline/gentile baptism did not involve conversion/repentance even in the baptism of Saul is difficult to maintain in the light of 22:16, where Ananias tells Saul, "Get up and have yourself baptized and your sins washed away." Quesnel's attempt to explain this away (pp. 77-78) is unconvincing, as is his attempt to dismiss 1 Corinthians 6:11: "You have been washed . . . in the name of the Lord Jesus Christ (*en tô ono-*

---

[21] Quesnel, *Baptisés dans l'Esprit*, 101.

[22] Ibid., 180.

[23] Ibid., 118–19.

[24] Luke 10:21; Acts 11:23-24; 13:52. So Lampe, "The Holy Spirit," 198.

mati, not *eis to onoma!)* and in the Spirit of our God," which indicates the reception of the Spirit in baptism. To deny this,
Quesnel is forced to claim a purely metaphorical meaning of
"washed" here (p. 155-156). Finally, in the Pauline literature itself, we have no reference to Paul or any other person laying
on hands for the initial gift of the Spirit.

Thus the hypothesis that Philip's baptism would not under
any conditions have conveyed the Spirit must be abandoned.
What then was wrong?

Two reasons, not necessarily exclusive, are given for this
anomalous situation. Dunn is representative of the first, that
the dispositions of the Samaritans were sufficiently inadequate
to nullify the effect of their baptism. Luke suggests this by
amalgamating the reaction of Philip with that to Simon, whose
magic had held many spellbound, so that even Simon's baptism
is followed by an infatuation with the person of Philip and the
miracles. This is further suggested by Luke's unique expression
here, that the Samaritans "believed Philip" (8:12). "They believed" *(episteusan)* is not followed here by *in* or *on the Lord* but
by "Philip" in the dative *(tô Philippô)*, an indication of Luke's
reservations about the solidity of their faith commitment.[25]

The second reason has to do with Luke's overarching theological interest. It was to the apostles that Jesus had said, "You
are to be my witnesses in Jerusalem, throughout Judea and
Samaria . . . " (Acts 1:8). Philip's mission to Samaria was not
commissioned by the apostles; he simply left Jerusalem because
of persecution. The resulting turn of events raised a new question concerning the incorporation of this mission under the supervision of the apostles. The delay of the Spirit in Samaria,
and its coming through the apostles Peter and John, permits
Jesus' programmatic commissioning to be fulfilled. It was to the
apostles, not to Philip, that Jesus had given the commission to
witness "in Jerusalem, thoughout Judea and Samaria, and to
the ends of the earth" (Acts 1:2, 8). It thus preserves the unity
of the apostolic church under the mother community.[26] In pass-

[25] Dunn, *Baptism*, 65. For a similar Evangelical view *see* D. G. Bloesch,
"The Charismatic Revival: A Theological Critique," in *Religion in Life* 35
(1966) 370.

[26] *See* E. Käsemann, *Exegetische Versuche und Besinnungen* (Göttingen, 1965)
165, and C. Grappe, *D'un temple à l'autre* (Paris: Presses Universitaires de

ing, this is an appropriate occasion to note that for Luke there is no opposition between the "charismatic" church and the "institutional" church if by the latter we understand a community that is under an authority structure. The Twelve must be brought to completion by the choice of a replacement for Judas before the Spirit can come (1:15-26), and among the four traits in Luke's description of the primordial Spirit-filled community, devotion to the teaching of the apostles ranks first (Acts 2:42).

What conclusions, then, can be drawn from this passage? Luke certainly considers the Samaritan situation unusual, and therefore not one which sets a standard for Christian practice. It is not the normal situation that the dispositions of the recipient would be so defective as to nullify the effect of baptism. Nor, on the other hand, should we conclude that the laying on of apostolic hands is necessary for the reception of the Spirit, since Paul receives the Holy Spirit through the laying on of Ananias' hands (9:17).[27] The only conclusion to be drawn, then, is that the gift of the Holy Spirit was considered to be an essential element of Christian initiation.

France, 1992) 121. E. Haenchen even thinks that for this purpose Luke broke up an originally unified experience: "Luke has done no less than to take the combination of baptism, laying on of hands, and reception of the Spirit, which in the belief and custom of his time formed one indissoluble whole, and divide it among Philip and the Apostles in such a way that the former got the beginning and the latter the end." *The Acts of the Apostles* (Philadelphia: Westminster, 1971) 308.

[27] Catholics have pressed Acts 8:9-25 to imply that the imposition of hands was reserved to the apostles (e.g., P. T. Camelot, "Confirmation," 145; Neunheuser, *Baptism*, 44). But Luke could hardly have been making the laying on of apostolic hands a universal condition for conveying the Spirit and then go on at once to relate the conversion and baptism of the eunuch by the same unqualified Philip (Dunn, *Baptism*, 58), without any presence of the apostles. For we may assume from the eunuch's rejoicing that he also received the Holy Spirit. Some important early manuscripts also read: "the Holy Spirit fell on the eunuch." Cf. B. M. Metzger, *A Textual Commentary on the Greek New Testament* (United Bible Societies, 1971) on Acts 8:39. It is important for Luke, who is concerned to unify the various traditions of his day, to bring the Samaritan mission under the authority of the Twelve. But to see this text authorizing the sacrament of confirmation as distinct from Christian baptism or as grounding the need for the laying on of apostolic hands to receive the Spirit goes beyond its exegetical limits. So, among others, Lampe, "The Holy Spirit," 198; Bovon, *Luke the The-*

Acts 10:44—11:18: The Cornelius Event and Peter's Explanation
This event is likewise unusual in that the Holy Spirit fell upon
the gentile listeners during Peter's preaching, prior to baptism
or the laying on of hands. Peter identifies the experience as the
same as the ''baptism with the Holy Spirit'' which the one
hundred and twenty experienced in the upper room (11:16-17),
but he orders them subsequently to be baptized in the name of
Jesus Christ. Cornelius and his men had received neither Johannine nor Christian baptism prior to the descent of the Spirit.
Their baptism here makes sense only if it is seen, as Peter indeed sees it, as the visible sign of belonging to the new Israel
to whom the Spirit is given. If God took the initiative to give
the pagans the Spirit that normally comes by baptism into the
community of believers, then this important sign of their belonging is not to be denied them. In any case, the baptism of
the Cornelius group would be utterly meaningless if it were
only symbolic and forward-pointing to the Spirit, for in the
presence of the reality, what further use would the symbol have?[28]

The Cornelius event is of central importance in the narrative
of Acts. Time and again Peter refers to it, tying it to the Pentecost event in Acts 2, both of which were not only an empowering but a being ''saved by grace'' (15:11). The action of God is
manifested by their bursting into tongues and ''glorifying God''

---

ologian, 231. What may be said is that Luke, concerned with the unity of
the church under the original Twelve, considers authentic Christian ministry to be only that done under the authorization of the apostles or at least
in communion with them.

The realization that confirmation forms an integral part of the initiation
of adults led to the insistence both in the new Roman Catholic Code of
Canon Law (Canons 883 and 885) and in the *National Statutes for Christian
Initiation* (voted by the United States Catholic Conference November 11,
1986, and subsequently approved by the Roman Congregation for Divine
Worship, and now published as Appendix 3 of the RCIA) that the priest-
minister of adult baptism also be the minister of confirmation. In the
United States, if a bishop wants to confirm an RCIA candidate, he must
also administer baptism (Statutes 12, 13). In this matter, the present legislation has abandoned the imperative of the laying on of ''apostolic hands''
as necessary for confirmation—a direction in keeping with our interpretation of the data of the Acts of the Apostles.

[28] Contra Dunn, *Baptism*, 20, 99.

(10:46),[29] another of Luke's indications that the presence of the Spirit is manifested charismatically.

In the Cornelius event the Spirit came first, and baptism followed consequentially. If that atypical sequence could be attributed to divine intervention, what is to be said of the sequence in the initiation of Saul in Acts 9:17-18? There was divine intervention in the Lord's appearance to Saul, but not in Ananias' determination to lay hands on Saul for the infilling of the Holy Spirit *prior* to Saul's baptism. Nowhere is it clearer than in these two texts (the Cornelius and the Ananias events) that for Luke the gift of the Holy Spirit is the primary and essential effect of initiation. The gift of the Spirit is "the way of incorporating converts into the community of disciples."[30] The laying on of hands appears in this case as the rite through which the Spirit is imparted. Still, baptism was considered necessary for Saul, just as for Cornelius, to complete the integral rite of initiation.

Acts 19:1-7: The "Disciples" at Ephesus

This text, which speaks of a later coming of the Spirit on those who were already "disciples," is another used by Classical Pentecostals and neo-Pentecostals in support of a "baptism in the Holy Spirit" subsequent to water-baptism.[31] But who are these "disciples"? The case for their being Christians lies in two points of the text: (1) "Disciples" elsewhere in Luke always means "Christians," and a number of authorities would see no exception here.[32] (2) The verb "believe" (*pisteuein*) used here ordinarily means the act of Christian faith.

In response to the first, it has been pointed out that the use of "disciples" here is unique in that it lacks the definite article

[29] "Glorifying God" could be a Lukan equivalent for prophesying, since for Luke an act of inspired and spontaneous praise can be called prophecy: Luke 1:67.

[30] Fitzmyer, *Luke the Theologian*, 133.

[31] See the references to Classical Pentecostal and neo-Pentecostal literature in Dunn, *Baptism*, 83.

[32] So. E. Haenchen, citing also Wellhausen, Knopf, Preuschen, Loisy, Zahn, and Käsemann.

or some qualification habitually used elsewhere, an indication that these disciples did not belong to the central Christian community in Ephesus.[33] And in the light of the whole passage, it is obvious that the expression "when you came to believe" (*pisteusantes*) cannot mean full Christian faith, though it does suggest that somehow they were in the orbit of it. Having received the baptism of John, they were aware of his messianiac preaching without knowing Jesus as its fulfillment. This latter point sufficed for Luke to classify them as "disciples" of sorts, that is, implicit believers, open to completion, though obviously they are of "a somewhat peculiar type."[34] In any case, the significant question for Paul, the litmus test to determine whether they were Christians, was whether they had received the Holy Spirit. For Luke, as for Paul (Rom 8:9), one cannot really belong to Christ unless one has the Spirit of Christ. The Holy Spirit is the essential effect of Christian initiation.

Nevertheless, the point to be remedied in their experience is baptism into the name of Jesus.[35] Far from demonstrating the possibility of a separation between baptismal initiation and the gift of the Spirit, this text does just the opposite. Though in this case the Spirit comes as Paul lays hands on the baptized, the gesture follows immediately and is considered integral to

[33] Dunn, *Baptism,* 84.

[34] L. Cerfaux and J. Dupont, *Les Actes des Apôtres,* "La Sainte Bible," 3d rev. edition (Paris: Cerf, 1964) 166. Acts represents Luke's efforts to integrate into a unifying view of the church various early trends, some of which went in contrary directions. It is not entirely unlikely that some early Jewish-Christian groups considered themselves Christians, but, like Apollos (18:24-28), were not instructed in what became the prevailing understanding of Spirit-baptism in the name of Jesus, and thus they continued the practice of John's baptism.

[35] The thesis of W. Wilkens, "Wassertaufe," 42, and S. Brown, "Water-Baptism and Spirit-Baptism in Luke-Acts" *ATR* 59/2 (1977) 135–51, that Christian baptism in Luke-Acts in no way differed from John's baptism collapses, as Quesnel has well seen *(Baptisés,* 69, n. 53), on the basis of this text. If there was no difference, why would the disciples have been rebaptized in the name of Jesus? Bruner, *A Theology of the Holy Spirit,* 211, argues convincingly: "The missing link in the Ephesians' spiritual formation, therefore, was not teaching on how to be baptized in the Holy Spirit, it was faith and baptism in Jesus."

the initiation rite which brings the Spirit.[36] The two elements
are as closely united here as in 2:38.[37]

Again the presence of the Holy Spirit is manifested by tongues and prophecy (19:6). It is difficult to see how Bruner could
dismiss the significance of this charismatic expression thus:
"That the Ephesian converts here spoke in tongues is merely
interesting—nothing more."[38] On the contrary, for Luke it is the
proof that the Spirit has been received. Whether Luke considered this the *only* possible proof of the reception of the Spirit is
surely questionable, but that he expected *some* experiential or
charismatic manifestation to follow reception of the Spirit is certain.

Conclusion: Christian Initiation in Luke

From our examination we can draw the following conclusions
about Luke's understanding of the "baptism in the Holy
Spirit":

(1) As the rite of Christian initiation, there is only one baptism, an integral rite that involves water and the gift of the
Holy Spirit. The rite of initiation may have varied, and it is not
clear that the laying on of hands was always practiced, but
when it was, it was part of the initiation rite. A delay in the imposition of hands for the Spirit was not normative practice.
Against Bovon (236-37), we do not believe the textual evidence
permits us to establish a consistent distinction in Luke of the effect of baptism (forgiveness of sins) and the laying on of hands
(gift of the Spirit). It is possible that early Christian communities had differing understandings of the specific effects of the

[36] The active, personal form, *"Paul* having laid hands on them" follows
the impersonal passive "they were baptized in the name of the Lord
Jesus." Some see this as an indication that the laying on of hands was reserved to a leader of the community or to an apostle. But see our remarks
above concerning Ananias.

[37] Bultmann is surely correct in concluding: "It has to be emphasized
that Acts, like Paul, conceived of Baptism, as did Hellenistic Christianity,
as the sacrament of the gift of the Spirit. The apparent exceptions actually
go to prove that for Acts baptism and the reception of the Spirit belong together. . . . Most of all the contrast of John's baptism with the Christian
rite in 19:1-7 shows that for the latter the gift of the Spirit is characteristic."
History of the Synoptic Tradition (New York: Harper & Row, 1968) 247, note 1.

[38] Bruner, *A Theology of the Holy Spirit*, 212.

two rites, if indeed such distinctions were made at that early hour.[39]

(2) Though the Holy Spirit is not explicitly mentioned in the baptisms of the Ethiopian (Acts 8:38-39), Lydia and her household (Acts 16:15), the jailer in Philippi (Acts 16:33), and the group of Corinthians (18:8), it is clear from the paradigmatic nature of Acts 2:1-38, 10:44-48, and 19:5 not only that the gift of the Spirit belongs essentially to Christian initiation, but that some external expression of its reception is normal.[40] Among these expressions, tongues and prophecy have a privileged place. If I may phrase Luke's view another way: the Spirit cannot be known to have been poured *in* unless it somehow pours *out*. Thus the initiate, receiving the Spirit through the ministration of the community, ordinarily shares his or her new experience in some way with the community for its upbuilding. It is not surprising, then, that Luke should conclude his account of the first mass conversion and baptism by a description of the growth of the community as *koinōnia* (Acts 2:42-44). No doubt it would be a mistake to make the charismatic expectation into a rigid law; on the contrary, Luke sees the charismatic expression as a marvelous confirmation of God's action in the event of Christian initiation.

(3) Even for the primitive community (and by implication for the later church), the fact that the Holy Spirit filled them once does not exclude later "fillings." And for such experiences there is no need to repeat baptism: prayer suffices. This is abundantly clear in Luke's catechism of prayer, where the gift of the Holy Spirit can be had for the asking (Luke 11:13). Since the teaching in the entire section 11:1-13 is about prayer rather than about conversion and initiation, and is directed to the dis-

[39] "From Tertullian *(De Baptismo, 8)* onwards there was a tendency to regard the bishop's imposition of hands upon, or 'consignation' of, the newly baptized as the particular sacramental sign of the coming of the Spirit, but of this, as a regular practice, there is no evidence in the New Testament, apart from Hebrews 6:2, a passage whose meaning is itself in doubt." Lampe, "Acts," in *Peake's Commentary on the Bible* (London: Nelson, 1962) on Acts 8:14-25.

[40] It is true that the charismatic manifestations at Pentecost (Acts 2:1-11), in Samaria (implicitly, Acts 8:17), with Cornelius (Acts 10:44-46) and at Ephesus (Acts 19:6) all occur at strategic turning points in Luke's program-

ciples, the implied readers are those already baptized (as is evident already from Luke 1:1-4). And since the whole section was introduced by the disciples' watching Jesus pray, there is no doubt here a flashback to Jesus' prayer following his baptism during which the Spirit descended in manifest form (3:21-22). The context suggests that the Holy Spirit in 11:13 is the Spirit that cries "Abba, Father" (cf. Gal 4:6; Rom 8:15), as can be seen both from the word "Father" introducing the Lord's prayer as well as the image of "Father" in 11:11-13. But since the expression also provides an introduction to one of Jesus' exorcisms and the discussion of the Spirit by which he expels demons (11:14-23), the charismatic Spirit is also envisaged. So it is also in Acts, where, in response to the prayer of the community, the disciples are filled again with the Holy Spirit and manifest this renewal in charismatic ministry (Acts 4:23-31). Since there is no evidence that the request for the Holy Spirit in Luke 11:13 is tied to initiation, it would be logical to conclude that if the effects of the Spirit are not manifest, or not fully manifest, at baptism (or confirmation), as may easily happen in infant baptism, subsequent prayer for the outpouring of the Spirit (such as the contemporary "baptism in the Holy Spirit") is wholly appropriate. In this way the baptized may effectively claim their patrimony.

matic description of the expansion of the church: Samaritans, gentiles, and disciples of John the Baptist. But Luke is far from suggesting that the phenomenon was unusual or given only on these occasions of "new beginnings." At times the whole initiation process is summarized by the simple remark that the converts were "baptized" (Acts 2:41; 8:38; 16:15, 33; 18:8).

Chapter Four:

Spiritual Body and Spiritual Rock: Spirit-Baptism in the Pauline Tradition and Hebrews

The Pauline letters antedate the synoptics. Concerned as they are, not with the events and teaching of Jesus' ministry but with the significance of the risen Lord and the Spirit for the church, they are a theological mine, particularly for the information they furnish on the topic at hand, the role of the Holy Spirit in Christian initiation. For convenience, we include in this chapter Titus and Hebrews, letters which are related to the Pauline tradition, though not generally accepted as authored by the apostle.

1 Corinthians 12:13: One Body, One Spirit

The Pauline text which comes closest to the expression "baptized in the Holy Spirit" is 1 Corinthians 12:13:

a: "For in [by/with] one Spirit we all were baptized into one body,
b: whether Jews or Greeks, whether slaves or free,
c: and we all were given to drink of the one Spirit."

Among the commentators, Dunn stands in almost solitary splendor in taking "baptized" here only in a metaphorical sense, not as referring to a water-rite.[1] Exegetes have found his

[1] Dunn, *Baptism*, 127–31.

position hard to sustain. The fact that the meaning of the verb "baptize" is metaphorical in Mark 10:38 and Luke 12:50 (and Dunn would also claim its metaphorical sense in the "baptized in the Holy Spirit" texts, a sense which we rejected above) is shaky ground indeed for sustaining a purely metaphorical sense in a text referring to Christian initiation, which clearly involved water-baptism. Hence, we must accept the majority position here that "baptized," while not excluding some metaphorical resonance, refers primarily to the Christian sacrament of water-baptism. Dunn's further position that in verse 13c *epostithemen*, which we, like most versions, have translated "we were given to drink," means rather to "water" or "irrigate" here is also difficult to sustain grammatically, and is not favored by the majority of exegetes.[2]

The question of whether *en* in 13a should be translated locally ('in') or instrumentally ("by" or "with") is more difficult to determine. The translations vary. Ervin is correct in pointing out that in the immediately preceding context, 1 Corinthians 12:3 and 9, *en* is instrumental, and that would favor the instrumental sense here, but he goes on to use this to exclude the Spirit from the element of baptism (i.e., he maintains that baptism by the Spirit does not involve the gift of the Spirit, at least not the same gift of the Spirit as 13c).[3]

Ervin's position appears to put more theological weight on the instrumental versus local meaning than the preposition can bear. It does lead us however to consider the three interpretations given to this verse: (1) 13a and c are synonymous metaphors for the same reception of the Spirit in baptism.[4] (2) 13a refers to baptism as the initiatory rite, 13c to the outpouring of the Holy Spirit and the spiritual gifts after baptism, either in the Classical Pentecostal sense[5] or in confirmation.[6] (3) 13a refers to baptism, 13c to the eucharist.[7]

---

[2] Dunn, *Baptism*, 131 and G. J. Cuming, "*Epotisthemen* (1 Corinthians 12, 13)" NTS 27 (1980/81) 283–85; *see* the response of H. M. Ervin, *Conversion-Initiation*, 100.

[3] Ervin, *Conversion-Initiation*, 99.

[4] Bachmann, Robertson-Plummer, Lietzmann, J. Weiss, Allo.

[5] Ervin, *Conversion-Initiation*, 100–101.

[6] J. Hanimann sees this text as evidence of the laying on of hands, though there is no reference in any of the Pauline letters to such a rite,

The eucharistic interpretation of 13c is not a new one,[8] but it is difficult to prove. Its major base is the eucharistic interpretation of "spiritual drink" in 1 Corinthians 10:4; but here the aorist *epotisthemen* ("we were given to drink") points to a single, initial act, not a repeated one (*epinon* in 10:4). The Classical Pentecostals who hold to position (2) at least do not claim any delay in the gift of the Spirit, thus avoiding the position that in the Pauline churches there were some that had received the Spirit and some who had not (yet). Such a position would be impossible to maintain in view of the repeated *pantes* ("all") here—all have received the Spirit. This means, in fact, therefore, that the question of how and when the Spirit is given in the rite of initiation becomes somewhat academic. Christian initiation involved baptism *and* the gift of the Spirit, however this was ritually expressed.

The Spirit here is obviously charismatic, as the whole purpose of introducing the *one* Spirit is to show the one source of the charisms. The theme of unity is once more reinforced by the expression *baptized into one body*. Some translators and exegetes understand the "body" here to mean the church, but a strong case can be made for it signifying in the first place the risen body of the Lord Jesus.[9] (1) The surrounding verses show that

"Nous avons été abreuvés d'un seul Esprit: Note sur 1 Co 12, 13b," *NRT* 94 (1972) 400–405. Bisping, Belser, Cornely, Gutjahr, Sickenberger, Huby, Prat, and Meinertz are listed as holding a confirmational interpretation by A. Feuillet, *Le Christ Sagesse de Dieu d'après les épîtres pauliniennes* (Paris: Gabalda, 1966) 102.

[7] E. Käsemann, *Essays on New Testament Themes*, trans. W. R. Montague (London: SCM, 1964) 113–14; W. Bieder, *Die Verheissung der Taufe nach dem Neuen Testament* (Zürich: EVZ Verlag, 1966) 122; A. Feuillet, *Le Christ Sagesse*, 101–2.

[8] Feuillet, *Le Christ Sagesse*, 101–2 lists Cyril of Alexandria (PG 74, 889B), Thomas Aquinas, Estius, Cornelius a Lapide, Natalis Alexander, and moderns Cerfaux, M. M. Bourke, and Schlatter.

[9] See L. Cerfaux, *The Church in the Theology of St. Paul* (New York: Herder & Herder, 1959) 266–82; J. A. T. Robinson, *The Body* (London: SCM, 1952) 47; R. Schnackenburg, *Baptism*, 26; D. M. Stanley, *Christ's Resurrection in Pauline Soteriology* (Rome: Pontifical Biblical Institute, 1961) 181; A. Wikenhauser, *Pauline Mysticism* (Freiburg: Herder, 1960) 20, citing in favor of this view: Percy, Casel, Kümmel.

the problem for Paul is not to show how the many can be one, but how the one can be many:[10]

12:12: "As a body is one though it has many parts, and all the parts of the body, though many, are one body, so also Christ. 12:14: Now the body is not a single part, but many."

(2) Earlier in the same letter Paul had used sexual imagery to show that "the Lord is for the body. . . . Do you not know that your bodies are members of Christ? . . . Anyone who joins himself to a prostitute becomes one body with her. . . . But whoever is joined to the Lord becomes one spirit with him" (1 Cor 6:13-17). Christian life is a union with the Lord so real that Paul can use the very same verb *(kollōmenos)* for union with the prostitute and union with the Lord. Both unions have a visible physicality about them (the Christian's body is a *member* of Christ), but the effect of this quasi-physical incorporation into Christ is that the Christian *also* becomes one spirit with him, i.e., enjoys the same life-giving Spirit that animates his risen body (Rom 1:4), for his risen body is the spirit-giving body (1 Cor 15:44-45).

The same underlying understanding appears in Paul's use of the "spiritual rock" imagery in 10:1-4:

"Our ancestors were all under the cloud and all passed through the sea, and all of them were baptized into Moses in the cloud and in the sea. All ate the same spiritual food, and all drank the same spiritual drink, for they drank from the spiritual rock that followed them, and the rock was Christ."

Exodus imagery underlies Paul's appeal to the Corinthians here. "Cloud" stands for the Spirit, the sea for baptism. Moses is a figure of Christ *into whom* the Christian is baptized (Gal 3:27). Water and the Spirit are therefore associated here with baptism into Christ, as all part of one initiation rite. The "spiritual drink" can stand for the Spirit or for the drink of the eucharist (paralleling "food"). But in any case, the rock which Moses tapped was an image of Christ, spiritual source (cf. John 7:37-39).

In speaking of the eucharistic body of the Lord, Paul says that the unity of the body as community derives from the unity of

[10] Robinson, *The Body,* 58–67.

the body of the Lord received in the eucharist: "Because the bread is one, we the many, are one body, since we all partake of the same bread" (1 Cor 10:17). Consequently, there is every reason to believe that the "body" into which the Christian is baptized in 12:13a is the risen body of the Lord. This body is source of the Spirit, whose gifts are distributed for the building up of the body of Christ, the community (12:7, 11). If, then, baptism joins one to the risen body of Christ, it automatically puts one in touch with the Spirit dwelling in him. And this Spirit is the one common source of the charisms.

1 Corinthians 6:11: Washed in the Spirit

Let us turn to another text of the letter to which we alluded earlier, 1 Corinthians 6:11:

"You were washed, you were sanctified, you were justified in the name of the Lord Jesus Christ and in the Spirit of our God."

"Washed" here is taken by most commentators as an allusion to baptism, though Dunn and Quesnel hold for a metaphorical meaning.[11] The purely metaphorical meaning is difficult to maintain, particularly in view of the fact that the only other usage of the verb *apolouesthai* ("wash") in the New Testament is Acts 22:16, where the baptismal context is unmistakable: "Rise and be baptized, and wash away your sins, calling on his name."[12] The "in" in this Corinthian text is not *eis* (into) but *en* (in) in both cases. This usage tells fatally against the attempt to establish a Pauline/gentile baptism "into the name" over against a Jewish baptism "in the name," as we noted above. And it is clear that the "Lord Jesus Christ" and the "Spirit of our God" are paralleled in such a way as to indicate a coordination in the activity of Christian initiation. The Spirit comes at baptism and is not reserved for a later moment.

In this single letter, then, Paul makes it abundantly clear that the Holy Spirit is given at the moment of Christian initiation, that is, baptism—a rite that involves both water and the Spirit.

[11] Dunn, *Baptism*, 121; Quesnel, *Baptisés*, 165–66.
[12] So Ervin, *Conversion-Initiation*, 93.

Furthermore, he presents the Spirit thus received as the source of various charisms. This appears from the opening lines of the letter (1 Cor 1:4-7) and is confirmed by the fact that in 12:13 it is precisely the matter of charisms that occasions the discussion of the Holy Spirit. The fact that the charisms are so evident that they need to be regulated is a challenge to today's church, in which there is often no awareness or concern about the charismatic dimension of the Spirit's activity.

Galatians 3:1-5: The Experience of the Spirit

"O stupid Galatians! Who has bewitched you, before whose eyes Jesus Christ was publicly portrayed as crucified? I want to learn only this from you: did you receive the Spirit from works of the law or from faith in what you heard? Are you so stupid? After beginning with the Spirit, are you now ending with the flesh? Did you experience so many things in vain?—if indeed, it was in vain. Does, then, the one who supplies the Spirit to you and works mighty deeds among you do so from works of the law or from faith in what you heard?"

In this text Paul recalls to his readers their beginnings in the faith, which he describes as "receiving the Spirit" and "beginning in the Spirit," clearly a reference to their Christian initiation. Then, in discussing the superiority of the Spirit to the law, he asks, "Did you experience so many things in vain?" (v. 4), explaining "so many things" thus: "Does the one who *supplies the Spirit* to you and *works mighty deeds among you* do so from works of the law or from faith in what you heard?" (v. 5). The close association here of the Spirit received and the *mighty deeds* makes it virtually certain Paul is speaking of the charisms poured out on the community at their baptism, and continuing even into the present. The presence and charismatic activity of the Spirit was so taken for granted by Paul as the birthright of Christians that he uses the Galatians' experience of the Spirit at their initiation and subsequent to it as an argument for the superiority of their Christian faith over the law. This text, then, shows both the experiential and charismatic dimensions of the Holy Spirit received upon Christian initiation.

2 Corinthians 1:21-22: Anointed and Sealed

Another text that merits brief consideration is 2 Corinthians 1:21-22, which speaks of the Spirit in the context of anointing and sealing:

"But the one who gives us security with you in Christ and who anointed us is God; he has also put his seal upon us and given the Spirit in our hearts as a first installment."

There is no doubt that Paul is here referring to the initial gift of the Spirit—the words *anointed, put his seal,* and *given* are all in the aorist tense in the Greek, indicating a single past action. It is this past act of anointing, sealing, and giving the "first installment" that is the ground of the present assurance God gives of salvation with and in Christ.

A significant number of exegetes see, in addition, references to the baptismal rite[13] and some even to confirmation or the anointing that followed baptism.[14] I. de la Potterie, insisting that the anointing here precedes the sealing of baptism, maintains that the word anointing refers not to a rite but, in a sequence similar to Ephesians 1:13, to "the act of God arousing faith in the heart of those who hear the word of truth."[15] Indeed, since the word "anointing" of itself can suggest the Spirit (Luke 4:18; Acts 10:38; 1 John 2:20), it is impossible to prove from this text whether the anointing with the Spirit was also expressed in a rite, as appears clearly only with Tertullian *(On Baptism, 7).*[16] Since the anointing of Christians *(kai chrisas,* "anointed us") was suggested by the mention of Christ, the anointed one *(eis Christon),* it is more plausible that the allusion would be to the coming of the Spirit upon Jesus at his baptism in the Jordan (cf. Luke 3:22; 4:18), an anointing in which Christians share from the moment of their initiation. If so, this would be the only reference in Paul to Jesus' baptism as the foundation and model for Christian baptism, a relationship we

[13] Bultmann, Plummer, Allo, Windisch, Belser, Schlier, Lampe, Hanson, Wendlund, Beasley-Murray, Barrett, Lietzmann, Halter, Dinkler, Furnish.
[14] Allo, Thornton, Belser.
[15] *The Christian Lives by the Spirit* (Staten Island: Alba House, 1971) 93.
[16] *See* R. Schnackenburg, *Baptism in the Theology of St. Paul* (New York: Herder & Herder, 1964) 89–91.

see clearly in Matthew and Luke (and one that will be the favorite in the Syriac tradition).[17] Paul's preferred model is the death-resurrection of Jesus. The text in any case does not allow a temporal delay in the gift of the Spirit. Christian initiation implies the gift of the Spirit: "Whoever does not have the Spirit of Christ does not belong to him" (Rom 8:9).

Romans 6:1-5: Baptized into Christ's Death

There is one final text which must be examined, if only because it became so influential in baptismal catechesis in the later church, and in a way that obscured the gift of the Holy Spirit in baptism:

"What then shall we say? Shall we persist in sin that grace may abound? Of course not! How can we who died to sin yet live in it? Or are you unaware that we who were baptized in Christ Jesus were baptized into his death? We were indeed buried with him through baptism into death, so that, just as Christ was raised from the dead by the glory of the Father, we too might live in newness of life. For if we have grown into union with him through a death like his, we shall also be united with him in the resurrection" (Rom 6:1-5).

The imagery here is graphic and powerful, easily lending itself to a catechesis on the symbolism of immersion as death and emergence from the water as resurrection. Because there is no mention of the Spirit here, it is also easy to see that such catechesis, if limited to this text, could easily lose sight of the Holy Spirit as the essential effect of baptism—as actually happened in the later centuries of the church. It is important to note, first, that Paul is here in the midst of a parenesis, i.e., a moral exhortation on the importance of breaking definitively with sin—a limited perspective but an important element of baptismal catechesis! He roots this exhortation in the meaning of baptism, which is a participation in the death and resurrection of Christ.

[17] Some scholars think there is a baptismal liturgy behind Galatians 4:6 (O. Betz, Ebeling, Mussner, Oepke) but the allusion is not certain and even less certain is the reference to Jesus' baptism.

By baptism one has died with Christ and risen to new life in him. If Paul prefers to attribute the resurrection of Jesus to the Father rather than explicitly to the Holy Spirit, it is nonetheless abundantly clear that the body of the risen Lord possesses the Spirit in its fullness to be given to the church.[18] Unlike the first Adam, who became only "a soul having life," the risen Christ, the second Adam, became "a spirit imparting life" (1 Cor 15:45), and he who clings to the risen Lord becomes "one spirit with him" (1 Cor 6:17). And, as we saw in 1 Corinthians 12:13, the effect of being baptized into the (risen) body of Jesus is to drink of the Spirit flowing from him.[19] Thus, limiting the effects of baptism to participating in Christ's death-resurrection without incorporating the Spirit is indeed to read the text of Romans 6 too narrowly, certainly not in the context of the whole of Paul's theology of initiation.

Conclusions: Christian Initiation in Paul

We may now draw the following conclusions concerning Paul's understanding of Christian initiation: (1) There is one rite of initiation involving baptism and the gift of the Holy Spirit, although the texts do not permit a conclusive distinction as to which element of the initiatory rite the reception of the Spirit was associated, if indeed such a distinction was ever in Paul's

[18] We are in agreement with J. D. G. Dunn that Paul never explicitly attributes the resurrection of Jesus to the Spirit, though he comes close to doing so in the older formula of Romans 1:4: "established as Son of God in power according to the spirit of holiness through resurrection from the dead." *Christology in the Making: A New Testament Inquiry into the Origins of the Doctrine of the Incarnation* (Philadelphia: Westminster, 1980) 144. If we may hazard a reason for this, it is that Paul wishes to attribute the raising of Jesus to the Father. In doing so, however, as the rest of the Pauline texts show, the Father so endows and empowers the risen Jesus with the Spirit that Jesus becomes source of the Spirit for the church. *See* 1 Corinthians 15:45; 2 Corinthians 3:18.

[19] In the light of the other Pauline texts even in 1 Corinthians, the "body" of 1 Corinthians 12:13 means first and foremost, as we have shown, the body of the risen Christ. However, "body" can also evoke death, as Cerfaux demonstrates in detail [*The Church*, 271, note 16], and thus Paul's use of the term "baptized into his death" in Romans 6:2, 4, found a foothold already provided in the term "body" used in 1 Corinthians 12:13.

mind. (2) The Spirit is the effect of baptismal contact with the risen Lord, source of the Spirit. (3) There is no evidence anywhere in the Pauline literature of a delay of the coming of the Spirit upon those initiated. (4) The Holy Spirit received from the beginning is manifested through charisms in the Pauline communities, though in different ways in different persons. Paul does not expect every initiated member to have all the gifts, and he allows for some gifts to be given later through prayer. Whether received upon initiation or later, the gifts are given for ministry to the church. Likewise, the Holy Spirit has other functions as well, such as sanctification, the experience of the fatherhood of God and the Lordship of Jesus, strengthening for endurance in the Christian journey, a life obvious by the fruits of love, joy, peace, and the other attitudes listed in Galatians 5:22.[20]

Titus 3:4-7: The Renewing Action of the Spirit

"But when the goodness and loving kindness of God our Savior appeared, he saved us, not because of deeds done by us in righteousness, but in virtue of his own mercy, *by the washing of regeneration and renewal in the Holy Spirit*, which he poured out upon us richly through Jesus Christ our Savior, so that we might be justified by his grace and become heirs in hope of eternal life."

That this post-Pauline text refers to baptism is admitted by virtually all commentators. Instead of saying, as Paul would usually do, that "he saved us through Jesus Christ," the thought is interrupted by one affirming the instrumentality of the *loutron*, which some versions translate "bath," and others, like the RSV, "washing." The difficulty comes in the train of

[20] For a full development of the Spirit in Paul, *see* Montague, *The Holy Spirit: Growth of a Biblical Tradition* (New York: Paulist, 1976) 127-228. *See also* R. P. Martin, *The Spirit in the Congregation: Studies in 1 Corinthians 12-15* (Grand Rapids: Eerdmans, 1984). On the gifts in general, *see* E. E. Ellis, "Spiritual Gifts in the Pauline Community," *NTS* 20 (1973-74) 128-44. On prophecy in particular, *see* D. E. Aune, *Prophecy in Early Christianity and the Ancient Mediterranean World* (Grand Rapids: Eerdmans, 1983) and D. Hill, *New Testament Prophecy* (Atlanta: John Knox, 1979).

genitives which follow: "of regeneration and of renewal of the Holy Spirit." Is the bath both of regeneration *and* of renewal? Or is the renewal *parallel* to bath, thus justifying the Classical Pentecostal doctrine of a second blessing, the "baptism in the Holy Spirit"?

The case is strong for seeing all as one event, the renewal being tied, like the regeneration, to "bath": (1) The entire section is governed by the expression "he saved us," which encompasses the whole of what follows. (2) As the text stands, the single preposition *dia* (through) is used only once and hence governs both "regeneration and renewal."[21] Ervin calls for an elliptical understanding of *dia* before "renewal," but that would have to be proved on other than grammatical grounds.

On the basis of these arguments, Dunn holds that "regeneration" and "renewal" are virtually synonymous.[22] But this is not the case. "Regeneration" *(palingenesia)* is not a Pauline way of referring to baptism. It is more Johannine (John 3:5). "Renewal" *(anakainōsis)*, however, is not only typically Pauline. Since it appears nowhere in Greek prior to Paul, the assumption is that it is a word of Paul's own coining. It is key to his understanding of the role of the Holy Spirit. Now all of Paul's usages of both verb and noun refer, not to the initial rite of baptism, but to the ongoing process of the Christian life. Thus the inward person is being renewed day by day (2 Cor 4:6); they must walk in newness of life *(kainoteti,* Rom 6:4) and be renewed in the spirit of their mind and put on the new person (Rom 12:2; cf. Eph 4:23-24), who is being renewed unto knowledge (Col 3:10). As R. C. Trench long ago pointed out, "rebirth" is a word taken from the realm of nature, "renewal" from the realm of art.[23] Like an artist carefully restoring a faded or damaged masterpiece, the Holy Spirit works upon the Christian until the divine image is restored (2 Cor 3:18).

Now, while the author of Titus may not be Paul, he certainly intends to write in the Apostle's name, and there can be no doubt that he has drawn this word from Paul, who apparently

[21] So A. Oepke, *TDNT* IV, 304; Bruner, *Theology,* 259; Dunn, *Baptism,* 166.
[22] Dunn, *Baptism,* 166.
[23] R. C. Trench, *Synonyms of the New Testament* (London: Macmillan, 1894) 65–66.

invented it. Ervin is certainly correct, then, in stating that the renewal by the Holy Spirit "equals the ongoing work of the Holy Spirit subsequent to the initial conversion experience."[24] But, because of the close tie with *loutron* ("bath") here, this work begins with the baptismal bath (or possibly the laying on of hands which accompanied the rite), and there is no ground for supposing a delay. It is furthermore a lifelong process. This would cohere well with Paul's teaching that the Holy Spirit is being constantly given (1 Thess 4:8) and that the Spirit's work of transformation goes from one degree of glory to the next (2 Cor 3:18).

This text, then, suggests a middle ground between a strict sacramentalism and the Classical Pentecostal doctrine of the "second blessing." Much of the anti-Pentecostal polemic has been aimed at showing that "everything is given in baptism," while the Pentecostals, working off their obvious experience of an explosion of "Holy Spirit power" at a later moment in the Christian life, have insisted that the "baptism in the Holy Spirit" is distinct from conversion-initiation. The analysis of this text suggests that the rite of initiation itself involves the gift of the Holy Spirit with his renewing power and, in the light of other texts we have seen, with charismatic power as well. But what is given is like a seed which develops according to certain rhythms; and there is nothing to gainsay that at certain moments, or even at a single critical moment in one's subsequent life, that life should "break through" with the amazing newness of a sprout bursting through the soil. If the Pentecostal must be cautioned against downplaying the power of baptismal initiation, the sacramentalist must be cautioned against downplaying the real newness of life experienced in what the Classical Pentecostals and neo-Pentecostals call the "baptism in the Holy Spirit."

Hebrews 6:1-5: Tasting the Gift and the Powers

"Therefore let us leave the elementary doctrines of Christ and go on to maturity, not laying again a foundation of repentance from dead works and of faith toward God, with instruction

[24] Ervin, *Conversion-Initiation*, 128.

about ablutions *(baptismôn)*, the laying on of hands *(epitheseos te cheirôn)*, the resurrection of the dead, and eternal judgment. . . . For it is impossible to restore again to repentance those who have once been enlightened, who have tasted the heavenly gift, and have become partakers of the Holy Spirit, and have tasted the goodness of the word of God and the powers of the age to come. . . ."

There is general agreement among the commentators that the strange plural, translated by the Revised Standard Version as "ablutions" but basically meaning "baptisms," is understandable as part of early instructions of catechumens about the various kinds of baptisms, that of John and that of Jesus, as well as Jewish purification ablutions. And the use of *baptismos* instead of *baptisma*, though unusual, is not unique in light of the same usage in Colossians 2:12. The interest of the text is that the laying on of hands, absent from the Pauline initiation texts, is explicitly mentioned here, as it is occasionally in Acts, as part of the rite of initiation. Sacramental interpreters want to pull the laying on of hands into the orbit of baptism, while Pentecostals (and confirmationists, we might add) stress the distinction of the two and seek to pull it into the orbit of the conveying of the Holy Spirit mentioned in verse 4.

The major argument in favor of the close connection with baptism is the enclitic *te* ("and") following *epitheseos* ("laying on"), instead of *kai* (the more usual "and") preceding.[25] Such usage for "and" indicates a very close connection of the words or phrases so joined.[26] Both Dunn and Bruner lean on this argument,[27] but Ervin correctly points out that *te* is also used in the immediately following expression as well ("and the resurrection of the dead"), thus nullifying the force of the *te* argument in this case. The alternation of *kai* and *te* in this series,

[25] For those less familiar with the details of Greek grammar, the usual word for "and" is *kai* preceding the word or phrase. Occasionally, however, especially for variety of style, the particle *te*, also meaning "and" is used instead, and it is placed *after* the word.

[26] W. Bauer, *A Greek-English Lexicon of the New Testament and Other Early Christian Literature.* ET, ed., W. F. Arndt and F. W. Gingrich (University of Chicago, 1957) 815.

[27] Dunn, *Baptism*, 207; Bruner, *Theology*, 211.

then, seems to be motivated more by a desire for variation in the listings rather than on a strict conjoining of elements. Once again, it appears evident that while both baptism and the laying on of hands are mentioned here, the attempt to assign the gift of the Spirit to one or the other element of the initiation rite to the exclusion of the other is a misguided effort. What can be said is that there is an *experiential* dimension to the rite of initiation (as the repeated "tasted" indicates) and a *charismatic* dimension, the latter being indicated by the expression, "having tasted . . . the powers of the age to come." There is little doubt that the word "powers" *(dynameis)* here means the wondrous works which the Spirit empowers the Christian to do in Jesus' name, which are anticipations of the coming kingdom just as they were in the ministry of Jesus.

One other text of Hebrews should be mentioned here before concluding. In describing the initial preaching and reception of the gospel, the author says: "God added his testimony by signs, wonders, various acts of power, and distribution of the gifts of the Holy Spirit according to his will" (Heb 2:4). Though not connected here with any rite like baptism or anointing or laying on of hands, the charismatic dimension appears at the very beginning of the Christian life (connected in some way, we may presume, with initiation), and this not only in the preacher but in the neophytes as well, as is indicated by the words "distribution of gifts."

On three points, then, Paul and the Letter to the Hebrews are in agreement: (1) The gift of the Spirit belongs integrally to Christian initiation; (2) There is an experiential dimension to the reception of the Spirit; (3) There is also a charismatic dimension. To this Titus brings the note of the baptismal bath that initiates the ongoing work of the Holy Spirit continually renewing the Christian.

Chapter Five

The Witness of Rome—1 Peter: Baptismal Grace Is Saving and Charismatic

Author and Date

The academic community has not reached a consensus concerning the authorship and the dating of 1 Peter.[1] Until modern times no one questioned the claim that the author was indeed the apostle Peter (1:1), the first among Jesus' disciples. Consequently a date for the letter was assumed prior to the apostle's death under Nero, between 64 and 67 A.D.

Beginning in the nineteenth century, doubts were raised on several critical grounds: (1) The cultivated Greek in which the letter is written and the citations from the Greek Old Testament could hardly have come from an Aramaic-speaking Galilean fisherman. (2) There are evident similarities with the thought and expressions of the Pauline letters. (3) The allusion to a world-wide persecution (5:9) would fit better the time of Domitian (81–96 A.D.). (4) It is unlikely that Peter would have addressed a letter to Pauline communities in Asia minor while

[1] A survey of research up to 1976 was made by J. H. Elliott, "The Rehabilitation of an Exegetical Step-child: 1 Peter in Recent Research," *JBL* 95 (1976) 243–54.

their founder, Paul, was still alive.[2]

These arguments have been countered by other scholars who hold for Petrine authenticity.[3] Ancient authors often made use of a secretary, who would be given considerable liberty in formulating the author's thought. In this case Silvanus is explicitly mentioned as the one "through whom" the author writes (5:12). Silvanus' role could easily explain not only the letter's stylistic peculiarities but also its reflection of Paul's thought, for Silvanus (or Silas) had been a journey-companion of Paul (2 Cor 1:19; 1 Thess 1:1; 2 Thess 1;1).[4] The reference to persecutions (5:11) could refer to widespread local harassments rather than a universal program of extermination. The same letter counsels respect for government and emperor (2:13-17)! As for Peter writing to communities founded by Paul, it is plausible that with the beginning of the Jewish revolt, the church in Rome under Peter's leadership assumed the role earlier held by the mother-church in Jerusalem. Hence an exhortatory letter (which 1 Peter is, rather than being disciplinary, like 1 Corinthians) would not be out of place. Granting an important role of Silvanus in the composition of the letter, these authors find no grounds to deny Petrine authorship and its consequent early date.[5]

[2] A late date was proposed as early as 1913 by O. D. Foster, *The Literary Relations of "The First Epistle of Peter" with their bearing on Date and Place of Authorship* (New Haven, CT: Yale University Press, 1913) and also F. W. Beare, who held that it was a "pseudonymous work of the post-apostolic age." *The First Epistle of Peter*, 3rd ed. (Oxford: Blackwell, 1970) vii, 215-16.

[3] *See*, for example, W. J. Dalton in *NJBC*, 903; J. Ramsey Michaels, *1 Peter*, Word Biblical Commentary 49 (Waco: Word, 1988) lxvi. Earlier, C. Bigg, *A Critical and Exegetical Commentary on the Epistles of St. Peter and St. Jude* (Edinburgh: T. & T. Clark, 1902) 87; E. G. Selwyn, *The First Epistle of St. Peter*, 2nd ed. (London: Macmillan, 1947) 32; A. M. Stibbs, *The First Epistle General of Peter* (Grand Rapids: Eerdmans, 1959) 30; Bo Reicke, *The Epistles of James, Peter and Jude*, AB 37 (Garden City: Doubleday, 1964) 71; C.E.B. Cranfield, *I & II Peter and Jude* (London: SCM, 1960) 13-16; C. Spicq, *Les Épitres de Saint Pierre* (Paris: Gabalda, 1966) 17-26.

[4] The letter is entirely attributed to Silvanus by E. Schweizer, *Der Erste Petrusbrief*3 (Zürich: Theologischer Verlag, 1972), 12; by Silvanus at the direction of Peter, according to P. H. Davids, *The First Epistle of Peter* (NICNT; Grand Rapids: Eerdmans, 1990).

[5] J. N. D. Kelly (*A Commentary on the Epistles of Peter and Jude* [New York: Harper & Row, 1969] 33), after a balanced consideration of all the

Still others have sought a middle ground. On the one hand, they take seriously the difference in style and the objection that Peter would probably not have written to Pauline churches during Paul's lifetime. They also doubt that the shift from Jerusalem to Rome took place before the fall of Jerusalem in 70 and thus whether the consequent re-adjustment and reformulation of the gentile mission would have happened before Peter's death. These facts would point to a later date and author. On the other hand, the similarities with Paul, James and 1 John, need not prove direct dependence. Quite the contrary, as is increasingly recognized today, all these writings draw on a common fund of earlier theological conceptions and formulations, many of which are of Palestinian origin. This is especially true of liturgical and hymnic materials, such as we find abundantly in 1 Peter. These scholars therefore opt for an author who is a disciple of Peter, writing sometime between 70 and 90 A.D. and reflecting the concerns of a Petrine school which was seeking to formulate a theology of the gentile mission from a new geographical and, in some sense, theological base.[6]

In any case, for our purposes it suffices to say that in the opinion of the majority of scholars, we are dealing with a church document of either late first or early second generation provenance, a document that can be safely assigned to the first century Roman community and witnesses to even earlier liturgical tradition.[7]

arguments, writes: ". . . taken as a whole, the evidence inclines towards an early date, and the earlier we place it the more difficult it becomes to deny some connection, indirect if not direct, with the Apostle."

[6] See E. Best, *1 Peter* (London: Oliphants, 1971) 49–63. J. H. Elliott in his extensive sociological study of 1 Peter, *A Home for the Homeless* (Philadelphia: Fortress, 1981) 85, suggests a date in the middle years of the Flavian age, i.e., between 69 and 96 A.D. N. Brox, *Der erste Petrusbrief* (Zürich: Benziger, 1979) 43, dates it between 70–100. *See* also D. Senior, *1 and 2 Peter* (Wilmington DL: Michael Glazier, 1980).

[7] Eusebius takes the canonicity of 1 Peter for granted, for he includes it among the writings which have been accepted from ancient times. The earliest attribution of it to the apostle comes from the New Testament itself—2 Peter 3:1 in the early second century at the latest. Polycarp, around 135 A.D., quotes from it several times, and Eusebius tells us that Papias (of Hierapolis in Phrygia, c. 60–130 A.D.) used it. Irenaeus (c. 185) speaks of it as the work of Peter, and Clement of Alexandria (c. 150–212) quotes from

As we have it now, 1 Peter is a letter. Unlike the Pauline epistles, which are customarily addressed to the Christians of a restricted locality, this letter is addressed to the Roman provinces which at that time covered nearly all of modern Turkey. It was evidently intended to be a circular letter for the widest possible Christian audience.

Liturgical Influence: Baptism

That the letter has been heavily influenced by the liturgy is generally admitted.[8] For some, represented by R. Perdelwitz, the entire section 1:3–4:11 is largely a baptismal homily.[9] H. Preisker has gone further and claimed that the entire epistle is substantially a Roman baptismal liturgy in which eight successive stages can be distinguished. Silvanus, a second or third generation Christian, put together the various parts and circulated the whole as a letter of the apostle.[10] F. L. Cross notes that not only is the liturgical dimension of the letter of great antiquity but also that the hope for the Second Coming and the undeveloped trinitarian formulas betray an early theology.[11] M.-E. Boismard has found and analyzed four baptismal hymns in the letter.[12] Even those scholars who maintain that the author composed the entire letter as a unity are compelled to admit its strong liturgical and baptismal character.[13] Certainly it is a rich

every chapter of it. Curiously, it is missing from the Muratorian Canon, those books accepted in Rome in the latter part of the second century. But there are possible echoes of it in Hermas' *Shepherd* (c. 140) and the Gnostic *Gospel of Truth* (before 145), both of which originated in Rome. See J. N. D. Kelly, *Commentary*, 2.

[8] J. H. Elliott in *The Elect and the Holy* (Leiden: Brill, 1966) 12, n. 3, lists W. Bornemann, B. H. Streeter, Jülicher-Fascher, H. Windisch, F. Hauck, F. W. Beare, E. Fascher, I. Fransen, J. Schneider, Ph. Carrington, E. M. Llopart, A. Strobel, M. E. Boismard, G. Braumann.

[9] R. Perdelwitz, *Die Mysterienreligion und das Problem des I. Petrusbriefes* (Giessen, 1911); cited by Elliott, *Elect*, 12, n. 3.

[10] H. Preisker, in his revision of H. Windisch's *Die Katholischen Briefe* (Tübingen: Mohr, 1951) 80–81.

[11] F. L. Cross, *1 Peter, A Paschal Liturgy* (London: Mowbray, 1954) 43–44.

[12] *Quatre hymnes baptismales dans la première épitre de Pierre* (Paris: Cerf, 1961).

[13] For a discussion of the debate and authors who react against a wholesale liturgical explanation of the letter see J. H. Elliott, *Elect*, p. 13, n. 3.

mine for understanding what Christian initiation meant in the Roman community in the first century.

Baptism, a Birth Event

What is baptism and what are its effects according to 1 Peter?

The word baptism appears only once in the letter, in a text we shall examine momentarily (3:21). But the role of the Holy Spirit in the initiation of the readers appears in the very address, which is trinitarian: "in the foreknowledge of God the Father, through *sanctification by the Spirit,* for obedience and sprinkling with the blood of Jesus Christ" (1:2). The identical phrase, *sanctification by the Spirit,* occurs in 2 Thessalonians 2:13, where it is connected, as here, with the initial call to faith in Jesus Christ. The Thessalonian text does not mention baptism, but a trinitarian initiation text of Paul does so under the image of washing in 1 Corinthians 6:11: "You were washed, you were *sanctified* . . . in the name of the Lord Jesus Christ and in the *Spirit* of our God."

The body of the letter begins with a reference to initiation (1:3-5). "Born again" is clearly an allusion to Christian initiation, to which the author returns in 1:23 and 2:2. Here, as in John 3:5-8, baptism is a birth event. It makes one a child of God, capable of calling God Father (1:17). Although the letter will have much to say about the sufferings of Christ and the sufferings of Christians, and even sees the blood of Christ as sealing the new covenant (1:2) and the price of redemption (1:18-19), it is remarkable that the birth event is linked to Christ's resurrection (1:3; 3:21) and not to his death. And, as in 1 Thessalonians 1:10, Christ's resurrection is viewed as a promise of his glorious revelation or parousia (1:4-5, 13). There is also a remarkable similarity with Titus 3:5-7, where the themes of rebirth, inheritance, hope, life and God "saving us by his mercy" appear.

Remarkable, too, is the emphasis on joy experienced by the newly baptized in the absence of vision, on the one hand (1:8), and in the presence of suffering on the other (1:6-7; 4:13). Joy is often linked to the Holy Spirit in the New Testament (Luke 10:12; Acts 13:52), especially in the Pauline literature (1 Thess 1:6; Rom 14:17; 15:13; Gal 5:22), and in Acts 8:39; 13:48; 16:34 and 1 Thessalonians 1:6 it is specifically tied to the moment of conversion and Christian initiation. Here the joy is described as *un-speakable* and *glorious*. These adjectives could be, of course, rhetorical flourishes; it is remarkable, however, that the author is not exhorting his readers to rejoice but actually describing their rejoicing. This and the broader New Testament context suggests that the process of becoming a Christian, from the inner consent of faith to the full rite of initiation, was normally an experience of great joy. In the post-biblical period this theme will be picked up by Hilary, as Kilian McDonnell will show.

Role of the Holy Spirit

The Holy Spirit reappears in the author's reflection on the Old Testament prophets and their New Testament counterparts, the preachers of the gospel. The prophets were inspired by "the Spirit of Christ," a rather unusual way of speaking about the Holy Spirit, for it means the "Spirit of the Messiah" (1:11). In the author's view the Spirit that inspired the prophets was in fact Christ's spirit and therefore Christ himself pre-existing through his Spirit in the prophets (see 2 Cor 3:12-18). It was also the Holy Spirit that accompanied the apostolic preaching with signs and wonders both in the preachers (Acts 1:8; 5:32; 1 Cor 2:4; 1 Thess 1:5; Heb 2:4) and in the listeners (Gal 3:1-5). That this Spirit was "sent from heaven" might allude to the Pentecost event described by Luke (Acts 2), but equally well, it might merely indicate the Spirit's divine origin.

Role of the Word

Particularly significant in the birth image is its relation in 1:23-25 not precisely to the sacrament or to the Holy Spirit but to the word proclaimed, imaged as seed (see James 1:18).[14] Though not meant to deny the role of baptism and the Spirit (the preaching is Spirit-inspired), this text is a reminder to the church of all times that persons can be sacramentalized without being evangelized. The role of faith in response to the preaching of

[14] The image of seed for the word is imbedded in the synoptic parables in which the seed also stands for the respondents to the word (Mark 4:1-34 and par.), without, of course, the image of birth. See J. P. Heil, "Reader-Response and the Narrative Context of the Parables about Growing Seed in Mark 4:1-34," *CBQ* 54 (1992) 271-86.

the word receives particular stress (1:5, 7-9). The influence of the word (*logos*) carries over into 2:2, where the expression usually translated "spiritual milk" is *logikon gala*, which retains its relation to the word (*logos*) of the previous section and justifies the AV translation, "milk of the word."[15]

We know that in the earliest liturgies of which we have witnesses, milk and honey were given to initiates to symbolize their entrance into the promised land.[16] Here, beyond the meaning of milk as word, a eucharistic meaning is quite likely, at least in the author's citation of Psalm 34:8, "Taste and see that the Lord is good," followed as it is by an allusion to the royal priesthood of the believers (2:5, 9). To whatever moment of the initiation rite this text refers, it certainly confirms what we have seen elsewhere, that there was an expectation of some life-changing experience in the process of becoming a Christian.

"Saved through Water"

We now come to the single text which mentions baptism, 3:21: "This [Noah's family "saved through water," v. 20] prefigured baptism, which saves you now." Again there is an echo of Titus 3:5: "he saved us through the bath of rebirth . . .," the emphasis falling upon the sacrament as the instrument of salvation. The water of baptism is a counterpart or "antitype" of the waters of the flood. By passing through the water of baptism, Christians, like Noah, are saved. There is no mention of the Holy Spirit here as there is in Titus 3:5: "and renewal by the Holy Spirit." Nor is there mention of any other rite such as anointing or the laying on of hands. Not much can be made from the silence of texts, but it is clear that the water rite here is considered the efficacious instrument of salvation for the believer. The sanctifying role of the Holy Spirit is, of course, presumed (1:2).

Charisms, Love and Stewardship

The lengthy exhortations concerning the new ethical life of

[15] See Kelly 85–86.

[16] Hippolytus, *Trad. apost.* xxiii. 2; Tertullian, *Adv. Marcion* i. 14; *De cor.* iii.3).

Christians and their duties according to their state of life (2:11–4:9) reflect the baptismal catechesis common in the ancient church. This section climaxes with the exhortation to charity (4:7-9) and—significant for our inquiry—with an exhortation to use the gifts:

"Above all, let your love for one another be intense, because love covers a multitude of sins. Be hospitable to one another without complaining. *As each one has received a gift, use it to serve one another as good stewards of God's varied grace. Whoever preaches, let it be with the words of God; whoever serves, let it be with the strength that God supplies,* so that in all things God may be glorified through Jesus Christ, to whom belong glory and dominion forever and ever. Amen" (4:8-11).

We are in an atmosphere very much like 1 Corinthians 12-14, where Paul sets the charismatic gifts in the context both of baptism (1 Cor 12:13) and of charity (1 Cor 13).[17] Likewise in Ephesians 4:1-16 the gifts and offices given by the Spirit are set in the context of baptismal grace (Eph 4:5) and love (Eph 4:16). There is thus every evidence that instruction on the charismatic nature of the Christian life and one's anointing for service to the community was part of the earliest Christian catechesis.

Here in 1 Peter each Christian is called a *steward* (*oikonomos*), that is, one responsible for the household. What is remarkable is that the role of steward is not limited to the elders or the authorities in the community (5:1) though obedience to them is counseled (5:5).[18] The distributive terms here ("if anyone," "each," "to each," "manifold") indicate, as in 3:8 and 5:5b, that it is all Christians who are household stewards of God's manifold grace. Whatever their specific ministry, all Christians are stewards responsible for the household of God, the family which is the church.[19]

[17] For a discussion of the relation of this text to the Pauline literature see Horst Goldstein, *Paulinische Gemeinde im Ersten Petrusbrief* (Stuttgart: KBW, 1975) 12–17.

[18] In 1 Corinthians 4:1-2 the stewards are the apostles; in Titus 1:7 they are overseers or bishops.

[19] So Elliott, *A Home for the Homeless*, 147-48. The text emphasizes interdependence of the gifts. No gift is to be exercised in isolation. Each Christian is both to give and receive ministry. See Stibbs, *Peter*, 156.

The *grace* (*charis*) of God is called manifold, the same word used in Hebrews 2:4, "*various* acts of power and distribution of the gifts of the Holy Spirit. . . ." And it expresses itself in charismatic gifts (*charisma* is the word for "gift" in 4:10). *Each one has received such a gift.*

The author provides only two illustrations of the varied gifts. The first, understood by the Revised NAB as "preaching" is in the Greek the much broader verb *lalein,* more literally translated "he who speaks." While it is surely a question here not of conversation but of addressing the community, much more is involved than preaching, as Michaels has correctly observed:

"The term ["he who speaks"] could embrace all that Paul includes under "prophecy" (Rom 12:6), "teaching" (Rom 12:7) and "exhortation" (Rom 12:8), as well as "wisdom" and "knowledge" (1 Cor 12:8). "Tongues" (1 Cor 12:10) are less likely to have been included because they seem to have been regarded more as a form of prayer to God (1 Cor 14:2, 28) than as *logia theou,* . . . intelligible words of God to the congregation. The interpretation of tongues, however, cannot be excluded."[20]

The author further emphasizes that such gifts of speaking are not mere human talents, though they may be in continuity with them. Rather the gifts are meant to be exercised as divinely given powers. He who speaks should do it "with the words of God," that is, in some way it must be an exercise of prophecy, divinely inspired.[21]

The second example is of the most general nature. "Service" occasionally means official ministry (2 Cor 11:8; 2 Tim 4:11), sometimes merely table service (Luke 10:40) or the distribution

[20] Michaels, *1 Peter,* 250.

[21] Some authors hold that "the words of God" here simply mean the authentic gospel, passing on the authorized tradition, as in Romans 3:2 and Hebrews 5:12, where the definite articles are used (W. J. Dalton, NJBC 908; Kelly, 180). However, the absence of the definite articles here and the context indicate more than that. He who speaks "the words of God," like the OT prophet, speaks under divine inspiration (so Michaels, 250). The simplest believer in the pew knows the difference between a preacher who parrots someone else's words, even the inspired word of Scripture, and one who breaks the word open with fresh and immediate meaning.

of goods (Acts 6:2). But frequently it means any kind of service in the household (1 Cor 16:15) or for the church (Eph 4:12; Rev 2:19). This sense seems preferable here. In any case it does not refer exclusively to the leaders of the community. Words addressed to them are found later in 5:1-5a. Consequently the less spectacular gifts are also seen here precisely as gifts, and while exteriorly they may seem little different from the exercise of natural talents, the Christian has a special anointing to use them "with the strength that God gives."

From this document of the Roman community in the last third of the first century, we can draw the following conclusions: (1) Christian initiation involves a trinitarian relationship in which sanctification is attributed to the Holy Spirit. (2) Baptism is a saving, birth event which initiates one into the life of the risen Christ. (3) The Spirit-inspired word of God, both in the Old Testament prophets and in the preachers of the word, is instrumental in effecting the new birth. (4) The mention of the water-rite alone suffices to describe the ritualization of the saving action of God. (5) Each of the baptized receives a charism and becomes a steward responsible for the household which is the church. (6) The charisms involve word gifts and gifts of service. They are not mere natural talents but are to be exercised under divine impulse, in love and mutual service.

Chapter Six

Living Water:
Spirit-Baptism in John

The pneumatology of the fourth evangelist is quite rich.[1] Following the tendency already observable in Luke to separate the gift of the Spirit from John's water-baptism, the evangelist omits entirely the account of Jesus' baptism in the Jordan and focuses solely upon the descent of the Spirit in the form of a dove. To this tradition John adds that the Spirit *abides* on Jesus, i.e., rests there in a permanent way, thus separating him from all preceding prophets on whom the Spirit came in a passing way:

"I saw the Spirit come down like a dove from the sky and *remain* upon him. I did not know him, but the one who sent me to baptize with water told me, 'On whomever you see the Spirit come down and *remain*, he is the one who will baptize with the Holy Spirit'" (John 1:32-34).

Thus, through his permanent possession of the Spirit, Jesus

[1] Besides the commentaries on individual passages, *see* G. M. Burge, *The Anointed Community: The Holy Spirit in the Johannine Tradition* (Grand Rapids: Eerdmans, 1987) with extensive bibliography; R. E. Brown, "The Paraclete in the Fourth Gospel," NTS 13 (1966–67) 113–32; "The Paraclete in Light of Modern Research," SE (1968) 158–65; G. Johnston, *The Spirit-Paraclete in the Gospel of John*, NovTSup 12 (Cambridge: University Press, 1970); Montague, *Holy Spirit*, 333–65.

"will be able to anoint with power those who believe."[2] There is, however, a significant shift in the way Jesus shows that he is endowed with the Spirit. In John there is no temptation story, nor is there a single exorcism. Likewise the dispute about the spirit by which Jesus casts out demons is missing. Instead, we have the graver accusation that Jesus is possessed by the devil (7:20; 8:48; 10:20), and the battle with Satan turns on who Jesus is (8:49-53). The conquest of Satan is focused entirely on the cross (12:31; 13:27; 14:30; 16:11). And the word *pneuma* is not associated with any of Jesus' miracles. The latter are limited to seven and are called *signs*, since the evangelist wishes to focus on the revelatory nature of Jesus' miracles.

John's view of Jesus' baptizing in the Holy Spirit must be interpreted against this background. Only the fourth evangelist tells us of Jesus' disciples baptizing during his public ministry (3:22; 4:2). Was this a "baptism in the Holy Spirit"? That could hardly be so, since the Spirit would not be given until Jesus was glorified (7:39). It is likely, then, that the rite was similar to that of John the Baptist. Certainly nothing can be drawn from it concerning Christian baptism subsequent to the resurrection of Jesus. The focus in John rather seems to be entirely upon the death-resurrection of Jesus as the source of the Spirit. The "signs" Jesus works all point to that great event, and perhaps for that reason they lack the mention of the Spirit. What John denies to the "signs," he lavishly grants to the moment of Jesus' glorification. The life-giving Spirit, promised in 4:10 and 7:39, is breathed out symbolically and proleptically as Jesus dies on the cross (19:30).[3] And the water flowing from Jesus' side is a symbolic fulfillment of the promise that from within him would flow rivers of living water, a further symbol of the Spirit (7:37-39; cf. 4:7-15).[4]

After the resurrection Jesus breathes upon his disciples and says, "Receive the Holy Spirit. Whose sins you forgive are forgiven them, and whose sins you retained are retained" (20:22-23). This has been called the Johannine Pentecost. Though

[2] Burge, *Anointed Community*, 62.
[3] Ibid., 133; R. E. Brown, *The Gospel According to John*, AB 29A (Garden City, N.Y.: Doubleday, 1970) 913.
[4] Burge, *Anointed Community*, 135.

John does not set the gift of the Spirit in the framework of the Jewish Feast of Weeks, as Luke does (and modern critical scholarship has given up efforts at harmonization of the two accounts), there can be no doubt that the Easter encounter of the risen Lord with the disciples is, in John's view, the fulfillment of the promises made earlier in the gospel concerning the eschatological gift of the Spirit (14:26; 15:26; 16:7). Jesus' breathing upon his disciples bespeaks a new creation which affects the disciples not merely as the Twelve but as representative of all disciples (cf. Gen 2:7). Moreover, the sending of the disciples is modeled on the Father-Son relationship (v. 21), which elsewhere is meant for all the disciples, not just for the Twelve (15:9).[5] Further, the word *receive* is a traditional expression for the initial gift of the Spirit.[6] Thus verse 22 would appear to be the fulfillment of the Baptist's prophecy that Jesus would baptize with the Holy Spirit.[7] "The present scene serves as the baptism of Jesus' immediate disciples and as a pledge of divine begetting to all believers of a future period represented by the disciples."[8]

There is a difficulty raised, however, by the immediately attached verse 23, for it seems that the Spirit given here is specifically for the power to forgive or retain sins. This aspect need not detain us long, for while there is dispute as to whether the text refers to the power to forgive sins *after* baptism, there is a broad consensus that it in any case includes the forgiveness of sins *in* baptism.[9]

John 3:5-8: Born of Water and Spirit
The New Testament tradition already departs from that of the Old Testament in introducing a human agent as conveyor of the

[5] Brown, *The Gospel According to John*, AB 29A, 1034–35.

[6] *See* the extensive references given in Burge, *Anointed Community*, 126.

[7] "Thus it seems that in some fashion the disciples were experiencing in John 20 the eschatological Spirit predicted in 1:33. . . . This is the time of their 'recreation' and new birth. This is the advent of the Paraclete." Burge, *Anointed Community*, 149.

[8] Brown, *John*, 1037. Brown also notes that the baptismal ritual of breathing on the subject to be baptized has preserved this ancient symbolism.

[9] For a complete discussion see Brown, *John*, 1039–45 and J. Schmitt, "Simples remarques sur le fragment Jo., XX, 22–23," *Mélanges en l'honneur de Monseigneur Michel Andrieu* (Université de Strasbourg, 1956) 415–23.

Spirit,[10] and, as we have seen, John carries this further in stating that the Spirit Jesus gives is the one that abides in or on him in its fullness (3:34).[11] It is also clear, in the rich imagery of the Fourth Gospel, that the Spirit flows from the exalted Jesus to the one who believes in him (7:39; 19:37) and that for the first disciples the moment of Jesus' gift of the Spirit is Easter Day when Jesus breathes the Holy Spirit upon them.[12] We are now in a position to examine more closely how subsequent believers receive the Spirit, and the pertinent text is given earlier in the gospel:

"Truly, truly, I say to you, unless one is born of water and the Spirit, he cannot enter the kingdom of God. That which is born of the flesh is flesh, and that which is born of the Spirit is spirit. Do not marvel that I said to you, 'You must be born anew.' The wind blows where it wills, and you hear the sound of it, but you do not know whence it comes or whither it goes; so it is with every one who is born of the Spirit" (3:5-8).

The connection of this text with the "Johannine Pentecost" of 20:22 is suggested by the common link of *pneuma* but also in the close relationship of its meanings as "wind" and "breath."[13] But of the many questions raised by this text, the one that interests us here is the relation of water and the Spirit to being born *anōthen* (v. 3), which can mean either "from above" or "again." In the Greek both "water" and "Spirit" lack the definite article, and both are governed by the preposition *ex*, indicating a very close relationship between the two. There can therefore be no question of two rebirths or two baptisms, as even a Pentecostal scholar like H. D. Hunter admits.[14] To speak of a "born again" event for Christians already baptized is therefore quite un-Scriptural. In Bruner's words, "A man must be 'born again' but not 'again and again.' "[15]

---

[10] Cf. F. Martin, *Baptism*, 9.

[11] Burge, *Anointed Community*, 54–56.

[12] Ibid., 95, 100.

[13] Brown, *John*, 1030, 1037; Burge, *Anointed Community*, 169.

[14] H. D. Hunter, *Spirit Baptism*, 99. Charismatically oriented Baptist Howard Ervin makes no attempt to use this text to support a subsequent "baptism in the Holy Spirit," *Conversion-Initiation*, 143–44.

[15] Bruner, *Theology*, 258.

On the other hand, to speak of the expression as a *hendiadys* (two nouns joined by *and* but standing for a noun and a modifier), as Dunn does, is not particularly helpful. It would mean either that the water has subsumed the Spirit (a position first witnessed by Tertullian[16]), or that the Spirit has subsumed the water, water being merely a metaphor for the Spirit. The latter alternative is, of course, possible, given the relation of water to the Spirit in Ezekiel 36:25-26, Isaiah 44:3, and 1QS IV 19-21. And in the Book of Jubilees, dating from the second century B.C., there is a loose connection between the Spirit and divine filiation: "I will create in them a Holy Spirit and I will cleanse them . . . I will be their Father, and they will be my children."[17]

But to exclude an allusion to baptism, at least at some level of the text, is a narrow exegesis indeed, in the light of the following considerations: (1) "Water" appears to many exegetes as an intrusion into the text.[18] Left out, the text makes perfect sense, and is consonant with verse 8, where there is no mention of water. Yet "water" appears in all the manuscripts, and therefore is obviously intentional either by the original author or the Ecclesiastical Redactor responsible for the final version of John. No reasonable motive can be assigned for the author/editor's insisting on "water" in a text that could do without it, unless he had a sacramental interest.[19] (2) By the time of the publishing of John's Gospel, water-baptism in the name of Jesus (or the "trinity" of Matt 28:19) was universally practiced, and that meaning of "water" could not have escaped John's readers, particularly in view of the positive references to baptism in 3:22-26 and 4:1-2.[20] "Water" here as a word for baptism need not obscure the more important context of the role of the Spirit and of Jesus himself in the conferring of the new birth.[21] The

[16] *See* chapter 3, note 14 above.

[17] *Jub.* I 23-25.

[18] Brown, *The Gospel According to John* AB 29, 142, lists as holding this position in one form or another: Bultmann, K. Lake, Wellhausen, Lohse; and Catholics: Braun, Léon Dufour, Van den Bussche, Feuillet, Leal, De la Potterie. To these could be added Wendt, Haenchen, and Bernard.

[19] *See* also O. Cullmann, *Early Christian Worship* (Philadelphia: Westminster, 1953) 76-77.

[20] So Burge, *Anointed Community*, 171.

[21] *See* G. R. Beasley-Murray, "John 3:3, 5: Baptism, Spirit and the King-

exegetical contortions Dunn exhibits in trying to escape a sacramental reference in John 3:5 reveal his anti-sacramental bias.[22]

For our purposes, it suffices to show that this text confirms what we have seen elsewhere, that the Holy Spirit is conferred in the rite of initiation, which includes as a necessary element water-baptism.

Charisms in John?

The charismatic dimension of the life of the Spirit might well appear at first sight to be muted in John. There is no doubt that the role of the Paraclete in the Last Discourse is depicted primarily in terms of witnessing to Jesus against the world. But the Paraclete also will relate the "more" which Jesus could not tell in his earthly ministry, and he will declare the things that are to come (16:12-13). Exegetes dispute whether this refers to prophecy as experienced in other New Testament communities or whether it means the ongoing interpretation of the meaning of Jesus for each age.[23] From what we have seen in previous chapters, however, the concept of prophecy was broad enough to include both these functions (see, e.g., Luke 1:67). Other charisms are implied in Jesus' promise that his disciples will do even greater works than he did (14:12), and his works were the works of a prophet (4:44; 6:14; 7:40; 4:19). Consequently, though the manner of describing the Spirit-impelled life may be different in John, the charismatic nature of it is clearly present.

The Johannine epistles assume that each Christian has an anointing enabling him or her to judge the truth or falsity of external teachers (1 John 2:20-27). Though it is obvious that the writer of the letter does not exclude himself as teacher, the character of the Johannine communities appears to be such that more emphasis is placed on this interior anointing than upon

dom," *ExpTim* 97 (1985) 167-70. Burge, *Anointed Community*, 167-68, who holds for a sacramental meaning of "water," is at pains to point out that it is quite secondary to the role of the Spirit and ultimately of Jesus himself in his death and glorification as the agent of the rebirth.

[22] Dunn, *Baptism*, 183-94; answered by Ervin, *Conversion-Initiation*, 144-46.

[23] Wikenhauser, Bernard and Windisch are among the former, Bultmann and Brown among the latter. Brown, *The Gospel According to John* AB, 298, 715-16.

external control. The author, as a matter of fact, does not invoke his own authority as settling the issue; he appeals rather to the inner anointing which enables the authentic disciples to identify his teaching as that which was "from the beginning."[24] The inner anointing is that of the Holy Spirit given in baptism.

We can conclude, then, that in the rich symbolism of John, the life-giving and regenerating Spirit, given proleptically and symbolically from the crucified Jesus and actually by insufflation on Easter Sunday, is received by the Christian at baptism. There is no delay envisioned to the coming of the Spirit to achieve his effects. The Spirit's new life is manifested in various ways, particularly in his testimony to Jesus, in the inner enlightenment he gives concerning right teaching, in empowering the disciples to forgive sins and to do Jesus' works, and in guiding them into the future.

The prophetic dimension of the Spirit's action is given greater prominence in another witness of the Johannine tradition, the Book of Revelation. The entire work is called prophecy (Rev 22:18-19); in it the Spirit speaks to the churches (2:7, 11, 17, 29; 3:6, 13, 22). Though from an author other than the fourth evangelist, the Book of Revelation shares many of the rich symbols of the gospel. The living water symbolized and already experienced in baptism becomes the eternal reward of the faithful conquerors (21:6-7; 22:17). It is the river of life that flows from the throne of God and the Lamb for the healing of the nations (22:1-2).

In sum, the Johannine picture, though at times expressed differently, coheres well with what we have seen elsewhere in the New Testament: the Holy Spirit is conferred at the moment of baptism, empowering with knowledge that is both true and experiential, and manifesting itself in the community through prophetic and healing gifts.

---

[24] Such a situation certainly had its pitfalls, and eventually, if we are to accept the reconstruction of R. E. Brown, in the face of the schism within the community, it survived only by accepting the more visible authority structure of the larger church. R. E. Brown, *The Epistles of John* AB 30 (Garden City: Doubleday, 1982) 103–15; *The Community of the Beloved Disciple* (New York: Paulist, 1979) 138–42, 155–62; Burge, *Anointed Community*, 217–21.

Chapter Seven

Charism and Community: Spirit-Baptism and the Building of the Church

Though the expectation of charismatic expression is not always expressed, it is so pervasive, especially in Luke and Paul, and so neglected in the usual contemporary catechesis of initiation, that it deserves special attention before concluding our study. For the baptism in the Spirit does not terminate at personal regeneration and renewal but is aimed at building up the Christian community.

Leaving to rest the question of whether the gift of the Spirit is given in baptism or in the laying on of hands, it can be said without hesitation that the integral rite of initiation involved the gift of the Holy Spirit, and that gift manifested itself in various ways, an important one of which was gifts *(charismata)* aimed at the upbuilding of the community or at the creation of *koinōnia*.

We saw this clear expectation in the Markan conclusion (Mark 16:9-20), where Christian baptism appears to be modeled upon Jesus' own baptism, as an empowerment by the Holy Spirit for ministry. In Matthew's community, the gift of prophecy was still highly regarded, though it appears to be moving toward a recognized ministry in certain individuals. In John the gift of the Spirit is more sacramentalized and identified with "life" under the symbol of water and wind. But the prophetic Spirit underlies such passages as John 16:12-15, where the promised Spirit will reveal the things of Jesus and declare the things that are to come. The letters of John reveal an even more daring "anointing" of each individual, by which he can, in the face of false teaching, identify the teaching which was "from the beginning." In another stream of the Johannine tradition, the Book of Revelation teems with prophetic words and, in fact, is in its entirety an example of early Christian prophecy (22:18-19). It is in Luke-Acts, of course, that the Spirit appears primarily as the prophetic spirit. Luke's paradigmatic descriptions of Christian initiation describe the Spirit manifesting itself through the prophetic gifts.

Koinōnia

The goal and term of the charisms in Jesus' ministry was the announcing and manifestation of the kingdom (Mark 1:15; Matt 12:28; Luke 11:20). In the disciples' ministry it is the same (Matt 10:1, 5-8), but in the post-resurrection church the charisms are more ecclesially oriented. This appears most strikingly when Luke lists the four effects of the Pentecostal Spirit upon the first gathering of believers: "They devoted themselves to the teaching of the apostles and to the communal life, to the breaking of the bread and to the prayers" (2:42). This verse in Greek is grammatically tied closely to the preceding Pentecostal event.[1] To this the wonders and signs done by the apostles are added (v. 43). This summary description is paradigmatic for Luke.

The word translated "communal life" is koinōnia. Of the wide spectrum of meanings, the one intended here is best determined from the context. It is a communal life that "has its basis in faith . . . its expression in cult . . . and its concrete realization in the sharing of material goods. . . ."[2] The context, as we

---

[1] The Greek particle de concludes the phrase introduced by the preceding Greek particle mèn of verse 41.

[2] G. Panikulam, Koinōnia in the New Testament: A Dynamic Expression of Christian Life (Rome: Biblical Institute 1979) 124. For further literature on koinōnia in the New Testament: L. Sabourin, "Koinōnia in the New Testament," Religious Studies Bulletin (Sudbury) 1 (1981) 109-15; M. J. Suggs, "Koinōnia in the New Testament," Midstream 23 (1984) 351-62; M. Vellanickal,

have seen, also makes it clear that this new community is the work of the Holy Spirit that descended at Pentecost. The community is the visible and permanent manifestation of which the Pentecostal theophany was the passing sign. It is the new people God vitalized by the Spirit of God (Ezek 36:27).[3]

This is Luke's only use of *koinōnia* in Acts. Thereafter the reality described by *koinōnia* becomes *ekklēsia*.[4] In the idyllic description of the primitive community here, Luke appears to have drawn *koinōnia* from the Pauline tradition, where it is an important ecclesial concept. Of the eighteen times the word appears in the New Testament, thirteen of them are in Paul. Central to the term for him is Christ-centered fellowship. It is never used for an individual's union with Christ (for which Paul's preferred term is "to be in Christ"[5]). Thus it functions not only statically as an image of the church ("community" or "communion") but dynamically as an ongoing reality progressively created by the *participation* or *sharing* of faith (Phlm 6), of the gospel (Phil 1:5), of the eucharist (1 Cor 10:16), of the sufferings of Christ (Phil 3:10), and even of material goods (2 Cor 8:4; 9:13; Rom 15:26). It is not surprising then that the Spirit should also appear in this context twice. In Philippians 2:1, Paul says, "If there is any fellowship in the Spirit"—a phrase that lends itself to many possible translations, but the most likely one takes Spirit here to be the Holy Spirit, in the sense in which the term also appears in the "trinitarian" blessing of 2 Corinthians 13:13: "The grace of our Lord Jesus Christ and the love of God and

"Ecclesial Communio: A Biblical Perpsective," *Bible Bhashyam* 12 (1986) 182–95; and the older literature: J. Y. Campbell, "*Koinōnia* and its Cognates in the NT," *JBL* 51 (1932) 352–80; H. W. Ford, "The NT Conception of Fellowship," *Shane Quarterly* 6 (1945) 188–215; G. V. Jourdan, "*Koinōnia* in 1 Cor 10:16," *JBL* 67 (1948) 111–24; S. Lyonnet, "La *koinōnia* de l'église primitive et la sainte èglise (Act. 2:42-7)," 35 *Congresso Eucharistico Internationale, Sess. de estud.* I, Barcelona (1954) 511–15; F. Hauck, *koinos*, etc., TDNT III, 789–809.

[3] "As through the interior transformation of the law (Jer 31:33) and the permanence of the Spirit (Ezek 36:27) Yahweh made Israel a new people, so also here we have . . . a new community. . . . It is the Spirit that forms and vitalizes the community into this realisation, giving it a spiritual basis and an external realisation." Panikulam, *Koinonia*, 124.

[4] Fitzmyer, *Luke the Theologian*, 139.

[5] Panikulam, *Koinōnia*, 5.

the *fellowship of the Holy Spirit* be with all of you." The genitive "of the Holy Spirit" may be objective, with the sense, "fellowship in (or with) the Holy Spirit,"[6] but the parallel expressions "grace of . . . Christ" and "love of God" as a blessing imparted suggest that the genitive is subjective, i.e, the fellowship created or given by the Holy Spirit.[7] G. Panikulam in his extensive study concludes that *koinōnia* here is so comprehensive it cannot be limited to either objective or subjective meanings.[8]

The term is thus one that is rich and extensive, reaching from the idea of union together with the Father (1 John 1:3) or in God's son, Jesus (1 Cor 1:9) to the very pragmatic sharing of economic life. And the whole is attributed to the Holy Spirit. In the post-New Testament church the term becomes a major ecclesiological locus, a testing ground for who belongs to the church and who does not (a process already discernible in 1 John), but in the more irenic atmosphere of Paul it is simply a rich symbol for a dynamic church life.

Perhaps it was precisely the embarrassment of riches in the polyvalent meanings of *koinōnia* that led Paul to choose another term and image in treating more specifically of the purpose of the charisms. He connects the charisms to his image of the *body* of Christ and sees them as given for its *upbuilding*. The body image is intimately connected with *koinōnia*, even another way of describing the same reality, as appears from 1 Corinthians 10:16: "The bread that we break, is it not a *communion* (*koinōnia*) in the *body* of Christ?" But "body" and "building" are clearer and more versatile images for developing the themes of growth and ministry within the communion.

Paul: Charisms for Community[9]

Paul assumes that the Holy Spirit functions in the Christian community through the charisms. This appears from his very

[6] The number of exegetes who hold this position is impressive: Dunn, *Jesus and the Spirit* (Philadelphia: Westminster, 1975) 261; Hauck, *TDNT*, 3:807; Windisch, Kümmel, Barrett, George, Lietzmann, Furnish.

[7] So Plummer, Bruce, Jourdan, Spicq, Zerwick, Heinrici, Bachmann, Bousset.

[8] Panikulam, *Koinōnia*, 70.

[9] Besides the commentaries, *see:* D. E. Aune, *Prophecy*,; S. M. Burgess, *The Spirit and the Church: Antiquity* (Peabody, Mass.: Hendrickson, 1984);

first letter: "Do not quench the Spirit. Do not despise prophetic utterances" (1 Thess 5:19-20). In Galatians 3:2-5 Paul appeals to his readers' experience of the wonder-working Spirit as an argument for the superiority of the gospel over the works of the law. It is in 1 Corinthians 12-14, however, that the Apostle's major treatment of the charisms occurs. In the very introduction to the letter, Paul praises the community for its being endowed "with every kind of discourse and knowledge, as the testimony to Christ was confirmed among you, so that you are not lacking in any spiritual gift" (1 Cor 1:5-7). Since the "testimony of Christ" is doubtless Paul's preaching of the gospel which the Corinthians accepted,[10] the outpouring of the gifts of the Spirit is tied to their initiation into the Christian life. The same sequence of events appears in Hebrews 2:4: "God added his testimony by signs, wonders, various acts of power, and distribution of the gifts of the Holy Spirit according to his will." The last item, according to the consensus of commentators, refers to the manifestation of charismatic gifts.[11] Hence it may be assumed that in the early church there was a widespread, if not universal, expectation that the baptized would manifest their reception of the Spirit charismatically. The letter to the Romans (12:6-8) indicates that this was so not only in the communities Paul founded, but elsewhere as well, in fact, in the capital of the empire.

In the major treatment of the charisms later in 1 Corinthians, Paul states that "to each one the manifestation of the Spirit is

W. A. Grudem, *The Gift of Prophecy in First Corinthians* (Washington: University Press of America, 1982); R. P. Martin, *The Spirit and the Congregation;* D. Hill, *New Testament Prophecy;* T. Callan, "Prophecy and Ecstasy in Greco-Roman Religion and in 1 Corinthians" *NT* 27 (1985) 125-40; J. Behm, "Glossa," *TDNT* 1:719-27; A. Bittlinger, *Gifts and Graces: A Commentary on 1 Corinthians 12-14,* trans. H. Klassen (Grand Rapids: Eerdmans, 1968); E. E. Ellis, " 'Spiritual' Gifts"; R. H. Gundry, " 'Ecstatic Utterance' (NEB)?" *JTS* 17 (1966) 299-307; A. A. Hoekema, *What About Tongue-Speaking?* (Grand Rapids: Eerdmans, 1966); E. Schweizer, "Pneuma, pneumatikos" *TDNT* 6:332-455; R. L. Thomas, *Understanding Spiritual Gifts* (Chicago: Moody, 1978); G. T. Montague, *The Spirit and His Gifts* (New York: Paulist, 1974) and *The Holy Spirit,* 145-84.

[10] This meaning of *martyrion* also appears in 1 Corinthians 2:1; 2 Thessalonians 1:10; 2 Timothy 1:8.

[11] Spicq, Graf, Hughes, Jewett, and others.

given for a good purpose" (12:7), thus implying that some manifestation of the Spirit appears in each of the baptized:

"To one is given through the Spirit the expression of wisdom; to another the expression of knowledge according to the same Spirit; to another faith by the same Spirit; to another gifts of healing by the one Spirit; to another mighty deeds; to another prophecy; to another discernment of spirits; to another varieties of tongues; to another interpretation of tongues. But one and the same Spirit produces all of these, distributing them individually to each person as he wishes" (12:8-11).[12]

Paul apparently considers that a baptized person who would not have received some manifest gift of the Spirit to be an anomaly. The normal Christian life is charismatic.[13]

Later Paul indicates that the gifts fall into a certain order:

"First, apostles; second, prophets; third, teachers; then, mighty deeds; then gifts of healing, assistance, administration, and varieties of tongues" (12:28).

This passage reveals the evolution beginning to take place even in this early period from gift to recognized office, and it is apparent that some of the gifts are less "dramatic" than others: teaching, assistance, administration, for example.[14] Paul's own

[12] A discussion of each of the charisms would go beyond the scope of our study. Paul himself discusses several of them in 1 Corinthians 14. On tongues, prophecy, and interpretation, see my study, The Spirit and His Gifts, 18-50. For other studies see the bibliography in note 9, esp. the work of R. L. Thomas.

[13] "Every single Christian . . . possesses a spiritual endowment. The discussion [here] returns to this common characteristic. For example, in verses 8-10 the words 'to one . . . to another . . .' and so on, take their cue from this universal characteristic. The same strain is carried in the words 'to each one individually' (v. 11). . . . In the companion section of Romans, it is 'as God has allotted to each a measure of faith' (12:3). In Ephesians also . . . : 'But to each one of us grace was given according to the measure of Christ's gift' (4:7). If there is one teaching that is well established in this field, it is that every Christian has at least one gift." Thomas, Understanding, 33.

[14] Antilēmpseis ("assistance") means "acts of helping." Kybernēseis ("administration") comes from the term for helmsman of a ship and was popu-

gift/office as apostle is being exercised in this very letter in his teaching and regulation of matters in the community. Nevertheless, it is clear that it is not Paul who endows the community with different gifts and ministries; at most he coordinates and regulates the gifts and ministries each has received from the Spirit.

However, though the Spirit is understood to manifest itself in each one from the moment of his or her initiation into the faith, it is possible to progress to other gifts, since Paul encourages the faithful to "seek after the greater spiritual gifts" (12:31; 14:1), and especially to seek the gift of prophecy (14:1). The gift of tongues appears to be so highly esteemed by the Corinthians that there was no concern to bring this "pre-conceptual" type of praise, thanksgiving, or message (14:14-16) to intelligible term so that more of the community could benefit by it. They should therefore move on and seek gifts that would more clearly build up the community (14:26).[15]

This admonition to seek the gifts is helpful when considering the contemporary situation in which many Christians are baptized in infancy or in adulthood without any expectation of a charismatic expression. In such cases, awakening the individual to the charismatic potential of his or her baptism, and praying with him through the laying on of hands, as is done in the "baptism of the Holy Spirit," could be a way of activating gifts and ministries of which he or she was previously unaware.[16]

larly used as an image for governing. *See* H. Conzelmann, *1 Corinthians* (Philadelphia: Fortress, 1975) 215. We can assume therefore that some gifts, like tongues, prophecy, and healing came "unexpectedly," i.e., beyond the natural dispositions of the recipient, while others appear to be an elevation of natural gifts or at least in some continuity with them.

[15] As Conzelmann, *1 Corinthians*, 233, notes, whereas the governing norm for the charisms in 1 Corinthians 13 is *agape* (love), the governing norm in 1 Corinthians 14 is *oikodome* (upbuilding). The two will be combined in Ephesians 4:16: the body "builds itself up in love."

[16] It is crucial not to reduce the charisms to natural talents. Though the spiritual gifts often perfect the natural gifts and function according to the individual's temperament and personality, the gifts are to be sought in prayer (1 Cor 14:1), and even when the gift received is one of "helping" or "administrating," it is to be done under the movement of the Holy Spirit.

Ephesians: Building the Body[17]

The author of Ephesians calls upon the Pauline tradition in his concise synthesis of the common and the diverse gifts in the church. After the long hymn of praise and thanksgiving (following the Jewish *berakah* pattern) in which the author rehearses the wonders of salvation history that have brought Jew and Gentile together in Christ, he exhorts his readers to embody this unifying mystery in their lives. He does so first by recalling the gifts common to all: one call, one body, one Spirit, one Lord, one faith, one baptism, one God and Father of all (4:1-6). Then he shows that the very diversity of gifts in the church, the charisms and offices, are aimed at the same unity (4:7-16).

J. C. Kirby has argued that Ephesians is the transformation into a letter of what was originally a liturgy. The primitive "canon" developed a theology of baptism for which the most plausible setting was the Christian celebration of Pentecost. There are, in fact, numerous direct or indirect allusions to baptism in the text, the most explicit being the "one baptism" of 4:5.[18] Moreover, Psalm 68, which is used in 4:8 for the charisms, was one of the readings prescribed for the Jewish feast of Pentecost, and there are other indications that the Christian celebration of Pentecost underlies the original liturgical text.[19] If this is so, then Ephesians 4:1-16 is a fascinating confirmation of the thesis of our earlier chapters, that baptism (or at least the integral initiation rite, which in some cases, if not all, included the imposition of hands) was understood by the early church

[17] In this section, besides the commentaries, I have drawn on the more extensive treatment in my doctoral thesis, *Growth in Christ* (Fribourg, Switzerland: St. Paul's Press, 1961) 144–62, later popularized in *Maturing in Christ* (Milwaukee: Bruce, 1964) 221–30, updating both. *See also* K. Usami, *Somatic Comprehension of Unity: The Church in Ephesus* (Rome: Biblical Institute Press, 1983) 136–42.

[18] The others: the "bath of water with the word" (5:26), the "seal of the Spirit" (1:13-14; 4:30); brought to life, raised, and ascended with Christ (2:4-6); the contrast with Jewish circumcision (2:11-22); the new creation (4:22-24); the fragment of a baptismal hymn, "Awake, O sleeper, and arise from the dead, and Christ shall give you light" (5:14 concluding the longer section beginning with 5:8).

[19] J. C. Kirby, *Ephesians: Baptism and Pentecost* (Montreal: McGill University Press, 1968) 145–64.

not only to confer the grace that saves but the charismatic Spirit as well.

That such is the underlying assumption in Ephesians becomes clear from the ease with which the text flows from the "one baptism" to charismatic grace: "But *(dè)* to each of us grace was given according to the measure of Christ's gift" (4:7). Contrasting this grace with the common graces just listed (the Greek *dè* has the sense of a slightly adversative addition: "but also"), the author clearly is referring to charismatic grace, for unlike the grace that saves, which is always poured out in abundance, without measure (Rom 5:5, 17, 20; 1 Thess 3:12; Phil 1:9; Eph 1:8), this grace is carefully measured for each one: "We have gifts that differ according to the grace given to us" (Rom 12:6). It is not said that *some* received these gifts and others not. Everyone in the community has received some gift, diverse and measured though it may be.[20]

Then, adapting a text from Psalm 68:18,[21] the writer ascribes the outpouring of these spiritual gifts to the glorified Christ, "who ascended far above the heavens, that he might fill all things" (4:8-10). Ephesians reflects here the Lukan tradition of Acts 2:33, which attributes the outpouring of the Spirit to the exalted Christ. "All things" refers not to the church but to the universe of matter and spirit, in keeping with the cosmic wisdom concept developed in Colossians-Ephesians, and the church as the channel of this "cosmic" redemption.[22] The text continues:

[20] Against Schlier, Merklein, and Zerwick, who take the "we" as already a reference to the office-bearers in verse 11, R. Schnackenburg devotes a lengthy and adequate refutation in *Der Brief an die Epheser* (Zürich: Benziger, 1982) 177–78.

[21] The Hebrew originally read, "You have ascended on high, taken captives, received men as gifts" (NAB), but the Ephesian text reflects a rabbinic tradition which interpreted this verse of Moses who ascended Mount Sinai to receive gifts *for* men, that is, the law. By the first century the Jewish feast of Pentecost celebrated the giving of the Law through Moses. The author of Ephesians now applies this to Christ, who ascended into heaven and poured out the Spirit (Christian Pentecost) upon the church. Cf. Kirby, *Ephesians*, 146.

[22] B. F. Westcott's excursus ("The Expression *ta panta*" in *St. Paul's Epistle to the Ephesians* [London, 1906] 186–87) is still one of the best commentaries on this passage. *See also* H. Schlier, *Der Brief an die Epheser* (Düsseldorf: Patmos Verlag, 1957) 194; P. Benoît, "Corps, tête et plérôme dans les

"It was he who gave some as apostles, others as prophets, others as evangelists, others as shepherds and teachers, so as to organize the saints for active service in building up the body of Christ, until we all as a whole perfectly attain to the unity of the faith and of the thorough knowledge of the Son of God, to perfect manhood, to the mature stature that belongs to Christ's fullness—so that we may no longer be children tossed about and swung round by every wind of teaching that cheating people contrive in craftiness that leads to the trap error has laid. Rather, by embodying the truth in love, let us grow up unto him in every respect. He is the head, Christ. From him the whole body, growing more and more compact and closely knit together through every life-feeding contact (according to the measured activity each single part deploys), the whole body, I say, works out its increase for the building up of itself in love" (Eph 4:11-16—my translation).

The author's point in enumerating five of the offices is not to give an exhaustive list of the "each one of us" mentioned in verse 7, but rather to list some of the more important roles as representative of the diversity of graces.[23] In view of the approaching verses 13 and 14 on faith, knowledge, and doctrine, he chooses such gifts as have a stable character and engage functions of authority and teaching. The fact that Christ "gave" the persons who exercise these offices indicates that they were not merely a matter of appointment but that he also gifted them to be of service to the church.[24]

The aim of these offices is expressed in a dense pile-up of prepositional phrases: *pros ton katartismon tōn agiōn eis ergon diakonias, eis oikodomēn toû sōmatos toû Christoû*, which we have translated "so as to organize the saints for active service in building up the body of Christ." The punctuation of these

épîtres de la captivité," *RB* 49 (1956) 5-44; F. Mussner, *Christus Das All und die Kirche* (Trier: Paulinus Verlag, 1955) 29-39.

[23] He omits "miraculous powers, gifts of healing, services of help, powers of administration, diverse kinds of tongues," inserts "evangelists and pastors," but otherwise keeps the same order as in 1 Corinthians 12:28: "first apostles, secondly prophets, thirdly teachers; after that, miraculous powers, etc."

[24] Westcott, *Ephesians, ad loc.*

phrases is crucial to their interpretation. Some translations take the first two phrases coordinately: "to equip the saints, for a work of service."[25] This punctuation easily lends itself to taking "saints" here as those holding the offices just mentioned. In this interpretation the ministry to the church and the upbuilding of the body is the role of the ministers just mentioned, the "service" is taken as "official" service, and the body of Christ is the direct recipient of their ministry.[26] However, this would be a strange understanding of "saints," which is a Pauline word for all the faithful, and it would furthermore limit the up-building power to certain offices, whereas elsewhere in Pauline thought the upbuilding function is that of every member, and it is the purpose of all the gifts given to the church (1 Cor 14:26). It also assumes that official service is the only meaning of *diakonia*, whereas elsewhere in the New Testament and in Paul in particular, it has a much broader sense. When Paul speaks of the "service *(diakonian)* to the saints" to which the household of Stephanas devoted themselves, this is certainly not "official" service (1 Cor 15:16). Thus "service" here is to be taken in a sense as broad as the grace from which it flows—each has received his or her share (v. 7).

Furthermore, the word *katartismos*, which we have translated "to organize" does not really mean "to perfect" (as some older translations had it), but, as modern translations render, "equip" or "ready." The root word *arō*, "to join, adjust," in-tensified by *kata*, gives the idea of a plentitude achieved by har-monious assemblage of parts. When the verb is used of parts in relation to the whole, the idea is not only that all the parts fit together harmoniously but also that they are ready and apt for the purpose for which the whole is destined.[27] It is used in pro-fane Greek for mobilizing an army.[28] This sense fits perfectly

[25] Chrysostom, Textus Receptus, the Authorized, Revised, American Standard, and Revised Standard Versions, Segond, R. Knox, Conybeare, Dibelius.

[26] This hierarchical interpretation is found in Chrysostom, Theophylact, Calvin, Bengel, and more recently was espoused by C. Masson, *Epître aux Ephésiens* (Neuchatel: Delachaux & Niestlé, 1953) and Zerwick, *Der Brief an die Epheser* (Düsseldorf: Patmos Verlag, 1962) *ad loc*.

[27] R. Trench, *Synonyms*, 78.

[28] Polybius I, 221, 4; 29, 1; 36, 5; III, 95, 2.

here. Consequently, the better interpretation, that followed by most modern versions and translations,[29] takes the phrases as telescoped, as we have done in our translation: "to organize the saints for active service in building up the body of Christ."[30] The consequences are crucial: The role of the official ministers in building the church is to release and direct the church building power latent by divine gift in every Christian.[31]

It is in this fashion that the body (and not merely the official ministers) builds itself up in love. The concluding verse 16 summarizes this activity in a highly condensed way. All the building grace and activity comes from Christ the head, but it is mediated through the activity of every single member. Here the author combines the images of a building and a body in a dramatic way. He uses the architectural language of the day in the term *synarmologoumenon*, which, without the prefix *syn-* "represents the whole elaborate process by which stones are fitted together; the preparation of the surfaces, including the cutting, rubbing and testing; the preparation of the dowels and the dowel-holes, and finally the fixing of the dowels with molten lead."[32] To this the author of Ephesians adds the prefix *syn-*, so that the metaphor is one of the church as a building pulling its parts together into one unified whole. Hence "growing more and more compact."

The second metaphor, "closely knit together *(symbibazomenon)* . . . etc.," is that of a living organism such as the body, in which ligaments bind the body together, or in which each

[29] Luther, Westcott-Hort, Bover, Nestle, British & Foreign Bible Society, NEB, NABR, Bible de Jérusalem, NIV, NAS, Rotherham, Twentieth Century NT, Weymouth, Montgomery, Williams, Beck.

[30] "To organize" is the translation also of J. Lilly and P. Benoît (Bible de Jérusalem).

[31] The text is thoroughly exegeted in this sense, with its far-reaching theological implications, by Markus Barth, *Ephesians 4–6* AB 34A (Garden City: Doubleday, 1974) 478–84. See also R. P. Meyer, *Kirche und Mission im Epheserbrief* (Stuttgart: Verlag Katholisches Bibelwerk, 1977) 65. J. Gnilka, *Der Epheserbrief* (Freiburg: Herder, 1971) 213; F. Foulkes, *The Epistle of Paul to the Ephesians* (Grand Rapids: Eerdmans, 1963) 120; C. L. Mitton, *Ephesians* (Grand Rapids: Eerdmans, 1973); O. Betz, *Einsein in Christus* (Kassel: J. G. Onken Verlag, 1969).

[32] J. A. Robinson, *Saint Paul's Epistle to the Ephesians* (London: 1928) 262.

member supplies life to the next by interaction with it. It is more readily transferable to members capable of interlacing themselves and interacting spiritually, as the text wishes to specify concerning the members of the church.[33]

The point of all this is that the charismatic life given to each member of the body is oriented to building up the body of Christ, to creating that *koinōnia* which the church is meant to be. These gifts are manifested already from the moment of Christian initiation, although they may grow and increase as the individual seeks them in prayer (according to 1 Cor 12-14). Thomas Aquinas saw this clearly in his perceptive commentary on this passage:

"From Christ our head comes not only the increasing compactness of the members of the Church through faith, nor merely the connection or binding through the mutual help of charity, but certainly from him comes the members' actual operation or movement to action, according to the measure and ability of each member . . . for not only by faith is the mystical body compacted, nor merely by charity's connecting assistance does the body grow; but likewise *by the effectual composing activity springing from each member*, according to the measure of grace given him, and the actual motion to operation which God effects in us."[34]

The passage climaxes with the word *agape*, indicating not the goal (this is Christ, v. 15) but the energy and the life that empowers the interaction of the members as well as the effect of their interaction. When Paul dealt with the relation of charity to the charisms in 1 Corinthians 12-14, the excesses of the Corinthians forced him to stress the difference and superiority of charity over the charisms. Here in the more pacific atmosphere of Ephesians, we have the integration of charisms and charity, with the proper roles assigned to each. Charismatic grace is not superfluous; it is a normal channel through which the church builds itself up in love.

[33] "That the members among themselves as *living* should cohere and live, grow and function as one." I. M. Vosté, *Commentarius in Epistulam ad Ephesios,* 2nd edition (Rome-Paris, 1932) *ad loc.* G. Delling, *TDNT* 7:764 also takes *aphē* to mean "contact" and not merely "ligament."

[34] Aquinas, *Comment. in Epist. S. Pauli, ad loc.;* my translation.

Chapter Eight

Conclusions: Spirit-Baptism in the New Testament

Our study has covered the key texts relating to the question of Christian initiation and the "baptism in the Holy Spirit." A broader study of the role of the Holy Spirit in the Old and New Testaments would be a helpful context, but it goes beyond the limits of this study and has been treated elsewhere. On the basis of our analysis of the texts, the following conclusions seem to impose themselves:

1. The texts do not permit us to reconstruct with certainty a consistent rite of initiation in the church in New Testament times. The essential elements of the *integral rite of initiation, however, always included water-baptism in the name of Jesus (or the later trinitarian formula) and the gift of the Holy Spirit.* It is not clear that the water-baptism was always accompanied by the laying on of hands and even less clear whether anointing was part of the rite in the apostolic period. When accompanying baptism, the laying on of hands was probably seen to symbolize the imparting of the Holy Spirit.

2. Concerning the *manner* in which the baptismal union with Jesus through the Spirit was *imaged,* the Pauline tradition thought of the risen Christ as the spiritual or life-giving body to

which one is joined by baptism and from which ones receives the Spirit. This was further developed, for parenetic purposes, into the "baptism into his death," an image that lent itself to later ritual development which unfortunately lost sight of the gift of the Spirit as the primary effect of union with Christ. In the Matthean and Lukan traditions (and perhaps already in the Markan), the model was the Spirit-baptism of Jesus himself, which was not a mere repetition of John's baptism but a union of water and Spirit, a model which the fourth evangelist and the author of the letter to Titus develop in terms of rebirth.

3. Concerning the *evidence* of one's having received the Holy Spirit, it is assumed in many of the texts that there is an *experiential* dimension. Eduard Schweizer's comment cited earlier bears repeating: "Long before the Spirit was a theme of doctrine, He was a fact in the experience of the community."[1] Barrett adds: "No more certain statement can be made about the Christians of the first generation than this: they believed themselves to be living under the immediate government of the Spirit."[2] Though caution should be exercised lest "experience" be equated too narrowly with "feelings" in the modern sense, it is nevertheless a reminder that the effects of receiving the Holy Spirit should somehow be manifest.

4. Furthermore, a strong case can be made for the expectation of a *charismatic* expression on the part of the receiver. Such a charismatic expression was often tongues and prophecy (the gifts that have a privileged place in Acts), but other wonder-working powers also were manifested, as well as less spectacular service gifts, in different ways in different members. This appears not only from many of the accounts of Christian baptism but from the fact that Christian initiation was modeled upon Jesus' baptism in the Spirit, which anointed him with power to proclaim the kingdom, to heal, deliver from oppression of evil spirits, and to work miracles. There is no evidence, however, that any *one* charismatic gift, such as tongues, was *always* expected to reveal itself. These gifts were manifested from the very beginning of one's initiation for the upbuilding of the

[1] Schweizer, *TDNT* 6: 396.
[2] Barrett, *Holy Spirit*, 1.

community and the spread of the gospel. Other gifts could, however, be sought after and exercised later (1 Cor 14:1). Ephesians 4:1-16 assumes that charismatic grace is received by every Christian at baptism. It could be argued that some gifts might manifest themselves later, just as their recognition by the church and the appointment to office in the community would normally come later.

Our interest here, of course, is the relationship of the charisms to Christian initiation. If we ask the broader question, "How widespread was the actual charismatic phenomenon in the life and worship of the first century communities?" we need only to scan the New Testament canon. The four gospels, Acts, and Paul all take for granted that charisms are among the ordinary manifestations of the Christian life. So do Hebrews, Ephesians, the pastorals (which, despite their emphasis on church order, give prophecy a place of honor, 1 Tim 1:18), and even James, who speaks of the ministry of healing through prayer and anointing (James 5:14-15). 1 Peter attributes even Old Testament prophecy to the Spirit of *Christ* (1 Pt 1:11); he speaks of an experiential dimension of the new Christian life (1 Pt 2:2-3) and of the varied gifts received by each Christian for the service of the community (1 Pt 4:10-11). 2 Peter 1:20 speaks of the divine inspiration of authentic prophecy. The letters of John assume the illuminating role of the Holy Spirit as an argument not against prophecy but against *false* prophecy and teaching (itinerant prophets seem to be presumed in 2 John 10 and 3 John 5-10). So it is with Jude (8-13), who, as an antidote to false teaching and prophecy, urges the faithful to "pray in the holy Spirit" (v. 20), an expression virtually equivalent to Paul's description of tongues (1 Cor 14:15; cf. Rom 8:26-27). The Book of Revelation is an extended example of early Christian prophecy (Rev 22:7, 18). Colossians speaks of the gift of "spiritual wisdom and understanding" (1:9) and urges the readers to "teach and admonish one another, singing psalms, hymns, and spiritual songs" (Col 3:16). Teaching here is not related to office but seems to presume a charismatic gift; "spiritual songs" is a possible allusion to tongues.[3] In short, only the brief letter to Phile-

---

[3] *See* Montague, *Holy Spirit*, 216-19.

mon (a mere 25 verses) has no allusion to the charisms, a fact easily explained by the practical subject matter of the letter.

Of course, not all the charisms are listed in each book, and sometimes the allusions are not certain, so we have no way of knowing whether all the gifts, or only certain ones, functioned in specific communities. The near ubiquity of prophecy, however, is impressive. No matter how much a given New Testament document may attack false prophecy or seek to regulate the charisms, there is not a single instance in which the widespread phenomenon of the prophetic gifts is condemned or even questioned. It is part of the normal Christian life which Paul defends (1 Thess 5:19-20) and promotes (1 Cor 14:1). But besides the charisms, the Spirit's presence was manifested in various other ways as well: through the fruits of the Spirit (Gal 5:22), holiness, bearing witness, endurance and wisdom in persecution, identifying the true teaching of Jesus in the face of false teaching or prophecy, and following Jesus to the cross. In the Last Discourse in John, various functions are attributed to the Paraclete, including prophecy (16:13), and any of these could be evidences of having received the Spirit.

5. *The initial gift of the Spirit is not static but is meant to grow.* This appeared most clearly in our study of *anakainōsis* (''renewal') in Titus 3:5, and it is confirmed by 2 Corinthians 3:18. We may reasonably assume that such growth, like growth in nature, may at times be gradual and at other times dramatic. Such a range of growth-rhythms would provide ample room for the kind of spiritual awakening which we witness in those already baptized when they receive a new outpouring of the Spirit, which the Classical Pentecostals have called the ''baptism in the Holy Spirit.'' Thus this ''baptism in the Holy Spirit'' is not to be dismissed as irrelevant simply because in the sacramental view the Spirit is given at baptism. The Pentecostal experience is a reality in the modern church, and the fact that as a means of evangelization it is far outdistancing the efforts of the mainline churches should make the more sacramentally oriented pay attention. The element which the Pentecostals have touched on is the one largely neglected in the mainline sacramental churches—that the Spirit received is manifested charismatically and will indeed do so, if one has such an expec-

tation and has not *a priori* excluded it. God, of course, is not limited by our subjective dispositions. But ordinarily God takes us where we are.

6. Christian initiation of *adults* (which includes what we now recognize as baptism and confirmation) should therefore follow the pattern in the New Testament and create the *expectation* not only of an *experience* of the Spirit but of some *charismatic* manifestation as evidence of the reception of the Holy Spirit. While this should not be made an object of distracting introspection, and it should also be made clear that the Holy Spirit manifests himself in many ways other than the more spectacular gifts, the range of reception is often related to the range of expectations, and Paul's advice to "seek the gifts, especially that you may prophesy" (1 Cor 14:1) remains valid.

7. Finally, it should be pointed out that charisms are of *great variety*, including some that are no less anointed by the Spirit for their being humble services. In all cases, the charismatic empowerment is destined not for personal fanfare but for the *building up of the church* and evangelization. The charismatic dimension of the Spirit's life is therefore crucial to the survival and growth of the church. The gifts are not toys but tools. They are not optional accessories but part of the church's essential equipment for its upbuilding, and every one of the baptized has received a charismatic grace to be ministered to the community. The role of the authority-bearing offices in the church is, among other things, to call forth, facilitate, and coordinate the church-building power present by divine gift in every baptized Christian (Eph 4:7-16).

It now remains to be seen to what extent this vision of Christian initiation shaped the church's rites and expectations in the succeeding centuries.

Part Two:

The Early Post-Biblical Evidence

Introduction

Before plunging into the vast waters of the post-apostolic age, it will be helpful to refocus the theological issues which have prompted our investigation. Scholars, both Catholic and Protestant, have sought an explanation of the current phenomenon of baptism in the Holy Spirit in our common sources. In Roman Catholicism there are at least two dominant ways of theologizing about the baptism in the Holy Spirit.[1] One view, promoted by Francis Sullivan of the Gregorian University in Rome, looks upon the baptism in the Spirit as a special grace, a new imparting of the Spirit unrelated to any immediate sacramental context.[2] This view is based on the quite valid supposition that there can be multiple impartings of the Spirit. Among the early Christian authors the question of multiple impartings of the

[1] I do not intend to make a survey of Catholic views on the baptism in the Holy Spirit.

[2] Sullivan, "Baptism in the Spirit," *Charisms and Charismatic Renewal* (Ann Arbor: Servant, 1982) 59–75. *See also* Sullivan, " 'Baptism in the Holy Spirit': A Catholic Interpretation of the Pentecostal Experience," *Gregorianum* 55 (174) 49–68. In support of his view that there can be multiple non-sacramental impartings of the Spirit, Sullivan cites Thomas Aquinas, *Summa Theologiae* I, q43, a6, and I, q43, a6, ad2.

Spirit was widely discussed.[3] The non-sacramental view of the baptism in the Spirit has many advantages, among them its ecumenical appeal to the evangelical churches, which do not have a highly sacramental polity.[4]

The other view, which was the principal theological stance adopted at the beginning of the Catholic charismatic renewal, relates the baptism in the Spirit to water-baptism or to the rites of initiation (water-baptism, sign for the imparting of the Spirit, eucharist). The baptism in the Spirit in this instance is a bringing to awareness and a new actuality the graces of initiation already received. In no way does this imply that the "original act of baptism was deficient or inadequate."[5] Nor is it just a psychological moment. Rather it is the sovereign act of Christ now actualized in a new way in the new subjective dispositions and openness.[6] The sacraments are acts of Christ; Jesus is the one who baptizes in the Holy Spirit.

Such an actualization of a previously bestowed grace can already be found in the New Testament. The author of the 2 Timothy writes: "I remind you to rekindle the gift of God that is within you through the laying on of hands" (1:6. *See also* 1 Tim 4:14). Augustine and the pre-scholastics develop the theology of an actualization of the sacrament of baptism given to infants, which is the issue here. In Augustine's view the Holy Spirit indwells a baptized infant. Still there is lacking a dimension of actualization, which is later achieved through knowledge and experience. Within Augustine's own thought this actualization theology underwent some development, which can be

[3] J. Lecuyer, "La confirmation chez les pères," *Maison Dieu* 54 (1958) 23–52.

[4] Francis Sullivan maintains that the sacramental view of the baptism in the Spirit is based on the supposition that such an important conferring of charisms could only take place within a sacramental context. *See* Sullivan, *Charisms*, 62, 69, 70, 71; Sullivan, "Catholic Chrismatic Renewal," *Dictionary of Pentecostal and Charismatic Movements*, ed. S. M. Burgess and G. McGee (Grand Rapids: Zondervan, 1988) 118–20. No such supposition to the sacramental view exists. Yet Sullivan is correct in pointing to a danger of a kind of sacramental imperialism. "The sacred liturgy does not exhaust the entire activity of the church." *The Constitution on the Sacred Liturgy* art. 9.

[5] K. Leech, *Experiencing God: Theology as Spirituality* (New York: Harper & Row, 1985) 212.

[6] In an earlier day this would have been expressed in the vocabulary of *ex opere operato* and *ex opere operantis*.

dated rather clearly. In 408 Augustine said that infants, because incapable of faith, were justified by the faith of the church.[7] Four years later (411–12) he explained that God justifies infants by a hidden grace, a grace not yet manifested in works.[8] Five years later in 417 he added that the divine indwelling is always related to some knowledge or experience. On this basis he held that the Spirit indwells baptized infants, but that they do not yet know the Spirit. Some persons both possess and know or experience the Spirit, and others know the Spirit but do not possess the Spirit [sic]. Baptized infants are indwelt by the Spirit, but this indwelling still lacks a dimension of experiential actualization. Comparing the indwelling Spirit to reason, Augustine says that the child has reason but is not aware of it. Reason is "like a covered spark waiting to be kindled by oncoming age."[9] In the East Symeon the New Theologian (949–1022) held similar actualizing suppositions in relationship to infant baptism, though he applied them in an unacceptable way.[10]

An actualizing theology has formed the supposition of those who hold a sacramental view of the baptism in the Spirit.[11] Such an actualization does not take place in a void, but is part of the daily proclamation of the Word and the faith life of the church.[12] With some variations the Catholics who have supported

[7] Augustine, *Letter* 98:10; CSEL 34:532

[8] Augustine, *On Merits and the Remission of Sins and the Baptism of Infants*; CSEL 60:11.

[9] Augustine, *Letter* 187:6:21; CSEL 57:99, 100, 103, 104.

[10] Symeon, *Ethics* 10:318; SC 129:282. These texts are gathered in C. Moeller and G. Philips, *The Theology of Grace and the Ecumenical Movement* (London: Mowbray, 1961) 12–15.

[11] This has been caricatured as "the time bomb theory." Lederle, *Treasures*, 223. This is based on the supposition that charisms are spiritual objects, or commodities, whereas they are gifts of the Spirit coming to "visibility" in a service to the body of Christ.

[12] This emphasis is found in Peter Hocken. Hocken's view on the actualization of the previously received sacrament of baptism has evolved. He has argued for the essentially ecumenical character of the charismatic movement and its characteristic grace of the baptism in the Spirit. Hocken wrote "that any attempt to formulate a *doctrine* of 'spirit-baptism' that can be harmonized with Catholic teaching on the sacraments of baptism and confirmation is *a misguided effort*." "Catholic Pentecostalism: Some Key Questions," *HeyJ* (1974) 140. In an unpublished paper, "A Clarification on

the sacramental approach to baptism in the Spirit are Cardinal
Suenens,[13] Kevin and Dorothy Ranaghan,[14] Heribert Mühlen,[15]
René Laurentin,[16] Donald Gelpi,[17] Simon Tugwell,[18] and my-
self.[19] No attempt is made here to give a complete list of those
holding a sacramental view, but the first *Malines Document*
should be mentioned.[20] The Anglican,[21] Lutheran,[22] and Ortho-

Baptism in the Spirit" (August 23, 1989), Hocken has indicated that this
was written at a time when he objected to the "spirit-baptism" terminology. For Hocken, the received categories of particular Christian traditions
are not adequate on their own to grasp this grace. The Catholic explanation of the baptism in the Spirit as an actualization of the sacrament of
baptism "does not really explain anything" because such an explanation
does not "give prominent place to the Word of God and faith." *One Lord,
One Spirit, One Body* (Gaithersburg: Word Among Us, 1987) 98, 99. Hock-
en's objection here may be to the pastoral way the actualization of baptismal grace is approached, rather than to the theological position itself.
While Hocken accepts the necessity of relating the baptism in the Spirit to
the liturgical process of ecclesial initiation, he holds that it is more than
actualization of graces objectively conferred. It is related to the contemporary proclamation of the Word and the faith expectation of the community in which the fuller Word is proclaimed. Still Hocken's formulations
are unusual: "As a Catholic I believe the eucharist to be very important.
But I know that who Jesus is and what he came to do are more basic"
(Ibid., 117). Hocken questions the unique character of the apostolic age
(Ibid., 52). *See* Lederle, *Treasures,* 85–90; Schmieder, *Geisttaufe: Ein Beitrag
zur neueren Glaubensgeschichte,* 420–25. My view set forth in this present
book supposes that the actualization of baptismal graces takes place in a
community of faith in which the Word is daily proclaimed. Hocken is correct in calling for a more explicit expression of this supposition.

[13] Suenens, *A New Pentecost?* (New York: Seabury, 1974) 81.

[14] Ranaghan, *Catholic Pentecostals* (New York: Paulist, 1969) 107–56.

[15] Mühlen, *Einübung in die christliche Grunderfahrung,* 2 vols. (Mainz:
Matthias-Grünewald, 1976) 1:92-101; *A Charismatic Theology: Initiation in the
Spirit* (New York: Paulist, 1978) 140–43. Mühlen concentrates in a rather ex-
clusive way on confirmation as over against baptism.

[16] Laurentin, *Catholic Pentecostalism* (Doubleday: Garden City, 1978) 45, 46.

[17] Gelpi, *Pentecostalism: A Theological Viewpoint* (New York: Paulist, 1971) 173–86.

[18] Tugwell, *Did you Receive the Spirit?* (New York: Paulist, 1972) 48.

[19] McDonnell, "The Holy Spirit and Christian Initiation," *The Holy Spirit
and Power: The Catholic Charismatic Renewal,* ed. K. McDonnell (Garden
City: Doubleday, 1975) 57–85.

[20] *Theological and Pastoral Orientations on the Catholic Charismatic Renewal*
reprinted in *Presence, Power, Praise: Documents on the Charismatic Renewal,* 3
vols.; ed. K. McDonnell (Collegeville: The Liturgical Press, 1980) 3:13–70.

dox renewal gave some support to this position.[23] But there has been a slight shift: the 1980 document from the German Catholic bishops still sees the liturgical context as the "appropriate" (*angemessen*) locus for "Spirit-Renewal,"[24] a lead which is followed by the document from the bishops of the German speaking areas of Switzerland and Austria.[25] In both cases the focus is no longer on initiation. In the last document issued by the German bishops the sacramental and non-sacramental views are placed side by side.[26]

Both views of the baptism in the Holy Spirit can find support within the Catholic tradition. The sacramental view has its basis in the rites of initiation, and also in one of the ways the church identified itself during the first one thousand years, namely, the ecclesiology of communion, or *koinōnia* ecclesiology. During this period no one wrote tracts on the church; the first to do that

The same theological perspective on the baptism in the Holy Spirit can also be found in an earlier international document, "Statement of the Theological Basis of the Catholic Charismatic Renewal," issued at the First International Leaders Conference at Grottaferrata, October, 1973, reprinted in *Presence, Power, Praise* 3:1–11. The *Malines Document* is not based on the supposition that grace of this importance can only be imparted in a sacramental act.

[21] J. Gunstone, *Greater Things Than These: A Personal Account of the Charismatic Movement* (New York: Morehouse, 1974) 31.

[22] A. Bittlinger, "Baptism in Water and in Spirit: Aspects of Christian Initiation," K. McDonnell and A. Bittlinger, *The Baptism in the Holy Spirit as an Ecumenical Problem* (Notre Dame: Charismatic Renewal Services, 1972) 11, 12, 19, 20. The international Lutheran charismatic document recognizes a diversity within the Lutheran churches, including the sacramental perspective. *Welcome, Holy Spirit: A Study of Charismatic Renewal in the Church*, ed. L. Christensen (Minneapolis: Augsburg, 1987) 81–84. C. Lindberg, "Charismatic Renewal and the Lutheran Tradition," *Lutheran World Federation Report* 21 (1985) 29, 30. A fuller treatment is found in Lindberg, *The Third Reformation: Charismatic Movements and the Lutheran Tradition* (Macon: Mercer University, 1983). Lindberg's publications in this area are a critique, sometimes severe, of the Lutheran charismatic renewal.

[23] Lederle, *Treasures*, 235–41.

[24] *Erneuerung der Kirche aus dem Geist Gottes* 2.5 reprinted in *Erneuerung in Kirche und Gesellschaft* 10 (1981) 2–31.

[25] "Der eigentliche Ort der Geist-Erneuerung ist die Liturgie," *Geistliche Gemeinde Erneuerung: Grundentscheidung: Sakramente: Charismen* 137, reprinted in *Erneuerung in Kirche und Gesellschaft* 22 (1985) 1–41.

[26] *Der Geist Macht Lebendig* reprinted in *Jesus ist Herr*, ed. N. Baumert (Münsterschwarzach: Vier-Türmer, 1987) 35, 36.

seems to have been Jean de Paris (1240?–1306).[27] But the early authors, Tertullian, for instance, did betray their ecclesiological suppositions.[28]

The Focus of the Study

Some clarification of how "baptism in the Holy Spirit" is used in the study of post-biblical authors is needed. The Pentecostal/charismatic movements use baptism in the Holy Spirit to identify an experience existing in some patterned way in texts in Acts (1:2-5; 2:1-4: 8:14-17; 10:44-47; 19:1-7). Though these texts present problems, not the least of which is chronology, though the elements are not always the same, there is an imposition of the hands, a prayer for the descent of the Spirit, either an expectation that a charism will be manifested, and/or the actual manifestation (tongues and prophecy). The baptism in the Holy Spirit is modeled on Pentecost; Peter notes the recipients receive the Spirit "just as we have" (Acts 10:47), a reference back to the Pentecost where the coming of the Spirit is manifested in some charismatic gift. The experience is the baptism in the Spirit.

In order to locate and identify this experience within the rites of initiation in the authors being studied (Tertullian, Origen, Hilary of Poitiers, Cyril of Jerusalem, John Chrysostom, Philoxenus, John of Apamea, Theodoret, Severus, and Joseph Hazzaya), I will look for (1) a sign of the prayer for the descent of the Spirit, usually the imposition of hands, but also anointing, (2) praying for the descent of the Spirit, (3) an expectation that charisms will be manifested, and/or the actual manifestation.[29] These are usually found among those who claim they have received the baptism in the Holy Spirit. Some of the authors I

[27] *De Potestate Regia et Papali* (New York: Columbia, 1974).

[28] W. Elert, *Eucharist and Church Fellowship in the First Four Centuries* (St. Louis: Concordia, 1966); A. Houssiau, "Incarnation et communion selon les pères Grecs," *Irénikon* 45 (1972) 457–68.

[29] When the baptism in the Spirit is prayed for, imposition of hands is usually the gesture used. Anointing is not used. But if it were used within the Catholic charismatic renewal, no objection would be made on theological grounds. As we shall see, anointing and imposition of hands were sometimes a composite rite.

present write of Christian initiation or baptism without any reference to specific ritual elements. In these cases I note that the charisms are situated within baptism or in relation to it.

In the next two chapters I am going to examine a text from Tertullian, but first I will situate it in its historical ecclesiological context. Very briefly, I am going to sketch communion ecclesiology as found in the early post-biblical period, with special reference to Tertullian. After some reference to the architectural setting of the rites of initiation in North Africa in the second and third centuries, I will attempt to show how Tertullian saw the communion actively incorporating new members through one liturgy, which is both Christian initiation and what many would identify as the baptism in the Spirit.

The Ecclesiology of Koinōnia/Communion

After the Pentecost event Peter went out and preached, not on the Spirit, but on Jesus Christ, crucified and risen (Acts 2:22-24). Those who heard the proclamation were "cut to the heart," and said to Peter and the other apostles, "What shall we do?" To which Peter responded: "Repent, and be baptized every one of you in the name of Jesus Christ for the forgiveness of your sins, and you shall receive the gift of the Spirit" (2:37, 38). The dynamic is thus: Pentecost, preaching of Jesus Christ, conversion, baptism, imparting of the Spirit.[30] But there is a further development. "And all who believed were together and had all things in common; and they sold their possessions and goods and distributed them to all, as any had need. And day by day, attending the temple together and breaking bread in their homes, they partook of food with glad and generous hearts" (2:44-46; see also 4:32-33). This gathering of the community for the breaking of bread seems to have a eucharistic dimension.[31] So if

[30] Luke does not have a uniform chronology of how these elements occur.
[31] Hans Conzelmann suggested that Luke "is thinking of the ordinary daily meal here [Acts 2:44-46], but he does not make a distinction between it and the Eucharist. The unity of the two is part of the ideal picture of the earliest church." Acts of Apostles: A Commentary, 2nd edition (Philadelphia: Fortress, 1987) 23. See also A. Wikenhauser, Die Apostelgeschichte (Regensburg: Pustet, 1956) 55, 56; D. M. Stanley, The Apostolic Church in the New Testament (Westminster: Newman, 1965) 13. Ernst Haenchen has nothing

one is true to the dynamics of Acts one would add immediately after the imparting of the Spirit, *koinōnia*/communion, that is, community formation together with its eucharistic expression. The language of Luke is communion language. These passages had a great influence in post-biblical ecclesiology.[32] In order to be more specific about the meaning of communion let me give a short definition: "a sharing in one reality held in common."[33] Synonyms for *koinōnia* are sharing, participation, community, communion.

But the early post-biblical development incorporated the other communion texts from the New Testament in order to lay bare the inner source of the church's life, the mystery of the church as it is hidden in the mystery of God, always returning to divine communion, communion in the life of God. Without repeating what George Montague has written I want to call to mind some of the texts in relation to specific systematic themes.

The fountain of the church's life is rooted in the many-faceted mystery of God. There is a pneumatological dimension: "The grace of the Lord Jesus Christ and the love of God and the fellowship (*koinōnia*) of the Spirit be with you" (2 Cor 13:14. *See also* Phil 2:1). The church is a communion in the Spirit. There is also a specific christological expression: "For as we have abundant sharing in Christ's sufferings, so through Christ we have abundant communion in the consolation too" (2 Cor 1:5. *See also* Phil 3:10). The one reality all in the church share is the sufferings and resurrection of Christ; for this reason we are one. But there is also a participation in the mutuality of Father and Son: "That which we have heard, which we have seen with our eyes

specific to say on the eucharistic import of these texts. *See The Acts of the Apostles: A Commentary* (Philadelphia: Westminster, 1971) 192–96; 232–35.

[32] *Communio sanctorum,* Mélanges offerts à Jean-Jacques von Allmen, ed. B. Bobrinskoy and others (Geneva: Labor et Fides, 1982); J. M. R. Tillard, *The Eucharist: Pasch of God's People* (New York: Alba, 1967). Communion categories also influenced fourth century monasticism. *See* H. Bacht, "Koinōnia, Dans le monachism," *Dictionnaire de Spiritualité* (Paris: Beauchesne, 1974) 8, 1754–58; A. Veilleux, *Pachomian Koinōnia: The Lives, Rules, and Other Writings of Saint Pachomius and His Disciples,* 3 vols. (Kalamazoo: Cistercican Publications, 1980, 1981, 1982).

[33] John Cardinal Willebrands, "The Future of Ecumenism," *One in Christ* 11 (1975) 313.

. . . the life which is manifest . . . we proclaim to you so you may have a share with us; and our communion is with the Father and with his Son Jesus Christ" (1 John 1-4; 3:24).[34] The life of the church is that one reality, that one life, shared by the Father and Son.

One could ask, has this sharing in one reality held in common no expression perceivable to the senses? Yes, there is the sharing in the gospel of which Paul writes (Phil 1:5). But there is another perceivable level, which is sacramental: "The cup of blessing which we bless, is it not a sharing in the blood of Christ? The bread which we break, is it not a sharing in the body of Christ? Because there is one loaf, we who are many are one body, for we all share in the same loaf" (1 Cor 10:16-17).[35] Where the sharing in the Spirit, in the sufferings and resurrection of Christ, in the life common to Father, Son, and Holy Spirit, come to outward expression is in the proclamation of the gospel and in the sharing in the eucharistic bread and wine. For Paul this divine and eucharistic communion has economic expressions, namely, in alms for the poor, "sharing in the relief of the saints" (2 Cor 8:3-5). One cannot expect trinitarian and eucharistic communion to be real when it is not also real in the world we all experience. If there is a communion from above, into which we are invited to enter, there has to be a corresponding communion from below (of earthly goods).[36]

This points to the importance of communion ecclesiology as offering a participatory category which integrates spiritual and material sharing.[37] Communion ecclesiology offers the possibil-

[34] The text of 1 John 1:1-4 is sometimes interpreted in relation to 3:24, giving the text a more explicit triadic character. See J. Ratzinger, "Kommentar zum 1 Kapitel *Dei Verbum*," LTK (Freiburg: Herder, 1967) 504–506.

[35] G. Panikulam, *Koinōnia*, 25, 26; J. Hainz, *Koinōnia: 'Kirche' als Gemeinschaft bei Paulus* (Biblische Untersuchungen 16; Regensburg: Pustet, 1982) 232–72. S. Brown, "Koinōnia as the Basis of New Testament Ecclesiology," *One in Christ* 12 (1976) 157–67.

[36] K. McDonnell, "Vatican II (1962–65), Puebla (1979), Synod (1985): *Koinōnia/communio* as an Integral Ecclesiology," *JES* 25 (1988) 399–427.

[37] "Christ reveals to us that the divine life is trinitarian communion. Father, Son, and Spirit live the supreme mystery of oneness in perfect, loving intercommunion. It is the source of all love and all other communion that gives dignity and grandeur to human existence." *Puebla: Evangelization*

ity of an integral view of the church in which there are various
levels of participation: in the life of God, the Spirit, Christ, in
the gospel, the bread and wine, and material wealth. No other
category offers the possibility of an integral ecclesiology of such
breadth and depth.[38] To become a Christian one needs to hear
the gospel proclaimed, to be converted, to have communion in
the Spirit, to share in the death and resurrection of Jesus, thus
becoming a member of the body of Christ, one participating in
the local worshipping communion. There are no isolated Christians.

Peace and Communion

These communion themes, especially the eucharistic one, constituted the ecclesiological supposition "for most, if not all, of
the earliest councils," and remained a force as an ecclesiological
model for about the first thousand years.[39] As early as Justin
Martyr (c. 100–c. 165) communion was being used as a way of
identifying ecclesial relationships.[40] Irenaeus (c. 130–c. 200) em-
ployed eucharistic communion as a way of validating doctrine:
"Our way of thinking ought to accord with the eucharist, and

at *Present and in the Future of Latin America* (Washington: National Conference of Catholic Bishops, 1979) art. 212. The 1985 Synod of Catholic bishops
declared: "The ecclesiology of communion is the central and fundamental
idea of the council's [Vatican II] documents. *Koinōnia*/communion, founded
on Sacred Scripture, have been held in great honor in the early church
and in the Eastern churches to this day . . . the ecclesiology of communion cannot be reduced to purely organizational questions or to problems which simply relate to powers. Still, the ecclesiology of communion is
also the foundation for order in the church, and especially for a correct
relationship between unity and pluriformity in the church. . . . This is of
great importance especially today because the church, inasmuch as she is
one and unique, is as a sacrament, a sign and instrument of unity and of
reconciliation, of peace among men, nations, classes and peoples." *Origins*
15 (December 19, 1985) 448. *Koinōnia*/communion has been the topic of discussion in the international dialogues between the Catholic church and the
following denominations: Anglican, Baptist, Classical Pentecostal, Disciples,
and the Orthodox. *See* Tillard, *The Eucharist: Pasch of God's People*; Tillard,
Eglise d'Eglises (Paris: du Cerf, 1987).

[38] K. McDonnell, *"Koinōnia/communio* as an Integral Ecclesiology," 399–427.

[39] J. D. Zizioulas, *Being as Communion* (Crestwood: St. Vladimir, 1985) 156.

[40] Justin, *Dialogue with Trypho* 35, 5; *Die ältesten Apologeten*, ed. E. J. Goodspeed (Göttingen: Vandenhoeck & Ruprecht, 1914) 131.

the eucharist, on the other hand, confirms our way of think-ing.''[41] Irenaeus used communion language to speak of the salvation God gives through the Christ or the Spirit,[42] and to speak of salvation as a progressive introduction of believers into communion with God.[43] As I turn to the individual texts I will be able to demonstrate how the early Christian writers, especially the Latins and the Greeks, situate the rites of initiation within the eccesiology of communion.

[41] ''*Nostra autem consonans est sententia Eucharistiae, et Eucharistia rursus confirmat sententiam nostram. Against the Heresies* (hereafter cited as *AH*) 4, 18, 5; SC 100:610. *See also* 5, 2, 2; SC 153:31, 33.

[42] Ibid., 3, 18, 7; SC 211:366; 5, 1, 1; SC 153:21; 5, 14, 3; SC 153:191.

[43] Ibid. 4, 14, 2; SC 100:543, 545.

Chapter Nine

Tertullian:
African/Enthusiast/Rigorist

The communion themes were already in place in North Africa
when Tertullian (c. 160–c. 225) wanted to speak of ecclesial realities. For Tertullian communion had its origin in that transcen-
dent move of God toward the world in sending the Son, who
in turn commissioned the apostles, who founded churches in
various cities. Each church in each city is a communion, but
that which binds apostolic city to apostolic city and to other
churches in other cities is communion in doctrine. Tertullian
wrote: "We are in communion with the apostolic churches because our doctrine in no way differs from theirs; this is a sign
of truth."[1] All of the apostolic churches and all the churches in
communion with the apostolic churches constitute "one primitive apostolic church. . . . To prove that this unity [exists between them], they give to each other the peace, they call each
other brothers, and they show hospitality to one another, rights
which no other law directs except the unique tradition of the

---

[1] "*Communicamus cum ecclesiis apostolicis quod nulla doctrina diuersa: hoc est
testimonium ueritatis.*" Prescription Against the Heretics (hereafter cited as PH)
21:7; SC 46:115.

sacrament."[2] To give each other the peace is to be in communion because they mutually recognize in each other the full apostolic life. The one reality which binds all is the unique tradition of the sacrament, a global concept for all of the saving truths and mysteries of the faith.[3] Included under the handing on of the sacrament are faith in one God, Creator of the universe, Jesus Christ, born of Mary, and son of the Creator, the resurrection of the flesh, the scriptures. "From these mysteries the church nourishes her faith."[4]

Each believer is introduced to these mysteries by initiation into the communion. Thus Christian initiation is that unique bearer of apostolic faith, apostolic life, and apostolic practice. Peace and communion are not distinct realities, but have the same theological content.[5] To give each other the peace means to admit each other to the full life of each other's church, including eucharistic life and hospitality. Of churches which have fallen into heresy Tertullian said that "under no pretext do the apostolic churches receive them in the peace and communion. . . ."[6] Tertullian could turn the argument around and contend that the exclusion of heretics from communion means they have a different baptism: "the very fact of their [heretics] being deprived of communion is witness to their being aliens . . . they do not have the same baptism."[7] Though this reasoning

---

[2] "*Omne genus ad originem suam censeatur necesse est. Itaque tot ac tantae ecclesiae una est illa ab apostolis prima, ex qua omnes. Sic omnes primae et omnes apostolicae, dum una omnes. Probant unitatem communicatio pacis et appellatio fraternitatis et contesseratio hospitalitatis. Quae iura non alia ratio regit quam eiusdem sacramenti una traditio.*" Ibid., 20, 7, 8; SC 46:113, 114.

[3] J. De Ghellinck and others, *Pour l'historie du mot "sacramentum"* (Paris: Champion, 1924) 79.

[4] *PH* 4; SC 46:138.

[5] L. Hertling, *Communio: Church and Papacy in Early Christianity* (Chicago: Loyola University, 1972) 21. Though dated, especially in regard to Rome's relationship to other churches within the universal communion, this small study is still useful.

[6] "*Sed adeo nec sunt nec probare possunt quod non sunt, nec recipiuntur in pacem et communicationem ab ecclesiis quoquo modo apostolicis, scilicet ob diuersitatem sacramenti nullo modo apostolicae.*" PH 32: SC 46:132.

[7] "*Ad nos enim editum est, haeretici autem nullum consortium habent nostrae disciplinae quos extraneos utique testatur ipsa ademptio communicationis. non debeo in illis cognoscere quod mihi est praeceptum quia non idem deus est nobis et illis*

would ultimately be rejected by the church, behind Tertullian's sacramental exclusion is a profound communion ecclesiology.

The articulation of communion ecclesiology became more nuanced after Tertullian, especially in Cyprian and Augustine. In the development beyond Tertullian the universal church became the communion of communions, as in Augustine's formulation: "The church consists of the communion of the whole world."[8] Communion is one of the ecclesiological categories used by the authors studied.

The Architecture of Communion

The early church used to have baptisms twice a year, during the season of Easter and Pentecost, but there could also be baptisms at other times. In the early centuries the candidates for baptism entered the catechumenate, an extended period of instruction. Already St. Paul admonishes the catechumen to provide for the needs of the instructor (Gal 6:6). Some forms of instruction were developed in the "Two Ways" of the *Didache*, component blocks of which are generally conceded to date from the first century.[9] By 215 there is a full blown catechumenate, as

nec unus Christus, id est idem: ergo nec baptismum unum quia non idem." On Baptism (hereafter cited as *OB*) 15; SC 35:87.

[8] "Quamobrem si nulla interprete indigent canonicarum Scripturarum testimonia quae commendant Ecclesiam in totius orbis communione consistere. . . . " On the Unity of the Church: Against the Donatists 20, 56; PL 43:434. Augustine also commented on the vertical and horizontal communion: "Through what is common to the Father and the Son, they wished us to be in communion among ourselves and with them, and through this gift [the eucharist] gather us into one so that what both have, one has." Sermon 71, 12, 18; PL 38:454. A fourth-century text reads: "The holy communion of the Father, the Son, and the Holy Spirit is the place where the faithful are bound to receive communion on Sundays." From a Gallic Commentary on the Creed quoted by F. J. Babcock, "Sanctorum communio," JTS 21 (1920) 109. Making even more explicit the eucharistic dimensions of communion ecclesiology is the formulation of John Damascene (c. 675–c. 749): "We say koinōnia and so it is, for through it [the eucharistic celebration] we have communion with Christ and partake of his flesh and deity. But through it we also have communion among ourselves, and are united to one another. Since we receive one bread, we all become one body of Christ, one blood, and members of one another. We are united in the one body of Christ." On the Orthodox Faith 4:14; PG 94:1153.

[9] Didache 1–6; SC 248:141-68.

seen in the *Apostolic Tradition* of Hippolytus (16–20), a document which is contemporary with Tertullian's *On Baptism*.[10] Tertullian also witnessed to the existence of the catechumenate, which might be as long as three years. During this time the catechumens were admonished to frequent prayer, fasting, and other penitential exercises.[11] As Easter approached there was an announcement such as St. Augustine gave in a later period: "Easter is coming; register for baptism."[12] The rite of initiation as Tertullian knew it consisted of a water–bath, anointing, laying on of hands, and the celebration of the eucharist.[13] Referring to the imposition of hands Tertullian described its purpose as "inviting and welcoming the Holy Spirit."[14] In the West, in contrast to the tradition of the East (where the anointing was given heavier theological content), the imposition of hands was of great significance.

Now we can visualize how they thought of the theological aspects of initiation by looking at how they used their church buildings during initiation. There was a widely divergent tradition as to shapes and sizes of churches in what is called Roman Africa, which would be North Africa of the Mediterranean seaboard.[15] Without attempting to universalize the architecture of the early church in Roman Africa, I am using the model of a separate baptistery, related to, but separate from, a building with an anteroom and a larger room with an altar. In the baptistery there is a large circular pit filled with water so that, if an

[10] *The Treatise on the Apostolic Tradition of St. Hippolytus of Rome*, ed. G. Dix (London: SPCK, 1937) 23–30.

[11] *OB* 20; SC 35:94.

[12] *"Ecce Pascha est, da nomen ad Baptismum."* Augustine, *Sermon*, 132:1; PL 38:735.

[13] An exception to this pattern is in the baptismal practice of the early Syriac church in which the water-bath was preceded by a pneumatic anointing. *See* G. Winkler, "The Original Meaning of the Prebaptismal Anointing and its Implications," *Worship* 52 (1978) 24–45. A much later western mentality would see in that anointing a "confirmation-like" act. To the ancient Syrian Christian such a term, and any separation of the anointing from the water-bath, would be unthinkable.

[14] *"Dehinc manus inponitur per benedictionem advocans et invitans spiritum sanctum."* *OB* 8; SC 35:76.

[15] A. Khatchatrian, *Les Baptistères Paléochrétiens: Plans, Notices et Bibliographie* (Paris: Centre National de la Recherche Scientifique, 1962) 27–39.

adult stands in it, the water reaches to about the waist. On the side nearest the door there are steps down into the pool, and on the opposite side steps up.

Asking for the Inheritance

Tertullian presupposes that those coming to baptism will be adults. Nonetheless infant baptism is practiced, against which Tertullian issues a minority report, saying quite boldly, "Let them be made Christians when they are capable of knowing Christ."[16] However, two generations after Tertullian the baptism of children is a general practice in North Africa.[17]

At the very end of the treatise *On Baptism* Tertullian exhorts the adult neophytes: "Therefore, you blessed ones, for whom the grace of God is waiting, when you come up from the most sacred bath of the new birth, when you spread out your hands for the first time in your mother's house with your brethren, ask your Father, ask your Lord, for the special gift of his inheritance, the distributed charisms, which form an additional, underlying feature [of baptism]. Ask, he says, and you shall receive. In fact, you have sought, and you have found: you have knocked, and it has been opened to you."[18]

The sequence of events as Tertullian knows them must be noted. Tertullian calls attention to the moment when the neophytes come up from the water, (which corresponds to ascending the steps up on the far side of the baptismal pool) after being immersed. This is in the baptistery, which may be a sepa-

[16] "*Veniant ergo dum adolescunt, veniant dum discunt, dum quo veniant docentur; fiant Christiani cum Christum nosse potuerint.*" OB 18; SC 35:92, 93.

[17] E. Dekkers, *Tertullianus en de Geschiedenis der Liturgie* (Brussels: Desclee de Brouwer, 1947) 167.

[18] "*Igitur benedicti quos gratia dei expectat, cum de illo sanctissimo lavacro novi natalis ascenditis et primas manus apud matrem cum fratribus aperitis, petite de patre, petite de domino, peculia gratiae distributiones charismatum subiacere; petite et accipietis inquit; quaesistis enim et invenistis, pulsastis et apertum est nobis.*" OB 20; SC 35:96. The last phrase is very difficult to render in English, and, in part, I have been guided by the Sources Chrétiennes translation and by the suggestions of Francis Sullivan. According to *Oxford Latin Dictionary*, the force of *subiacere* is "to form an additional, underlying feature." I thank Cecil M. Robeck, Jr., who called my attention to the text of Tertullian.

rate building, or possibly they used a river.[19] Then there is an indirect reference to the neophytes entering the eucharistic area proper ("when you spread out your hands for the first time in your mother's house").

Tertullian's phrase "when you spread out your hands for the first time" (*primas manus . . . aperitis*) refers to the neophytes lifting up and spreading out the hands in a prayer gesture.[20] The posture of standing with arms outstretched and palms open was customary when the community entered into the prayer of praise, in contrast to a penitential prayer made on one's knees.[21]

The expression "in your mother's house" (*apud matrem*) is a reference to the church, both as a physical place in which to gather, and as the mystery of God's grace.[22] As far as can be determined Tertullian is the first to use the title "mother" for the church, a theme he returns to several times.[23] Odo Casel

[19] Justin Martyr in his First Apology, 61, writes: "Then they are brought by us where there is water, and are reborn by the same manner by which we ourselves were reborn." Goodspeed, *Die ältesten Apologeten* 70.

[20] In his treatise *On Prayer*, 14, Tertullian said that those who killed the prophets do not dare to lift their hands in prayer. "We however not only lift them up, but also spread them out, and modulating them by the Lord's passion (*dominica passione modula[ta]*), in our prayers also express our faith in Christ." CChr 1:265. "Modulating" the hands according to the passion seems to be referring to the outstretched arms of Christ on the cross.

[21] *Against Marcion* 1:23; CChr 1:466. F. J. Dölger proposed that the first prayer the newly baptized prayed was the Lord's Prayer. "Das erste Gebet der Täuflinge in der Gemeinschaft der Bruder," *Antike und Christentum: Kultur- und religionsgeschichtliche Studien*, 2nd edition (Münster: Aschendorff, 1974) 142–55.

[22] R. F. Refoulé, Introduction, *Traité du Baptême*; SC 35:16, note 2.

[23] Tertullian, *On Prayer*, 2; CChr 1:258; *On the Soul*, 43:10; CChr 1:847. The last mentioned work belongs to the Montanist period. For the place of Tertullian in the development of the church as mother *see* Joseph C. Plumpe, "The Mater Ecclesia of Tertullian," *An Inquiry into the Concept of the Church as Mother in Early Christianity* (Washington: Catholic University of America, 1943) 45–62. Plumpe has demonstrated that the presumption for an understanding of the church as mother would have been in place already before Tertullian. *Mater Ecclesiae* 35–44. For the early patristic, including pre-Tertullian, understanding of the baptismal font as the mother or womb of the church *see* W. M. Bedard, *The Symbolism of the Baptismal Font in Early Christian Thought* (Washington: Catholic University of America, 1951) 17–36. The use

remarked that Tertullian used the phrase *apud matrem* for the church, without any further explanation, as though it were understood by all.[24] The neophytes are reminded that they have entered the church—understood as both community and building—using this prayer gesture for the first time as they pray together with sisters and brothers in the faith to ask for charisms from God. There is no doubt that the eucharistic celebration took place at this point. Elsewhere Tertullian is more explicit about the eucharistic celebration following the water-bath and the imposition of hands. He sums it all up in a lapidary phrase: The church "seals with water [the water-bath], clothes with the Holy Spirit [imposition of hands], and feeds with the eucharist [celebration with the local communion]."[25]

What is essential to keep in mind is that the neophytes are moving from the water-bath phase (which in passing Tertullian places in relation to the waters of Jesus' own baptism),[26] and from the imposition of hands phase, to the eucharistic part of the rite of initiation. What transpires now, happens within the context of the local communion, sisters and brothers, gathering around the bishop (or presbyter) for the celebration of the eucharist.

At this point Tertullian offers pastoral advice. He suggests that the occasion for asking and receiving the charisms, which form an additional, underlying feature of baptism, is after the water-bath and the anointing, when the neophytes are gathering in the eucharistic room with the rest of the community, with hands raised and extended in prayer.[27] He uses the Greek

of "mother" for the church was picked up in the tradition after Tertullian, by Cyprian, for example, who had such a profound respect for Tertullian, though, because of his later Montanism, he never quoted him directly. Cyprian wrote: "You cannot have God for your father if you do not have the church for your mother;" "*Habere non potest Deum patrem qui ecclesiam non habet matrem.*" *On the Unity of the Church* 6; CSEL 1:214. *See also* Karl Adam, *Der Kirchenbegriff Tertullians* (Paderborn: Schöningh, 1907) 71–120.

[24] "Antike und christliche Tempelaufschriften," *Jahrbuch für Liturgiewissenschaft* 10 (1930) 144, note 7.

[25] "*Eam aqua signat, sancto spiritu uestit, eucharistia pascit, martyrium exhortatur et ita aduersus hanc institutionem neminem recipit.*" PH 36; SC 46:138, 139. Brackets mine. *See also* Dekkers, *Tertullianus en de Geschiedenis der Liturgie* 163, 164.

[26] *OB* 9; SC 35:79.

[27] The editors of Tertullian's works in CSEL 20:218 and in the *Corpus*

transliteration of *charisma* instead of the more general word *donum*. The technical sense of *charisma*, as used today, is a later development, which may begin about the fourth century. In the Vulgate translation *charisma* is used only once: "Earnestly desire the higher charisms" (1 Cor 12:31). Mostly Jerome uses *gratia*, a translation which borrows from the affinity with *charis*. This solution is not helpful because it blurs, if not wipes out, the difference between grace and charism. Sometimes the Vulgate employs *donum* (Rom 5:15; 11:29; 1 Cor 7:7) which makes *charisma* the equivalent to the more generic *dōrea*. In other cases Jerome uses *donatio* (Rom 12:6; 2 Cor 1:11).[28] Jerome may be shy of using *charisma* because of the increasing necessity of distancing the church from Montanism, a factor which I will discuss in the chapters on Cyril of Jerusalem, Jerome's contemporary. Given the wide acceptance of the prophetic gifts in the early church, Tertullian's use of *charisma* for what later became charisms in the technical sense, the prophetic gifts among them, seems unexceptional. This more technical sense is further recommended by the effort Tertullian uses to indicate their special character: "ask the Father, ask the Lord, for the special gift of his inheritance, the distribution of charisms" (*petite de patre, petite de domino peculia gratiae distributiones charismatum subiacere*). What Tertullian is straining to say may be found in a distinction made in the later Latin tradition: *gratia gratum faciens* (grace given for the good of the receiver, such as sanctifying grace) and *gratia gratis data* (grace given for the good of others). When treating of

Scriptorvm Latinorvm Paravianvm (Paravia: 1960) 34, noted that Adolf Harnack considered the words *"distributiones charismatum subiacere"* a gloss which should be deleted, without indicating either the reason for this judgment or the source in Harnack's writings where such a note is to be found. In neither case did the editors feel the evidence sufficient to delete the phrase. No such note is printed by Refoulé, Introduction, SC 35 or in A. d'Alès' 1933 edition in the Textus et Documenta series published by the Gregorian University, or in the CChr, Series Latina. The last named edition does record, not a recommended deletion, but a variant expansion, namely, *"sicut 'pater' charismatum, i.e. donorum, distributiones largitur, ita peculia gratiae 'dominus.'"* CChr 1:295.

[28] A. Vanhoye, "The Biblical Question of 'Charisms' After Vatican II," *Vatican II: Assessment and Perspectives*, 2 vols.; ed. R. Latourelle (New York: Paulist Press, 1988) 1:443.

the latter Thomas Aquinas listed prophecy, tongues, word of knowledge, and miracles.[29] Two editors of Tertullian's *On Baptism* identify the spiritual gifts of which he writes in the present text as those of 1 Corinthians 12.[30]

Tertullian went beyond saying that the newly baptized should expect the charisms to manifest themselves at this time. Twice he suggests that the neophytes ask for the charisms to be imparted to them: "*ask* of your Father, *ask* of your Lord" (*petite de patre, petite de domino*). The nature of this prayer is not specified, and there is a suggestion that it is the Lord's Prayer, which has some probability.[31] Luke lends some credence to this possibility. Shortly after the Lord's Prayer we read: "how much more will the heavenly Father give the Holy Spirit to those who ask

[29] Thomas Aquinas, *Summa Theologiae* II–II, 171–78.

[30] Refoulé, Tertullien, *Traité du Baptême;* SC 35:96, note 6, and A. D'Ales in *Tertulliani De Baptismo* (Rome: Gregorian University, 1933) 48.

[31] Dölger, "Das erste Gebet," 142–55. Dölger cited *On Prayer* by Cyprian, written a little more than a generation later than Tertullian's treatise of the same name, and like Tertullian's, essentially a commentary on the Lord's Prayer and oriented to the baptismal liturgy. Cyprian said that "by the very first words of one's new birth . . . [the new born Christian should] confess that God is his Father in heaven." *On Prayer,* 9; Michel Réveillaud, *Saint Cyprien, L'Oraison Dominicale* (Paris: Presses Universitaires de France, 1964) 88. This, Dölger suggested, means that the neophytes prayed the Lord's Prayer. He gave other patristic witnesses to the liturgical practice of praying the Lord's Prayer immediately after baptism (this would include prayer within the eucharistic celebration). He has also pointed out the variant reading of the petition "your kingdom come," as "may your Holy Spirit come over us and cleanse us," found in Gregory of Nyssa (c. 330–c. 395) *On the Lord's Prayer,* 3; PG 44:1157, in Evagrius Ponticus (346–99) PG 79:1180 (in a text falsely attributed to St. Nilus), and in Maximus the Confessor (c. 580–662) *On the Lord's Prayer* PG 90:885. Evagrius and Maximus did not actually give the variant but seem to be citing the text, that is, when commenting on the phrase "your kingdom come," Maximus wrote, "that is the Holy Spirit." This variant was first found in Marcion, against whom Tertullian wrote his tract. Marcion had this variant in his edited recension of the Gospel of Luke, dated about 144, the only gospel he accepted, a work which Tertullian had in front of him when he wrote his treatise against him. If this variant were current and accepted in North Africa at the time Tertullian wrote, it would add force to Tertullian's note that the newly baptized should pray for the charisms. But Tertullian in his own commentary on the Lord's Prayer, though he comments on one petition after the other, made no mention of the variant reading.

him?" The prayer in Tertullian is directed first to the Father, and then to Christ, a rather insistent formula.[32]

Specifically the neophytes are to ask for the charisms (*peculia gratiae distributiones charismatum subiacere*) which, ostensibly, one expected to find in a normal, healthy local communion. Tertullian uses the expression *peculium*. This refers to the inheritance, or rather to that special part of the whole inheritance, the *Sondergut*, which the *pater familias* handed on to the sons or slaves.[33] Implicit is the presumption that the part of the inheritance which is given is handed over with a kind of open-handed liberality, gratuitously, without the sons or slaves having any right to it.[34] The persons who receive it do not possess it as proprietors, but as something which still belongs to the *pater familias*, of which the sons or slaves have the use. In this case the special part of the inheritance is the charisms which form an additional, underlying feature (*subiacere*) of baptism.[35] The requests for the part of the inheritance, which are the charisms, are made with the expectation that the petitioners will receive what is requested: "Ask, he says, and you shall receive."[36] Finally, Tertullian suggests that the prayer has been effective, the

[32] The early Christians would not have found it awkward to address the Our Father to Christ. *The Acts of Justin Martyr and His Companions*, recension B, 4, a text from the middle of the second century has the martyr, Hierax, replying to a question about his father, saying: "Christ is our true father, and our faith in him is our mother." *The Acts of the Christian Martyrs*, ed. Herbert Musurillo (Oxford: Clarendon, 1972) 50. The apochryphal *Second Letter to the Corinthians*, 2, 1, 4 which dates from about 150, and is the earliest extant sermon, said of Christ that "he gave us light; as a father he called us sons; he saved us when we were perishing" PG 1, 332. In *AH*, 4, 31, 3; SC 100, 793 Irenaeus, a younger contemporary of Tertullian, with whose works Tertullian was acquainted, wrote: "The Word of God is the Father of the human race." *See also AH* 4, 21, 3; SC 100:792. Later the tradition of Christ as Father found its way into the monastic tradition and into *The Rule of St. Benedict*, 2, which said that the superior of the monastery holds the place of Christ and should be addressed as "Abba." *The Rule of St. Benedict*, ed. Timothy Fry and others (Collegeville: The Liturgical Press, 1980) 172. *See* appendix "The Fatherhood of Christ," 356–63.

[33] "Peculium," PWK, 37th half volume (1937) 13–16.

[34] Refoulé, Introduction, SC 35:96, note 5.

[35] *OB* 10; SC 35:80.

[36] *OB* 20; SC 35:95.

charisms prayed for have been given: "So now, you have sought, and have found; you have knocked, and it has been opened to you."[37] The most obvious sense of the words indicates that, at least for some of the neophytes, there is some observable phenomena, something experiential, perhaps the first expression of a charism, which leads the onlooker to conclude that prayer has been answered. Tertullian is not speaking in a vacuum. The presence and exercise of the charisms is a fact of ecclesial life in the second and third centuries.[38]

Tertullian encourages the neophytes to pray for the charisms within the context of the rite of initiation. What prompts Tertullian to give such advice? If the charisms belong to the normal life of the ordinary local communion, it seems a likely object of exhortation. God, being sovereign and free, is in no way dependent on a person's subjective dispositions. God can and does give gifts of which individuals were not previously aware. But God usually takes persons where they are. And if persons have no awareness that the whole spectrum of charisms are gifts which belong to the normal functioning of the ordinary local communion, then very likely such gifts will not be operative in the church. So Tertullian ostensibly wants the newly baptized to be aware that such charisms (which he does not specify) are associated with baptism, that the charisms are expected, and that the neophytes should even, at this most appropriate moment, request them.

In summary, we have seen the broad framework of communion ecclesiology operative in the ancient church. Communion/ *koinōnia* makes an integral ecclesiology possible, embracing as it does various sacral and sociological levels. Communion is that

[37] Ibid.
[38] E. Schweizer, "pneuma," *TDNT* 6: 396; Hans von Campenhausen, *Ecclesiastical Authority and Spiritual Power in the Church of the First Three Centuries* (Stanford: Stanford University Press, 1969) 178–212; George H. Williams and Edith Waldvogel, "A History of Speaking in Tongues and Related Gifts," *The Charismatic Movement*, ed. Michael P. Hamilton (Grand Rapids: Eerdmans, 1975) 61–113. *See* note of J. H. Waszink in Tertullian, *De Anima* (Amsterdam: Meulenhoff, 1947) 166, 167; Cecil M. Robeck, Jr., "The Role and Function of Prophetic Gifts for the Church at Carthage AD 202–58" (Ph.D. diss., Fuller Theological Seminary, 1984) 191–277; Harold D. Hunter, *Spirit-Baptism.*

primary level of sharing, transcendental in its origins, namely, participation in the life common to Father, Son, and Spirit; but is also participation in the depth of the Christian mysteries, namely, communion in the death and resurrection of Jesus, sharing in the one bread and one cup, fellowship in the one gospel. Beyond these levels there is also sharing in material wealth.

The rites of initiation show how communion ecclesiology was expressed architecturally, namely, a baptistery, an anteroom, and a larger eucharistic room. Moving through the rites performed in these different spaces, Tertullian shows how neophytes are introduced into the communion. Among other rites hands are laid upon the neophytes, asking for the Spirit to come down. Tertullian exhorts the neophytes, as they are coming up from the water, to raise their hands and pray with insistence that the special part of the inheritance, the bounty of charisms, will be given to them. Such a prayer indicates that the charisms belonged to the normal, day to day life of the ordinary Christian community. In addition to urging this petition, Tertullian suggests that it was granted. Charisms were facts of church life in the first centuries; therefore expectations that they would be granted within the rites of initiation do not seem unusual.

If the baptism in the Spirit as understood today usually involves laying on of hands, a prayer for the descent of the Spirit, and some expectation that the charisms will be imparted, then the baptism in the Holy Spirit is integral to the whole rite of Christian initiation as Tertullian understood it, even though he did not name it so. If this is so, why are there not more witnesses among the early authors to the charisms within the liturgy of initiation? How could such a striking element be lost? To this question we now turn.

Chapter Ten

Tertullian: Montanism and Reluctant Withdrawal of Communion

The disappearance of the prophetic charisms from the rites of Christian initiation seems to be related to the rise of Montanism. Montanists gave much attention to the charisms. This enthusiastic, apocalyptic movement traces its origin to one Montanus in Phrygia. The followers of Montanus lived in the expectation of a new outpouring of the Holy Spirit on the church. The earnest of the coming New Pentecost was the presence of prophets, male and female, within Montanism. Soon, the Montanists are reported to have said, the Heavenly Jerusalem will descend near Pepuza in Phrygia—although it is not certain that this declaration can be traced back to the founders of the movement.[1]

In this chapter I will note the church's reaction to the New Prophecy, as Montanism was originally called, at least by its supporters. I will look at Tertullian's account of the reigning pope's initial response, as well as the welcome Gaul gave the news of the movement in Phrygia. Tertullian eventually became a Montanist, making necessary an examination of the relationship to Montanism of his treatise *On Baptism*, which contains the reference to charisms within the rite of initiation. Some at-

[1] W. Tabbernee, "Revelation 21 and the Montanist 'New Jerusalem'," *Australian Biblical Review* 37 (1989) 52–60.

tention will be given to the impact on the church of Tertullian's exodus from the Catholic communion, and to how his peers in succeeding centuries related to him.

The exact date of Montanism's emergence is not clear, but G. S. P. Freeman-Grenville, agreeing with Epiphanius,[2] has cogently argued that the movement began in 156/157,[3] though Eusebius and Jerome both give 172.[4] The movement spread from Asia Minor to Rome and the North Africa of Tertullian's time. In Rome it attracted only a small number of adherents, but in North Africa it was to find large numbers of followers. Judged by the Catholic norms of the last decade of the second century, it was not inherently heretical, nor was it necessarily always heretical, even though later it was consistently treated as such. News of the movement reached Rome possibly as early as 177.[5] Eusebius reported that Irenaeus took letters from the Martyrs of Lyons (who were still in prison) to Pope Eleutherius (c. 174/5–c. 189) in which the Martyrs gave their unsolicited opinion on Montanism. The same letters were sent to Asia, and in particular to Phrygia.[6] These letters could not have been written without Irenaeus being involved in some manner. The letters he handed over to the Roman bishop were essentially conciliatory.[7]

[2] Epiphanius, *Against Heresies*, 68:1; PG 41:855.

[3] "The Date of the Outbreak of Montanism," JEH 5 (1954) 7–15. R. Grant accepts the 156–57. *Augustus to Constantine* (New York: Harper & Row, 1970). In the 19th century the Tübingen school argued that Montanism was simply a convenient name given by scholars to certain styles of life and currents of thought in the second and third centuries, a thesis now long abandoned.

[4] Eusebius, *Chronology*; PG 19:563, 564; Jerome, *Chronology*; PL 27:627. H. von Campenhausen contends that 172 or 173 is the date favored by the majority of scholars. *Ecclesiastical Authority* 181, note 15. See also W. H. C. Frend, "A Note on the Chronology of the Martyrdom of Polycarp and the Outbreak of Montanism," *Oikomene: Studi paleocristiani publicati in onore del Concilio Ecumenico Vaticano II* (Rom: 1964) 499–506, and T. D. Barnes, "The Chronology of Montanism," *JThS*, n.s. 21 (1970) 403–07.

[5] Frend, *The Early Church*, 3d edition (Philadelphia: Westminster, 1985) 69, 70.

[6] Eusebius, *Ecclesiastical History* 5, 3, 4; SC 41:27.

[7] Pierre de Labriolle, *La Crise Montaniste* (Paris: Leroux, 1913) 269. But see the different interpretation of these texts in P. Monceaux, *Histoire Littéraire de L'Afrique Chrétienne*, 7 vols. (Paris: Leroux, 1901) 1: 402–405.

Eleutherius took no action against Montanism, though Eusebius reported that there were difficulties in Asia Minor. The first councils or synods in the history of the church (be it noted, including laity) were held in Asia Minor to deal with the strong reaction to the new movement.[8] The problems the New Prophecy, as it was called, raised in Asia must have been considerable. Neither the threat of gnosticism, nor Marcionism had ever pressed the church into calling councils. Montanism was threat enough to institute the first council since Jerusalem (Acts 15); it is not surprising that there were excommunications.

Nonetheless Tertullian wrote of a bishop of Rome, most likely Pope Victor, Eleutherius' successor, who had decided in favor of the New Prophecy. According to Tertullian this pope, though he knew of the prophecies of Montanus, Prisca, and Maximilla, had "bestowed his peace (*inferentem pacem*) on the churches of Asia and Phrygia," and this by writing "letters of peace" (*litteras pacis*).[9] The pope could not have given his peace unless the prophecies of the three prophets, as he knew them, were within the bounds of orthodoxy. Peace, it will be recalled, was a synonym for ecclesial communion, both personal and ecclesial.[10] Hippolytus (c. 170–c. 236), a younger contemporary, a conservative who wanted to retain the ancient customs, said that at the end of the rite of initiation the kiss of peace is to be exchanged, signifying that the newly baptized now fully belong to the communion.[11] To give the peace to the churches had a specific sense of acknowledging communion. For the bishop of Rome to send peace to the Montanist churches in Asia and Phrygia was to say "we belong to the same communion, we celebrate the same Eucharist, we hold the same faith." Tertullian said that the bishop of Rome had "already sent" (*iam emissas*) letters to these churches in which he expressed the giving

---

[8] J. Lebreton, "Le developpement des institutions ecclésiastiques à la fin du second siècle et au début du troisième," *RevScRel* 24 (1934) 158–61.

[9] "*Nam idem tunc episcopum Romanum, agnoscentem iam prophetias Montani, Priscae, Maximillae, et ex ea agnitione pacem ecclesiis Asiae et Phrygiae inferentem, falsa de ipsis prophetis et ecclesiis eorum adseuerando et praecessorum eius auctoritates defendendo coegit et litteras pacis reuocare iam emissas et a proposito recipiendorum charismatum concessare.*" Against Praxeas, 1:5; CChr 2:1159.

[10] Hertling, *Communio*, 18, 19.

[11] Hippolytus, *Apostolic Tradition*, 21; SC 53:91.

of the peace, the exchange of such letters of communion being a common practice.[12] However, Praxeas, a traveler from Asia and a heretic in his own right (he introduced Patripassian Monarchianism into Rome), succeeded in turning the pope against the Montanists. The pope reluctantly recalled the letters he had already sent, put them on hold, and withdrew his intention of recognizing the charisms.[13]

The character of Montanism was not universally the same, but there were serious abuses and excesses, if the sources are to be trusted. Montanism was condemned before 200 by Asian synods and then, with reluctance, by Rome after the turn of the century, probably by Victor's successor, Pope Zepherinus (198/9–217). If Montanism reached Rome in 177, and the condemnation by the hesitant Zepherinus came about twenty-three years later, then Rome did not panic into condemnation. In part the hesitancy must have been due to the recognition that prophecy belonged to the apostolic witness. If the church is built upon "the foundation of the apostles and prophets" (Eph 2:20), the charismatic-prophetic element belongs to the church in some constitutive sense.[14] In the *Didache*, which contains material perhaps older than the later books of the New Testament,

---

[12] When Tertullian described the letters as "already sent" (*iam emissas*), this does not necessarily mean that they were already on the road to Asia Minor. Rather it could mean that they were already written, sealed with the official stamp, and, perhaps known to the public. De Labriolle, *La Crise Montaniste*, 259, 261.

[13] George La Piana, "The Roman Church at the End of the Second Century," *Harvard Theological Review* 18 (1925) 244–51. We know of Praxeas and his adherence to Patripassianism only from Tertullian's book *Against Praxeas* (CChr 2:1159–205). Tertullian may have somewhat misrepresented him. Tabbernee claims that Victor's *litteras pacis* were written to the Asiatic Christian communities in Rome under Victor's pastoral care, some of which contained Montanists, rather than to churches *in* Asia Minor. See his "Opposition to Montanism from Church and State: A Study of the History of Theology of the Montanist Movement as Shown by the Writings and Legislation of the Orthodox Opponents of Montanism" (Ph.D. diss., University of Melbourne, 1978) 46–49.

[14] "Just as Deuteronomy 18:15, 18 promised that Israel would again be given a 'prophet,' so the author of Ephesians cannot imagine the church living on solid ground without the service of 'prophets.' " Markus Barth, *Ephesians*, 2 vols. (Garden City: Doubleday, 1974) 1:317.

the prophets still play a large role, quite likely even presiding at the eucharist (10:7).[15] Justin Martyr (c. 100–c. 165), who may have perceived that the charismatic prophetic dimension of the Old Testament belonged constitutively to Jahwism,[16] boasted to the Jewish Trypho "that the prophetic gifts remain with us," having been transferred from the Jews.[17] Irenaeus witnessed to the presence in the church of his time of "prophetic charisms" and "tongues."[18] Though Irenaeus did not support Montanism, neither did he attack it. Irenaeus did take the occasion in his *Against Heresies* to chide those who rejected the Fourth Gospel precisely because it contains the promise of the Spirit, thereby rejecting at the same time "the Gospel and the grace of prophecy."[19] "They are truly unfortunate," continued Irenaeus, "who, realizing there are false prophets, take this as a pretext for expelling the grace of prophecy from the church."[20]

Even anti-Montanist polemicists recognized that "the prophetic charisms must exist in the church until the final com-

[15] A. Tuilier, Introduction, *La Doctrine des Douze Apôtres (Didachè)*; SC 248:52, 53; J. P. Audet, *La Didachè: Instructions des Apôtres* (Paris: Lecoffre, 1958) 432, 433.

[16] "It is therefore evident that the charismatic was an absolutely constitutive factor in Jahwism." Gerhard von Rad, *Old Testament Theology*, 2 vols. (New York: Harper & Row, 1962) 1:100, 102: "Israelite religion . . . is *a creation of that spirit* which bloweth where it listeth. . . . *At the very beginning of Israelite religion we find the charisma*, the special individual endowment of a person; and to such an extent is the whole structure based on it, that without it it would be inconceivable." Walther Eichrodt, *Theology of the Old Testament*, 2 vols.; 5th edition (Philadelphia: Westminster, 1960) 1:292. Emphasis in the original.

[17] Justin, like Irenaeus, also acknowledged that the openness to true prophets brought with it the problem of false prophets. *Dialogue with Trypho*, 82; *Die ältesten Apologeten*, 194.

[18] *AH* 5, 6, 1; SC 153:74. *See* note in SC 152:229. *See also AH* 1, 13, 4; SC 264:198; *AH* 3, 24, 1; SC 211:472, 474; *AH* 4, 26, 5; SC 100:728.

[19] "*Alii uero ut donum Spiritus frustrentur quod in nouissimis temporibus secundum placitum Patris effusum est in humanum genus, illam speciem non admittunt eius quod est secundum Iohannem Euangelium, in qua Paraclitum se missurum Dominus promisit, sed simul et Euangelium et propheticum repellunt Spiritum.*" *AH* 3, 11, 9; SC 211, 170, 172. *See* SC 210:289 for the discussion of a possible negative having been dropped from the text.

[20] "*Infelices uere qui pseudoprophetas quidem esse nolunt, propheticam uero gratiam repellunt ab Ecclesia.*" Ibid.

ing."[21] How justified was the final reprobation of Montanism, and a long trail of condemnations, need not detain us.[22] The provocation must have been grave. The condemnation of a movement in which the charisms played a large role made it difficult to support prayer for charisms within the rite of initiation. This was true even though it was recognized that the charismatic element belonged to the nature of the church.

What gives this special relevance is the ecclesiological context in which Tertullian situated baptism, namely, the ecclesiology of communion. Tertullian asserted that the heretics against whom he was writing did not have the same God, nor the same Christ, consequently they did not have the same baptism.[23] Tertullian understood baptism as the law of faith.[24] As we have seen, the sign that the heretics were alien to the true discipline (*haeretici autem nullum consortium habent nostrae disciplinae*), by which Tertullian here understood sacramental doctrine, was their exclusion from communion (*quos extraneos utique testatur ipsa ademptio communicationis*).[25] The explicit use of communion ecclesiology is not extensive in Tertullian, but it is an operative category.

Tertullian's Taint

Would not Tertullian be a tainted source because of his eventual turn to Montanism? His relationship to Montanism leads us into the notoriously difficult chronology of his life and writings. Already in the last century Adolf Harnack had voiced the complaint

[21] "*Etenim prophetiae donum in omni ecclesia ad ultimum usque Domini adventum permanere debere auctor est Apostolus.*" Eusebius, *Ecclesiastical History* 5:17, 4; SC 41, 54. Here Eusebius was quoting an anti-Montanist source.

[22] von Campenhausen, *Ecclesiastical Authority*, 149–212; J. L. Ash, "The Decline of Prophecy in the Early Church" *Theological Studies* 37 (1976) 227–52, especially 251, 252; Cecil M. Robeck, Jr., "Canon, Regulae Fidei, and Continuing Revelation in the Early Church" *Church, Word, and Spirit*, ed. J. E. Bradley and R. A. Muller (Grand Rapids: Eerdmans) 65–92. This last essay I read in galley form.

[23] He was arguing from their heretical theology to the nullity of their baptism.

[24] *OB* 13; SC 35:86; *PH* 14:4; SC 46:107.

[25] *OB* 15; SC 35:87. *See* Valentin Morel, "Disciplina: Le mot et l'idée représentée par lui dans les oeuvres de Tertullien" RHE 40 (1944) 19, 20, 22.

that the question had been repeatedly worked and reworked so that it was difficult to see how more light could be shed.[26]

The conversion of Tertullian to Christianity could be placed in the years 190–95. The evidence suggests that his treatise *On Baptism* was written early in these Christian years, rather than late.[27] After Tertullian wrote *On Baptism*, he wrote five, possibly six, books before he showed signs of Montanist influence.[28] The editors of Tertullian's writings in the *Corpus Christianorum, Series Latina*, dated *On Baptism* in the years between 198 and 204.[29] P. Monceaux and R. F. Refoulé placed it in the years 200–206.[30] No agreement has been reached on the date of his becoming a Montanist. Barnes places it before 206,[31] Quasten gave it as 207,[32] Refoulé as 213,[33] and the editors of *Corpus Christianorum* between 208–12.[34] Despite the difficulties which chronology presents, *On Baptism* is recognized as "certainly" belonging to his Catholic period.[35] "Nowhere in these homilies does Tertullian show any interest in Montanism."[36]

Quasten agreed, but seems to be of two minds concerning any Montanist influence whatsoever in this Catholic tract. Commenting on Tertullian's contention that "where there are three, that is, Father, Son, and Holy Spirit, there is the church, which

[26] *Die Chronologie der altchristliche Litteratur bis Eusebius*, 2 vols. (Leipzig: Hinrichs, 1904) 2:256.

[27] Ibid., 269. For a contemporary treatment of the problem of chronology in Tertullian *see* C. Becker, "Zur Chronologie der Schriften Tertullians," *Tertullians Apologeticum: Werden und Leistung* (Munich: Kösel, 1954) 346–55. See also Barnes, *Tertullian: A Historical and Literary Study* (Oxford: Clarendon, 1971) 42–48.

[28] "Tabvla Chronologica"; CChr 2:1627.

[29] Ibid.

[30] Monceaux, *Histoire Littéraire de l'Afrique Chrétienne*, 1:208; Refoulé, Introduction, Tertullien, *Traité du Baptême; SC* 35:12.

[31] Barnes, *Tertullian*, 46–47.

[32] Johannes Quasten, *Patrology*, 4 vols. (New York: Herder and Herder, 1961, 1963, 1986) 2:166.

[33] Refoulé, Introduction, *Traité du Baptême; SC* 35:8.

[34] CChr 2:1627.

[35] Refoulé, Introduction, *Traité du Baptême; SC* 36:12. *See also* de Labriolle, *La Crise Montaniste*, 356.

[36] E. Evans, Introduction, *Tertullian's Homily on Baptism* (London: SPCK, 1964) xi.

is a body of three,"[37] Quasten suggested that "the more . . .
Tertullian leaned to Montanism, the more he came to regard the
body of believers as a purely and exclusively spiritual group."[38]
Since opposition to the episcopate was pragmatically built into
the New Prophecy, one can doubt that there were any Montanist leanings in *On Baptism* when in the same tract Tertullian
gave bishops, presbyters, and deacons such preference in conferring baptism (though a layperson could also baptize).[39] No
one tainted with Montanist inclinations could have written in
the same baptismal treatise, "jealousy of the episcopate is the
mother of schisms."[40]

It is true that even in his Catholic period Tertullian so stressed
the heavenly saving power in the church that the visible aspect
of the church did not receive its due; but the stark contrast,
even opposition, between the empirical church and the graced
church, so typical of his Montanist period, was not a theme of
his Catholic years.[41] What Tertullian wished to say in the
trinitarian expression in his *On Baptism* was that the church is
necessary in the work of salvation, which is itself trinitarian.
Karl Adam, in explicit reference to the problematic trinitarian
formulation ("where there are three, that is, Father, Son, and
Holy Spirit, there is the church, which is a body of three"),
only appeared to overstate the case when he wrote: "In every
saving act the efficacy of the church is just as necessary as the
efficacy of the Trinity."[42] Adam's bold assertion is based on
Tertullian's daring ecclesiological insight in his tract *On Prayer.*
Tertullian was interpreting the Lord's Prayer for catechumens
and was writing between 198 and 200, about the same time as
he wrote *On Baptism*, at a period when he was most probably
active as a catechist in the catechumenate at Carthage.[43] When
one prays the Lord's Prayer and speaks the name "Father,"
Tertullian noted, one thereby calls upon the "Son." More than

---

[37] *OB* 6; SC 35:75.
[38] Quasten, *Patrology* 2:331.
[39] 17; SC 35:89-91.
[40] *"Episcopatus aemulatio schismatum mater est."* Ibid. 17; SC 35:90.
[41] Adam, *Der Kirchenbegriff Tertullians*, 90.
[42] Ibid., 92.
[43] Plume, *Mater Ecclesia*, 45.

that: "Even our mother the church is not omitted, seeing that in 'son' and 'father' there is a recognition of 'mother': for the name of both father and son has its actuality from her."[44] The necessity of the church is rooted in the trinitarian order of salvation.[45] This is not yet early Montanism, but advance preparations for a purely spiritual church have been made, even if unconsciously.[46]

But there is that other mind of Quasten on Tertullian's relationship to the New Prophecy in the tract *On Baptism*, namely, that it is "free of every trace of Montanism."[47] He was moved to this conclusion by Tertullian's considerable respect at this period for clerical authority, not a characteristic of the New Prophecy.

Tertullian's *On Baptism* is, therefore, a reliable source of Catholic baptismal practice in North Africa at the end of the second century. The tract *On Baptism* was not written as a proposal as to how baptism might be carried out in Carthage. Rather, the originality of the text is that it furnishes us with liturgical details of how the Carthaginian church actually celebrated initiation. On the basis of liturgical practice Tertullian reflected theologically. He wrote with enough precision that we can reconstitute the general lines of the North African baptismal liturgy of his day. Given the general tendency of ritual patterns

---

[44] "*Ne mater quidem Ecclesia praeteritur, siquidem in filio et patre mater recognoscitur, de qua constat et patris et filii nomen. On Prayer 2; CChr 1:258.*

[45] The omission of the spirit in the formulation could have at least two reasons. The first is that spirit does not bring the argument forward, because spirit does not demand mother, as do father and son. The second is that in his Montanist period Tertullian identified the church with the Spirit, not as an "autonomous" person, but precisely in the Spirit's trinitarian relationship: "*Nam et ipsa ecclesia proprie et principaliter ipse est spiritus, in quo est trinitas unius diuinitatis, Pater et Filius et Spiritus sanctus. Illam ecclesiam congregat quam Dominus in tribus posuit.*" On Modesty 21; CChr 2:1328. See Adhémar d'Alès, *La Théologie de Tertullien* (Paris: Beauchesne, 1905) 215–18; Robert E. Roberts, *The Theology of Tertullian* (London: Epworth, 1924) 184–90.

[46] Refoulé commented on the trinitarian formula, but failed to remark any Montanist tendencies here. Rather he saw Tertullian, who was a jurist, as being inspired by the juridic principle "*Tres faciunt collegium.*" SC 35:75, note 3. But see Barnes, *Tertullian*, 22–29 who argues against the identification of Tertullian with the jurist Tertullianus.

[47] Quasten, *Patrology* 2:280.

to be conservative, Tertullian is very likely giving us the baptismal practice which had been in force for some years. In the first chapter Tertullian made a specific appeal to "the roots of tradition," and later in the same book returned to the traditional rules to be observed in baptizing.[48] Later, when he did become a Montanist, he wrote again about the liturgy of baptism in his *The Chaplet*. In this description of baptism, in which the Montanist Tertullian would not differ from the earlier Tertullian, he cited the rite of baptism as a way of demonstrating the argument from antiquity.[49] Tertullian had a developed conception of tradition and had obviously given the matter much thought.[50] Together with Origen, he attached a value to tradition analogous to that which he attached to the letter of scriptures.[51] His appeal to tradition expresses a desire to retain the rites and doctrine which had been handed down from the earlier days. His treatise *On Baptism* is of greatest importance for the liturgical history of the rites of Christian initiation, being "not merely the earliest work on the subject . . . (but also) the only Ante-Nicene treatise on any of the sacraments."[52] This gives the treatise *On Baptism* the character of a *locus theologicus*.[53]

The Fall of a Giant

Tertullian's entry into the ranks of the Montanists greatly compromised his reputation and influence. The traditional view that Tertullian ultimately left the Catholic church to join a separate

[48] "*De sacramento aquae nostrae qua ablutis delictis pristinae caecitatis in vitam aeternam liberamur non erit otiosum digestum istud instruens tam eos qui cum maxime formantur quam et illos qui similiter, credidisse contenti, non exploratis rationibus traditionum temptabilem fidem per imperitiam portant.*" OB 1 (SC 35, 64). Here tradition refers both to doctrine and rites which had been handed down. Refoulé, Introduction, *Traité du Baptême*; SC 35:65, note 5. "*Superest ad concludendam materiolam de observatione quoque dandi et accipiendi baptismi commonefacere.*" OB 17; SC 35:89.

[49] Tertullian, *The Chaplet*, 3; CChr 2:1042.

[50] Quasten, "Tertullian and 'Traditio'" *Traditio* 2 (1944) 481–84.

[51] D. van den Eynde, *Les normes de l'enseignement Chrétien dans la littérature patristique des trois premiers siècles* (Paris: Gabalda & Fils, 1933) 277, note 2. *See also* 197–212. Frans de Pauw, "La justification des traditions non écrites chez Tertullien" *Ephemerides Theologicae Lovanienses* 19 (1942) 5–46.

[52] Quasten, *Patrology*, 2:278.

[53] Refoulé, Introduction, Tertullien, *Traité du Baptême*; SC 35:29.

Montanist community, which he also eventually left to found his own sect,[54] has been challenged recently. It is claimed that Tertullian, in fact, never left the Catholic church at Carthage but remained a leading member of a pro-Montanist group which, if it separated at all, did so well after Cyprian's time.[55] Even if this view is correct, it is evident that Tertullian's adherence to the New Prophecy greatly compromised his reputation and influence. His Montanism made it difficult to recognize his positive contributions. Tertullian was not just another ecclesiastical scribbler. By any standards he was, Augustine excepted, "the most important and original ecclesiastical author in Latin."[56] With great intelligence, both penetrating and witty, with a restless mind, taking no account of due measure, he confronted his readers with what was striking and out of the ordinary. He was "incapable of being dull."[57] Not with studied genteel elegance, but with appeals to the heart and to the imagination, with rapid shifts of thought, with truculence and carefully chosen vulgarities, he sometimes persuaded, more often captured. The opposition was not to be vanquished; it had to be obliterated. Relentless in his convictions, unrepentant in his violation of the old classical norms for artistic behavior, he refused to subordinate his personality to the anonymity of the tradition.[58] Tertullian would have none of it. He it was who introduced the individual element into Latin ecclesiastical literature.[59] Direct to the point of a fault, the force of his personality was everywhere obtrusive in his writings.[60] "No one raised Latin to such a

[54] Augustine, On Heresies 8:6; CChr 46:338, 339.
[55] Tabbernee, "Remnants of the New Prophecy: Literary and Epigraphical Sources of the Montanist Movement," Studia Patristica 21 (1989) 195–97. See also D. Powell, "Tertullianists and Cataphrygians," VC 29 (1975) 33–35, and Tabbernee, "Opposition to Montanism from Church and State," 76–79, 134–40, 368–71.
[56] Quasten, Patrology, 2:247.
[57] H. von Campenhausen, The Fathers of the Latin Church (London: Adam & Charles Black, 1964) 9.
[58] E. Norden, Die Antike Kunstprosa, 2 vols. (Stuttgart: Teubner, 1958) 2:606; C. Mohrmann, "Observations sur la langue et le style de Tertullien," Etudes sur le Latin des Chrétiens, 4 vols. (Rome: Edizioni di Storia et Letteratura, 1961) 2:246.
[59] Monceaux, Histoire Littéraire de l'Afrique Chrétienne, 1:458.
[60] Mohrmann, "Observations," 246.

height of passion."[61] He used all the refinements and strata-
gems of rhetoric, all the clarity of law, confident that he was
sweeping all before him. The language he forged "was without
precedent in the literary field."[62]

An injustice would be done if he were to be considered a
literary technician. In addition to his stylistic talents in Latin he
also wrote Greek, and, like Hilary after him, referred to the
Greek text when quoting the Bible. H. von Campenhausen
judges him to have been "the most penetrating exegete of the
whole ancient church, whose detailed accuracy and understanding was out-done by none of the later theologians."[63] Jerome
said it best: "Who is more educated than Tertullian? Who more
acute?"[64] "A learned man on fire."[65] "His *Apology* and his *To
the Heathens* contain all profane science."[66]

Those who read him paid a price. Even in antiquity the
groans of those who unpacked his sentences could be heard.
Lactantius (c. 240–c. 320) maintained that the obscurity of Tertullian's style is one of the reasons he was little known.[67] Norden
names him as "without question the most difficult author in
the Latin language. He makes unreasonable demands on the
reader."[68] Nonetheless the claim is made that he is "the real
creator of church Latin."[69] Christine Mohrmann believes Tertullian to be less the isolated genius and more the participator in
the "collective creation of a linguistic community."[70]

Whether he was a priest or not is disputed. Jerome twice
within a short space called him a priest.[71] However, the recluse

[61] Norden, *Antike Kunstprosa*, 606.
[62] von Campenhausen, *The Fathers of the Latin Church*, 8.
[63] Ibid., 7.
[64] Jerome, *Letter* 70:4; CSEL 54:707.
[65] Jerome, *Letter* 84:2; CSEL 55:122.
[66] Jerome, *Letter* 70:5; CSEL 54:707.
[67] Lactantius, *Divine Institutions*, 5:1; CSEL 19:402.
[68] Norden, *Antike Kunst*, 2:606.
[69] A. Harnack, *Geschichte der altchristlichen Litteratur bis Eusebius*, 4 vols.
(Leipzig: J. C. Hinrich, 1893) 1/2:667. *See also* M. Bardenhewer, *Geschichte der
alchristlichen Literatur*, 5 vols. (Freiburg im Br.: Herder, 1903) 2:340.
[70] "Observations," 2:236; Mohrmann, "Saint Jérôme et Saint Augustin
sur Tertullien," *Etudes sur le Latin des Chrétiens* 3:387, 388.
[71] Jerome, *On Famous Men*, 53; PL 22:661.

of Bethlehem is not a disinterested historian, but may have wanted to shore up the priesthood over against what he thought were the pretensions of the bishops. Quasten thinks Tertullian was a priest, otherwise how account for the eminent position he attained as a teacher, a role he scarcely could have fulfilled as a layman.[72] This does not seem to be a compelling argument. Justin Martyr was a layman, teacher, and theologian. Tertullian, a man of some vanity, would not have left his priestly dignity unremarked in all of his writings.[73] This is not an idle point. He was probably active as a catechist, possibly giving the catecheses to candidates in preparation for their initiation.[74] On Baptism might itself be the composite of a series of baptismal homilies.[75] If this is true, then the presence of the elements of the baptism in the Spirit in the rite of initiation would have greater weight. Then, one is not dealing with a casual lecture on baptism, but with a catechesis which was itself part of the larger liturgy of initiation itself. It is quite possible that a person of Tertullian's obvious attainments gave the baptismal catecheses to the candidates even though he were a layman.

Tertullian at the Bar of his Peers

Cyprian (d. 258), who became bishop of Tertullian's home town, Carthage, some 23 years after Tertullian's death, was an assiduous student of his writings. As recorded by Jerome, Cyprian's secretary told of Cyprian's unwillingness to let a day pass without reading a page of Tertullian. Each day Cyprian was accustomed to say to his secretary, "*Da Magistrum*" ("Give me one of the Master's books").[76] Cyprian knew how to distinguish between the central tradition and the distorted views of "the Master." Though comfortable with Tertullian himself, though drawing on Tertullian for his own writings, Cyprian

[72] Quasten, *Patrology*, 2:246.
[73] I am indebted to Godfrey Diekmann for these reflections.
[74] von Campenhausen, *Fathers of the Latin Church*, 7.
[75] Evans, "Introduction," *Tertullian's Homily on Baptism*, xi.
[76] Jerome, *On Famous Men*, 53: PL 23:664. The fact that all but one of Tertullian's Montanist works have survived may support the contention that Tertullian never formally separated from the Catholic church. Tabbernee, "Remnants of the New Prophecy," 197.

never once mentioned his name, never acknowledged his specific indebtedness to him. Does this not seem a little small-minded, seeing that Cyprian was "entirely dependent on Tertullian."[77] This is shunning of a high order.

Hilary of Poitiers (c. 315–67) acted more magnanimously, even recommending Tertullian's treatise *On Prayer*.[78] At the same time, he recognized that Tertullian's authority had been compromised by his departure from the Catholic communion and his adherence to the Montanists.[79] Hilary had been influenced by Tertullian's treatises *On the Soul, On Baptism, The Prescription of Heretics, Against Praxeas,* and *On the Resurrection.*[80] Given the breadth of his indebtedness to Tertullian, the one explicit mention of Tertullian in *On Matthew* seems less than generous. But Hilary had done more than most.

Augustine was more unbending. While he granted with Jerome that Tertullian had a "penetrating" (*acutus*) mind,[81] he placed him squarely among the weightier heretics, namely, Pelagius, Donatus, Arius, and Manes.[82] Augustine ridiculed Tertullian as having "cheeks full of sound, not wisdom."[83] This disdain did not dissuade Augustine from several times appropriating, without attribution, Tertullian's golden aphorism, "the seed is the blood of Christians,"[84] casting it in more Augustinian modes, as "sparse is the seed of blood, up looms the church's field of corn."[85] Mohrmann, whom I am summarizing, judges this to be a transposition from the sublime lapidary formulation of Tertullian to the pathetic rhetoric of Augustine.[86]

Jerome did what he could to salvage Tertullian's writings, but in the end he had to say "we praise his genius, but we con-

---

[77] Quasten, *Patrology* 2:340.
[78] Hilary, *On Matthew,* 5:1; SC 254:151.
[79] Ibid.
[80] J. Doignon, "Introduction," *On Matthew;* SC 254:32, 33.
[81] Augustine, *On Genesis, a Literal and Unfinished Book,* 10:25, 41; PL 34:427.
[82] Augustine, *On Heresies,* 86; CChr 46:338, 339.
[83] Augustine, *On the Good of Widowhood,* 4:6; PL 40:433.
[84] Augustine, *Apology,* 50:13; CChr 1:171.
[85] Augustine, *Sermon,* 22:4; CChr 41:294. *See* Mohrmann, "Saint Jérôme et Saint Augustin sur Tertullien," 388, note 2.
[86] Mohrmann, "Observations," 388.

demn his heresy."[87] Mohrmann suggests that Jerome was bending over backwards to sympathize with the wayward Tertullian.[88] The reason: Tertullian was a soul-brother. Jerome contended that Tertullian was pushed into Montanism by the envy and insults he had suffered at the hands of Roman clerics.[89] Envy and insults were what Jerome remembered most from his own years in Rome.[90] Jerome's memory of the Roman church was that of a "whore decked in purple," "the senate of the pharisees."[91] Then, too, he may have felt the necessity of sympathizing with Tertullian whose polemical treatises were a quarry in which Jerome would dig and enrich himself. In fact, Jerome used Tertullian as a source, without attribution, almost as a matter of habit.[92]

The ancients had a much more relaxed attitude about borrowing without attribution, but Jerome is less than honest if we remember what he had said about Ambrose's heavy borrowing from Didymus the Blind's treatise *On the Holy Spirit*. Ambrose was, in Jerome's words, "a crow garmented in the feathers of a peacock,"[93] a *bon mot* which Rufinus maliciously repeated for posterity.[94] According to Jerome, Ambrose's crime was even greater: he turned Didymus' good Greek into Ambrose's bad Latin.[95] A castigator of those who borrowed from others without attribution, Jerome should have been more generous in acknowledging his own indebtedness to Tertullian, which was sometimes exceedingly great, even verbal.[96]

[87] Jerome, *Against Rufinus*, 3:27; CChr 79:98.

[88] Mohrmann, "Saint Jérôme et Saint Augustin sur Tertullien," 389.

[89] *"invidia postea et contumeliis clericorum Romanae ecclesiae ad Montani dogma delapsus."* Jerome, *On Famous Men*, 53; PL 23:663.

[90] J. N. D. Kelly, *Jerome* (New York: Harper & Row, 1975) 104–15.

[91] Jerome's Preface to Didymus the Blind's *On the Holy Spirit*; PL 39:1031.

[92] Kelly, *Jerome*, 64; Y. M. Duval, "Tertullien contre Origène sur la résurrection de la chair dans le *Contra Iohannem Hierosolymitanum* 23–36 de Saint Jérôme," *Revue des Etudes Augustiniennes* 17 (1971) 227–78, especially 248, 274–78; Y. M. Duval, "Saint Jérôme devant le baptême des hérétiques," ibid. 14 (1968) 145–80.

[93] Jerome, Preface to Didymus the Blind's *On the Holy Spirit*; PL 39:1031.

[94] Rufinus, *Apology Against Jerome*, 2:25; PL 21:604.

[95] Jerome, Preface to Didymus the Blind's *On the Holy Spirit*; PL 39:1032.

[96] F. Schultzen, "Die Benutzung der Schriften Tertullians de monogamia und de ieiunio bei Hieronymus adv. Iovinianum," *Neue Jahrbucher für deutsche Theologie* 3 (1894) 493, 496–98, 502.

Tertullian the Montanist turned against the Catholic communion all the literary skills, all the passion, all the exegetical knowledge he had formerly used in its defense. His peers in subsequent centuries may want in magnanimity, but their response is not without solid foundation, nor untypical of how those were regarded, who were thought to have departed from the faith of the church. To call in question the central doctrinal tradition was to put salvation, one's own and others', at peril.

Cyprian and Augustine had large pastoral concerns. Cyprian was pastor of the very church at Carthage to which Tertullian had belonged. The memory of such a man would have been a living reality. Augustine, bishop of Hippo, a city near Carthage, must still have felt the scandal of the giant's fall.

In summary, *koinōnia/communio* was a way of identifying the church from the earliest post-biblical days of theological reflection. A primary paradigm for the communion was the rite of initiation (baptism, sign of the giving of the Spirit, eucharist). Tertullian's *On Baptism*, as the first treatise on initiation from either East or West, is of greatest importance for the history of liturgy. When Tertullian described the initiatory celebration in Carthage at the end of the second and beginning of the third centuries he was not innovating, but setting forth the practice of the church which already had a tradition, to which he made explicit reference. There is no reason to doubt that the Catholic Tertullian is a reliable witness to the liturgical practice in North Africa at this period, rites which already for him had some antiquity. Within the celebration of initiation, that is, after the water-bath and the imposition of hands (with the prayer "inviting and welcoming the Holy Spirit"), as they entered the eucharistic room, Tertullian exhorted the newly baptized to pray that they might receive that special honored part of the inheritance, the charisms. The whole context would suggest that what many today call the baptism in the Spirit was integral to the rite of initiation as presented by Tertullian at the end of the second century of the church's life.

If that is so, it seems appropriate to draw on the actualist categories of the author of 2 Timothy 1:6, of Augustine, the prescholastics, and Symeon the New Theologian. For a church which has infant baptism, the baptism in the Spirit is a new actualization, of what was received at baptism as an infant.

Why would the mention of the charisms within the rite of initiation disappear? The reaction to Montanism and to Tertullian, the Montanist, was stronger than to either gnosticism or Marcionism, as is seen in the calling of the first council since that recorded in Acts 15. Montanism was also one of the forces which prompted the church to make a decision about the New Testament canon. Given Tertullian's aggressive, passionate style, it cannot be a matter of surprise that Cyprian and Hilary would distance themselves, that Jerome and Augustine would condemn him. Because the charisms were identified with Montanism, the charisms themselves, by contagion, probably became suspect. Would one promote at the heart of the rites of initiation the very charisms, especially the prophetic, which the Montanists championed, which had proved so problematic?

Chapter Eleven

Origen:
"Baptism Is the Principle and
Source of the Divine Charisms"

Origen (c. 185–c. 254) forces one to take sides. Fierce battles
were fought after Origen's death concerning this catechist,
exegete, theologian, apologist, mystic, spiritual master, church-
man, schoolman, creative scholar of prodigious output, and undoubted man of genius. In the fourth century the unbending
rigidity of Epiphanius (c. 315–403) was joined to the irascibility of
Jerome (c. 342–420) to defame the man whom Harnack calls "the
only true scholar which the early church possessed."[1] More
than any scholar before Jerome, he respected the Hebrew text
of the Old Testament and maintained high standards for textual
criticism.[2] Origen is a towering figure in whose shadow the
whole of the pre-Nicene church stood for good and ill. The
post-Nicene era, on both sides of the ledger, was paying its
debts to him. Still today we pay our dues.

Purporting to be citing the western view, George Scholarius,
the fifteenth-century Byzantine scholar, wrote: "Where Origen

---

[1] Adolph Harnack, "Origen," *Twentieth-Century Theology in the Making*,
ed. Jaroslav Pelikan (New York: Harper & Row, 1969) 3, 196.

[2] R. P. C. Hanson, *Origen's Doctrine of Tradition* (London: SPCK, 1954) 85.

was good, no one is better; where he was bad, no one is worse."[3] Scholarius indicates that this ambiguity drew down on Origen's head the distinction of being called the Father of Orthodoxy and the Father of Arianism. At least Jerome, that sometime friend, was convinced that Origen had spawned the heresy of Arius,[4] a view difficult to demonstrate. Jerome's new-found animosity toward a man he had extolled did not prevent him from copying *verbatim* sizable blocks of Origen's text into his own mediocre commentaries.

In the next two chapters I will discuss the tentative, provisional character of Origen's theological speculations, his commitment to the church and its apostolic tradition, his teaching on the relation of the charisms to initiation, the support such teaching finds in Basil, Jerome's deteriorating relation to Origen, Origen's proposal of the Jordan experience as the model for Christian initiation, his own personal role in preparing new converts for initiation, how Origen ties the exercise of the charisms to "the worthy," and his special predilection for the intellectual charisms.

The probable city of Origen's birth and the scene of much of his early teaching and composition is Alexandria, in size and importance the second city of the Roman Empire. Founded by Alexander the Great, a city with two harbors, it was a port strategically situated for commerce with the whole of the Mediterranean seaboard, and through the Red Sea with Southeast Asia. Ptolemy Philadelphus founded one of the great libraries of antiquity there, which supported the vibrant intellectual life of the city, including Philo (c. 20 B.C.–c. A.D. 50), who influences Clement of Alexandria (c. 150–c. 215) and Origen, but also gnostic thinkers Basilides and Valentinus. Ammonius Saccas, the founder of Neoplatonism lectured there. Besides being a center for Hellenism, it had the largest Jewish population of any city in the ancient world. The western text of Acts 18:25 notes that Apollos became a Christian in Alexandria, so there were Jewish Christians in the city at a very early date.[5] Eusebius records the

[3] Quoted in Henry Chadwick, *Early Christian Thought and the Classical Tradition* (New York: Oxford University, 1966) 95.

[4] *Letter 84, To Pachomius and Oceanus* 4; CSEL 55:125, 126.

[5] F. F. Bruce, *The Book of the Acts* (Grand Rapids: Eerdmans, 1954) 381.

legend that Mark evangelized Egypt.[6] Though unproven, it is not to be ruled out.[7] A newly discovered letter of Clement demonstrates the influence of Mark in the second-century church in Alexandria.[8] Adolf von Harnack notes our "almost complete ignorance" of early Christian history in Egypt.[9] We moved beyond this since Harnack wrote, but very little.[10]

Research Theology

It is not surprising that a city with these cultural credentials should produce a theologian of such scope, force, and originality as Origen. He is a maker of decisions. If one compares his theology to that of his predecessor, Clement of Alexandria, one is struck by the gain in definiteness.[11] Yet it is an open-ended determination, aware that the tradition is undeveloped, questions are unsettled. If his decisions are bold, they are also exploratory, tentative. Pamphilius (c. 240–309), Origen's younger contemporary, says in his defense, "rather than affirming he was discussing and exploring the broad reaches of the faith."[12] He speculates, not teaching as incontrovertibly true, that God is finite. The reason: were God not finite, God could not reflect on the divine self. Further, he speculates that God creates all spirits equal, but by the exercise of free will they develop a hierarchy of order. Some sinned and fell into sin and became either demons or souls imprisoned in bodies. Death does not irrevocably decide the fate of a soul. In the final consummation (*apocatastasis*) all free moral creatures, including the devil, will attain salvation. This doctrine of *apocatastasis*, later condemned, probably by the First Council of Constantinople in 543, is also

6 *Ecclesiastical History* 2:16; SC 31:71.

7 B. A. Pearson, "Earliest Christianity in Egypt: Some Observations," *The Roots of Egyptian Christianity*, eds. B. A. Pearson, J. E. Goehring (Philadelphia: Fortress, 1986) 144.

8 M. Smith, *Clement of Alexandria and a Secret Gospel of Mark* (Cambridge: Harvard University, 1973).

9 *Die Mission und Ausbreitung des Christentums*, 4th ed. (Leipzig, Hinrichs, 1924) 2:706.

10 A. F. J. Klijn, "Jewish Christianity in Egypt," *The Roots of Egyptian Christianity*, 161–75.

11 Hanson, *Origen's Doctrine of Tradition*, 183.

12 *Apology for Origen* 1; PG 17:552.

found in some form before Origen in Clement of Alexandria (c. 150–c. 215), and after him in Gregory of Nyssa (c. 330–c. 395), the latter declared a Doctor of the Church centuries later.[13] The subordinationism evident in Origen's trinitarian teaching is part of his groping for answers not yet available. Here he cannot be faulted. Until 355 everyone, with the exception of Athanasius (c. 296–373), is a subordinationist.[14] Given his readiness to take positions together with the knowledge that much was free speculation, one is astonished at how much of his doctrine of the trinity anticipated Nicaea by a hundred years. Judged by the Cappadocian settlement, Origen's doctrine of the trinity, without benefit of the theological discussion and development immediately before and after Nicaea, is largely on target. An achievement of some magnitude!

The fourth-century defenders of the divinity of the Holy Spirit were all indebted to him. Gregory Nazianzus (329–89) summed it up when he said that "Origen is the stone on which all of us were sharpened."[15] Basil (c. 330–79) and Gregory Nazianzus, as a mark of their admiration, sifted through the writings of their master to produce an Origen anthology, the *Philocalia*, containing many passages whose Greek text would otherwise have been lost to posterity. A close look at the selections shows that discretion was used in the choice, especially in avoiding trinitarian passages which might be interpreted as subordinationist. Perhaps even more than the other two Cappadocians, Gregory of Nyssa remained under his influence, which "seriously imperiled his reputation for orthodoxy."[16] Nonetheless, he was

[13] G. May, "Eschatologie," *Theologische Realenzyklopädie* (Berlin: de Gruyter, 1982) 10:301, 302; C. Lenz, "Apokatastasis," *Reallexikon für Antike und Christentum* (Stuttgart: Hiersmann, 1950) 1:514. Gregory of Nyssa, *Life of Moses* 2:82; SC lbis:54; Gregory of Nyssa, *On the Soul and Resurrection; PG* 46:67–72.

[14] R. P. C. Hanson, *The Search for the Christian Doctrine of God* (Edinburgh: T. & T. Clark, 1988) xix, 64.

[15] Recorded by Hesychius and found as an entry in *Svidae Lexicon*, ed. A. Adler (Stuttgart: Teubner, 1933) 3, 619.

[16] W. Fairweather, *Origen and Greek Patristic Theology*, (New York: Charles Scribner, 1901) 243; Hans Urs von Balthasar, "Introduction," *Origen: Spirit and Fire*, ed. R. J. Daly (Washington, D.C.: Catholic University of America, 1984) 1.

not slavish. When Origen's anthropology needed correcting, Gregory of Nyssa did not hesitate to set the master right.[17] The Cappadocians, together with Athanasius, defended Origen, even when they took different positions, and admitted that he was not without error.

Origen wrote in a time of persecution, when the public life of the church was restricted and the question of "authorized" theology unsettled. He taught before Nicaea, when many questions were still open, and the creedal situation more fluid. With great love for the church and the rule of faith, he put forth a number of hypotheses—tentative, hesitant options. Over-confident certitude in theological matters, he contended, was "to ignore one's ignorance."[18] After Nicaea, when the church was free and creedal lines firmer, some persons dogmatized his speculations, and set forth his hypotheses as absolute truth, bringing down condemnation upon his grave. No one raised large objections to his doctrinal positions during his lifetime, precisely because they were unconventional. What had been acceptable in the evangelical freedom of the hunted church, what passed muster in the theology of a persecuted community, was looked upon as perilous deviation by a church now free and given to more precise ordering of life and theology. Origen had not changed; the church had.[19] Few, even of his most ardent defenders, would suggest that he is to be followed without discernment. He was a pilgrim of truth, a third-century seeker when theology was groping, and he was judged wanting by those who were hemmed in by a kind of dogmatic fundamentalism, unable to grasp the dynamics of historical development.

"I Am a Man of the Church"

Though Origen's doctrine of penance and eucharist have been the object of controversy, this is less true of his teaching on

[17] J. Laplace, "Introduction," to Gregory of Nyssa's The Creation of Man, SC 6:30-33; D. L. Balas, "Origenes," Theologische Realenzyklopädie 14:177.

[18] Pamphilius preserves a fragment of Origen's Commentary on Genesis in his Apology, Preface; PG 17:545. See J. W. Trigg, "Origen's Modesty," Studia Patristica 23 (1989) 349-55.

[19] See Crouzel and Simonetti, "Introduction," SC 252:32-36.

baptism. His *Commentary on John,* considered his masterpiece,[20] gives an insight into his teaching on the inner life of the Christian, more particularly the call to the ascetic life and perfection. His teacher, Clement of Alexandria (c. 150–c. 215), had announced a forthcoming treatise on the perfect initiation of the Christian, which would also describe the final stages of the ascent of the human soul. Though Clement never carried out this intention, Origen adopted it as his program in composing his *On John,*[21] as he also carried out Clement's unfulfilled promise of a treatise *On Principles.*[22] At various stages of his early life he composed, more correctly dictated, his *On John,* in which is found the pertinent text. After returning to Alexandria from a voyage to Rome and Arabia, he begins dictating Volumes 1–4. Volume 5 is written at Antioch in 231–32. During a brief sojourn in Alexandria, he sketches out Volume 6, in which we find the text we are reviewing. Before finishing, he goes to Greece and Athens via Caesarea, where he is ordained a priest. After returning from Athens, he completes Volume 6 of *On John* at Caesarea in 234.[23]

Ambrose, Origen's wealthy lay convert from Valentinian gnosticism, specifically requested the commentary from his master. He was evidently influenced by a highly allegorizing commentary on John written by Heracleon (fl.c. 145–80), a Valentinian with less objectional views. Origen's convert wants instruction in true Christian gnosis, something his master was already engaged in expounding, following Irenaeus and Clement. Origen develops a method for presenting Christian gnosis and, more importantly, wants to lead the reader from knowledge to re-experience the mysteries of the church already shared,[24] in this case Christian initiation. He wants to be a

[20] H. Crouzel, *Origen* (San Francisco: Harper & Row, 1989) 42.

[21] R. Cadiou, *Origen: His Life at Alexandria* (St. Louis: Herder, 1944) 4.

[22] C. Kannengiesser, "Divine Trinity and the Structure of *Peri Archon,*" *Origen of Alexandria: His World and His Legacy,* eds. C. Kannengiesser, W. L. Petersen (Notre Dame: University of Notre Dame, 1988) 238–42.

[23] P. Nautin, *Origène: Sa Vie et Son Oeuvre* (Paris: Beauchesne, 1977) 377–80, 410.

[24] R. Gögler, "Einfuhrung," Origenes, *Das Evangelium nach Johannes* (Einsiedeln: Benziger, 1959) 35.

faithful dispenser of the divine mysteries,[25] as one who establishes his identity in relation to the church: "I, a man of the church, living in the faith of Christ and placed in the middle of the church . . ."[26] While Clement and Tatian (c. 160) were educated in Greek philosophy before their conversion, Origen was born a Christian, and drank in the scriptures from his earliest years as a student of his holy father, Leonidas.[27] His sense of the church is native, not acquired.

"By Itself"

At the beginning of the passage on Christian initiation, Origen is speaking of the great wonders of Jesus, themselves "symbols of those delivered by the word of God in all ages from every kind of sickness and weakness."[28] Even though these miracles were corporal in character, they were just the same calls to faith. "This is true of the water of baptism, symbol of the purification of the soul washed of every stain of sin, and it (baptism) is in itself the principle and source of the divine charisms for anyone who offers one's self to the divinity through the powerful epiclesis of the adorable trinity."[29]

The context for speaking of baptism is the healing miracles of Jesus, which, though they concern physical bodies, are a call to faith, an invitation to enter the kingdom, and to begin the ascent to perfection. Baptism is the true beginning, and only baptism equips one for the pilgrimage road which leads to the Father. Origen makes a parallelism between two "symbols (symbola)," the one the healing miracles of Jesus and the other baptism as principle and source of the charisms. By virtue of the word spoken by the Word, the healings of Jesus are "the symbol" of the larger deliverance from sickness and weakness operative at all times in history. Even though these miracles of Jesus are physical in nature, they are beneficial for those healed beyond the physical restoration, because they are a call to faith. Likewise the baptism, "the symbol" of purification and a wash-

[25] *On John* 20:2; SC 290:160.
[26] *Homilies on Joshua* 9:8; SC 71:260.
[27] Eusebius, *Ecclesiastical History* 6:1, 2; 6:2, 7; SC 41:82-86.
[28] *On John* 6 33; SC 157:254.
[29] Ibid.

ing of every stain of sin, is by itself the effective principle and source of the divine charisms because of the naming of Father, Son, and Holy Spirit. As in the healings of Jesus there is a physical element and an address to the soul, so in the waters of baptism. In both, the material element acts in real relation to the spiritual effect. In the physical healing miracles there is a purification and the call to faith; in the physical waters of baptism, a purification and the imparting of the charisms.

Negatively, baptism is the effective symbol of interior purification. Positively, baptism is "the principle and source of the divine charisms." "Principle" (*arche*) and "source" (*pege*) are strong expressions having almost identical meanings of essential basis, origin, beginning, fountainhead. Placed next to one another they are an intensive formulation. This concentration of force is itself the object of a further intensification. Origen says that baptism "in itself" or "by itself" (*kath hauto*) is the principle and source of the divine charisms for the believer who surrenders (*emparexonti*) to the divinity (*theioteti*) which acts in the water-bath by virtue of the trinitarian epiclesis, the calling down of Father, Son, and Holy Spirit.

The delivering over of one's self to the divinity indicates that the baptismal rite is not magic, not a species of sacramental objectivism apart from any faith commitment or moral engagement on the part of the believer. Elsewhere Origen complains that though baptism is a dying to sin and being buried with Christ, some do not die to sin and are therefore not rightly baptized.[30] Origen combines the objective and subjective elements of the sacramental action. One can recognize the lineaments of the later doctrine of *ex opere operato* and *ex opere operantis*. The sacrament is not effective because of the believer's faith, but by virtue of the divine act in the sacrament. The sovereign act of God is, however, not fruitful in the believer if there is no subjective yielding to the divinity.[31] Baptism is therefore the source and origin of the charisms in baptism in virtue of "the adorable trinity," by the naming of the names.

[30] *On Romans* 5:8; PG 14:1038.
[31] Crouzel, Origen, 226; Gögler, "Einführung," *Das Evangelium nach Johannes*, 186, footnote 1.

The Authority of Basil

Basil lends his authority to the authentic doctrine Origen proposes concerning the relationship of baptism to the charisms. In the whole of the Basilian corpus there is only one explicit reference to Origen by name, and this has to do with the citation of this passage as a support for the divinity of the Holy Spirit.[32] First Basil remarks that Origen's ideas on the Holy Spirit "are not always absolutely sound,"[33] a reference to some passages subordinating the Spirit to the Son and the Father in an unacceptable way (there is an acceptable subordination in the trinity: "The Father is greater than I" [John 14:28]). Then he contends that in "many places, moved by the force of custom, he (Origen) speaks in an orthodox way of the Holy Spirit."[34] Basil then quotes Origen's passage on baptism being the principle and source of the charisms from the *Commentary on John*.[35] Basil's attention is on the phrase "surrenders oneself to the *divinity* which acts in the water by virtue of the trinitarian epiclesis." This declaration regarding the divinity of the Holy Spirit, because one of the trinity, is Basil's central concern in his *On the Holy Spirit*. But Basil, the great champion of orthodoxy, would not be citing so important a text on Christian initiation, were it not within the great central tradition. Indeed, as we shall see, he himself, in a different context, proposes a similar relation between baptism and the charisms. Basil feels no constraint to affirm (or deny) the relation of initiation to the charisms, because Origen expounds the traditional doctrine.

Texts and Translations

There are two pertinent manuscript traditions of Origen's text. The text established by A. E. Brook[36] and E. Preuschen,[37] which is the one used in the Sources Chrétiennes edition of Origen's

---

[32] J. Gribomont, "L'Origènisme de Saint Basile," *L'Homme devant Dieu: Mélanges offerts au Père Henri de Lubac* (Paris: Aubier, 1963) 1:230; *On the Holy Spirit* 29:73; SC 17bis:506.

[33] Ibid.

[34] Ibid.

[35] Ibid.; Origen, *On John* 6, 33, 166; SC 157:254.

[36] *The Commentary of Origen on S. John's Gospel* (Cambridge: University Press, 1896).

[37] *Der Johannes Kommentar*, Die griechischen christlichen Schriftsteller der

On John,[38] reads "baptism is (*estin*) in itself the principle and source of the divine charisms," while the text found in the quotation from Origen preserved by Basil reads "baptism has (*exei*) in itself the principle and source. . . ."[39] As C. Blanc remarks, the two texts mean the same thing.[40]

H. Crouzel translates the passage differently. In the last phrase of the text, Crouzel makes the trinity rather than baptism the principle and source of the charisms. ". . . (baptism washes the soul free of the stain of sin, and) does so by itself for the one who yields to the divine power which comes from the invocations of the adorable trinity, origin and source of the divine charisms."[41] H. Urs von Balthasar inexplicably leaves out "priniciple and source" from his translation, though the Greek is clear.[42] A look at the Greek indicates that the translation given above, where baptism is the principle and source, is more faithful to the original and is the translation given by J. Danielou[43] and H. Rahner.[44] C. Blanc gives the same French translation in the Sources Chrétiennes edition of Origen's *On John,*[45] and R. Gögler renders the German translation of the text in the same sense.[46] Finally, B. Pruche gives the same French translation of this text which Basil preserves in his *On the Holy Spirit.*[47] The

---

ersten drei Jahrhunderte (Leipzig: Hinrichs, 1897–1941) 10. Hereafter cited as GCS.

[38] SC 157.

[39] Basil, *On the Holy Spirit* 29:73; SC 17bis:506.

[40] *SC* 157:256, footnote 1.

[41] *Origen,* 225, 226; H. Crouzel, "Origène et la structure du sacrement," *Bulletin de Littérature Ecclésiastique* 2 (1962) 91.

[42] *Parole et Mystère chez Origène* (Paris: du Cerf, 1957) 100.

[43] *Origen* (New York: Sheed & Ward, 1955) 55.

[44] "Taufe und geistliches Leben bei Origenes," *Zeitschrift für Aszese und Mystik* 7 (1932) 208, 211.

[45] SC 157:254, 256.

[46] Origenes, *Das Evangelium nach Johannes* (Einsiedeln: Benziger, 1959) 186.

[47] 29:72; SC 17bis:506. Because of the massive destruction of Origen's writings which took place after the Origenist controversies of the fourth and sixth centuries, we have only about a fourth of the total text of Origen's *On John.* One isolated fragment reproduces a similar doctrine of baptism with its large trinitarian accent, but without explicit mention of the charisms. Fraggment 36; GCS 10; Origenes Werke 4:511-13.

difference between Crouzel's translation and that of other scholars should not be pressed. Crouzel situates the trinity, which is the principle and source of the charisms, within baptism.

As we shall see, *charisma*, either in New Testament or in the post-biblical tradition, does not always mean prophetic charisms, such as tongues, prophecy, and healing. It can have a meaning more general than the charisms mentioned in 1 Corinthians. But in this passage Origen specifies the meaning. He introduces this passage by reference to the healing miracles of Jesus. He ends the passage with a quotation from 1 Corinthians 12:4, namely, "there are a variety of charisms."[48] He further specifies by adding that his witness to baptism as the principle and source of the charisms "is confirmed by the history recounted in the Acts of the Apostles: the Spirit descended in a manifest way on the baptized."[49] The reference to "a manifest way" is to the charisms which accompanied the receiving of the Spirit. Origen alludes to Luke's stress on the "manifest" character of this reception, when he refers to the charismatic manifestations accompanying the Pentecost event as the Exalted Christ pouring out "this that you both see and hear" (Acts 2:33). Origen continues relating the evidence of the Spirit's coming in the charisms upon the baptized saying that this outpouring occurred "after the water had prepared the way for those who present themselves there (in baptism) with a sincere heart."[50]

Origen both names baptism as the principle and source of the charisms and indicates that he has principally in mind the charisms listed in 1 Corinthians 12.

---

[48] *On John* 6:33; SC 157:256.
[49] Ibid.
[50] Ibid.

Chapter Twelve

Origen:
"No River Is Good
Except the Jordan"

In Tertullian, the imparting of the charisms is clearly set within the rite of baptism, and the other authors yet to be examined all relate the charisms to Christian initiation. Nowhere, however, do we find such an explicit formal statement that baptism is the principle and source of the charisms. That Origen's position here represents common teaching in the early third century seems to be indicated by the lack of any protest within the tradition. The first great attack on Origen's speculations was inaugurated by that intrepid heresy hunter Epiphanius of Salamis between 375 and 377, about one hundred twenty-five years after Origen's death. Epiphanius, "able but anti-intellectualist, of wide but ill-digested learning . . . inordinately lacking in judgment, tact and charity," poisoned the atmosphere by giving a one-sided account of Origen's positions.[1] Through the influence of Epiphanius, Jerome was persuaded to defect from Origen's camp, though in Jerome's *On Famous Men* he had lauded Origen's breadth of learning in scripture, his knowledge of Hebrew, his learned commentaries, his teaching in "dialectics, geometry, arithmetic, music, grammar, rhetoric, all parts of philosophy," and hailed him as an "immortal genius."[2] During

[1] J. N. D. Kelly, *Jerome* (New York: Harper & Row, 1975) 197.
[2] 54; PL 23:665, 667.

the period of his admiration, Jerome writes of the Roman synod which condemned Origen "not on account of innovations in dogma, nor to accuse him of heresy, as many of these mad dogs claim nowadays, but because they could not stand the splendid effect of his eloquence and scholarship: when he spoke all were speechless."[3] In Jerome's preface to his Latin translation of Origen's *Homilies on Ezechiel,* Jerome, following Didymus the Blind, lauds Origen as "the second master of the church after the apostle (Paul)."[4] Scholars are unclear as to the reason for Jerome's about-face. Epiphanius had courted Jerome, having him accompany him to Rome in 382. Jerome and Paula had enjoyed his hospitality in Cyprus in 385, and Jerome received Epiphanius as a guest in his Jerusalem monastery. To this one could add Jerome's friendship with the monks who were opposed to Origen, and his deteriorating relationship to his childhood friend, Rufinus, a great admirer of Origen. The passing of Jerome to the anti-Origenist camp is a major coup for Epiphanius. The wit, the brilliance, the scorn wielded in Origen's defense with Jerome's considerable literary skill, is now turned against him with equal effect. The prestige of Jerome is a significant factor in opposition to Origen in the fourth century and beyond.

In the sixth century the bitter controversy flares again, especially among the monks in Palestine, with the resulting condemnation of Origenist speculations by the Council of Constantinople in 543, a condemnation supported by both Pope Vigilius and the eastern patriarchs. Those who scoured his writings, eager to find offense during the first and second Origenist controversies, never cited his teaching that baptism is the principle and source of the charisms. Neither friend nor foe took exception. The reason? Origen was expressing the common faith of the church. Basil of Caesarea seems to concur.

Origen as Catechist

In the beginning Origen was a catechist. He reconstituted the catechetical school founded by Pantaenus (d. c. 190) and subsequently directed by Clement. Though it was founded on the

[3] *Letter* 33; CSEL 54:259.
[4] Preface; SC 352:30.

private initiative of Pantaenus, and refounded by Origen as his own enterprise after it had ceased to exist, Bishop Demetrius later extended his official patronage to it and made Origen, at the age of 18, its head. As established by Pantaenus, the school found its authority in affirming the tradition (*pareilephamen*).[5] In its beginnings, and for a time under Origen, the school had as its goal the instruction of candidates for baptism. Later, Origen added further instructions for mature Christians. Under Clement we know the formation period lasted at least three years after enrollment. So there was a catechumenate in Alexandria around the year 200. The predecessors of Origen in the school, Pantaenus and Clement, were essentially catechists oriented toward Christian initiation, as was Origen at the beginning.

We know from his general teaching, for instance, that he proposed the baptism of Jesus in the Jordan as the model of Christian baptism. This would have been part of his catechetical instruction for prospective candidates for baptism. The Jordan which cleanses Naaman the Syrian is "of sovereign virtue and very good to drink. Just as no man is good save God the Father, so no river is good except the Jordan."[6] As Naaman was cleansed in the Jordan, so we can receive baptism only in the Jordan, where Jesus was baptized, only from it can we draw those great benefits in the measure of our need.[7] Those who deposit their uncleanness in the Jordan will be purer than the foulest leper, "capable of receiving twice-over the graces (or charisms—*charismatōn*) of the Spirit and ready to welcome the Spirit. The dove of the Spirit does not fly over any other river."[8] Christ himself is our true Jordan;[9] more than that, Christ is both the minister and the river in which the baptized are plunged.[10] Jesus' baptism in the Jordan is his baptism in the

---

[5] E. de Faye, "L'Ecole Catéchétique d'Alexandrie," *Clement d'Alexandrie* (Paris: Minerva, 1906) 34; *Ecclesiastical History* 5:10, 1; 6:3, 3; SC 41:39, 87. Eusebius' treatment of the catechetical school is inaccurate in details. See G. Bardy, "Aux origines de l'école d'Alexandrie," *Recherches de Science Religieuse* 27 (1937) 65–90.

[6] *On John* 6:47; SC 157:314.

[7] *On John* 6:48; SC 157:318.

[8] Ibid.

[9] *Homilies on Luke* 21:4; SC 87:294.

[10] Crouzel, "Origène et la structure du sacrement," 87.

Spirit, and it is this same baptism in the Spirit, explicitly so called by Origen, that he extends to us.[11] Before Origen, Justin Martyr had called Christian initiation "baptism in the Holy Spirit."[12]

From the references scattered in his works, we know that Origen has precise ideas on how to instruct catechumens in preparation for baptism. He is profoundly serious about authentic Christianity, baptismal formation, and a quality catechumenate. Origen divides the catechumens into two groups: beginners and the more advanced.[13] In a Christian culture still close to its Jewish roots, Origen thinks that catechumens should be instructed in the books of Esther, Judith, Tobit, and Wisdom, which he considers the basic moral teaching for beginners.[14] To describe the progress through the catechumenate, he uses the image of the Exodus.[15] Not everyone is admitted to the catechumenate, but only those who have demonstrated the intent to live a moral life.[16] The very entrance to the catechumenate is itself a covenant commitment, which may or may not have been actualized within a liturgical rite.[17] Only after catechumens are taught not to sin, to progress toward real blessedness, only then "do we call them to our mysteries."[18] To assure that such admission not be lightly given, the members of the already existing community are called to witness that the transformation, moral and religious, has taken place in the candidate.[19]

Origen's insistent concern for the catechumenate is the background for evaluating his teaching that baptism is the principle and source of the divine charisms. Here he speaks not simply as the scholar of great breadth who knows the tradition, the textual critique, the biblical commentator, but as a pastoral person who knows the burgeoning catechumenate system in which

[11] *Homilies on Luke* 24:1; SC 87:324.

[12] *Dialogue with Trypho* 29:1; PG 6:537.

[13] *Against Celsus* 3:51; SC 136:121-125.

[14] *Homilies on Numbers* 27:1; SC 27:513.

[15] *Homilies on Joshua* 4; SC 71:146-59.

[16] *Against Celsus* 3:57-59; SC 136:133-39.

[17] *Exhortation to Martyrdom* 17; PG 11:584, 585; M. Dujarier, *A History of the Catechumenate: The First Six Centuries* (New York: Sadlier, 1979) 62.

[18] *Against Celsus* 3:59; SC 136:138.

[19] Ibid.

he himself, as a catechist, engaged in preparing new believers for Christian initiation.

Mystery and Moral

For Origen, "the baptismal mystery is the one, great, all-decisive event of the spiritual life."[20] However much Origen is interested in moral earnestness manifested in ascetic discipline, baptism is not just an ascetic experience. Rather it is a supernatural event touching the deepest faith identity of the Christian. In this context, Hugo Rahner situates Origen's declaration that baptism is the principle and source of all graces.[21]

The mystery of baptism is hidden in the trinitarian mystery.[22] The water of baptism "is no longer simply water, for it is consecrated by a mystical epiclesis."[23] Our baptism must be celebrated "with the authority of the whole most excellent trinity, that is, by the naming of Father, Son and Holy Spirit."[24] The Christian life begins in the Father,[25] flows from the Father, and the return ascent to the source, the Father, begins in baptism.[26] In naming the three persons, the baptismal waters share "in the power of the holy trinity," conferring on them "an ethical and contemplative virtue."[27] Here Origen gives the discipline of conversion its sacramental base, insuring that in baptism the outpouring of baptismal grace is bonded with moral initiative.[28] In Origen, baptism is a fountain which continues to flow. The

[20] Rahner, "Taufe und geistliches Leben bei Origenes," 208.

[21] Ibid. Rahner uses the more generic "grace," rather than the specific "charism." One can translate *charisma* as grace both in New Testament and post-apostolic texts. See, A. Schindler, "Gnade," *Reallexikon für Antike und Christentum* (Stuttgart: Hiersmann, 1979). However Rahner seems not to have averted to the specific reference Origen makes to 1 Corinthians 12:4, which would indicate that here the more restricted "charism" is appropriate.

[22] *Homilies on Jeremiah* 18:9; SC 238:210; *Homilies on Genesis* 2:5; SC 7bis:98-100.

[23] *On John*, Fragment 36; GCS 10; Origenes Werke 4:511-13.

[24] *On First Principles* 1, 3, 2; SC 252:146. Hereafter cited as *OFP*.

[25] *Homilies on Genesis* 2:5; SC 7bis:98, 100.

[26] *Homilies on Jeremiah* 18:9; SC 238:210.

[27] *On John*, Fragment 36; GCS 10; Origenes Werke 4:512.

[28] Rahner, "Taufe und geistliches Leben bei Origenes," 217.

ascetical dimension of Origen's teaching is important for his teaching on the charisms, for their exercise does not take place apart from the ascetical discipline, that is, the ethical and contemplative virtue.

As baptism is a trinitarian mystery, so also the charisms therein imparted. Origen discusses charisms in a section of the *Commentary on John* devoted to the Holy Spirit. He identifies the Spirit as the "matter" or "substance" (*hyle*) of the charisms; however, they are "produced by God, procured by Christ, and subsist according to the Holy Spirit," demonstrating both the special work of the Spirit and the unity of the triune act, a point of some sophistication.[29] He immediately refers to Paul's triadic formulation concerning varieties of charisms, services, ministries, but the same Spirit, Lord, and God (1 Cor 12:4, 5).[30] The charisms are placed in a pronounced trinitarian context. In some way he refers twelve times in *On First Principles* to Paul's list of charisms in 1 Corinthians 12.[31]

The Worthy and the Intellectual Charisms

Though Origen recalls that "the rain . . . of the divine charisms" which Christ gives to the church makes it glad,[32] and reminds us that "the vestiges and traces (of the charisms of healing) continue to manifest themselves in the churches,"[33] he singles out for special attention the charisms of wisdom, knowledge, and faith, and names those who exercise them "the worthy."[34] This formulation raises two issues: the concentration on the Christians who have attained perfection as the ones who exercise the charisms, and the prominence given to the intellectual charisms.

Origen has been accused of elitism because he distinguishes between the simple Christian and the spiritual or perfect believer. Actually this is a borrowing from St. Paul (1 Cor 1:1-3;

[29] *On John* 2, 10, 73-77; SC 120:252-56.
[30] SC 120:252, footnote 1.
[31] Preface 4 and 8; 1, 3, 7, three times; 1, 3, 8, twice; 2, 1, 3; 2, 7, 3; 2, 10, 7; 3, 1, 17. See SC 312:63.
[32] *Commentary on the Psalms* 64:11; PG 12:1496.
[33] *On John* 8:48; SC 290:311.
[34] OFP 2, 7, 3; SC 252:330.

3:3, 4; Gal 6:1). For Origen, all things have a double aspect, one bodily, perceptible to all through the senses, the other spiritual and mystical, known only to the perfect. Obviously the perfect is still *in via*, and has not reached ultimate purity. The depth of engagement is the sign that one is more than a simple Christian. Using this framework and basing himself on Paul's distinction between the simple Christian who possesses the Spirit, but lives according to the flesh (*sarkikoi*), and the perfect, who is fully led by the Spirit (*pneumatikoi*),[35] Origen develops his doctrine of the charisms, which is a sprawling intuition rather than a neat systematization.[36]

Though the charisms are given either "through baptism or the grace of the Spirit,"[37] they are fully operative, not in the fleshly (*sarkikoi*) but in those who live by the Spirit, the *pneumatikoi*, who are "worthy" (*axios*). Christ, who is wisdom, does not exert the power of wisdom in all, but only in those who through ascetic discipline apply themselves to wisdom. Though "in the Spirit is found the whole nature of the charisms," the word of wisdom, the word of knowledge, and faith are given only to the one who is worthy.[38] The operation of the charisms belongs to a more advanced stage, to those who are "purer and more single-minded."[39]

He returns to the charisms of wisdom and knowledge.[40] Origen is especially drawn to these two charisms, saying they have "greater eminence" and belong to "a higher intellectual order," while other charisms such as miracles and healings are of a lower order.[41] He carefully notes that the word of wisdom has the primacy, then word of knowledge, and only then comes faith, which is also of a lower order.[42] Even lower on the hier-

---

[35] H. Conzelmann, *A Commentary on the First Epistle to the Corinthians* (Philadelphia: Fortress, 1975) 57; H. D. Wendland, *Die Briefe an die Korinther* (Göttingen: Vandenhoeck & Ruprecht, 1968) 30, 31.

[36] H. Crouzel, *Origène et la "Connaissance Mystique"* (Brouwer: Desclée, 1961) 126.

[37] *OFP* 2, 10, 7; SC 252:390-392.

[38] *OFP* 2, 7, 3; SC 252:330.

[39] *OFP* 1, 3, 8; SC 268:162, 164.

[40] *OFP* 2, 7, 3; SC 252:330.

[41] *Against Celsus* 3:46; SC 136:110; *Homilies on Jeremiah* 8:5; SC 232:368.

[42] Ibid.

archy are the charisms of miracles and healing, because they lack the intellectual character.[43]

Origen, in a fragment of his *Homilies on Proverbs*, ties the absence of truly wise persons to the absence of the "outstanding charisms." "Do not wonder," says Origen, "if now a person truly wise according to God cannot be found. For the majority of the outstanding charisms (*exaireton charismaton*) fail, so that they are not at all, or scarcely, to be found."[44] The persons wise according to God and the outstanding charisms stand and fall together.

In a fragment of his *Commentary on 1 Corinthians*, Origen quite explicitly says that the charism of wisdom is not for beginners but for the perfect. Only those who have striven against their passions and have demonstrated that they lead a healthy Christian life exercise this charism.[45] In even a more pointed way, he calls attention to the moral preparation necessary for the exercise of the charisms of wisdom by quoting Sirach 1:26: "If you desire wisdom, keep the commandments."[46]

In the preface to *On First Principles* he presents the charisms as necessary for elaborating the teaching of the apostles. Because the apostles did not say everything, and left many things unclear as to "the how and why," God gives "the higher charisms," by which he means "language (*sermonis*), wisdom, and knowledge," to those who are "worthy and capable."[47] The intellectual charisms of which Paul writes in 1 Corinthians 12:8, 9 are therefore in the service of a "research theology," a questing theology which relies not just on human intelligence to exegete those areas which the apostolic tradition has left unsaid or unclear. Here Origen places the charisms in the service of "the teaching of the church handed down in unbroken succession from the apostles, which is preserved and continues to exist in the churches to the present day."[48]

---

[43] Ibid.

[44] Fragment from *Homilies on Proverbs*; PG 13:25.

[45] *On 1 Corinthians*, fragment 9; text found in C. Jenkins, "Origen on I Corinthians," *Journal of Theological Studies* 9 (1908) 238.

[46] Ibid. See Crouzel, *Origène et la "Connaissance Mystique,"* 443–60.

[47] OFP, Preface, 3; SC 252:78, 80.

[48] *OFP* Preface, 2; SC 252:78.

Prophecy and The Spiritual Senses

The charism of prophecy is necessary if one wishes to interpret correctly the wondrous deeds of Moses and Aaron. How could it be otherwise, as the Spirit is power, indeed the agent, of these mighty acts. The principle: the Paraclete is the only real exegete.[49] Or more precisely: there must be a proportionality between the Spirit in the deeds of Moses and Aaron and the Spirit in the soul of the biblical exegete. Those who interpret prophetic deeds need the prophetic charism: "the apostles commanded us to be imitators of this grace, that is, the gift of prophecy, as belonging to our equipment."[50] We need to ask and expect "the plenitude of this gift (of prophecy)."[51]

Origen's doctrine on "the spiritual senses," or "the divine senses," belongs with his teaching on the charisms. He believes that just as the body has sense organs ordered to the perception of the physical world, so the believer has organs ordered to divine realities, spiritual and immaterial. "The knowledge of God does not depend on the eye of the body, but (on the eye) of the Spirit."[52] This divine sense belongs to "a different order" because it is directed to divine realities.[53] Though it is one faculty, it expresses itself in sight, smell, touch, hearing, and taste.[54] Basing himself on the biblical witness, especially 1 John 1:1-4 ("we declare to you what was from the beginning, what we have heard, what we have seen with our eyes, what

[49] H. de Lubac, *Histoire et Esprit: L'Intelligence de l'Ecriture d'après Origène* (Paris: Aubier, 1950) 316.

[50] *Homilies on Exodus* 4:5; SC 321:129, 130.

[51] Ibid.

[52] *Against Celsus* 7:33; SC 150:88.

[53] *Against Celsus* 7:34; SC 150:92.

[54] Ibid. 1:48; SC 132:200-08; Origen, *Spirit and Fire: A Thematic Anthology of His Writings*, ed. H. Urs von Balthasar (Washington, D.C.: Catholic University, 1984) 190; M. Harl holds that though expressions are diverse, the spiritual sense is one. See Harl "La 'bouche' et le 'coeur' de l'apôtre: deux images bibliques du 'sens divin' de l'homme ('Proverbes' 2, 5) chez Origène," *Forma Futuri* Studi in onore del Cardinale Michele Pellegrino (Turin: Erasmo, 1975) 17–42. K. Rahner, however, holds that the spiritual senses are multiple, not just varied in expression. See Rahner, "Le Début d'une Doctrine des Cinq Sens Spirituels chez Origène," *Revue d'Ascétique et de Mystique* 30 (1932) 113–45.

we have looked at and touched with our hands . . .''), Origen teaches that just as there is a proportionality between a sense organ and what it senses, so in the spiritual order. The eyes illumined by the Spirit acquire a knowledge of spiritual realities by a kind of connaturality in Christ and the Spirit, a knowledge which is immediate and intuitive. Such knowledge is the result of an "encounter between two freedoms": the freedom of God wanting to reveal the divine self, and the freedom of the human person who by ascetic discipline prepares for God's act of revelation.[55] However profound this seeing with spiritual eyes, it falls short of the face-to-face vision beyond all human analogies. Like the charisms, only the pure in heart, the perfect, exercise the spiritual senses.[56]

In summary, Origen, man of the church, the finest scholar of the first millennium of the church's life, the theologian of prodigious range, the catechist preparing converts for their baptismal initiation, presents baptism as the principle and source of the divine charisms at the beginning of the third century. In this he differs from Tertullian and the other authors to be examined. They situate the imparting of the charisms within the rite of initiation or in relation to it. Origen does more. In a most emphatic way, using strong intensive forms (the use of "principle" and "source" both meaning the same thing, the forceful "by itself") he elevates the relation between Christian initiation and the charisms to a formal one, touching the constitutive nature of baptism through the trinitarian epiclesis, the calling down on the waters of Father, Son, and Holy Spirit. The great champion of orthodoxy Basil of Caesarea quotes the relevant text as authoritative for establishing the divinity of the Spirit, something he would not have done had the text's teaching on the relation of the charisms to baptism not stood in the great central tradition. To the authority of Origen, Basil adds his own.

Even during the two Origenist controversies of the fourth and sixth centuries, when enemies diligently read Origen in order to find scandalous passages to justify their condemnation of him,

[55] Crouzel, *Origen*, 114, 132.
[56] *Commentary on the Canticle of Canticles* 1:1; SC 375:82.

no one, not even his bitterest opponents, cited Origen's passage on baptism being the principle and source of the divine charisms. This is an argument from silence, with all of its limitations, but given the ferocity of the repeated anti-Origenist attacks during the two controversies, given the eagerness with which his enemies searched his writings for heresy, it carries probability. No voice is raised against Origen's teaching on this point because it is unexceptional, the received doctrine.

From the explicit references to 1 Corinthians 12:4, it is clear that Origen includes the whole Pauline range of charisms, including the prophetic. Though Origen acknowledges the traces of the charism of healing in the church, though he frequently returns to Paul's full list of charisms in 1 Corinthians 12, he concentrates especially on the intellectual charisms: the word of wisdom, the word of knowledge, and faith. Like Philoxenus and the Syrians, as we shall discover, Origen sees the exercise of the charisms as the provenance not of simple Christians, those who have the Spirit but live according to the flesh. Rather those who are spiritual, that is, who are led by the Spirit, and give themselves to the required discipline for the ascent to the mountain of perfection—these exercise the intellectual charisms. Together with prophecy, the charisms of wisdom, knowledge, and faith are in the service of the church in "a research theology," questing for the meaning of the scriptures, searching out those areas which the apostles left unsaid or unclear.

Chapter Thirteen

Hilary of Poitiers:
The Poet Bishop as Bridge

In common with Tertullian Hilary of Poitiers (c. 315–67) very likely had a classical education, which would mean that he studied both Latin and Greek. Jerome, that man of small praise, deprecated Hilary's knowledge of Greek, saying that he possessed only "a slight tinge of Greek letters."[1] Though Hilary knew no Hebrew, Jerome conceded that he was nonetheless "learned, given the epoch in which he lived."[2] He studied rhetoric and was exposed to the philosophical and literary sources.[3] Jerome, not easily pleased in these matters, acknowledged that Gaul had schools of merit.[4]

We know little else of his life, though some consensus exists that he was born of pagan parents.[5] Apparently he was convert-

---

[1] Jerome, *Letter*, 34:3; CSEL 54:262.

[2] Jerome, *Letter*, 34:1; CSEL 54:259, 260.

[3] H. C. Bennecke, "Hilarius von Poitiers," *TRE* 15 (1986) 315.

[4] Jerome, *Letter*, 125:6; CSEL 56:123. J. H. Reinkens, *Hilarius von Poitiers* (Schaffhausen: Hurter, 1864) 7.

[5] C. F. A. Borchardt, *Hilary of Poitiers' Role in the Arian Struggle* (The Hague: Martinus Nijhoff, 1966) 3.

ed and baptized as an adult, and soon after was made bishop of Poitiers,[6] still dominantly a pagan city.[7] In 356 he was exiled to Phrygia. While in exile he wrote *On the Trinity*, his major work and significant here because of the attention he gives to the charisms.

Something of a poet, he, together with Ambrose, laid the foundations of western hymnody. Hilary places the poet in him at the service of proclamation: "He who treats the Word of God must do honor to that Word by the beauty of his phrasing. Just as those who compose the wording of a king's rescript must proceed with diligence and care in order to be worthy of the dignity due to a prince."[8] The love of art and the pursuit of the beautiful breaks through his theological writings. Together with Tertullian and Cyprian, he gave form to Latin theological vocabulary.[9]

The reason for ending his exile and his return to Gaul in 360 or 361 is no clearer than the grounds for his exile. Sulpicius Severus suggested that officials finally decided that Hilary, as an ardent defender of Nicaea, was a fomenter of discord in Asia Minor.[10] Possibly the authorities felt that he was doing more damage in exile than he had done at home. Better a quiet Hilary in Gaul than a noisy Hilary in Phrygia.

After his exile ended he lived in Gaul about seven years. During the last four years (364–67) he composed his *Tract on the Psalms*, the most important of his exegetical works, and the principal text of interest here. Like those of Origen and Eusebius, his commentary is very extensive. Its length encouraged copyists to choose only certain psalms, with the result that we today do not have the full text.[11]

[6] Jerome, *Commentary on Isaiah*, 17:60; PL 24:595. Hilary of Poitiers, *On Synods* 91: PL 10:545.

[7] Reinkens, *Hilarius von Poitiers*, 7; A. Feder, "Kulturge-schichtliches in den Werken des hl. Hilarius von Poitiers," *Stimmen aus Maria-Laach* 81 (1911) 36–42; Bennecke, "Hilarius von Poitiers," 316.

[8] Hilary, *Tract on the Psalms*, 13:1; CSEL 22:79.

[9] R. J. Kinnavey, *The Vocabulary of St. Hilary of Poitiers* (Washington: Catholic University of America, 1935) 309.

[10] Sulpicius Severus, *Chronology*, 2:45; CSEL 1:98.

[11] C. Kannengiesser, "L'exégèse d'Hilaire," *Hilaire et son Temps*: Actes du Colloque de Poitiers (29 Septembre–3 Octobre 1968) (Paris: Etudes Augustiniennes, 1969) 133.

Hilary calls his commentary on the psalms a *tractatus*, which, at that time, meant first of all exegetical preaching.[12] The determination of the title has some meaning for understanding the content. Theological speculation in a written text directed more specifically to a learned audience would give more liberty to challenge the received truths. If, on the other hand, the contents of the book on the psalms were first of all homilies, which were then reworked and edited, we would be to some degree in contact with the bishop of Poitiers as he proclaimed the faith to the people at the gathering of the community. As biblical catechesis, this work would find its place in the broad central tradition of the proclaimed faith.

Literary style will be a factor in effective transmission of the message. Hilary writes in a highly literary, self-conscious Latin when he wants to, making him "the Rhône of eloquence," as Jerome calls him.[13] When Hilary writes in his mannered style, as in his *Tract on the Psalms*, it draws the applause of those given to literature. But, as Jerome remarks, to the simpler

---

[12] Hilary, *Tract on the Psalms*, 130:1; 135:2; CSEL 22:675, 721. Cyprian, whom Hilary read, uses *tractatus* in the sense of exegetical preaching: *On Good Works and Alms* 12: CChr 3a:63. *See also Letter* to Cyprian from Nemesianus and others, 78:1; PL 4:420; Pseudo-Cyprian, *On Discipline and Modesty* 1; PL 4:820. The identity of Pseudo-Cyprian has been determined as Novatian, the third century Roman Priest. *See Clavis Patrum Latinorum*, ed. E. Dekkers (Bruges: Beyaert, 1961) 3, 14. Ambrose also used *tractatus* as exegetical preaching in *Letter* 2:7; PL 16:881. *See* C. Mohrmann, "Praedicare—Tractare—Sermo: Essai sur la terminologie de la prédication paléochrétienne," *Maison Dieu* 39 (1954) 104, 105. Hilary himself wrote of a reading that preceded his exposition, which lends credibility to the first text being a homily. *Tract on the Psalms* 13:2; 14:1; CSEL 22:79, 84. Both P. Coustant and P. Galtier, who held that it is essentially a written commentary, grant that there is internal evidence that the first texts on each psalm were homilies. Coustant, *Admonition on Hilary's Tract on the Psalms* 22; PL 9:231, 232. P. Galtier, *Hilaire de Poitiers* (Paris: Beauchesne, 1960) 161. O. Bardenhewer also thought the first text was that of a commentary or explanation *(Erklärung)* rather than a homily: *Geschichte der Altkirchlichen Literatur*, 3:372, note 4. In editing Hilary's exposition of Psalm 118 for Sources Chrétiennes 344, 347, M. Milhau chose "commentaire." M. F. Buttell, *The Rhetoric of Hilary of Poitiers* (Washington: Catholic University of America, 1934) 8, 11, thinks the bishop reworked and edited homilies.

[13] Jerome, *On Galatians*, 1:2, preface; PL 26:355.

people the *Tract* is inaccessible.[14] Coustant counts among the exasperations of Hilary's style long periods, dense sentences, opaque constructions, and disregard for the rules of grammar.[15] Even Jerome, himself a great stylist, finds Hilary difficult to decipher.[16] Modern readers can find the line of thought to be "meandering."[17] What Coustant finds worthy of censure in Hilary's style, namely, long involved sentences, E. Norden praises as "masterful periods" in the style of Cicero.[18] Further, Norden contends that, as a stylistic achievement, the *Tract on the Psalms* "stands higher than any other comparable writing coming to us from antiquity."[19] The commentary on the psalms is a work of the mature Hilary, embodying the wisdom of the East and infused with a deep personal fervor.

Because we are looking at the charisms, more specifically the prophetic charisms, and this in the context of Christian initiation, we should glance at how Hilary related to those who might influence his view of the charisms, most especially Tertullian, Irenaeus, Origen (c. 185–c. 254), and Eusebius of Caesarea (c. 260–c. 340). An ecclesiastic could appropriate that tradition slavishly or critically. Did Hilary move with freedom within the tradition, honoring it but retaining his originality? Would the office of bishop make him defensive and timorous in the face of the threat Montanism posed? Especially significant will be the impact on his theology of charisms by his exile from Gaul to Asia Minor, possibly to Phrygia, the place in which Montanism first arose and still existed. These are the issues in this chapter.

The North Africans: Tertullian and Cyprian

The writings of the two North African theologians, Tertullian and Cyprian, must have been easily obtainable in Gaul. Hilary recommended that his readers turn to their books on the Lord's

---

[14] " . . . *longis interdum periodis inuoluitur, et a lectione simpliciorum fratrum procul est.*'Jerome, *Letter*, 58:10; CSEL 54:539.

[15] Coustant, *General Preface*, 4:32: PL 9:26.

[16] Jerome, *Letter*, 58:10; CSEL 54:539.

[17] P. Camelot, "Hilaire de Poitiers," *Catholicisme*, 7:733.

[18] Norden, *Die Antike Kunstprosa*, 2:584.

[19] Ibid., 583.

Prayer, as Hilary did not wish to duplicate their volumes.[20] This explicit mention of Cyprian and Tertullian was exceptional. Hilary was careless about making direct references to books he had consulted.

Very likely Hilary knew Tertullian's *Against Praxeas* in which Tertullian recounted Rome's original favorable reception of the charismatic outbreak in Phrygia, which later became known as Montanism.[21] Hilary thought Tertullian's Montanism was not sufficient reason for restricting access to all of his writings, though it did detract from his authority.[22] If there were any Christian masters to whom Hilary looked before his exile it would be to Tertullian and Cyprian, and, to a lesser degree, Lactantius and Novatian.[23] In Hilary's early writings there is a kind of omnipresence of Tertullian, though the dependence is rarely literal.[24] Only points of contact between Irenaeus and Hilary can be established. How Hilary related to Irenaeus depends on the dating of the Latin translation of Irenaeus' *Against Heresies*.[25] In any case, acceptance of the charisms belonged to the traditions of Gaul as expressed by Irenaeus: "It is impossible to enumerate the charisms throughout the world the church has received from God."[26] As we have seen, the letters of the Martyrs of Lyons to Pope Eleutherius carried by Irenaeus seem to have been in favor of the prophetic charisms in Phrygia at the very beginning of Montanism.

[20] Hilary, *On Matthew*, 5:4; SC 254:150.

[21] J. Doignon, Introduction, Hilary, *Sur Matthieu*; SC 254:32; Borchardt, *Hilary and the Arian Struggle*, 136-40; J. Moignt, "La théologie trinitaire de S. Hilaire," *Hilaire et Son Temps* 170; M. Simonetti, "Hilary of Poitiers and the Arian Crisis in the West," in Quasten, *Patrology*, 4:42.

[22] Hilary, *On Matthew*, 5:1; SC 254:150.

[23] J. Doignon, *Hilaire de Poitiers avant l'Exil* (Paris: Etudes Augustiniennes, 1971) 521.

[24] Ibid.

[25] Doignon, *Hilaire de Poitiers*, 195; Moignt, "La théologie trinitaire de S. Hilaire," 170, 171; J. Daniélou, "Hilaire de Poitiers, evêque et docteur," *Hilaire de Poitiers, Evêque et Docteur, Cinque conférences données à Poitiers à l'occasion du XVIᵉ centenaire de sa mort* (Paris: Etudes Augustiniennes, 1968) 11; J. Doignon, "Un *Sermo temerarius* d'Hilaire de Poitiers sur sa Foi (*De Trinitate* 6, 20-22)," *Fides Sacramenti: Sacramentum Fidei*, ed. H. J. Auf der Maur and others (Assen: von Gorcum, 1981) 211-17.

[26] Irenaeus, *Against Heresies*, 2:32, 4; SC 294:340.

Hilary translated two commentaries on the psalms, one by Origen and another by Eusebius of Caesarea.[27] Origen's *Commentary on the Psalms,* composed between 214 and 218, was the first work he published beyond the circle of his students.[28] This commentary would markedly influence Hilary's own.[29] Very likely Hilary had a copy of Origen's commentary on forty-one psalms in front of him when he was composing his own *Tract on the Psalms.*[30] Origen's commentary has been lost, but through catenae and citations some can be recovered. Both Origen and Hilary write of the abundance of salvation, a theme to which Psalm 64 lends itself. Both use the Fourth Gospel's symbol for the Holy Spirit, namely, water. Hilary, however, will concentrate on the water image in a much more expansive manner.

Both are interested in the charisms. Possibly Origen intended *charisma* in the commentary on this psalm to mean the more generic gifts. Though possible, he elsewhere speaks of the prophetic charisms, and there is no reason why the more specific meaning should be excluded. If Hilary is following Origen here, he clearly interpreted Origen's usage of *charisma* in the specific sense.

When writing of the miracles Jesus worked, Origen claims that "the vestiges and traces [of the charism of healing] continue to manifest themselves in the churches."[31] Origen writes of "the rain . . . of the divine charisms," which Christ gives to the church, making it glad.[32] The shower of charisms means that Christ will give charisms to the church in a gradual way; also they germinate slowly. Hilary will give much attention to the rain, which gradually becomes creeks, which in turn, little by little, become a mighty river.

[27] Jerome, *Letter,* 112:20; CSEL 55:390.

[28] Origen, Preface, *Commentary on the Psalms,* 2; PG 12:1078-79.

[29] N. J. Gastaldi, *Hilario de Poitiers: Exégeta del Salterio* (Paris: Beauchesne, 1969) 279.

[30] C. Kannengiesser, "Hilaire de Poitiers," *Dictionnaire de Spiritualité* 7 (1969) 482.

[31] Origen, *On John,* 8:48; SC 290:311. In *Origen: His Life in Alexandria* (St. Louis: Herder, 1944) R. Cadiou suggests that in the days of Origen there *only* remained "scraps and vestiges" of these wonders. Origen's emphasis is slightly different. He says that the vestiges *continue* to this day in the churches.

[32] Origen, *Commentary on the Psalms* 64:11; PG 12:1496.

Origen cites the baptismal text of Luke 4:18: "The Spirit of the Lord is upon me, he has anointed me." Luke has conflated Isaiah 11:1-3 and Isaiah 61:2. This seems to be Luke's way of joining Spirit and baptism, as he does in Acts 10:38: "God anointed Jesus with the Holy Spirit and power." In Hilary this Lucan text is placed after the baptismal experience, and in relation to the abundant fruit. Whether Hilary understood the baptismal nuance in Luke's text, or whether Hilary read baptism into Origen's use of the water symbol, thus going beyond Origen's text, cannot be determined. Without a more explicit baptismal reference in Origen one cannot deduce that Hilary's baptismal interpretation of water is dependent on Origen.

Elsewhere Origen remarks that at Jesus' own baptism he was given the charism of wisdom.[33] The baptism which Jesus gives is "the baptism in the Holy Spirit."[34] The treasures which one finds in Christ are the charisms of wisdom, faith, knowledge, but, Origen vaguely indicates, there are others.[35] Origen reminds his readers that Paul asks us to strive for the charism of prophecy (which is among the higher gifts), at least insofar as it is within our capacity; we strive, but we await the fullness of this charism from the Lord. If we have the charism of prophecy, we shall know how to interpret the writings of the prophets. "The Spirit of the prophets is subject to the prophets" (1 Cor 14:32). "We should ask God for the plenitude of this charism (prophecy)."[36] Origen even suggests giving the Lord a helping hand. On the basis of Psalm 80:10 ("Open your mouth and I will fill it"), Origen wants us to make the first move toward receiving the charism of prophecy by opening the mouth. If you do not open your mouth, how can the Lord give the charism of prophecy?[37] Prophecy is a charism of interpreting the scriptures

[33] Origen, *Against Celsus*, 1:44; SC 132:192.

[34] Origen, *On Jeremiah*, 2:3; SC 232:244. Here Origen distinguishes between the baptism in the Holy Spirit and the baptism in fire.

[35] Ibid. 8:5, 25; SC 232:368.

[36] Origen, *On Exodus*, 4:5; SC 321:130; *On Ezeckiel*, 2:2; SC 352:104-6. In the extant fragments of Origen's *On Ephesians* he again links the charisms of wisdom and knowledge to understanding the scriptures. Origen, *On Ephesians*, 11; J. A. F. Gregg, "The Commentary of Origen upon the Epistle to the Ephesians," *JTS* 3 (1902) 240, lines 19-26.

[37] Origen, *On Exodus*, 4:4; SC 321:130.

and Origen is largely a lecturer on the Bible; given this supposition his advice seems apt.

How much did Origen influence Hilary? In Hilary's book on the psalms it is sure and extensive. The peculiarities and objectionable positions which distinguished Origen from other theologians, however, are attenuated in Origen's commentary.[38] Besides, Hilary was his own man; he related to Origen with some independence.[39] Therefore Hilary, in using Origen's commentary, would not be passing on those theological positions which drew the ire of posterity down on Origen's head. If Hilary was to look to Origen for some indication of how he viewed the charisms, Hilary would also read that the master had taken a position against the Montanist teaching on ecstasy.[40]

How much Hilary's tract owed to Origen's was a question discussed already in the fourth century.[41] Jerome seems almost compulsive about the way he returned again and again to the question of Hilary's originality, possibly because he had himself been accused of being a drudge,[42] wanting in real creativity.[43] These references to Hilary in Jerome's writings constitute one of the reasons why Hilary became so widely known already at the end of the fourth century.[44]

Jerome said that Hilary added his own material to what he adapted from Origen, implying that Hilary had not greatly exercised theological imagination in composing his commentary.[45] The discussion continues in the 20th century. Bardy also

[38] Kannengiesser, "Hilaire de Poitiers," 483.
[39] Reinkens, *Hilarius von Poitiers*, 283.
[40] Origen, *On First Principles*, 2:7, 3; SC 252:330.
[41] Borchardt, *Hilary and the Arian Struggle*, 182.
[42] In 392 or 393: Jerome, *On Famous Men*, 91; PL 23:700, 702. About 400: Jerome, *Letter*, 61:2; CSEL 54:577. In 401: Jerome, *Letter*, 84:7; CSEL 55:130; About the same time: Jerome, *Apology against Rufinus*, 1:2; CChr 79:2, 3; About 402: Jerome, *Letter against Rufinus*, 14; CChr 79:14; After 404: Jerome, *Letter*, 112:20; CSEL 55:390. These texts are gathered by G. Bardy, "Traducteurs et adaptateurs au quartrième siècle," *Recherches de Science Religieuse* 30 (1940) 272, note 2, 3.
[43] Preface to *Micah*, Book 2; CChr 76:473; G. Bardy, "Traducteurs et Adaptateurs," 271, 272.
[44] Kannengiesser, "L'heritage d'Hilaire," 440-43.
[45] Jerome, *On Famous Men*, 100; PL 23:699.

thought that Hilary was more of an adapter than an author, paraphrasing rather than translating.[46] Hilary's dependence on Origen seems both textual and literary, though he brought a critical mind to his sources.[47] He can recommend a specific work of Tertullian even when recognizing that he has been compromised by his later Montanism.[48] In Origen, Hilary knew he had a master. Just the same, he distanced himself from the master's mystique.[49] In particular he was less given to Origen's allegorical interpretation. He treaded a path between the allegorical and the literal, but in his work on the psalms he gave more attention to the literal sense. Usually he began with the latter.[50] The question of Hilary's originality and his relation to Origen, especially in the *Tract on the Psalms*, is significant for his teaching on the rites of initiation and the charisms.

Origen's Archivist: Eusebius

The distinction between Origen and Eusebius is a little blurred because Eusebius was an ardent follower of the Alexandrian scholar. Eusebius stands in a direct line of descent. Eusebius was a pupil of Pamphilus (c. 240–309), author of the *Apology* on Origen, a work now lost except for the first book. More than that Eusebius assisted Pamphilus in writing that defense. After Pamphilus' martyrdom, Eusebius succeeded him as curator of Origin's library and archives. A considerable section of the sixth book of the *Ecclesiastical History* is devoted to the life of Origen.[51]

Eusebius gives evidence in the *Ecclesiastical History* that he himself was interested in the prophetic charisms.[52] One is not

[46] Bardy, "Traducteurs et Adaptateurs," 273.

[47] Gastaldi, *Hilario de Poitiers*, 280.

[48] Hilary, *On Matthew*, 5:1; SC 254:150.

[49] Kannengiesser, "Hilaire de Poitiers," 491.

[50] X. LeBachelet, "Hilaire de Poitiers," DTC 6:2400.

[51] SC 41:82-163.

[52] The daughters of Philip possess the prophetic charisms *EH* 3:31, 4-5; 3:37, 1; SC 31:142, 151; Justin records the existence of prophetic charisms in the church of his day *EH* 4:18, 8; SC 31:197; a medical doctor from Alexandria possesses the prophetic charisms *EH* 5:1, 49; SC 41:19; the initial outbreak of prophecy in Asia is judged positively by the confessors in Gaul *EH* 5:3, 4; SC 41:27; the testimony of Irenaeus on prophecy in the early church *EH* 5:7, 2-6; SC 41:33, 34; the false prophets of the Montanists *EH*

surprised to find the same interest expressed in his *Commentary on the Psalms*, which was the work of his mature years, the last he wrote. The original is lost, though enough excerpts have been preserved that the whole of this extensive commentary may be reconstructed.[53] Judging by the extant fragments, Eusebius' whole commentary was a monumental work.[54]

The words of Psalm 64 dictate that there will be similarity of themes. Hilary, Eusebius, and Origen all mention the charisms; Origen once in this psalm commentary, Eusebius twice.[55] From the free scriptural quotations, that is, other than those of Psalm 64 itself, Hilary has only one in common with Origen,[56] while he has eleven in common with Eusebius, some following the same sequence.[57] If Hilary had Origen's commentary in front of him, he must also have had a copy of Eusebius'. In Hilary's *Tract on the Psalms* there is some literary dependence on Eusebius, and here and there, direct borrowing.[58]

Eusebius says that the church, as the house of God, still lives in the realm of the flesh; nonetheless, it already enjoys the goods which adorn God's house: "divine conversation, sacred instruction, the charisms of the Holy Spirit."[59] Among them are the word of wisdom, the word of knowledge, faith, healings, and tongues.[60] The River of God is the Holy Spirit, which inundates and makes the land "drunk . . . with the charisms of the Holy Spirit."[61] The force of God's torrents makes glad the city of God.

5:16, 8; 5:17, 4; SC 41:48, 50, 51; the necessity of prophecy continuing in the church until the parousia *EH* 5:17, 4; SC 41:54; martyrdom is the highest of the charisms *EH* 8:10, 3; SC 55:20.

[53] Quasten, *Patrology* 3:337.

[54] Ibid., 338.

[55] Origen, *Commentary on the Psalms*, 64:11; PG 12:1495; Eusebius, *Commentary on the Psalms*, 64:5-9, 10, 11; PG 23:640.

[56] Psalm 68:3.

[57] The scriptural quotations in common with Eusebius are: Galatians 4:26; Genesis 6:3, 12; 1 John 2:2; Psalm 83:3; 1 Timothy 3:15, 1 Corinthians 2:8f; 1 Corinthians 3:16; Micah 1:2; Psalm 17:8f; Psalm 68:3; Isaiah 61:1f; 1 Corinthians 15:53. Those underlined are in the same sequence in Hilary and Eusebius.

[58] Gastaldi, *Hilario de Poitiers*, 280.

[59] Eusebius, *Commentary on the Psalms*, 64:5-9; PG 23:631.

[60] Ibid.

[61] Ibid., 64:10, 11; PG 23:642.

Origen does, but Eusebius does not, mention the relation of the charisms to initiation as Hilary does. Montanism seems not to be an issue in Hilary's Gaul, though it is still a concern of Origen and Eusebius in the East. While Hilary knows of Montanism, he refuses to be intimidated by distant controversies.

Personal Reflections in a Formal Treatise?

Augustine's *On the Trinity* subsequently dwarfed Hilary's major work of the same name. It is distinguished from Augustine's, indeed from the whole corpus of ancient authors: it is the single case in those early centuries in which a book was written according to a predetermined outline.[62] The delineation went beyond indications of general contents of each book to a detailed plan.[63] Hilary included the charisms in book eight (29–34), then, not by chance; it is not a random topic on which he stumbled. "We have planned our work in such a manner that the books are connected and follow an order that is best adapted for the reader's progress. We have decided not to offer anything that was not well coordinated and assimilated, in order that the work might not appear like a tumultuous gathering of peasants who are shouting in confusion."[64]

The consensus that Hilary was an adult convert from paganism left unresolved the dispute whether any remembrance of that conversion process was left in the personal references at the beginning of his treatise *On the Trinity*. If Quintilian was his model in both the twelve chapter format and style, as Jerome remarked and others confirmed,[65] then it is likely that Hilary wrote something of his conversion into his first chapter of *On the Trinity*. Quintilian, writing on the training of the orator, recommended that the speaker tell a little about himself.[66] Most

[62] Augustine, *On the Trinity*, 1:20-36; CChr 62a:19-35.

[63] P. Smulders, *La doctrine trinitaire de S. Hilaire de Poitiers* (Rome: Gregorian University, 1944) 41. Of book eight in which much of the material on the charisms is to be found Hilary said: "Book 8 is entirely concerned with the evidence for the one God." Hilary, *On the Trinity*, 1:28; CChr 62:25.

[64] Hilary, *On the Trinity*, 1:20; CChr 62a:19, 20.

[65] Jerome, *Letter*, 70:5; CSEL 54:107. E. P. Meijering, *Hilary of Poitiers on the Trinity: De Trinitate 1, 1–19, 2, 3* (Leiden: Brill, 1982) 5–10.

[66] Quintilian, *Institutions of Oratory*, 4:1, 7; M. Fabi Qvintiliani Institutio-

scholars think that Hilary incorporated some aspects of his own conversion experience into this treatise.[67] The willingness to incorporate highly personal reflections into his more formal theological treatise on trinitarian doctrine gives likelihood that he would not hesitate to let his own baptismal experience come to expression in the less structured, less systematic *Tract on the Psalms*, in which Hilary wrote of the relationship of initiation to the charisms, our principal area of interest.

Both Sulpicius Severus (c. 360–c. 420),[68] and Venantius Fortunatus (c. 530–c. 610)[69] record Phrygia as the place of banishment, though their works do contain some legendary material. Jerome, too, in his translation of Eusebius' *Chronology* named Phrygia as the place of banishment and added that while there Hilary wrote.[70] Exile had become the favorite tool against adherents of the Nicaean definition that the Son was "of the same substance" (*homōusios*) as the Father. Hilary, who had been chosen bishop about 354, may have written the first three books of *On the Trinity* while still in Gaul, finishing it during his exile in Asia.[71] Hilary gives little place to philosophical considerations in his defense of the Nicaean faith, even though trinitarian doctrine had been weighted with philosophical speculation.[72]

Above all, Hilary was an exegete. His earlier work, the *On*

nis Oratoriae, 2 vols.; ed. L. Rademacher (Leipzig: Teubner, 1965) 1:7. Meijering, *Hilary of Poitiers*, 14.

[67] Against personal reflections in *De Trinitate* is Galtier, *Saint Hilaire de Poitiers*, 9–10. Galtier thinks that the personal references constitute an "itinéraire fictif," introduced for literary purposes. Other scholars see some measure of Hilary's personal experience in the first book of *On the Trinity*: H. Lietzmann, "Hilarius 11," *PWK* 8/2 (1913) 1601; Smulders, *Doctrine trinitaire de Hilaire de Poitiers*, 37; Bachelet, "Hilaire de Poitiers," 2389; Gastaldi, *Hilario de Poitiers*, 280; E. Boularand, "La conversion de saint Hilaire de Poitiers," *Bulletin de Littérature Ecclésiastique* 62 (1961) 102; Paul C. Burns, "Hilary of Poitiers' Confrontation with Arianism from 356 to 357," *Arianism: Historical and Theological Reassessments* (Philadelphia: Philadelphia Patristic Foundation, 1985) 291. Borchardt has gathered much of this research; *Hilary and the Arian Struggle*, 5.

[68] Severus, *Chronology*, 2:42; PL 20:152.

[69] Fortunatus, *Life of Hilary*, 1:5; PL 9:188.

[70] Jerome, *Chronicle*, year 359; PL 27:687.

[71] Borchardt, *Hilary and the Arian Struggle*, 40–43.

[72] Simonetti, "Hilary of Poitiers and the Arian Crisis," 4:54.

Matthew, made him the very first exegete in the West before Ambrose and Augustine to produce an important exegetical study.[73] When expounding the scriptures early in his career he repeated such phrases as "the catholic faith," "apostolic doctrine," "the faith of the gospel."[74] He had the same concern in exile when writing *On the Trinity;* he wanted to impart "the apostolic teaching."[75] But Hilary did not make a strong appeal to apostolic succession such as one finds in Irenaeus,[76] or Tertullian.[77] Apostolic tradition was not used as his point of departure for a theological exposition.[78] Nonetheless, he wanted to stand in the tradition.[79] He also had considerable awareness that, as a bishop, he expounded the mysteries of the scriptures "under the title of his own pastoral authority."[80] Authority was indeed invested in the living tradition, but a bishop had a special role in identifying the faith of the gospel. This desire to relate to the apostolic faith, the living experience of the church, should be kept in mind when he writes of his experience of initiation and the prophetic charisms.

In the Land of Montanus

Since Phrygia was the birthplace of Montanism, one is curious about the traces of this early charismatic movement in Hilary's writings. de Labriolle, who searched out references to Montanism, could find only two very brief allusions in the whole corpus of Hilary.[81] The first occurs in *Book II to Constantius*, written in 359, quite possibly in Constantinople just before Hilary returned to Gaul. Hilary asked the Emperor permission to return home in order to debate Saturninus of Arles who had been responsible

[73] J. P. Brisson, Introduction, Hilaire de Poitiers, *Traités des Mystères;* SC 19bis:9.
[74] Hilary, *On Matthew*, 10:9; 12:4; 20:9; SC 254:226, 272, 112.
[75] Hilary, *On the Trinity*, 8:2; CChr 62a:313. Smulders, *La doctrine trinitaire de S. Hilaire*, 107, note 1.
[76] *AH* 3:3, 4; 4:26; SC 34:104-14; 100:712-28.
[77] Tertullian, *The Prescription of Heretics*, 21:36; SC 46:115.
[78] C. Kannengiesser, "Hilaire de Poitiers," 489.
[79] Gastaldi, *Hilario de Poitiers*, 282.
[80] Ibid.
[81] P. de Labriolle, *Les sources de l'histoire du Montanisme*, (Paris: Leroux, 1913) 108.

for Hilary's unjust condemnation. The reference here is hardly flattering: "Montanus defended another Paraclete through his insane women."[82] This brief mention is found in a list of six (Marcellus of Ancyra, Photinus, Sabellius, Montanus, Manichaeus [Manes], and Marcion), who, in varying degrees, had wandered from the faith.

The second mention of Montanus, in *Against Constantius*, was very likely written also in 359, that is, while Hilary was still technically in exile. In a passing allusion in a somewhat corrupted text Hilary reproached Constantius for exiling the holy Paulinus of Trier to Phrygia because he would not sign the condemnation of Athanasius; in Phrygia Paulinus' situation was aggravated because he "could obtain food neither from the Emperor's granary, nor from the supplies belonging to Montanus and Maximilla."[83]

For one who had some acquaintance with Phrygia, and possibly with Montanism, Hilary showed almost no interest in the threat which the movement was believed to pose. In his *Tract on the Psalms* he mentioned the charisms of prophecy, healing and exorcism.[84] One would have expected that at least the charism of prophecy would have elicited a pastoral caveat. The *Tract on the Psalms* would have been an appropriate place to raise the question of the charisms because Hilary believed that each psalm was originally given in the Spirit of prophecy.[85] Though bishops were their chief antagonists, there is no mention of Montanism in the whole of the *Tract on the Psalms*.

Hilary spoke of being confined "in the East,"[86] but he also used a more expansive formulation and wrote "of the ten provinces of Asia, in which I am now staying."[87] This was an extensive territory including the smaller unit also called the province of Asia, and the provinces of Hellespontus, Lydia, Phrygia, Caria, Provincia Insularis, Pisidia, Pamphylia, and

---

[82] Hilary, *Book II to Constantius*, 9 PL 10:570; de Labriolle, *Sources de l'histoire du Montanisme*, 108.

[83] Hilary, *Against Constantius*, 11: PG 10:588.

[84] 64:15: CSEL 22:246.

[85] Hilary, *Tract on the Psalms*, 63:2-3; CSEL 22:225-26.

[86] Hilary, *On Synods* 8; PL 10:485.

[87] Ibid., 63; PL 10:522, 523.

Lycia.[88] While he seems to have passed most of his time in Phrygia, he was evidently free to move around the ten provinces, something not always granted to those in a similar situation.[89] He himself said that he had frequently written to the bishops of Gaul "from a great number of cities in the Roman province."[90] Hilary could have come upon the Montanists during this tour of the cities, though they were not numerous in the large cities due to the presence of monarchical bishops, their mortal enemies.[91] Beyond this we have no precise knowledge of what cities he visited, and no knowledge whatsoever that he came into contact with Montanists in Asia. But we do know that Montanists were there.

This enthusiastic charismatic movement, sometimes called "the New Prophecy," was often treated as a heresy. Hippolytus says that "[the Montanists] are thought to be orthodox about the beginning, and the fashioning of all (the doctrine of creation), and they do not accept unorthodox teachings with regard to Christ."[92] Even the relentless heresy hunter, Epiphanius (c. 315–403), witnessed that the Montanists were in agreement with the great church in matters of dogma.[93] Epiphanius, born about the same time as Hilary and Cyril, and a compatriot of Cyril of Jerusalem (he came from Gaza), recognized that Montanism taught the correct trinitarian doctrine, but included Montanism in his *Panarion*, a massive index of heresies, because it was still a threat.[94] The *Panarion* was begun about 375 and fin-

[88] Borchardt, *Hilary and the Arian Struggle*, 38.

[89] Simonetti, "Hilary of Poitiers and the Arian Crisis," 4:37.

[90] *"Nam cum frequenter vobis ex plurimis Romanarum provinciarum urbibus significassem."* Hilary, *On Synods*, 1; PL 10:479, 480. Borchardt has done the research in this area.

[91] R. M. Grant, *Augustus to Constantine* (New York: Harper & Row, 1970) 141; and W. Tabbernee, "Opposition to Montanism from Church and State," especially 542–51.

[92] Hippolytus, *Philosophumena*, 17:26: *Philosophumena* or *The Refutation of all Heresies*, 2 vols.; ed. F. Legge (London: SPCK, 1921) 2:168.

[93] Hippolytus, *Philosophumena*, 17:26; *The Refutation of all Heresies* 2:168. Epiphanius, *Panarion*, 2:1, 48; PG 41:856. de Labriolle, *Sources de l'histoire du Montanisme*, 114–44; PG 41:173-1200; 42:9-831.

[94] de Labriolle, *Sources de l'histoire du Montanisme*, 114–44; PG 41:173-1199; 42:9-831.

ished approximately three years later,[95] so his remarks about Montanism would very likely be based on their current significance. The *Panarion* appeared about 378, therefore from eleven to fourteen years after Hilary wrote his *Tract on the Psalms*. Epiphanius contended that the Montanists were still found in Cappadocia, Galatia, Phrygia, and above all in Cilicia and Constantinople.[96]

Far from being a dead heresy in the fourth century, it was, on the contrary, "still very strong . . . indeed flourishing" in parts of the empire.[97] Eusebius devoted four chapters of the fifth book of his *Ecclesiastical History* to Montanism and made other scattered references.[98] Didymus the Blind (c. 313–98), after saying that many heresies would not be referred to because they were then academic relics, went out of his way to treat of Montanism in several chapters, because the dangers were real and the faithful needed to be warned.[99] Jerome (c. 342–420) saw Montanist communities in Ancyra (the modern Ankara) when he was traveling through Galatia in 373.[100] Though flourishing, the Montanists were not numerous in the great cities because of the presence of the monarchical bishops. Montanism was, then, a living reality when both Hilary and Cyril of Jerusalem lived. Hilary's pages on the charisms in *On the Trinity* 8:29-34 were certainly written in Asia Minor, where Hilary had the greatest chance of coming into contact with the Montanists; if not actual contact, the geographical proximity would make Hilary more aware of their existence, and of the problematic nature of the prophetic charisms within Montanism.

[95] F. Williams, Introduction, *The Panarion of Epiphanius of Salamis*, ed. F. Williams (Leiden: Brill, 1987) xiii.

[96] Epiphanius, *Panarion*, 2:1, heresies 48, 49, 51; 2:2, heresy 79; PG 39:855; 880, 948; PG 42:741; de Labriolle, *La crise Montanist*, 493, 494.

[97] de Labriolle, "Le Montanisme oriental au IV siècle," *La Crise Montaniste*, 493.

[98] 5:16-21; SC 41:46-63; *Ecclesiastical History*, 2:25; 5:3, 4; 5:14; 6:20, 3; SC 31:92; SC 41:26, 27, 45, 120.

[99] Didymus, *On the Trinity*, 2:18; 3:18, 19, 23, 38, 41; PG 39:720, 881, 889, 891, 924, 977, 984.

[100] *Commentary on Galatians*, 2:2; PL 26:382. See de Labriolle, *La Crise Montaniste*, 492-95. These sources have been gathered by de Labriolle in *Sources de l'Histoire du Montanisme*.

In summation, Hilary moves with some freedom in respect to the tradition which he received. Tertullian's lapse into Montanism does not prevent Hilary from recommending the reading of the North African's *On Prayer*. When composing his own *Tract on the Psalms* he had before him the commentaries of both Origen and Eusebius. Because we are using a text reconstructed from quotations of Origen in the books of other authors, we cannot be sure of possessing the whole commentary on a particular psalm. The same can be said of Eusebius, though to a lesser degree. In both cases Hilary's indebtedness is certain.

Both Origen and Eusebius write of the divine largess, an outpouring like a rain of charisms. Origen relates that flood of charisms to the celebration of Christian initiation as Hilary does but Eusebius does not. While the presence of the prophetic charisms is not what it was in apostolic times, Origen assures us that the vestiges and traces still continue in the church.

Hilary's exile in Asia Minor raises the question of why there is no mention of Montanism in *On the Trinity*, a book written in the geographical area where Montanism was still flourishing. In this work Hilary gives more than a passing reference to the charisms. One expects some cautionary remarks from an attentive bishop. Hilary's nerves are steady. While he can be a formidable foe, as the Arians discovered, he is not easily alarmed and is not over-solicitous. As a good pastor Hilary does not raise issues, even extremely important controversies, if they are not actualities in Gaul. Arguments from silence are treacherous, but there is a degree of plausibility.

Hilary stands in that tradition expressed by his countryman, Irenaeus, and by the Martyrs of Lyons. Gaul does not panic at the noise of distant wars. If the prophetic charisms are problematic in Asia Minor, they are honored in Gaul.

When Hilary is writing a rather formal treatise, like *On the Trinity*, he probably incorporates his own personal experience, following the advice of Quintilian. This makes it all the more likely that when he is writing his much more personal, prayerful reflections on the psalms, he would not hesitate to include his own personal experience of Christian initiation, a topic to which we now turn.

Chapter Fourteen

Hilary of Poitiers:
The River of God and Intense Joy

At every period of his life, before the exile in *On Matthew* (therefore prior to 356), during the exile in *On the Trinity* (between 356 and 359), and after exile in the *Tract on the Psalms* (between 364 and 367), Hilary has something to say on the charisms, not always at great length, but some recognition that they belong to the Christian life.

In chronological order I am going to look at the writings of Hilary to note the presence in early works of the themes which will still be part of the religious universe of his last years, namely, the abundance of the charisms and their relation to initiation. Some attention needs to be paid to Hilary's teaching on the utility of the charisms. Why should the charisms be used? In what theological context does he set them? What is Hilary's dominant concern?

In his early years as a bishop, that is before 356,[1] he refers to the charisms in his *On Matthew*. Here he situates the charisms in the same baptismal context he will later use, after his exile, in his *Tract on the Psalms*. In the Matthew commentary Hilary

---

[1] Doignon, Introduction, Hilaire de Poitiers, *Sur Matthieu*; SC 254:19, 20.

says: "Those who will be coming to baptism *(Venturi enim ad baptismum)* first confess faith in the Son of God, in his passion and resurrection."[2] This verbal confession ought to correspond "to a certain truth in acts, especially by fasting during the time of the passion."[3] But as the Lord had pity on those who accompanied him for three days and had no food (Matt 15:32-39), except the seven loaves of bread and some fish, the Lord has pity also on us. The seven loaves are the seven gifts of the Holy Spirit, of which Isaiah wrote (11:2). The undetermined number of fish signify that believers are given a share in "diverse gifts and charisms."[4] The filling of the seven baskets indicates the excessive exuberance, the overflowing abundance of the seven-fold form of the Spirit. "The baskets are filled to the brim and beyond with that which they have to give. To satisfy our hunger they must always be rich and full."[5]

Hilary has little to say on the liturgy of initiation. The Gallican sacramentaries have only one anointing with chrism after the water-bath and no laying on of hands.[6] But in *On Matthew* Hilary writes of "the gift of the Spirit being bestowed on pagans through the imposition of the hands and prayer."[7] It is not clear here whether Hilary is referring to a rite, or simply exegeting the text of Matthew 19:14, which refers to Jesus laying hands on the children. Hilary interprets Jesus' saying "let the little children come to me" as a figure of the blessing being offered to the Gentiles.[8] Even if Hilary may have known of a laying on of hands, the anointing seems to have a greater importance for him.[9] To this degree, then, he has a more eastern view.

The Order of the Heavenly Mystery: the Baptism of Jesus

Important for the developing theology of initiation both as a christological and pneumatological event is Hilary's description

---

[2] Hilary, *On Matthew*, 15:8; SC 258:42, 44.
[3] Ibid.
[4] Ibid., 15:10; SC 258:47.
[5] Ibid.
[6] L. L. Mitchell, *Baptismal Anointing* (London: SPCK, 1966) 121.
[7] Hilary, *On Matthew*, 19:3; SC 258:93.
[8] Mitchell, *Baptismal Anointing*, 123.
[9] Ibid.

of the sequence of rites modeled on the baptism of Jesus. First Hilary proposed "the order of the heavenly mystery is expressed in it (baptism of Jesus)."[10] Jesus, of course, had no sin, and therefore no need of baptism. Nonetheless because he was human, and precisely to fulfill "the mysteries of human salvation," Jesus went down into the Jordan, "sanctifying the human person through his incarnation and baptism."[11] The order of the mystery in Jesus' baptism becomes the order in ours. We enter into the mystery of Jesus' own baptism to discover the identity of ours.

Hilary exegetes the baptism of Jesus: "In effect, after he had been baptized, the gates of heaven opened, the Spirit is sent and is recognized under the appearance of the dove, and he (Jesus) bathes in this sort of unction of the Father's love."[12]

Jesus goes down into the water and comes up. The anointing with the Spirit sent by the Father, descending upon him, is itself a kind of baptism. "A voice from the heavens speaks: 'You are my beloved son; today I have begotten you.' "[13] The voice of the Father on high proclaims the divine sonship below.

Here again we have an expression of Hilary's daring. The baptismal texts all have versions of "you are my beloved son, *in whom I am well pleased*" (Matt 3:17; Mark 1:11; Luke 3:22). Hilary chooses a variant reading, which in the second half of the verse substitutes the text of Psalm 2:7: "You are my beloved son. *Today I have begotten you.*"[14] The baptism of Jesus is the birth of the Son.[15] The birth event is initiatory to a new way of

[10] Hilary, *On Matthew*, 2:5; SC 254:110.

[11] Ibid.

[12] Ibid., 2:6; SC 254:110.

[13] Ibid.

[14] *Novum Testamentum, Graece et Latine*, ed. E. Nestle and K. Aland (Stuttgart: Württembergische Bibelanstalt, 1962) 149.

[15] The *Didascalia Apostolorum* from North Syria in the earlier half of the third century uses Psalm 2:7 in the same way. Speaking of the role of the bishop: "through whom the Lord gave you the Holy Spirit, and through whom you have learned the word and have known God, and through whom you have been known of God, and through whom you were sealed, and through whom you became sons of light, and through whom the Lord in baptism, by the imposition of hand of the bishop, bore witness to each one of you and uttered his holy voice saying: 'You are my son. I

existing and acting. In no sense is Hilary an adoptionist. To maintain the tradition which gives great importance to the baptism of Jesus Hilary risks using this variant reading. Hilary adds: "He (Jesus) is designated Son by the voice and vision."[16] This is why Hilary uses birth rhetoric for the Jordan event. The baptism of Jesus is the prototype. To know his baptism is to learn our own birth event: "This was done so that we in our time might learn what has been fully realized in Christ. After the water-bath, the Holy Spirit rushes upon us from the gate of heaven, that we might bathe in the anointing of the heavenly glory, and that we might become sons of God through adoption spoken by the voice of the Father."[17] Our baptism is an icon of Jesus'. Here, as at Pentecost, the Spirit envelops.

Hilary expounds a trinitarian dynamic: the Father reaches through the Spirit to endow and disclose the Son. The christological and the pneumatological moments are held in tension: the vision of the Spirit descending from the Father; the voice of the Father announcing Jesus as the eternal Son.

The primary effect of Jesus' own baptism in the Jordan is the imparting of the Spirit joined to divine sonship. Because the baptism of Jesus orders Christian baptism, the primary effect of Christian initiation is likewise the imparting of the Spirit coinhering in the adopting action of the Father, making sons and daughters of God. The anointing by the Spirit and the voice of the Father declares Jesus to be the eternal Son. Because this was fully realized in Christ when he came up from the waters, it is realized in us, that is, after the water-bath, the Spirit rushes down upon us, and we are anointed "with the unction of heavenly glory,"[18] and by the adopting voice of the Father we are declared adopted children. The baptism of Jesus at the Jordan constitutes the mystery of Christian baptism. Jesus is baptized in the Spirit; we are baptized in the Spirit.

In his *On Matthew* Hilary gives the impression that the imparting of the Spirit is distinct from and following baptism

this day have begotten you.' " *Didascalia Apostolorum* 9; *Didascalia Apostolorum*, ed. R. H. Connolly (Oxford: Clarendon, 1969) 93.

[16] Hilary, *On Matthew*, 2:6; SC 254:110.
[17] Ibid.
[18] Ibid.

when he writes of "the sacraments of baptism and of the Spirit."[19] J. Doignon thinks Hilary may be distinguishing between baptism and a later, more advanced stage of perfection in which the Spirit is imparted.[20] In this matter Hilary may be following Tertullian, who, in some passages, attributed the gift of the Spirit to the water-bath.[21] In spite of this evidence Tertullian also says elsewhere that the imparting of the Spirit is later: "I do not say that the Holy Spirit is given to us in the water, but that in the water we are made clean by the action of the angel, and made ready for the Spirit."[22] This discrepancy can be deceptive.[23] In both cases the later imparting of the Spirit is still within the same rite.

Both Tertullian and Hilary are still thinking of a single unified celebration of initiation made up of a series of discrete, interdependent rites. To speak of the meaning of specific elements in the one initiation liturgy was not to suggest that these elements stood apart from each other in a temporal sequence of some months or years. They all belonged to one integral liturgical celebration.

Hilary notes that salt contained water and fire, but that "out of the two substances one unique thing is made."[24] The image of the two elements constituting one is then applied to "the mystery of water and fire," the water–bath and the imparting of the Spirit.[25] He differentiates between "the sun and the rain in the sacraments of baptism and the Spirit."[26] Both belong to the one initiatory complex. While distinguishing the two, he wants to insist on their unity.

Before his exile, while still in Poitiers, Hilary recognized that the charisms were given in abundance in relation to initiation, and he had a pronounced theology of baptism modeled on the baptism of Jesus.

[19] Ibid., 4:27; SC 254:148.
[20] SC 254:149, note 29.
[21] Tertullian, On the Soul, 1:4; Tertullian, On Modesty, 9:9; CChr 2:782, 1297.
[22] Tertullian, On Baptism, 6:1; SC 35:75.
[23] Refoulé, Introduction; SC 35:42, 43.
[24] Hilary, On Matthew, 4:10; SC 254:126.
[25] Ibid., 4:10; SC 254:128.
[26] Ibid., 4:27; SC 254:148. See also Tract on Psalm 118, 3, 5; SC 344:152.

Before he left Gaul, or not later than the first year of his exile, Hilary writes in the first book of *On the Trinity* of his own need for guidance in the composition of *On the Trinity*: God "summons us to share in the prophetic and apostolic Spirit."[27] Here the prophetic Spirit seems to refer to inspired teaching.

In the eighth book of *On the Trinity*, written in Asia Minor where Montanism still flourished, Hilary gives his most expansive exposition of the charisms (8:29-34), and that in a context specifically trinitarian. He makes appeal to "the rare and difficult charisms" for understanding the God who is undeniably three, triumphantly one.[28] If the word of understanding is necessary for insight into the mystery, the charisms themselves manifest who such a God is when the Risen Savior tells the apostles that they will receive the Holy Spirit, the promise of the Father, that they will be baptized in the Holy Spirit. Within this trinitarian dynamic of the one God the charisms are introduced.

Hilary ties the charisms to the event to which the risen Savior referred when he said "Stay in Jerusalem . . . You shall be baptized by the Holy Spirit not many days hence," (Acts 1:5) which Hilary quotes.[29] Hilary, therefore, joins the imparting of the charisms to being baptized in the Holy Spirit.

In *On the Trinity* alone Hilary cites Paul's full list of charisms in 1 Corinthians 12 four times,[30] and twice repeats a partial list.[31] All in all he makes nineteen references to 1 Corinthians 12. Obviously the charisms are not a matter of minor significance. Whether *On the Trinity* or *On the Faith (against the Arians)* is Hilary's original title, he evidently thinks that the charisms belong in some significant way to the Christian faith, to the manner in which the trinitarian life of the one God is given visibility in ministry. The insistent repetition of the Corinthian text is not accidental.

---

[27] Hilary, *On the Trinity*, 1:38; CChr 62:36. *See* the discussion of the dating of book 1. Here I am following Smulders, *Doctrine trinitaire de Hilaire*, 41, and Borchardt, *Hilary and the Arian Struggle*, 41.

[28] Hilary, *On the Trinity*, 8:34; CChr 62a:346.

[29] Ibid., 8:30; CChr 62a:341.

[30] Ibid., 2:34, 8:29, 30, 33; CChr 62:70; 62a:340-42, 345.

[31] Ibid., 8:33, 34; CChr 62a:345-47.

The charisms have a double modality: they are given "by the Spirit in the Spirit."[32] "By the Spirit" indicates agent; the Spirit is God in action, God as Act. "In the Spirit" indicates environment, or, more precisely, the mystery which can only be appropriated from the inside. They are not found among those who are "living outside of the apostolic spirit,"[33] "outside the gospel."[34]

The charisms, here specifically the gifts of wisdom, knowledge, teaching, miracles, healing, tongues, and interpretation, are "ministries and workings (*ministeria et operationes*) of the church in which [church] is the body of Christ."[35] Or, in Hilary's more striking formulation, "the divisions of the charisms (charismata) are from the one Lord Jesus Christ, who is the body of all."[36] To avoid all suggestion that the charisms owe their existence to some ordinance of the church Hilary adds: "God has instituted them."[37] Charisms are to be used in the proclamation of the gospel. We should not leave the charisms dormant, as though the Spirit were absent from the church. For Hilary many of the charisms are miraculous manifestations, though perhaps not helpers, administrators, fasting, almsgiving, charity: "Through the miracles that have been granted for the profit of everyone the gift of the Holy Spirit does not remain hidden."[38] The charisms belong to the church on its way to its ultimate consummation: "Because the charisms are effective they are the pledge of our future hope."[39]

Gifts are Profitable: Use Them!

In the eighth book of *On the Trinity* Hilary returns to a theme he had developed at the end of the second book. In the earlier section he cites Paul's list from 1 Corinthians 12, and then adds that the gift of the Spirit is without ambiguity "since its manner

[32] Ibid., 8:31; CChr 62a:343.
[33] Ibid., 8:35; CChr 62a:348.
[34] Ibid., 8:30; CChr 62a:342.
[35] Ibid., 8:33; CChr 62a:345.
[36] Ibid., 8:32; CChr 62a:344.
[37] Ibid., 8:33; CChr 62a:345.
[38] Ibid. Also, Hilary of Poitiers, *Commentary on Psalm 118*, 12:14; SC 347:96.
[39] Hilary, *On the Trinity*, 2:35; CChr 62:71.

of acting and its power is clearly determined."[40] No obscurity
exists on this point; we have "absolute knowledge" *(absolutam
habet intelligentiam)*.[41] "The manifestation of the Spirit is through
the effects which these powers produce."[42] Doubt cannot remain.

Hilary returns rather insistently to the utility of the charisms.
We know, he said, that they are useful because in the gift, who
is the Spirit, is manifested a whole range of ministries, which
build up the church. He again cites Paul's list of charisms in
1 Corinthians 12.

Protesting that charisms are not just adornments, Hilary insists they are "profitable gifts" *(per quas dationum utilitates)*.[43]
Then he details how the charisms are profitable: when the
words of life are spoken; or when there is understanding of divine knowledge (which divides us from animals); when by faith
we stand inside the gospel; when healings and miracles are performed; when by prophecy we are taught of God;[44] when
spirits, holy or evil, are discerned; when sermons in foreign
languages are signs that the Holy Spirit is active; when interpretation makes intelligible the sermons in foreign languages.[45] In all of these gifts the presence of the Spirit is
manifested in concrete effects.[46] In short, the gifts make a difference; they are profitable. But divine effects come only from divine causes. If the charisms really make a difference it is
because they are expressions of the life of the one God, because
of their trinitarian nature; furthermore, charisms are given to
the church.[47] If the charisms are effective and profitable, then
"let us make use of such generous gifts."[48] Hilary is here appealing to the experience of the church. Though the appeal is

[40] Ibid., 2:34; CChr 62:70.
[41] Ibid., 8:30; CChr 62a:341.
[42] Ibid., 8:30; CChr 62a:340.
[43] Ibid., 8:30; CChr 62a:341.
[44] The actuality of prophecy seems to reside in the possession of divine
truths, a somewhat attenuated view of prophecy.
[45] Hilary thinks that speaking in tongues is a real language, used to proclaim the gospel to the nations.
[46] Hilary, *On the Trinity,* 8:30; CChr 62a:341, 342.
[47] Ibid., 8:29-33; CChr 62a:340-46.
[48] Ibid., 2:35; CChr 62:70, 71.

not forceful, falling short of Cyril of Jerusalem's similar appeal, yet it is real.

Why the Charisms in a Book on the Trinity?

Luis Ladaria suggests that Hilary treated the theme of the charisms "with much greater frequency" in his later works.[49] This is true if one considers *On the Trinity* as one of his later works, which seems unlikely. One must remember the short span of Hilary's public literary life was about a dozen years, 356–67. If *On Matthew* was written before 356,[50] and *On the Trinity* between 356 and 359, and *The Tract on the Psalms* between 364–67, then it is a little forced to say that *On the Trinity* belongs to his later works. In any case the frequency of his references to charisms in *On the Trinity* would have given him more opportunities to say something, at least in passing, about Montanism. But there is no mention of Montanism in this major treatise written in Asia Minor where Montanism still existed.

As we have seen, there is a substantial amount of teaching on the charisms in *On the Trinity*. There are nineteen citations of 1 Corinthians, direct or indirect, and one of Ephesians 4:11, all texts concerning the charisms;[51] this in a book meant to be the defense of the Nicaean faith. Whether one takes the present title, *On the Trinity*, or what was probably his name for the treatise, *On the Faith (against the Arians)*, Hilary could have omitted the charisms from consideration and not be accused of having excluded material immediately pertinent to the issue at hand. In a formal treatise, *On the Trinity*, which followed a preconceived, detailed outline, the repeated citation of 1 Corinthians 12, the repetitive listing of charisms signals a determination to protect and foster charisms in the church. He spoke boldly of the charisms which had brought the Montanists into disrepute and enmity with the bishops. No evidence can be

[49] Ladaria, *El Espiritu Santo en San Hilario de Poitiers* (Madrid: Eapsa, 1977) 177.

[50] Doignon, Introduction; SC 254:19, 20.

[51] In the order of the texts in 1 Corinthians: *On the Trinity*, 2:34; 8:28; 8:28; 8:31; 8:34; 8:29; 8:34; 8:39; 8:34; 8:33; 8:31; 8:34; 8:34; 8:29; 8:33; 8:31; 8:32; 8:33; CChr 62:70; CChr 62a:340, 340, 343, 346, 340, 346, 352, 346, 345, 343, 346, 346, 340, 345, 343, 344, 345. Ephesians 4:11: *On the Trinity*, 8:33; CChr 620:346.

found in the text to support the supposition that Hilary was proposing something new and unheard of. The impression is given that Hilary was handing on something important and traditional. No enthusiastic group at enmity with their bishops is going to drive out the charisms given at Christian baptism, an icon of Jesus' baptism in the Jordan.

The River of God

In Hilary's *Tract on the Psalms* one finds the pertinent text on initiation and the charisms in a context which is eucharistic and pneumatological.[52] Hilary isolated two elements: food, which for him is the eucharist, and the torrents of river water, which is the gift of the Holy Spirit.

Hilary had been commenting on Psalm 64:9. "You have visited the earth and watered it; you have multiplied the means of enriching it. The river of God is full of water, and you have prepared food for them." For Hilary this enrichment was a kind of drunkenness, which he wanted to specify in more detail.[53] The city of God was made joyous by the swelling streams with which it is fed. The River of God is a new kind of water.

To justify this reading Hilary calls on two texts. The first is John 4:14: "Whoever drinks of the water which I shall give him, from his belly shall flow rivers springing up into eternal life." Hilary here opts for what has been called the eastern, more anthropological reading, following Origen and Athanasius, where the subject from whom the water flows is the believer.[54] This is in contrast to the western, more christological reading, following Justin, Hippolytus, and Tertullian, where the subject from whom the water flows is Christ.[55]

Hilary applies John 7:39 to the earlier text with its reference to the flowing rivers: "Now this he said about the Spirit." For Hilary, therefore, the Spirit flowed as a river from within the believer. Hilary continues reaffirming the river's identity with

[52] I thank Harold Cohen and George Montague for calling my attention to this text.

[53] Hilary, *Tract on the Psalms*, 64:13; CSEL 22:244.

[54] L. F. Ladaria, "Juan 7, 38 en Hilario de Poitiers: Un Analisis de Tr.Ps. 64, 13-16," *Estudios Eclesiasticos* 52 (1977) 123-28.

[55] Burge, *Anointed Community*, 88-93.

the Spirit. Though the river of God flows within the believer, its source is in God. The abundance of waters makes the river overflow: "We are inundated with the gifts of the Spirit. That fountain of life, which is the river of God, spills over in us."[56] The charisms inundate like a mighty river, an image of embarrassing largess, of superabundance.

But water by itself is not sufficient; we also live from food. "We have food prepared for us."[57] The food, prepared in advance, is a new kind of food, carrying within it newness of life, directed to a specific function. "This food prepares us for the communion in the life with God through the communion of the holy Body [eucharist], and then in the communion of the assembled holy Body [church]."[58] There are different levels of communion: communion in the eucharist is communion in God, which demands communion in the gathering of believers. Here is that ancient communion ecclesiology where communion is "a sharing in one reality held in common."[59] Communion inheres in communion.

The Spirit: Presence of the Future

The three levels of communion form one complex mystery, each one being actualized at the interior of the other. The food, which is the body of Christ, is received in the present, but it also has an orientation to what is to come. "Although we are saved in the present, even more truly we are prepared for the future."[60] Life reaches out and forward to some more perfect, more lasting, communion still to come. The psalmist (who for Hilary is a prophet) lived in the past, but speaks of realities which are still to be realized in our future. The past of the prophetic writers now teaches us about our present, which impels us to our future. The Spirit is the presence of the future.

One prays the words of Psalm 64:9, 10: "Inebriate its rivers, multiply its generations. He will rejoice in its misty rain, when

---

[56] Hilary, *Tract on the Psalms*, 64:14; CSEL 22:245.

[57] Ibid.

[58] Ibid.

[59] John Cardinal Willebrands, "The Future of Ecumenism," *One in Christ* 11 (1975) 313.

[60] Hilary, *Tract on the Psalms*, 64:14; CSEL 22:245.

it arises." This text, spoken in the past, Hilary takes as the universal law of prayer for the present. "This is what is expressed in every prayer. What has been commemorated in the past, and all those things asked for in prayer, may God fulfill."[61] Hilary uses the Old Testament psalm text as a prayer that the abundance there promised will be realized.

Expanding the image of a swollen river, and a prolonged, heavy, misty rain, Hilary turns the text into a prayer for God's abundance in his day, expanding on themes both Origen and Eusebius treated extensively. Then Hilary asks how this prayer, uttered in the past, is fulfilled in the present. "The earth, which God has visited, has been made drunk. How does one understand streams being inebriated? In this way: we must be convinced that when someone has drunk from the water of the Lord, then streams will flow from the belly of that person. Now we must be sure that we drink the water of the Lord, so that the rivers will flow."[62] The new water in the torrent of the river is an image of a bounty beyond imagination or need.

A transposition of the sources of the water is evident. God is the source. With what force, what impetuosity, and power the river of water flows from God! Once we have drunk of God's river, we, in turn, have the source of living water within. This is not to say that the source within the believer is a source for others. Such a deduction would be alien to Hilary.[63] Nonetheless the task is to assure that we who have come to faith drink, and drink deeply.

Hilary further specifies the nature of this river. "The Holy Spirit is called a river. When we receive the Holy Spirit, we are made drunk. Because out of us, as a source, various streams of grace flow, the prophet prays that the Lord will inebriate us. The prophet wants the same persons to be made drunk, and filled to all fullness with the divine gifts, so that their generations may be multiplied. This means that the good earth is compared in the gospel simile to the seed of the word, bearing fruit thirty, sixty, and a hundred fold."[64]

[61] Ibid., 245, 246.
[62] Ibid., 246.
[63] Ladaria, "Juan 7, 38 en Hilario de Poitiers," 127.
[64] Hilary, *Tract on the Psalms*, 64:14 CSEL 22:246.

The accents in which Hilary writes of initiation are communal and personal. "We who have been reborn through the sacrament of baptism experience intense joy *(maximum gaudium)* when we feel within us the first stirrings *(initia sentimus)* of the Holy Spirit."[65] Now the torrents of new water within break through to conscious awareness.

Just as Hilary, in his more formal treatise *On the Trinity*, seems to be alluding to his own experience of conversion as an adult, so here also. From a random remark in his book *On the Synods* we know that Hilary was probably baptized shortly before he was made bishop, not an unusual practice at that time.[66] Hilary speaks of the intense joy when the first movements of the Spirit were felt at his own adult baptism.

The vocabulary is boldly concrete. Hilary uses a Latin word *(sentire)* which means to perceive with the senses. He "feels" the initial movements of the Spirit within. Not for the first time does Hilary use the vocabulary of feeling in relation to the Spirit. Hilary writes: "Among us there is no one who, from time to time, does not feel the gift of the grace of the Spirit *(donum spiritalis gratiae sentiat).*"[67] While the meaning is clear, namely, that spiritual graced events can have content at the level of conscious awareness, care must be taken not to press the text, as though Hilary were saying that only what was felt was real. Or that the presence of the Spirit is always perceivable by the senses. Nonetheless Hilary links the coming of the Spirit to experience.

In addition to perceiving the movement of the Spirit, the joy Hilary experiences is "intense." Hilary continues his description of initiation: "We begin to have insight into the mysteries of faith, we are able to prophesy and to speak with wisdom. We become steadfast in hope and receive the gifts (plural) of healing. Demons are made subject to our authority."[68] This is an obvious reference to 1 Corinthians 12. To Paul's list Hilary adds

---

[65] Ibid.

[66] " . . . *regeneratus pridem et in episcopatu aliquantisper manens . . .* " Hilary, *On Synods*, 91; PL 10:544.

[67] Hilary, *Tract on Psalm 118*, 118:12, 4; SC 347:76.

[68] Hilary, *Tract on the Psalms*, 64:15; CSEL 22:246.

exorcism, and in this matter he is following the tradition.[69] The impression is given of charisms which are not outside the realm of Hilary's or his readers' experience. The point at which the charisms begin to be experienced is Christian initiation.

Throughout the commentary on this psalm Hilary cites texts about the Spirit, the river of God, communion, which prepare for initiation. Earlier Hilary uses 1 Corinthians 12 on the charisms when speaking of the good things which are to be found in the house of God, which is the church. The reference is not generic; rather Hilary names the charisms, one after the other.[70]

The theme of charismatic gifts is further witnessed to by the text from Isaiah 61:1-2: "The Spirit of the Lord is upon me, because he has anointed me to preach the good news to the poor, to give sight to the blind, and to announce the acceptable year of the Lord." This is the announcement of the age of plenty, given in the synagogue at the beginning of Jesus' public ministry, characterizing it as a ministry in the Spirit (Luke 4:16-19).[71] Though it is unusual to speak of Jesus possessing charisms, that is what the text is saying. Charisms are ministries which make visible the power of the Spirit also in the case of Jesus. We enter into the mystery of Jesus' ministry in order to discover the identity of Christian ministry. Not only Jesus' baptism orders our baptism, Jesus' ministry orders our ministry. As Jesus begins his public ministry with an imparting of the charisms, so must also ours.

Hilary quotes the prophecy of Joel 2:28 ("I will pour out my spirit upon all flesh"), incorporated in the Pentecost account.[72] This last text characterizes the ministry of the church as one in the Spirit, based on the charisms. We have, therefore, both the ministry of Christ and the church presented in the optic of the charisms.

The abundance of the charisms is like that harvest Mark re-

[69] The *Apostolic Constitutions*, 8:23, 26; SC 336:228, 230, places exorcism among the charisms. An exorcist, like a healer, is not ordained. The reason is that "God has manifested it, and the grace is visible to all." There is a dependence here on *Diataxeis (Apostolic Tradition)* 15; SC 11bis:68.

[70] Hilary, *Tract on the Psalms*, 64:15; CSEL 22:246.

[71] Ibid., 64:16; CSEL 22:247.

[72] Ibid., 64:4; CSEL 22:235.

corded (4:8), bearing thirty, sixty, and a hundred fold. The great harvest is the plenty of the charisms.[73] Besides the charisms named explicitly there are "other full and perfect gifts," not to be reckoned as "carnal."[74]

The texts from Isaiah, Joel, and 1 Corinthians, together with the Marcan one, are in the same psalm commentary (64) in which is found the baptismal text we are considering. They demonstrate the logic of Hilary's argument: baptismal celebration is the locus for imparting the gifts.

Hilary wants to be even more insistent. The specific enumeration of the charisms from 1 Corinthians 12 given earlier in the commentary on this psalm is repeated immediately after Hilary speaks of the experience of intense joy at baptism. But they have a slightly different formulation: the understanding of mysteries, the knowledge of prophecy, the word of wisdom, the solidity of faith, the charisms of healing, and the subjugation of demons.[75] The charisms manifest themselves in relation to the celebration of initiation.

No Freestanding Charisms

Hilary continues explaining how the charisms are received in the church, and what the consequences are. "These gifts enter us like a gentle rain, and once having done so, little by little bring forth fruit in abundance."[76] The charisms are not just for embellishment. They are gifts which, when used, bear a great harvest. Then Hilary describes the great number and variety of charisms. "When this gentle rain falls, the earth rejoices. But the rains are multiplied so that [at first] there are small streams; the streams [then] become raging waters (inebriantur), so that they become mighty rivers."[77] A progression is noted: from a shower to a stream to a mighty river. Hilary is not disturbed that the image of river is used in two slightly different ways, namely, of the Spirit itself, and of the charisms, which is the Spirit coming to visibility in service to the body.

[73] Ibid., 64:6; CSEL 22:237.
[74] Ibid., 64:6; CSEL 22:237, 238.
[75] Ibid., 64:15; CSEL 22:246.
[76] Ibid.
[77] Ibid.

The rain of gifts, a power category, typifying the Acts of the Apostles, is easily identified here. "You shall receive power when the Holy Spirit has come upon you" (1:8); "(Peter proclaimed) how God anointed (a baptismal reference to Luke 3:16) Jesus of Nazareth with the Holy Spirit and with power; how he went about doing good and healing all that were oppressed by the devil for God was with him" (Acts 10:38). In Peter's sermon he joins Jesus' baptism at the Jordan with the charisms of power, healing and exorcism, which demonstrate the presence of the new reality.

The gifts enrich the church (*ecclesiae munera*).[78] The charismatic center is not, therefore, the individual, but the church. "These are true charisms, some of the many perfect gifts which adorn the house of God."[79] The church, as the house of God, is filled with God's charisms. Charisms, therefore, are not freestanding. Rather they are given in relation to the community's constitutive celebration of initiation. They are also ordered to the life of the local communion. Socially determined in this double sense, they are still eminently personal, even experiential.

One does not celebrate Christian initiation in order to receive the charisms. For Hilary that would have been exceedingly strange and would indicate that the candidate has not understood the gospel. On the contrary, because one has entered into the communion of the body of Christ (eucharist), into that other level of communion in the body of Christ (church), and into the communion in the life of God (grace), one receives charisms. All of this insures that each Christian serves the communion. Charisms are ministry to others.

One enters that communion through baptism, which is the central rite which in faith makes one a Christian. Hilary uses Psalm 64 to speak of "the spiritual and ecclesiastical chants" of the church, of "the morning and vesper hymns of the church."[80] The baptismal rite in which one becomes a Christian

[78] Ibid.

[79] Ibid., 64:6; CSEL 22:237.

[80] "*Hymnus ergo hic deo condecet, qui sit in Sion spiritali et ecclesiastico cantico innocens et dei laudibus dulcis. . . . Nam post praeparationes montium in accinctu potentiae et conturbatis maris fundum et sonitum fluctuum eius progressus ecclesiae in matutinum et uespertinorum hymnorum delectationes maximum misericordiae dei signum est.*" Ibid., 64:2, 11; CSEL 22:234, 244.

is part of a whole complex of liturgical rites in which the Word of God is proclaimed, hymns are sung, sins are forgiven. The local communion gathers for morning and evening prayers. Within this broad liturgical background Hilary situates his words on baptism, the Spirit, and the gifts of the Spirit, all in a communion ecclesiology, which is specifically eucharistic.

One should not think that Hilary has been carried away in a kind of charismatic ecstasy, where the wondrous and the unusual are normative. For Hilary, a good disciple of Origen, the charisms of first rank are wisdom, knowledge and faith.[81] Hilary gives privileged place to the charism of knowledge, partly because it is a specification of the charism of wisdom.[82] In addition to those named above, Hilary adds fasting, almsgiving, charity, solidity in the faith. "One does not expect that one person has all of the gifts."[83] The church is a web of mutually supporting charisms/ministries.

In summation, Hilary sees a clear trinitarian movement: the Father reaches through the Spirit to empower and reveal the Son. Communion in that life through the communion in the eucharistic body and communion in the ecclesial body is the locus for his teaching on the charisms. Communion inheres in communion.

Tertullian's text allows us to isolate certain specific baptismal gestures and acts. This made it possible to identify those elements which many associate with baptism in the Spirit. In his *Tract on the Psalms* Hilary has a different agenda. He is not concerned to identify, isolate, and then comment on the various gestures and acts in the liturgy of baptism. Therefore, in this text, he says nothing about an explicit prayer for imparting the Spirit, or other ritual elements, which undoubtedly were part of his rite of initiation. His concern is for the theological content and the experience.

But at the beginning of his public life as an author, Hilary, in *On Matthew*, does make one ritual remark on the anointing in Christian baptism. First he annunciates a principle: Jesus' baptism orders our baptism. Just as the Spirit came down on Jesus

[81] Hilary, *Commentary on Psalm 118:* Argument 4; SC 344:96.
[82] Ibid., 9, 3; 18, 10; SC 347:14, 242.
[83] Ibid., 12, 15: SC 347:96, 98.

as he ascended from the Jordan, so after the water-bath in Christian initiation there is an anointing with the unction of heavenly glory.[84] This reference to the rite of anointing in our baptism, given at the beginning of Hilary's public life, is given further content when, at the end of his life, he looks back and describes the same rite from the point of view of experience. At the first stirrings within of the Holy Spirit, Hilary and the other neophytes experience intense joy, and the charisms manifest themselves: words of understanding and wisdom, prophecy, healing, and exorcism. Christians are endowed with charisms as indeed Jesus was at the beginning of his public ministry. In quite personal terms Hilary speaks of the Spirit as the river of God inundating the community with charisms.

The two texts from the beginning and end of his life together give a consistent doctrine of the baptism in the Holy Spirit: as with Christ, so with us.

This experience of the Spirit at initiation is not a completely isolated event. From time to time the stirring of the grace of the Spirit within is experienced by all.

In *On the Trinity*, a book written in Asia Minor in areas where Montanism still flourished, Hilary relates the charisms to the words of the Risen Christ: "Stay in Jerusalem . . . You shall be baptized with the Holy Spirit." Christ imparts the charisms by the Spirit, in the Spirit. No one can claim the charisms from the outside. One must be inside the gospel. Nor are the charisms matters of speculation. Of their presence in the church we have absolute knowledge. Charisms are not decorative.

While we would see these gifts as real operations of God in the human acts, graced acts, and, in the older vocabulary, super-natural acts, we would not understand all these charisms to be miraculous. For Hilary at least the prophetic gifts are miraculous.

As Jesus' ministry orders ours, these charisms present in Jesus' public life are available for our work of evangelization. The Spirit, the River of God, flows within each believer, over-flowing its banks, inundating with the charisms, which are not freestanding, but are specifically gifts belonging to the church. The charisms are profitable; they make a difference. Use them!

---

[84] Hilary, *On Matthew*, 2:6; SC 254:110.

Hilary is more than just another theologian in that fertile and turbulent fourth century. The brief of Pope Pius IX declaring him a Doctor of the Church was signed May 13, 1851. He has special weight in identifying the faith, the experience, and the practice of the church.

Tertullian attending to ritual, Origen establishing a formal theology, and Hilary emphasizing experience, all write of charisms in relation to initiation. Cyril will combine ritual, theology, and experience in the very theater of salvation.

Chapter Fifteen

Cyril of Jerusalem:
Apostolic Memories
in the Very Theater of Salvation

A hundred and fifty years after Tertullian wrote *On Baptism*, a hundred and sixteen years after Origen dictated *On John*, Cyril of Jerusalem (c. 315–87), a contemporary of Hilary, possibly born in the same year, preached a series of twenty-four instructions, of which nineteen are called *Catechetical Lectures* (hereafter *CL*), and five *Mystagogical Catecheses* (hereafter *MC*).[1] All were delivered in the dedicated (335) Constantinian Church of the Sepulcher. The significance of these two series won for Cyril the title of "Doctor of the Church," conferred in the last century by Pope Leo XIII, a title he shares with Hilary and John Chrysostom.

The nineteen *CL* (one proto-catechesis and eighteen catecheses), in reality a Lenten series, were delivered between 348 and 350 either while Cyril was still a priest or as a new bishop.[2] The five *MC*, which are reflective instructions for the

---

[1] The usual date for Cyril's death is 386. P. Nautin, using Jerome's *On Famous Men*, has suggested that it is 387. "La date du 'de viris illustribus' de Jerome, de la mort de Cyrille de Jerusalem et de celle de Grégoire de Nazianze," *RHE* 56 (1961) 35.

[2] F. L. Cross suggested they might be as early as 347. *St. Cyril of Jerusalem's Lectures on the Christian Sacraments*, ed. F. L. Cross (London: SPCK, 1960) xxii.

days after Easter, were delivered sometime late in his life, sometime between 383 and 387.[3] These two sets of instructions represent "one of the most precious treasures of Christian antiquity."[4] No other early writer has given so detailed an account of baptism and the eucharist.[5] The first nineteen, called CL, are more formal instructions for catechumens preparing for baptism at the Holy Saturday-Easter vigil. These were delivered in the Martyrium of the Church of the Sepulcher to the candidates for baptism. The eighteen CL were very likely based on the Jerusalem creed, the creed itself figuring in the initiation rite.[6] In the liturgical act of handing over of the creed the catechumens were told to retain it "in the memory of the heart."[7] The MC were delivered in the Anastasis, a free standing rotunda.[8] The evidence for identifying initiation with what the contemporary Pentecostal/charismatic movement calls the baptism in the Spirit comes mostly from CL 16 and 17.

After situating the liturgical relationship of Jerusalem to Alexandria and Antioch, I will indicate aspects of the biblical teaching on charisms which are pertinent to this study. Irenaeus' teaching on the charisms, to which Cyril referred, is part of the tradition in which Cyril wanted to stand; I will give a summary statement of Irenaeus on charisms. I have chosen to study Irenaeus here because Cyril is the only one of our four authors to name him explicitly in a baptismal context, and in clear relationship to the charisms.

Alexandria: A Greek City in Egypt
We tend to think of Jerusalem as the chief city of Christendom, the Holy City, the place of pilgrimage visited by thousands who

[3] C. Beukers, " 'For our Emperors, Soldiers and Allies,' An Attempt at Dating the 23rd Catechesis by Cyrillus of Jerusalem," VC 15 (1961) 177–84.

[4] Quasten, *Patrology*, 3:363.

[5] Ibid., 372.

[6] A. A. Stephenson, "The Lenten Catechetical Syllabus in Fourth-Century Jerusalem," TS 15 (1954) 103, 116.

[7] CL 5:12; *Cyrilli Hierosolymarum Archiepiscopi Opera Quae Supersunt Omnia*, 2 vols.; ed. W. K. Reischl and J. Rupp (Munich: Keck, 1848/1850) 1:148 (hereafter cited as *CAO*).

[8] Stephenson presents some evidence against this commonly held supposition. *The Works of Saint Cyril of Jerusalem*, ed. L. P. McCauley and A. A. Stephenson (Washington: Catholic University of America, 1970) 150, 151.

came to feed their piety at the very ground of redemption. Such, however, was not how antiquity viewed Jerusalem. Nor was it perceived as a major religious center well into Cyril's years as a bishop. This much-diminished view of Jerusalem can start with its liturgical subservience.

The *CL* are structured according to a specific list of biblical readings, which determined the themes, among others, the Spirit and the charisms. Where did this reading list come from? Was Jerusalem a liturgically independent source? The answer is found in the relation of Jerusalem to two cities: Alexandria and Antioch.[9]

Alexandria presents its claims to apostolicity on Peter's pupil, Mark the evangelist, who, the legend held, brought the good news to Egypt. Though Jerusalem had an honorary precedence, both Alexandria and Antioch were recognized by the Council of Nicaea (325) as having positions which left Jerusalem subordinate and dependent. Alexandria was considered the first church of the orient. In the decrees of Nicaea Jerusalem is not even called by its historic name, but is still "Aelia," its secular name given by Hadrian after the Jewish revolt of 135.[10] Further, the Council of Nicaea subjected "Aelia" to Caesarea, which in turn was subject to Antioch. On the hierarchy of real episcopal power Jerusalem was rather low. One is therefore not entirely surprised to find some indications that Jerusalem's list of readings came from Egypt, more precisely, Alexandria.

The very earliest Christian history of Egypt is so misty that very little can be said for certain.[11] Eusebius of Caesarea, to whom our knowledge of this period is largely due, found the early history of Christianity in Egypt murky, and therefore passed on obscurities.[12] By the second century there were a large number of bishoprics, all centralized in the metropolitan city, Alexandria. The tradition of Mark being the bishop of Alexandria, though still unverified, was firmly established 120

---

[9] R. Zerfass, *Die Schriftlesung in Kathedraloffizium Jerusalems* (Münster: Aschendorffsche Verlagsbuchhandlung, 1968) 2; A. A. Stephenson, "Cyril of Jerusalem and the Alexandrian Heritage," *TS* (1954) 373–93.

[10] *Sacrorum Conciliorum Nova et Amplissima Collectio*, ed. J. D. Mansi (Paris: Welter, 1901) 2:679 (hereafter cited as Mansi).

[11] C. D. G. Müller, "Alexandrien," *TRE*, 2:248–61.

[12] R. M. Grant, "Early Alexandrian Christianity," *CH* 40 (1971) 142.

years after the period in which he would have lived.[13] One would have expected that Alexandria, as a strong Jewish city, would have become an early center of Christianity, but the Acts of the Apostles seem to indicate that the gospel went northwards. Even so, it is difficult to imagine that so vigorous a center of Jewish culture would have been left unevangelized in the early years of Christianity. One possible reason for the veil cast over Christianity's beginnings there is the hold which Gnosticism had on Egyptian Christianity in the early years, Alexandria being the home of Valentinus and Basilides.[14]

In the fourth century both Alexandria and Lower Egypt had Greek speaking populations; only as one moved into Upper Egypt was Copt spoken. Traces of Jerusalem's dependence on Alexandria are found in an Armenian text. The *Rituale Armenorum*, which is dated 440, is a borrowing from the Jerusalem liturgy of the previous century, therefore in temporal proximity to Cyril.[15] The *Old Armenian Lectionary*, which belongs to the same tradition, recorded the conviction that the biblical readings of Cyril's lectionary came from Alexandria: "Cyril sent to Alexandria to Peter (the bishop), and asked of him the lections ordained by James, the brother of the Lord."[16] Even though probably legendary, F. C. Conybeare judged that "it may well be true."[17] What is unusual is that Cyril had to go to Egypt to recover a tradition which went back to James, who was the dominant, authoritative leader in Jerusalem during the first generation of Christians in Jerusalem. Whatever the origin of the tradition, at the beginning of the fourth century "Egypt and Jerusalem were using essentially the same rite, which differed

---

[13] R. Trevijano, "The Early Christian Church of Alexandria," *ST* 12, part 1 (1975) 471–77; C. H. Roberts, *Manuscript, Society and Belief in Early Christian Egypt* (Oxford: Oxford University, 1979) 71–73; B. A. Pearson, "Earliest Christianity in Egypt: Some Observations," *The Roots of Egyptian Christianity* (Philadelphia: Fortress, 1986) 132–56.

[14] F. L. Cross, *The Early Christian Fathers* (London: Duckworth, 1960) 117.

[15] *Rituale Armenorum*, ed. F. C. Conybeare (Oxford: Clarendon, 1905).

[16] Appendix II, "The Old Armenian Lectionary and Calendar," ibid. 515; A. Renoux, Introduction, "Liturgie Hiérosolymitaine et vieux lectionnaire arménien," *PO* 35: 19–32.

[17] *Rituale Armenorum*, 515.

from that in use at Antioch."[18] This seems strange; however it seems to receive some support from a late Armenian source, *The Life of Cyril of Jerusalem*. This source also attributed the series of biblical lessons which it received from Jerusalem as coming from James, a tradition "which is not to be entirely rejected."[19] This is by no means a strong historical witness in itself, but it may bear traces of the contact between the Greek/Syriac life in Cyril's Jerusalem, and the rise of Armenian culture. The *CL* were among the first books to be translated into Armenian, an Indo-European language, in the fifth century, thus creating Armenian literature.[20]

Antioch: "The Beautiful City of the Greeks" in a Syrian Province

In the secular order the cities of first rank in the East were Alexandria and Seleucia, then Antioch, "the beautiful city of the Greeks," as Isaac of Antioch called it. For the general history of the universal church during the first four centuries Antioch played a role of greater significance than Jerusalem. Antioch was the center from which the early church sent missionaries. In part this was based on Peter's stay before he went to Rome. The Council of Nicaea gave it second place after Alexandria. As an administrative, military, and trade center it exceeds the importance of Jerusalem. Up into the fourth century it was often the residence of the emperor. As an administrative and military center of the civil government it far exceeded Jerusalem's role in the empire. Only at the end of the fourth and the beginning of the fifth centuries did Antioch give way to Constantinople and Jerusalem in religious influence. The dominant Greek character is manifested by the line of Greek bishops up to the end of the third century; among its influential theologian-bishops were Ignatius, Theophilus, Serapion, Paul of Samosata. Specific Greek/Antioch liturgical sources include *The Psalm Homilies of Easter Week* of Asterius (d. after 341) and other

[18] G. J. Cuming, "Egyptian Elements in the Jerusalem Liturgy," *JTS* 35 (1974) 123.

[19] E. Bihain, "Une vie arménienne de saint Cyrille de Jérusalem, *Muséon* 76 (1963) 334.

[20] G. Garitte, "Les Catéchèses de Cyrille de Jérusalem en Arménien: Fragments d'un Manuscrit du IXe Siècle," *Muséon* 76 (1963) 95.

similar homilies of his,[21] the *Catechetical Homilies* of Theodore of Mopsuestia (c. 350–428),[22] and the *Baptismal Catecheses* of John Chrysostom, the last of which will be treated extensively later. Within the city Greek was dominant; but once one passed the gates of the city it was Syriac.[23] As the metropolitan see of Syria, Antioch dominated the Syrian rite.[24]

The liturgical sources of the Syrian church are in an anomalous situation. In the period of the pre-Nicaean church we lack texts for the baptismal liturgy. On the other hand, for the period of the fourth to the sixth centuries no geographical area has so many and varied baptismal sources, though they are preserved mostly in Greek texts.[25] The first formal Eastern order of baptism is set out in the *Apostolic Constitutions* (hereafter *AC*), dated about 380, therefore during Cyril's life. I will be returning to the *AC* again in chapter 19. For present purposes I note that the *AC* have linguistic affinities to Cyril, and one of the four creeds given in the *AC* is also used by Cyril.[26] Given the great proliferation of creeds in the period after Nicaea this has some significance.

Liturgies are reflections of churches, and the *AC* mirror the confused situation in Antioch in the fourth century. The *AC* represent a concerted effort to impose order by learned use of the sources, false appeal to apostolicity, centralization of authority in the bishop, exhortations to obedience, and standardizing the charisms; what one would expect in a period of unrest.

The trinitarian and christological controversies after Nicaea made Antioch a city of turmoil. The church there was torn by

[21] PG 40 and 55. *See Clavis Patrum Graecorum*, 4 vols., ed. M. Geerard (Turnhout: Brepols, 1974) 2:137, 138.

[22] *Commentaries on the Lord's Prayer, Baptism and the Eucharist; Woodbrooke Studies* 6, ed. A. Mingana (Cambridge: Heffer, 1933); *Les Homélies Catéchétiques de Théodore de Mopsueste* (Studi e Testi 145), ed. R. Tonneau and R. Devreesse (Vatican City: Apostolic Vatican Library, 1949).

[23] Bardy, *Question des Langues*, 18, 19.

[24] H. M. Riley, *Christian Initiation* (Washington: Catholic University of America, 1974) 16.

[25] G. Kretschmar, "Die Geschichte des Taufgottesdienstes in der alten Kirche," *Leitourgia*, ed. K. F. Müller and W. Blankenburg (Kassel: Johannes Stauda, 1970) 133, 170; B. Botte, "Le baptême dans l'église syrienne," *OrSyr* 1 (1956) 136–55.

[26] M. Metzger, Introduction, *Les Constitutions Apostoliques*; SC 320:29.

schisms; three, then four, different bishops claimed the episcopal chair. For some years the bishops were Arian or Arianizing. The thunder of these quarrels reached Rome and Constantinople, and forced the involvement of the Council of Constantinople (381). The discord in Antioch, a Greek speaking city in a Syrian province, must have been heard in Greek and Syrian (and Latin) speaking populations of Jerusalem, and in the other churches with a Syrian population on their way to being taken over by Greek culture. The basic baptismal rite of Cyril, linguistically a Greek, was probably the old Syrian rite, which he modified.[27] At the time of Egeria the celebrations were in Greek, with translation for those speaking Syriac, a local dialect of Aramaic.[28]

As indicated, the rites being used in Egypt and Jerusalem were essentially the same at the beginning of the fourth century. At the end of that century another situation obtained; Jerusalem stood nearer Antioch because of developments in theology and liturgy during the preceding one hundred years.[29] Politically it was only under Juvenal (d. 458) who became bishop of Jerusalem in 422, that the mother of all churches broke free of the metropolitan Caesarea and the patriarchal Antioch. As if this new liberation were not enough, in 431 Juvenal announced that according to "the apostolic order and tradition," the see of Antioch should "be corrected and judged" by that of Jerusalem.[30] These bold claims were a threat to Caesarea and Antioch, but also to Alexandria and Rome.[31] Juvenal had gone far beyond Cyril in asserting independence, but Cyril had already marked out the path. Juvenal's was not a new initiative. Cyril gave the impetus to a new order, where Jerusalem set the liturgical agenda, Jerusalem sat in ritual judgment. What was left behind was subservience to Caesarea and Antioch, including liturgical submission.[32]

[27] E. J. Cutrone, "Cyril's Mystagogical Catecheses and the Evolution of the Jerusalem Anaphora," *OCP* 44 (1978) 53, 54.

[28] *Egeria's Travels*, 47:3; SC 296:314.

[29] Cuming, "Egyptian Elements," 123.

[30] E. Honigmann, "Juvenal of Jerusalem," *Dumbarton Oaks Papers* (Cambridge: Harvard University, 1950) 5:214, 215.

[31] Ibid., 217.

[32] Kretschmar, "Die Geschichte des Taufgottesdienstes," 34.

The determination of origin of the list of readings is related to this struggle. However one evaluates the verity of elements embedded in legendary material, it does seem probable that the list of biblical readings and the themes for catechizing (including the two on the Holy Spirit and the charisms), which Cyril used, were in place when he appeared on the scene, and that they were of some antiquity.[33] The list of scriptural readings "seems to have been very stable."[34] Indeed, the Bible readings remained the same for the successors of Cyril in the see of Jerusalem up until Juvenal, who became bishop of Jerusalem in 422.[35] Whether the succeeding bishops approached the subject matter of the 16th and 17th lectures on the Spirit and the charisms in the same manner in which Cyril did, is not determined. However if both the readings from scripture and the themes for the catecheses were determined by tradition, would not the same hold true for the teaching on the charisms and their relation to initiation? Stability and the search for apostolic links characterize the lists and themes.

A Sectarian? An Enthusiast?

The titles of catecheses 16 and 17 are quotations from 1 Corinthians 12:1-4 and 8. How does Cyril use *charisma*? Greek texts using *charisma*, whether biblical or post-biblical, need careful interpretation. In Paul there is no uniform meaning. In fact, a variety of meanings are found in Paul's later writings, as in Romans (12:6-8).[36] Salvation itself is a *charisma* (2 Cor 1:11; Rom 5:15). If one stays within the Pauline conceptuality there is no instrument for clearly distinguishing between structured ministries and ecclesiastical offices on the one hand, and on the

[33] Ibid., 338; Kretschmar, "Die frühe Geschichte der Jerusalemer Liturgie," *Jahrbuch für Liturgik und Hymnologie* (Kassel: Stauda, 1956) 2:23.

[34] E. Yarnold, "The Authorship of the Mystagogic Catecheses Attributed to Cyril of Jerusalem," *HeyJ* 19 (1978) 160.

[35] Kretschmar, "Die frühe Geschichte," 24.

[36] N. Baumert, "Charisma und Amt bei Paulus," *L'Apôtre Paul: Personalité, Style et Conception du Ministère,* ed. A. Vanhoye (Louvain: University Press, 1986) 207, 213-18. Baumert gives a useful overview of recent definitions of *charisma,* 203-06.

other, what later centuries will technically call *charismata*.[37]
Charisma cannot be placed in opposition to ecclesial authorities;
Paul intends to say the very opposite.[38] *Charisma* is also used to
indicate variety (1 Cor 7:7; 12:4-10; Rom 12:3-8; 1 Pet 4:10-11).
Some gifts are necessary for any form of Christian life: faith,
hope, and love (1 Cor 13:13). But Paul does not call these three
charismata. Others distinguish various forms of service: apostles,
prophets, teachers, helpers, administrators (1 Cor 12:28). Celibacy and marriage are both charisms (1 Cor 7:7), as is rescue
from mortal danger (2 Cor 1:11). In 1 Peter (4:10) any loving act
of service is a *charisma*. The more restrictive technical meaning
of prophetic gifts (miracles, healing, tongues, prophecy) as distinguished from teaching, helpers, administrators, has support
in the New Testament witness (Rom 12:6-8; 1 Cor 12:28), but is a
later development.[39] One can determine the meaning of *charisma*
in the New Testament, therefore, only from the context.[40]

Charisma in post-biblical Greek authors reflects and extends
the diversity of the New Testament usage. The range of meanings embraces divine and human gifts, gift of the Spirit, baptism, eucharist, endowment of the church, graces, special graces
(faith, prophecy, miracles); martyrdom, tears, theology.[41] Tertullian already begins to use charism in a more technical way,
with Origen giving it more clarity.[42]

In Cyril there are six explicit references to 1 Corinthians 12, including the titles of the two catecheses on the charisms, namely
16 and 17;[43] and there is one reference to Acts 19:6 ("when Paul
laid hands on them, the Holy Spirit came on them; and they

---

[37] A. Vanhoye, "The Biblical Question of Charisms," *Vatican II: Assessment and Perspectives*, 3 vols; ed. R. Latourelle (New York: Paulist, 1988)
1:464; E. Käsemann, "Ministry and Community in the New Testament,"
Essays on New Testament Themes (London: SCM, 1964) 63, 64.

[38] H. Conzelmann, "*charisma*," *TDNT*, 11:406; E. Käsemann, "Ministry
and Community," 63, 64; E. Cothenet, "Prophétisme et N.T. les grandes
Epitres de S. Paul," *DBSup* 8 (1972) 1302.

[39] Baumert, "Charisma und Amt," 205; Vanhoye, "The Biblical Question
of Charisms," 439–65.

[40] Conzelmann, "*charisma*," *TDNT* (1974) 9:403.

[41] *A Patristic Greek Lexicon*, ed. G. W. Lampe (Oxford: Clarendon, 1961).

[42] Baumert, "Charisma und Amt," 224.

[43] *CL* 5:11; *CAO* 1:146; *CL* 16:12; 17:2; 18:27; *CAO* 2:218, 220, 252, 330.

spoke with tongues and prophesied").[44] In the last catechesis before the celebration of the Easter Vigil Cyril lists "the heavenly charisms" of which the candidates should show themselves worthy. Some of the charisms included are miracles, healing, and tongues.[45] Cyril is no enthusiast, interested only in charismatic extravaganzas: exalted mountain-top experiences, dazzling miracles, exorcisms by the hundreds. Among the charisms which he mentions to the baptismal candidates are fasting, chastity or virginity, martyrdom, almsgiving, poverty, exorcism, wisdom, understanding, helpers, and administrators.[46] Cyril, then, does not have a narrow sectarian view of the charisms. He reflects the variety of the New Testament usage, including also the prophetic charisms.[47]

The Experience by which the Church Lives

Another link to antiquity is Irenaeus to whom Cyril refers toward the beginning of the two lectures on the Spirit and the charisms, but does not exploit.[48] Irenaeus is a witness to the historic faith of the church, the kerygmatic tradition, with which one has to reckon, a tradition which is, in Cyril's mind, apostolic and constant.[49] Cleaving to the permanent apostolic witness in the turbulent theological atmosphere after Nicaea,

---

[44] CL 17:30; CAO 2:288. Nowhere in the CL or in the MC does Cyril refer to the charisms as cited by Paul in Romans 12:6. There is one passing reference to Ephesians 4:11 in CL 13:29; CAO 2:88.

[45] CL 18:32; CAO 2:334.

[46] CL 16:12, 19, 21, 22, 31; 17:27 CAO 2:218, 228, 232, 234, 244, 246, 330. Beyond identifying the charisms, they get scant attention in C. Granado, "Pneumatologia de San Cirilo de Jerusalem," Estudios Eclesiasticos 58 (1983) 421–90, especially 481–83.

[47] Cyril sometimes uses dōrea, which in general Greek usage can also mean gift in a religious sense: gift of the Spirit, baptism, post-baptismal anointing, eucharist, Christ's teaching. Lampe, Patristic Lexicon, 395. Cyril can use forms of dōrea, sometimes in a context in which it is clear that he is using it as a synonym for charisma. In CL 18:29 (CAO 2:332), when speaking of "the heavenly charisms" he uses dōrea, while in CL 18:32 (CAO 2:334), when also referring to "the heavenly gifts," he uses charisma. Sometimes he will use a form of charis, e.g. CL 16:25; CAO 2:238.

[48] CL 16:6; CAO 2:210. The reference seems to be to AH 1, 2, 5; SC 264:44.

[49] CL 6:16; CAO 1:178.

Cyril avoids reference to contemporary controversies. For instance, Cyril never mentions the word which Nicaea employs to express the relation of the Son to the Father, *homōusios,* most likely because it was not found in the scriptures. Cyril wants to speak out of the pre-Nicaean church, of which Irenaeus is a major witness.[50] The experience of that history constitutes the kerygmatic tradition. Irenaeus recognizes the presence of "the prophetic charisms" in the tradition as he received it.[51] He will not allow the misuse of prophecy to disallow its use. The presence of false prophets is not to serve as a pretext "for expelling the grace of prophecy" from the church.[52]

Had Cyril read Irenaeus, or did he know Irenaeus through Eusebius (c. 260–339)? Though there is no evidence that Cyril had read Eusebius' *Ecclesiastical History* (hereafter *EH*), the first seven books were probably completed before 300, with further editions with new material in 315 and 325/326.[53] The earliest edition, therefore, was available about fifty years before Cyril preached his *CL* between 348 and 350. In addition, Eusebius was not a stranger to Jerusalem, being born in Palestine. He was present at the dedication of the Sepulcher, where he delivered not so much an oration as a treatise on the many virtues of Constantine, which are chapters 11–18 of the *Praises of Constantine.*[54] The Council of Tyre had been translated to Jerusalem at Constantine's request for the "lavish ceremonies" of dedication, which lasted a week (September 13–20, 335).[55] The dedication, then, was a conciliar event. Whatever else is thought of the reliability of Eusebius' reporting, the rather fulsome account of

---

[50] W. Telfer, General Introduction, *Cyril of Jerusalem and Nemesius of Emesa* (Philadelphia: Westminster, 1955) 63.

[51] *Demonstration of the Apostolic Preaching* 99; SC 62:169. *See also AH* 1:13, 4; SC 264:198; *AH* 4:26, 5; SC 100:726, 728.

[52] *AH* 3:11, 9; SC 211:172. "There are others who do not accept the charisms of the Holy Spirit, and thoroughly reject the prophetic charisms." *The Demonstration of the Apostolic Preaching* 99; SC 62:169. Cyril could have known this work directly, though, unlike *AH*, it is not cited by Eusebius in *Ecclesiastical History* (hereafter cited as *EH*).

[53] T. D. Barnes, *Constantine and Eusebius* (Cambridge: Harvard University, 1981) 277, 278.

[54] PG 20:1316-440. Quasten, *Patrology,* 3:327.

[55] Barnes, *Constantine and Eusebius,* 238, 248.

the Emperor's ambitious building program in Jerusalem which can be found in *The Life of Constantine* could stem from first hand observation.[56] In compiling the *Onomasticon*, a geographical index of the Bible, he seems to have used the libraries of both Caesarea and Jerusalem, a fact which does not exclude first hand personal knowledge of sites.[57] Further, writing the *Onomasticon* supposes an intimate knowledge of Jerusalem. Eusebius' interest would have gone beyond that of the normal devout seeker. In addition to the Sepulcher, there were, possibly, the basilicas on the Mount of Olives and in Bethlehem, built by Constantine's mother, Helen, who died about 330, five years before the dedication of the Holy Sepulcher. Cyril, who was ordained a priest by Maximus of Jerusalem about 345, was about 40 years old when the now aged Eusebius was in Jerusalem. Possibly Cyril gave the *CL* when he was still a comparatively young priest, though this role is usually reserved to the bishop. If he gave them while a priest, that would indicate that he was a person of distinction even before he became bishop.[58]

Some likelihood exists that Cyril had contact with Eusebius during the latter's stay in Jerusalem. If not contact, Cyril would have awareness of who Eusebius was, both because of Eusebius' role in the dedication and the books he wrote. This means that Cyril could be familiar with the teaching of Irenaeus either directly from the *Against the Heresies*, or *The Demonstration of the Apostolic Preaching*, or as the former is quoted by Eusebius in the *Ecclesiastical History*. Either way Cyril would have learned that the charisms belong both to the life of the church, and, significantly, to the apostolic proclamation of the gospel.

Irenaeus writes of the actuality of the charisms in the life of the church: "We have heard of many of the brethren who have foreknowledge of the future, visions, and prophetic utterances; others, by laying-on of hands, heal the sick and restore them to health."[59] Irenaeus hands on a further report of what he had heard: "We hear of many members of the church who have

---

[56] 3:25-43; PL 20:1086-101.

[57] D. E. Groh, "The *Onomasticon* of Eusebius and the Rise of Christian Palestine," *Studia Patristica* 18 (1975) 23-31.

[58] A. Paulin, *Saint Cyrille de Jérusalem Catéchète* (Paris: du Cerf, 1959) 25.

[59] *AH* 2:32, 4; SC 294:340, quoted by Eusebius in *EH* 5:7, 4; SC 41:34.

prophetic gifts, and, by the Spirit speak with all kinds of tongues, and bring men's secret thoughts to light for their own good, and expound the mysteries of God."[60] Some of the charisms were a matter of a report; not in all cases had he witnessed them himself. However for him the witnesses were reliable. The presence of the charisms was not a local phenomenon, but something which pertained to the universal church: "it is impossible to enumerate the charisms which throughout the world the church has received from God."[61] Eusebius, who quoted these texts in *EH*, concludes that the charisms were operative down to the time in which Irenaeus lived.[62] Though Eusebius is insistent in presenting Irenaeus' teaching on the charisms in a positive light, he tries to convey the impression that Irenaeus was inimical to Montanism, "an impression for which there is no evidence whatsoever."[63]

If Cyril had read Eusebius' *EH* he would also have found there some fragments of an anonymous second-century anti-Montanist who disapproved of Montanus' unnatural prophetic ecstasy. Montanus was "prophesying in a way that conflicted with the practice of the church handed down generation by generation from the beginning."[64] Prophecy itself was not reprobate; the manner was offensive. Finally, Eusebius quotes the anonymous author again to defend the continuing presence of prophecy in the church: "For the prophetic gifts must continue in the church until the final coming, as the apostle insists."[65] The position that the prophetic gifts belong constitutively to the church has biblical support (Eph 2:20).

If Cyril had read Irenaeus' *AH* instead of simply reading quotations from Irenaeus in Eusebius' *EH*, he would have seen that the charisms are presented in an ecclesiology of communion.

[60] *AH* 5:6, 1; SC 153:74, quoted by Eusebius in *EH* 5:7, 6; SC 41:34.
[61] *AH* 2:32, 4; SC 294:340, quoted by Eusebius in *EH* 5:7, 4; SC 41:34.
[62] *EH* 5:7, 6; SC 41:34.
[63] R. M. Grant, *Eusebius as Church Historian* (Oxford: Clarendon, 1980) 90.
[64] *EH* 5:16, 7; SC 41:48. On this anonymous author, who was probably a bishop or presbyter of one of the towns which together with Hieropolis and Otrous made up the Phrygian pentapolis situated in the region now known as Sandiliovasi near Sandikli in Turkey, see Tabbernee, "Opposition to Montanism from Church and State," 18–23.
[65] *EH* 5:17, 4; SC 41:54.

Although Irenaeus gives priority to the *teaching* charisms (apostles, prophets, teachers) he does recognize *all* the charisms in the church and sees the church as "the communion of Christ, that is, the Holy Spirit. . . . Where the church is, there also is the Spirit of God; where the Spirit of God is, there is the church and every grace."[66] The focus of Irenaeus' concern here is not theological speculation, but the life of the church.[67] Cyril may have also picked up the absence of any criticism of Montanism by Irenaeus, whereas the bishop of Lyons sharply criticizes those who use the excesses of Montanism as a pretext for extinguishing all prophecy.[68]

Dangerous Memories

Irenaeus' defense of the charisms should not be seen as an isolated instance. Quite the contrary; it was the general acceptability of prophecy in the life of the church which facilitated the spread of Montanism.[69] The New Prophecy had considerable credibility; it was "the most serious minded people who devoted themselves to the prophetic movement."[70]

Irenaeus and Apollinarius' teaching on the charisms belongs to the apostolic kerygmatic tradition out of which Cyril is operating.[71] He may be aware of other authors who would belong to the tradition of proclamation and are, at the same time, concerned with the charisms, such authors as Ignatius of Antioch,[72]

---

[66] *AH* 3:24, 1; SC 211:472, 474.

[67] A. Méhat, "Saint Irénée et les charismes," *Studia Patristica* 18 (1982) 723.

[68] Ibid., 720. Kretschmar, ["Le développement de la doctrine du Saint-Esprit du Nouveau Testament à Nicée," *VCaro* 22 (1968) 30] thinks that Irenaeus criticized the rigorist Montanists, to which Méhat replies that there are other expressions of rigorism than that found in Montanism. See also Tabbernee, "Opposition to Montanism from Church and State," 44–45.

[69] Ash, "The Decline of Prophecy," 236.

[70] W. Bauer, *Orthodoxy and Heresy in Earliest Christianity* (Philadelphia: Fortress, 1971) 137.

[71] It is not clear what other sources Cyril drew on, but teaching on the charisms would not be wanting. J. R. McRay, "*Charismata* in the Second Century," *Studia Patristica* 12, part 1, 232–37; H. von Camphenhausen, *Ecclesiastical Authority and Spiritual*, 178–212.

[72] Ignatius, Introduction to *Smyrnians*; *To Polycarp* 2:2; *To Philadelphians* 7:1, 2; SC 10:132, 148, 126.

Hermas,[73] Justin Martyr,[74] and the compiler of the *Didache*.[75]

In no sense is Cyril a scholar or speculative theologian. Rather, he is a pragmatic pastor who knows how to pass on the mysteries to baptismal candidates who are being received into the communion in the presence of ever increasing numbers of pilgrims. Cyril does not create "desk liturgies," that is, ideal liturgies thought up by academic liturgists in the privacy of their study. Rather he responds to the local situation which is full of dangerous and holy memories. Speaking of the opportunities which Jerusalem offers he says: "The most honored privileges are ours. Here Christ descended from heaven; here the Holy Spirit descended from heaven."[76] They are standing on the spot where the sacred blood was spilled, where the tongues of fire fell, where redemption was wrought. Cyril exploits the memories to capture the drama in symbol in the very "theater of salvation."[77] Most likely he is not thinking of the impact of what he is doing on Antioch, or Alexandria, or the universal church. He seems not to be looking beyond the religious needs of his own people and the pilgrims.[78]

In giving the catecheses which lead up to the Easter rites of initiation he remains the pastor; no attempt is made to play the theologian. Because of the theological uproar which had disturbed the church for decades (he was exiled and restored three times, the period after Nicaea being one of the most turbulent in the history of the church), Cyril states that he is only going to set forth what is in the scriptures.[79]

In summary: at the beginning of the fourth century Jerusalem was related liturgically to Alexandria and Antioch, the two nearest major metropolitan and cultural centers. One tradition

[73] Hermas, *The Shepherd*, "Mandates" 11:1-3, 9, 12; SC 53bis:192, 194, 196.
[74] Justin Martyr, *Dialogue with Trypho*, 30, 31, 82, 88; PG 6:540, 541, 669, 672, 685.
[75] *Didache*, 10, 11; SC 228.
[76] CL 16:4; CAO 2:208, 210.
[77] G. Dix, *The Shape of the Liturgy* (New York: Seabury, 1945, 1982) 352.
[78] Ibid.
[79] "Let us assert of the Holy Spirit only what is written: let us not busy ourselves about what is not written." CL 16:2. "For if it had been written, we would have spoken of it." CL 16:24; CAO 2:206, 236.

claims that Jerusalem received its reading list from Alexandria. Though possibly legendary, it may have a historical basis. If at the beginning of the fourth century the rite in Egypt and Jerusalem were the same, at the end of that century the theological and liturgical development in Jerusalem placed it nearer to Antioch. Whatever the liturgical and theological antecedents, the lists of readings and the teachings on the Spirit and the charisms were in place when Cyril appeared on the scene. Furthermore, they were probably of some antiquity.

Cyril was no enthusiast, all caught up in the prophetic charisms. His teaching on the charisms reflects the range of meanings found in the New Testament and in the other Greek authors of the first centuries. That spectrum of meanings included the prophetic charisms.

The broad range of charisms were witnessed to both in scripture and in the living experience of the church. Irenaeus is the only author Cyril mentions at the beginning of his two tracts on the charisms. Cyril could have known Irenaeus either directly or as mediated through Eusebius' *Ecclesiastical History*. Irenaeus reports the prophetic charisms actual in the church of his own day from witnesses whom he judged to be reliable. The bishop of Lyons understood the charisms to abound in the church with great variety. He is especially protective of prophecy. The abuse of prophecy must not lead to the church's rejection of prophecy. The tradition remained that prophecy must remain in the church until the Lord returns. In some way prophecy belongs to the deepest nature of the church. Prophecy and the other charisms found their primary context in the church as a communion in the Holy Spirit.

Chapter Sixteen

Cyril of Jerusalem:
The Geography and History
of the Spirit

Like Tertullian, and Hilary, Cyril speaks out of a communion ecclesiology. Within this context I will examine Cyril's teaching on the imposition of hands and anointing. From there I will move to a study of Cyril's temporal history of salvation and his spatial geography of salvation.

In the *CL* the communion is effected by the Holy Spirit in context of the resurrection. The risen Lord stands before the apostles, and breathes his breath upon them.[1] This, Cyril notes, was the second breathing; the first was at the creation of Adam's soul, which had been tarnished by sin. Not as a stranger does the Spirit come at Pentecost. Cyril notes the special quality of this second sending of the Spirit; Christ "imparted the communion of the Spirit to the apostles."[2]

The *CL* ends with a promise that in the post-Easter catecheses an explanation of "how they have received communion in the name of Christ, and how the seal of the communion of the Holy Spirit has been given."[3] As the *MC* are drawing to a close

[1] *CL* 17:12; *CAO* 2:262.
[2] *CL* 17:12; *CAO* 2:266.
[3] *CL* 18:33; *CAO* 2:336.

with the catechesis on the eucharist, Cyril reminds the new Christians that when the words "O taste and see that the Lord is good," are chanted they are being invited "by a sacred melody to communion in the holy mysteries."[4] After having "communion in the body of Christ" they extend their hands to receive the chalice of his blood. At the very end of *MC* Cyril gives one last exhortation: "Never cut yourself off from the communion," expressing that necessary bond between eucharistic communion and ecclesial communion.[5]

The rite of initiation brings about the communion in the sufferings of Christ; the communion is symbolic, and the salvation therein imparted is real.[6] In the *CL* Cyril explicitly states that "Peter imparted the Spirit by the imposition of hands."[7] He adds that the same Spirit will be given to the candidates. Then, very likely because of the discipline of the secret (certain matters were kept secret except from the fully initiated), he arouses the candidates' curiosity, saying, "in what manner I do not say, for I do not anticipate the proper time."[8] Cyril here acts as a mystagogue, one who leads others into the mysteries. Throughout the *CL*, in a gradual unfolding, step by step, he brings them not to behold, but to become actors, having communion in the mysteries which are proper to Christ.

---

[4] *MC* 5:20; SC 126:168.

[5] *MC* 5:23; SC 126:174. *See also* 1:4; 2:3, 5, 6, 7; 4:7; SC 126:88, 108, 112-18, 140, 141. That Cyril speaks a communion language common to the Jerusalem church as well as the church at large can be seen by the remark of Rufinus, who lived in a double monastery in Jerusalem between 381 and 397, therefore literally down the road, for the last six years of Cyril's life. Referring to Cyril's early reluctance to embrace the *homōusios* of Nicaea, to his problematic ordination, and to his promotion to the episcopacy by Acacius of Caesarea, who had heavy Arian proclivities, Rufinus called attention to Cyril's "acceptance of a confused priestly ordination, his penchant for sometimes varying in the faith, and often changing communions." "*Aliquando in fide, saepius in communione variabat.*" *Ecclesiastical History* 23; PL 21:495. Cyril, who did not have much sympathy for Athanasius' position, very likely objected to *homōusios* because it was non-scriptural. Eventually he associated himself with the neo-Nicenes. A. A. Stephenson, "S. Cyril of Jerusalem's Trinitarian Theology," *Studia Patristica* 11 (1972) 240.

[6] *MC* 2:5; SC 126:112, 114.

[7] *CL* 16:26: CAO 2:240.

[8] Ibid.

Cyril's formulation in the CL suggests that the laying on of hands, a rite imparting the Spirit, will be explained later. However, there is no mention of the imposition of hands in the MC.[9] Yarnold suggests that in CL there was a laying on of hands, which took place in the font, but this is not referred to in the text of CL because of the discipline of the secret.[10] The imposition of hands as part of the immersion rite is, as we shall see, in harmony with John Chrysostom. Whether with or without the laying on of hands, in the CL the Spirit is imparted while the candidate is still in the water,[11] while in MC the gift of the Spirit is given in chrismation after the water-bath.[12]

The candidates go down into the water-bath and rise out of the waters. What is the symbolic content of this descent into and ascent out of the baptismal waters? Is the primary locus in John 3 (birth image) or in Romans 6:3-11 (death and resurrection image)?[13] The theme of death and resurrection is not found in the earlier Syrian liturgies.[14] The early Armenian and Syriac churches chose the birth image, which they related to the baptism of Jesus, considering it the origin and living source of Christian baptism.[15] As Ephrem (c.306-73) said, Christ's baptism in the Jordan "opens up baptism."[16] In the older, purer Syriac tradition the Romans 6 passage seemingly made no impression on baptismal theology.[17]

---

[9] Cyril does allude to aiding someone by the imposition of hands in his *On the Paralytic* 16; CAO 2:422.

[10] Yarnold, "The Authorship of the Mystagogic Catecheses," 159.

[11] CL Proto.,4; 3:3, 4; CAO 1:8, 66, 68.

[12] MC 3:1, 2; CAO 2:364, 366.

[13] This is a major theme of Gabriele Winkler, *Das Armenische Initiationsrituale* (Rome: Pontifical Oriental Institute, 1982) 335-70; "The Original Meaning and Implications of the Prebaptismal Anointing," *Worship* 52 (1978) 24-45. This section is indebted to Winkler's research.

[14] E. C. Ratcliff, "The Old Syrian Baptismal Tradition and its Resettlement under the Influence of Jerusalem in the Fourth Century," *Liturgical Studies*, ed. A. H. Courtain and D. H. Tripp (London: SPCK, 1976) 142.

[15] S. Brock, *The Luminous Eye* (Rome: Centre for Indian and Inter-religious Studies, 1985) 70.

[16] Ephrem, *On Virginity*, 15:3; CSCO 224:50, 51.

[17] Ratcliff, "The Old Syrian Baptismal Tradition and its Resettlement under the Influence of Jerusalem in the Fourth Century," 142.

Cyril chooses both the mystery of Jesus' baptism in the Jordan and that of his death and resurrection. Here our concern is his use of the birth symbol in relation to the baptism of Jesus. At the Jordan Jesus was identified as the Messiah, the Anointed One, because on coming up from the waters Jesus was anointed, but not with perishable oil. "The Holy Spirit descended in substance upon him, like resting upon like."[18] The One from above rested on the One from above. This formulation, taken from Numbers 11:25, 26, presents the anointing with the Spirit as divine authentication of leadership, a new charismatic authority. "For Christ was not christened by men with oil of material ointment, but the Father, having appointed him to be the Savior of the whole world, anointed him with the Holy Spirit."[19] Cyril here appeals to Peter's sermon in the house of Cornelius, when Peter identified Christ as "Jesus from Nazareth, whom God anointed with the Holy Spirit" (Acts 10:38). The claim to be the One anointed with the Holy Spirit, Cyril notes, is also based on Jesus' own claim: "The Spirit of the Lord is upon me, because he has anointed me to preach the good news to the poor" (Isa 61:1; Luke 4:17).[20]

Christian baptism is "an imitation as in an icon" of Christ's baptism.[21] Referring to Christ's baptism Cyril says: "All of this was accomplished in you in a figure, because you are icons of Christ."[22] The outward form and the inward substance are the same in Christ and in us: "In the same manner for you also, after you had come up from the pool of the sacred streams, there was the anointing, the exact figure of that with which Christ was anointed. And this was the Holy Spirit."[23] The candidate is anointed on the forehead and on the organs of sense. Because of Cyril's realistic view of the *epiclēsis,* the anointing not only gives the indwelling divinity to the candidates, but makes them sensitive to things spiritual, arms them against the forces of evil, and saves them from the shame of sin.[24]

[18] *MC* 3:1; SC 126:122.
[19] *MC* 3:2; SC 126:122.
[20] Ibid.
[21] *MC* 2:5; SC 126:114.
[22] *MC* 3:1; SC 126:120.
[23] Ibid.
[24] *MC* 3:4, 7; SC 126:126, 130, 132.

Three times Cyril repeats an anti-Marcion control: the Spirit is the same in the Old and New Testaments.[25] Proceeding on this assumption Cyril traces the history of the Spirit from Moses through the prophets, the judges, the conception of Jesus, his baptism, the impartation of the Spirit to the apostles by the risen Christ, Pentecost, and the life of the church as recounted in Acts.[26] Of special significance are the titles of the two catecheses which narrate the geography and history of the Spirit. They are taken from Paul's double list of charisms in 1 Corinthians 12. Cyril, then, would have a broad understanding of charism. Within that expanse one finds the prophetic charisms.

Beginning, then, with Moses there is a continuous history of the Spirit, a charismatic succession. The Spirit who is the constant in this variable succession, Cyril insists, is like a vine which remains the same through the seasons (read Old and New Testaments), but brings forth new grapes. So too the Spirit is the same in both Testaments. Cyril stresses the continuity of the one plan of salvation, which in this instance is assured by the charismatic succession. At the same time he clearly states the newness: initiation has to do with "a new kind of water," "a new wine," namely, "the grace of the New Testament."[27] The grace given to the Old Testament leaders is now poured out in superabundance, "something new and marvelous."[28]

The spectrum of history—continuity—newness is Cyril's preoccupation. Cyril will range forward and backward along this extension. To Joshua who asked Moses to forbid Eldad and Medad to prophesy (Num 11:28) Moses replied: "Would that all the people of the Lord might prophesy whenever the Lord shall give them his spirit" (Num 11:29). When the spirit on Moses came down on the seventy elders, they began to prophesy. This, Cyril declares, is an image of "what was to come to pass among us on the day of Pentecost."[29] The God who gave par-

---

[25] *CL* 16:4, 6; 17:5, 18; *CAO* 2:208, 212, 258, 272.
[26] *CL* 16:25, 26; *CAO* 2:236, 238, 240.
[27] *CL* 16:11; 17:18; *CAO* 2:216, 272.
[28] *CL* 17:18; *CAO* 2:272.
[29] *CL* 16:26; *CAO* 2:240.

tially then, will give abundantly now.[30] The prophetic Spirit will come down on the Christian community. The history of the Spirit pours itself into baptism: "(The Spirit) heralded Christ in the prophets; (the Spirit) wrought (salvation) in the Apostles; and to this day (the Spirit) seals souls in Baptism."[31] During the rites of initiation the catechumens will be inserted into this history. The history of the Spirit goes on; but it is not an isolated history of the Spirit and the charisms. The continuing history is one because the Father reaches through the Son in the Spirit to bestow the charisms. "The charisms of the Father are not different from the charisms of the Son, or those of the Holy Spirit."[32] This trinitarian dynamic, in which the charisms belong, has as its goal "one salvation, one power, one faith."[33]

"A New Kind of Water"

The two lectures on the Holy Spirit, 16 and 17, are schematically commentaries on the pneumatological article of the Jerusalem creed, the first part of which reads "We believe . . . in the Holy Spirit and Paraclete who spoke in the prophets." That the Spirit spoke in the prophets is of considerable importance to Cyril. "All the saints" of the Old Testament had the Spirit, including the ones whose names we do not know.[34] The plan of salvation is one in the two Testaments.

The Spirit which spoke in Moses speaks also in Jesus. Before Jesus departed he committed himself to a continuation of the charismatic succession which began in Moses, and has its penultimate goal in the Pentecost experience. Basing himself on the promise Jesus made to his disciples ("I will ask the Father and he will give you another Paraclete," John 14:16), Cyril refers to the Pentecost event which took place in the very city in which he and his audience were, thus eliciting powerful memories still tied to Jerusalem. "Sacramental imagination" plays a large role in Cyril, a perspective to which Jerusalem lends it-

[30] *CL* 16:26; *CAO* 2:238.
[31] *CL* 16:24; *CAO* 2:236.
[32] Ibid.
[33] Ibid.
[34] *CL* 16:27; *CAO* 2:240.

self.[35] Altogether standing on Golgatha where the blood of Jesus flowed, or in the Upper Room in which the Spirit came as the rush of a mighty wind, in the very places where salvation was accomplished, walking on the stones on which Jesus walked, a new experience, another entrance into the mystery, is opened to the believer. That is why the Spirit is "a new kind of water."[36]

The Countries of the Spirit

Cyril chooses power categories to introduce the section on the charisms: "Great, omnipotent, and admirable is the Holy Spirit in the charisms."[37] Basing himself on the apostolic kerygmatic tradition, the living experience of the church, Cyril demonstrates the might of the Spirit in the charisms. In setting forth the tradition as a source of his teaching on baptism and the charisms, Cyril wanted to contrast the oneness of the Spirit with the diversity of those who receive. Charisms are given to each, because the Spirit knows what each says, or thinks, or believes. One Spirit is received by all, but experience differs according to the dispositions. No attempt was made to limit the charisms to bishops, priests, deacons. The experience also of solitaries, virgins, and, most significantly, "all the laity," are called to witness to the power of the Spirit in the charisms.[38] In the immediate context his appeal is to the experience throughout the world of the charisms of chastity, virginity, almsgiving, poverty, exorcism.[39] But in the same catechesis he recalls that the Spirit coming down as rain effects wisdom in one, in another prophecy, in another the power of exorcism, in yet another martyrdom.[40] Twice Cyril repeats the Pauline list of charisms in 1 Corinthians 12:7-11.[41] Cyril has a broad view of the charisms. While including the prophetic (tongues, healing, prophecy, miracles) the list extends beyond them to a variety of

[35] F. Cardman, "The Rhetoric of Holy Places," *Studia Patristica* 17 (1982) 1, 23.
[36] *CL* 16:11; *CAO* 2:216.
[37] *CL* 16:22; *CAO* 2:232.
[38] *CL* 16:22; *CAO* 2:234.
[39] Ibid.
[40] *CL* 16:12; *CAO* 2:218.
[41] *CL* 16:12; *CAO* 2:218, 330.

ministries and states.[42] The prophetic charisms are possibilities for the church.

Cyril plays on the contrast of the one Spirit in the many states of life. That is not enough for Cyril; he gives a geography of the Spirit. Beyond a casual allusion to Irenaeus as a representative of the church's experience, Cyril refers to the experience of the church in Jerusalem. Perhaps, he asks, the people of Jerusalem think it overly bold to assert that the Spirit and the charisms are present in such a great diversity of personalities. Actually, Cyril said, this is not bold enough. The truth is more glorious. Cyril then demonstrates the spectrum of diversity by appealing to the experience in his diocese, in the province of Palestine, and in the whole Roman Empire.[43] The full range of persons in the church demonstrates the presence of the charisms. For all in the church the Spirit is "the dispenser of their charisms."[44] Such an appeal to the whole of the local church, and to all the local churches in "the whole Roman Empire," and then "in the whole world" is an attempt to make a statement about the universal experience of the charisms, possibly an echo of Irenaeus: "It is impossible to enumerate the charisms which the church throughout the world has received from God."[45]

This experience "throughout the whole world," has shown that the Spirit is not a reluctant giver of the gifts, but pours them out "profusely."[46] No nationality is excluded from this lavish outpouring: "Let your mind range from this province (of Palestine) to the whole Roman Empire; then fix your gaze on the whole world; there are races of Persians, nations of Indians, Goths, Sarmatians, Gauls and Spaniards, Moors, Libyans, and Ethiopians."[47] Lest there be lands and nations unknown to Cyril, he adds "others whose names are unknown to us."[48] After reviewing the parade of races and nations endowed with

[42] CL 17:37; CAO 2:296.
[43] CL 16:22; CAO 2:232.
[44] CL 16:22; CAO 2:234.
[45] CL 16:22; CAO 2:232; AH 294:340.
[46] CL 16:26; CAO 2:238.
[47] CL 16:22; CAO 2:232.
[48] Ibid.

the charisms, Cyril concludes with a peroration. "You have seen . . . (the Spirit's) power exercised throughout the world."[49] From the geographic universality of the charisms and the presence of the charisms in all states of life, Cyril argues to the assurance that the candidates for baptism will not be excluded from the largess.

Completely Baptized

For Cyril the baptism of Jesus at the Jordan is a rite identification. The one on whom the Holy Spirit descended as a dove is the one who baptizes in the Holy Spirit. What is given to us is first manifested in the baptism of Jesus. The first fruits and gifts of the Spirit conferred on Jesus at the Jordan are his to impart to others,[50] especially at the resurrection. The Risen Savior appeared to the apostles and breathed the Spirit upon them, not for the first time, but the second. At creation God formed Adam from the dust of the earth and breathed into his nostrils the breath of life.[51]

Cyril then builds up a series of parallels between incomplete and complete, partially and fully. This breathing on the apostles immediately after the resurrection was an imparting of the Spirit. But it was partial. In the future, that is at Pentecost, the Risen Christ will be more lavish.

To give concreteness to his category of fullness Cyril joins the image of clothing to that of baptizing. The function of the Spirit at Pentecost is "to clothe with power and to baptize."[52] Piling image on image Cyril shifts to water encompassing the whole person who is immersed in it, joining Christian baptism to Pentecost. The grace given to the apostles "was not partial, but his [the Spirit's] power in all fullness. For just as one immersed in the waters of baptism is completely encompassed by the water, so they were completely baptized by the Spirit."[53]

Cyril takes up an image dear to the early authors: a piece of cold black iron thrust into the fire. As the fire penetrates the

---

[49] CL 16:23; CAO 2:234.
[50] CL 17:9; CAO 2:260.
[51] CL 17:12; CAO 2:266.
[52] CL 17:14; CAO 2:268.
[53] Ibid.

mass of the cold iron, it becomes hot, making what was black bright. So at baptism the Spirit penetrates completely into the most interior part of the soul. "The water encompasses the body externally, but the Holy Spirit baptizes the soul perfectly within."[54]

Now Cyril turns to the Pentecost event when the house where the apostles were gathered is filled with a mighty wind. "The disciples were within and the whole house was filled. Therefore they were baptized without anything wanting, according to the promise."[55] Or more literally, there was nothing wanting to their baptism. To approach completeness from a different perspective Cyril returns to a clothing image: the apostles "were clothed in body and soul with a divine and saving garment."[56] Because they were completely baptized in the Spirit the apostles spoke in tongues as the Spirit gave them utterance. The Spirit who had been manifested in the Old Testament prophets "now manifested something new and marvelous."[57] Though something of the Spirit had been given to the prophets, "now it came in superabundance; in their (the prophets) case they received a share of the Holy Spirit, now they (the apostles) were baptized in all fullness."[58]

When Cyril calls initiation the "baptism in the Holy Spirit" he is not innovating.[59] On the contrary, he is carrying on a living tradition as seen in Justin Martyr,[60] Origen,[61] and Didymus the Blind.[62] They either call the whole rite the baptism in the Holy Spirit, or apply to the initiatory rite the words of Jesus to the apostles, "before many days you shall be baptized with the Holy Spirit" (Acts 1:5).

Prepare to Receive the Heavenly Charism: Prophecy

Never does Cyril recommend that the faithful be open to the charism of tongues. Very likely this is due to his conviction that

[54] CL 17:14; CAO 2:268.
[55] CL 17:15; CAO 2:268, 270.
[56] Ibid.
[57] Ibid.
[58] CL 17:18; CAO 2:272.
[59] CL 16:6; CAO 2:213.
[60] Justin Martyr, *Dialogue with Trypho*, 29:1; PG 6:537.
[61] Origen, *On Jeremiah*, 2:3; SC 232:244.

tongues is a miraculous gift, more than that, a spectacularly miraculous gift. Following Luke he understands it as the gift of a foreign language. But he does see the relation between tongues and baptism. For him the Pentecost event was their baptism, indeed their water baptism, because the Spirit is a new kind of water. Because Pentecost is baptismal the apostles speak in tongues. Earlier Cyril had noted the link between tongues and water baptism.[63] Of all the charisms Cyril singled out one. Cyril cites Luke's presentation of the Pentecost event of Acts 2 as a fulfillment of Joel's prophecy: "I will pour forth my spirit upon all flesh; and your sons and daughters shall prophesy" (2:28). Then Cyril encourages his flock not to be concerned about worthiness because of social position. When the Spirit pours out the prophetic charism the Spirit is no respecter of persons, whether rich or poor. "Only let each one prepare oneself to receive the heavenly gift (singular)," namely, prophecy.[64] In the seventeenth catechesis, near the end of the whole Lenten series, Cyril expresses a wish: "God grant that you may be worthy of the charism of prophecy."[65] Those "who are about to be baptized even now in the Holy Spirit," should bring with them an expanded expectation.[66] They need only make large their awareness and "he will grant you charisms of every kind."[67] He speaks of the candidates' subjective openness to the charisms: "My final words, beloved brethren, in this instruction, will be words of exhortation, urging all of you to prepare your souls for the reception of the heavenly charisms (plural)."[68]

In summary, the laying on of hands in the CL may have been part of the immersion rite, as it will be in John Chrysostom. For Cyril in the MC the imparting of the Spirit is not a part of the going down into the water, but is tied to the post-baptismal anointing. Here the baptism of Jesus determines the ritual expression of the imparting of the Spirit: as Christ was anointed

[62] Didymus the Blind, *On the Trinity*, 2:12; PG 39:668, 673.
[63] CL 3:4; CAO 1:68.
[64] CL 17:19; CAO 2:274.
[65] CL 17:37; CAO 2:296.
[66] CL 16:6; CAO 2:212.
[67] CL 17:37; CAO 2:296.
[68] CL 18:32; CAO 2:334.

with the Holy Spirit on coming up out of the waters of the Jordan, so the Christian is anointed with oil after the water bath. The Jordan is Christ's baptism in the Holy Spirit, and the imitation of that mystery is the Christian's baptism in the Holy Spirit. Appealing to the transformative power of the Spirit, Cyril moves from the eucharist to the chrism. These mysteries bring one into a communion in the Spirit, which is baptismal, eucharistic, and ecclesial.

Communion in the Spirit belongs to a temporal succession. The same Spirit, given to Moses and the prophets, is given to the apostles. At Pentecost the history of the Spirit continues. In lavish abundance the Spirit, as "a new kind of water," is abundantly poured out on the church. A charismatic succession links the two testaments.

Cyril outlines a geography of salvation. The Spirit as the dispenser of the charisms, showers gifts upon the local church, the church in Palestine, and upon the whole world. The appeal is to a geographical universality. Another kind of universality is the common experience of all states of life, including the laity. Based on the experience of the church Cyril asks all those who are about to be baptized in the Holy Spirit to widen their expectations for the charisms. Of the experience of the apostles at Pentecost Cyril says that they were fully baptized. As a pastor he especially wants them to be found worthy of the charism of prophecy.

Chapter Seventeen

Cyril of Jerusalem: From Outside the Mystery to Inside

In the Proto-Catechesis which introduces the *CL* Cyril tells the candidates for baptism that they "will grasp by experience the sublimity of the doctrines."[1] What characterizes the *CL* is "knowledge" (*gnosis*), the word for the Easter Vigil celebration (and the other rites related to it) is "experience" (*peira*), the one word for *MC* is "memory" (*anamnēsis*), or more precisely "the memory of the experience." Whereas the *CL* are didactic and expansive, the *MC* are evocative and terse. Where the *CL* move outside the mystery of Christ's birth, baptism, death and resurrection, the *MC* move boldly within by participation. The *MC* call to remembrance the experience of the Easter celebration, the communion in the mysteries, when the catechumens fully realized the sublimity of the knowledge imparted to them during the whole course of the *CL*. I will be examining this passage from Martyrium to Anastasis, from knowledge to experience to memory, from outside the mystery to inside.

As indicated, the distinction between the *CL* and the *MC* was given architectural expression. The *CL* were delivered in the body of the church, while the *MC* in a building slightly set

[1] Cyril, Proto-Catechesis, 12; *CAO* 1:16.

apart, but architecturally related.[2] The neophytes gathering there were now clothed in their resplendent white garment received during the Easter Vigil celebration.

What the Spirit Touches, the Spirit Changes

According to Cyril's teaching in the *CL*, the charisms belong to the normal functioning of the ordinary Christian community. Cyril supports his teaching on the charisms by an appeal to the experience of the universal church, including the experience of the laity. Cyril wishes that the candidates prove themselves worthy of the charism of prophecy.

In the last catechesis of the *CL* before the Easter Vigil, Cyril told the candidates that during the days after the celebration of the mysteries, that is, the week after Easter, they will gather in the chapel of the Resurrection to hear "the reasons for everything which has been done."[3] While the *CL* are more doctrinal, given before the baptismal experience, the *MC* are clarifications, explanations, given after that experience. In the first catechesis after Easter Cyril enunciates the principle of mystagogy on which the *MC* are built: "seeing is far more persuasive than hearing."[4] Experience precedes explanation. Mystagogy, not didactic instructions, surrenders the ultimate reasons. From outside the mystery the teacher marks the road through knowledge to experience. From inside the mystery the mystagogue leads the way through memory to insight. The bishop/mystagogue, takes the neophytes on a journey into the center of the remembered experience where they have communion again in the mysteries of Christ's baptism, the mystery of his passion and death, the mystery of "the heavenly bread and the cup of salvation."[5] In the clarity of that memory they relive the meaning

[2] A. Grabar, *Martyrium: Recherches sur le Culte des Reliques et l'Art Chrétien Antique*, 3 vols. (Paris: Collège de France, 1946); *Egeria's Travels*, ed. J. Wilkinson (London: SPCK, 1971) 36–53; Telfer, *Cyril and Nemesius*, 43–54; C. Coüasnon, *The Church of the Holy Sepulchre in Jerusalem* (London: Oxford University, 1974). Stephenson raises some doubts as to where the *MC* were delivered. *The Works of Saint Cyril of Jerusalem*, 2:150, 151.

[3] *CL* 18:33; *CAO* 2:336.

[4] *MC* 1:1; *SC* 126:82.

[5] *MC* 4:5; *SC* 126:138.

of the mysteries which the rites themselves reveal. Memory expands the experience. They enter the full expanse of "the new truths," the reality of those who have been "renewed from oldness to newness."[6]

In the MC Cyril proposes a highly realistic conception of the role of the Spirit. Cyril annunciates the principle: "whatever the Holy Spirit touches is hallowed and changed."[7] The transformative function of the Spirit is seen first in relation to the eucharistic prayer for the Spirit to come down on the offerings (epiclēsis) of bread. The now elderly bishop draws on this teaching to explain the realistic conception of the anointing, in which the Holy Spirit is communicated.[8] "Your salvation began from him who was anointed by the Holy Spirit in truth."[9] As we have seen, Cyril taught that the Spirit descended on Jesus when he came up from the Jordan, so now the Spirit descends on the candidate after the neophyte comes up from the water-bath and is being anointed.[10] Cyril is concerned that the oil of chrism, used for the anointing, might be thought of as ordinary oil. Pushing the eucharistic analogy, Cyril asserts that just "as the bread of the Eucharist, after the invocation of the Holy Spirit, is no longer mere bread, but the Body of Christ, so also this holy ointment after the invocation is no longer simple ointment."[11] The transformed oil is "the gracious gift of Christ and the Spirit, producing [the presence of?] his deity."[12] Those anointed with this efficacious oil have "communion and participation in Christ."[13] Bold language even for a mystagogue.[14] Whatever differences may exist between the 348 theology of the CL in Cyril's younger years, and the 380s (sometime before 387) theology of the MC in his last years, the force of the Holy Spirit is in no way diminished.

[6] MC 2:1; SC 126:104.
[7] MC 5:7; SC 126:154.
[8] MC 3:3; SC 126:124.
[9] MC 3:6; SC 126:128, 130.
[10] MC 3:1; SC 126:120, 122.
[11] MC 3:3; SC 126:124.
[12] Ibid.
[13] MC 3:2; SC 126:124.
[14] Though the subsequent tradition will show special reverence for the oil

How does Cyril handle the charisms when one moves from the CL to the MC, from the more didactic catechesis to the realistic mystagogy? Strange to say, in the MC there is not one clear mention of the charisms.[15] The ambiguity in the one reference to the charisms in MC is by indirection. Wishing to highlight the spiritual riches which baptism confers, Cyril says that no one should think that these riches consist only of the remission of sins, or even merely adoption. "No, we know full well, that as it purges our sins, and conveys to us *the gift of the Holy Spirit*, so also it is the representation of Christ's sufferings."[16] Besides forgiveness of sins, adoption, and the communion/participation in the passion, Cyril adds "the gift of the Holy Spirit."

A. A. Stephenson noted that "the gift of the Spirit" or "the giving of the Spirit" "often denotes such inessential graces as charismata, speaking with tongues, working miracles, etc."[17] This interpretation is based on the usage in Acts, where the phrase "the gift of the Spirit" means the imparting or receiving of the Spirit itself and the charisms. Peter's sermon following the coming of the Spirit "makes the Pentecost event an essential part of the discourse."[18] Whoever repents and is baptized in the name of Jesus Christ will receive forgiveness of sins and "the gift of the Holy Spirit" (Acts 2:38). What the apostles received at Pentecost, the believers will receive at baptism.[19] "The gift of God" (Acts 8:20) which Simon wanted to buy was externally manifest in charisms.[20] Cyril uses this biblical shorthand phrase in the MC for the charisms.

after the invocation of the Spirit upon it, the church never fully accepted the parallel Cyril erected between the eucharistic and the chrism epiclesis.

[15] A case might be made for exorcism in MC 3:4, but this seems to be a grace enjoyed by the recipient, not a charism meant in service of others.

[16] MC 2:6; SC 126:114.

[17] Stephenson, *The Works of Saint Cyril of Jerusalem*, 2:176.

[18] R. F. Zehnle, *Peter's Pentecost Discourse* (Nashville: Abingdon, 1971) 42.

[19] J. D. G. Dunn, *Baptism in the Holy Spirit*, 56, 7–73; Dunn, *Jesus and the Spirit* 163–71.

[20] E. Haenchen, *The Acts of the Apostles* (Philadelphia: Westminster, 1971) 304; C. K. Barrett, *The Holy Spirit and the Gospel Tradition* (London: SPCK, 1947) 140–62.

But this is not a new development. Even in the *CL* he uses biblical shorthand. Pentecost is the paradigm. Cyril measures the gift of the Spirit with the charisms experienced in the mission of the church by the Pentecost experience in Acts 2, where the Spirit and the charisms also belong together: "They have received the Spirit just as we have . . . the Holy Spirit came down on them in the same way as it came on us at the beginning" (Acts 10:44; 11:15, 17). So "the gift of the Spirit," and "the gift of God," and "the grace of the Holy Spirit," seem to include the charisms also in *CL*.[21] Cyril has another expression for the charisms and graces, namely, "the communication of the Holy Spirit."[22] Cyril thinks the imparting of the charisms and graces is in proportion to the candidates' fervor. This includes, among other things, the charism of the special faith which moves mountains.[23]

"The communication of the Spirit" is twice related to the forgiveness of sins.[24] And it also seems to mean special graces,[25] which in one instance he identifies as being able "to accomplish deeds beyond human power," which in turn is itself followed by a wish that the candidates be worthy of the charism of prophecy.[26] In both cases there is a subjective disposition: "the communication of the Holy Spirit is granted in proportion to the faith of each" and "according to your capacity."[27] Cyril, therefore, uses biblical shorthand for charisms in both the *CL* and the *MC*. The charisms have not been abandoned in the *MC*.

False Windows or Pastoral Reality?

Could it be possible that Cyril and other fourth-century authors feel bound to issue a ritual, purely formal declaration asserting the theoretical permanence of prophecy in the church, while knowing that in reality it belongs to a distant past? Are they

---

[21] *CL*, 3:15; 16:10, 12; *CAO* 1:84; 2:216, 218.

[22] *CL* 1:5; *CAO* 1:34. *See* Stephenson, *The Works of Saint Cyril of Jerusalem*, 94, note 18.

[23] *CL* 5:11; *CAO* 1:146.

[24] *CL* 1:15; *CAO* 1:34; *CL* 17:37; *CAO* 2:296.

[25] Stephenson, *The Works of Saint Cyril of Jerusalem*, 1:94, note 18.

[26] Ibid.

[27] *CL* 1:15; *CAO* 1:34; *CL* 17:37; *CAO* 2:296.

designing false windows merely for show? Are they making theological assertions simply because without them the theological construction would lack symmetry and balance? In former times architects placed a window in the building plans, having no function, through which one could not see, but seemed called for by an exterior harmony of forms. The declaration concerning the enduring presence of prophecy and the prophetic gifts would rise out of the realization that, were the church to acknowledge the complete demise of prophecy, it would be recognizing that it lacked something of the apostolic substance.[28] Are the authors, therefore, designing theological false windows?

In responding to the first question one can look at how other authors handled charisms, authors belonging to the same Greek language group to which Cyril belonged, living about the same time.

In a letter written by Athanasius (c. 296–373) about 354 or 355, the Alexandrian bishop asserts that the charism of miracles is still to be found: "We know bishops who still work signs."[29] In fact, part of the response to Montanism was for the bishop to tame the charisms, prophecy for instance, by himself assuming prophetic functions. Already in Ignatius of Antioch (d. 107) the bishop has taken over the prophetic functions. No mention is made of prophets or teachers as ministers; Ignatius does refer to prophetic utterances which he himself had made.[30] The bishop triumphs over prophets by co-opting prophecy. "The relics of the gift (of prophecy) were to remain beneath the pastoral mitre."[31]

That scourge of heretics, Epiphanius, was by no means willing to let the Montanists appropriate the charisms. Writing in the mid 370s, therefore while Cyril was still alive, Epiphanius declares that "the charism (of prophecy) is not inoperative in the church. Quite the opposite. . . . The holy church of God welcomes the same (charisms) as the Montanists, but ours are real charisms, authenticated for the church by the Holy Spirit."[32] On the continuance of the charisms in the church, and more ex-

[28] Labriolle, La Crise Montaniste, 562.
[29] Athanasius, To Dracontius, 49:9; PG 25:533.
[30] Ignatius, Philadelphians, 7:2; SC 10:126.
[31] Ash, "The Decline of Ecstatic Prophecy," 250.
[32] Epiphanius, Panarion, 48; PG 41:857.

plicitly that of prophecy, the great church was in full agreement with the Montanists. No theological debate was necessary on this point: charisms belong to the continuous life of the church. For both parties the challenge was to find prophetic charisms actually operative in specific persons. Witnesses are scarce.

"A Dance with the Angels"

The more pressing question is not really about prophecy during the fourth century, but about prophecy and the prophetic gifts in relation to Christian initiation. Basil, for one, makes such a connection. He is writing very likely sometime between the end of 374 and the end of 375.[33] He borrows the category of "worthy" from Origen, asserting that the Spirit is always present to those who are deserving. Basil's principle: the totality is undivided in its parts. Basil's application: "The Spirit is conceived as the whole in its parts when it comes to the distribution of the charisms."[34] More specifically the Spirit is present in "prophecy, or healings, or other wonderful works," all of which are still to be found.[35] Of special significance is the baptismal context in which Basil speaks of charisms. The church is a body having members ministering in mutuality and reciprocity: "We are all members, the ones of the others, but according to the different charisms, in proportion to the grace God has given. . . . The diversity of the charisms corresponds to the diversity of members, but all are baptized in one sole Spirit."[36] Charism and baptism belong together.

When believers have communion in the Spirit, the light of the Spirit radiates in them and they themselves become spiritual. Then they can turn and minister to others through "knowledge of the future, understanding of the mysteries, the comprehension of what is hidden, the distribution of wonderful charisms, a citizenship in heaven, a dance with the angels, joy without end, resting in God, becoming like God, and, the highest of all desires, becoming God."[37] Basil here expresses the common

[33] B. Pruche, Introduction, Basil, *Sur le Saint-Esprit*; SC 17bis:56.
[34] Basil, *On the Holy Spirit*, 26:61: SC 17bis:468
[35] Ibid.
[36] Ibid.
[37] Ibid., 9:23; SC 17bis:328.

Greek understanding of the process of sanctification ending in a transformation, which is understood as divinization, not, of course, to be understood literally. In relation to the charisms Basil articulates a theology of spiritual illumination, the perfection of the image of God in the human person. Basil was giving expression to a broader tradition found earlier in Irenaeus. The bishop of Lyons had earlier developed a theology of transformation into the image of God, becoming spiritual through the communion in the Spirit, which came to expression in "the prophetic charisms."[38]

The Argument from Experience

Like Basil, Gregory Nazianzus (329–89) placed the charisms in a baptismal and divinization framework, when he delivered the five *Theological Discourses* between July and November of 380 in Constantinople.[39] "If the Spirit is not to be adored, how can (the Spirit) divinize me in baptism?"[40] The argument here starts with the interior transformation of the believer, which can only be accounted by the divinity of the Spirit. Gregory argues from experience to the divinity of the Spirit to the presence of charisms.

Gregory notes that the Spirit who divinizes can bring to perfection by bestowing the charisms even before baptism, as in the case of Cornelius (Acts 10:44-48). The Spirit came down upon Cornelius, who was endowed with the charism of tongues just as had happened at Pentecost. All of this is in anticipation of baptism.[41] Even after baptism the Spirit and the charisms are to be sought, as happened to the new converts in Samaria when Peter and John came down and laid hands on them (Acts 8:14-17). Also at Ephesus the believers were baptized in the name of Jesus, Paul laid hands on them, imparting the Spirit, so that they spoke in tongues and prophesied (Acts 19:1-7). "This Spirit does all that God does: dividing into tongues of fire, distributing charisms, coming to expression in apostles, prophets, evangelists, pastors, and doctors."[42] Geogra-

---

[38] *AH* 5:6, 1; SC 153:74.
[39] P. Gallay, Introduction, *Grégoire de Nazianze: Discours 27-31*; SC 250:14.
[40] Gregory Nazianzus, *Fifth Theological Discourse*, 28; SC 250:332.
[41] Ibid., 29; SC 250:334.
[42] Ibid., 29; SC 250:334, 336.

phy is no hindrance, because nothing can circumscribe the Spirit. The scope of the Spirit is universal. "This Spirit penetrates the apostolic and prophetic powers at the same instant in places distant from one another, because they are dispersed here and there."[43]

Care must be taken not to press the texts from Basil and Gregory. They both want to keep the charisms in the context of initiation, both recognize that the charisms are present in the church. But they do not promote the prophetic charisms. In an earlier treatise, *On Baptism* (from about 366), whose authenticity has only been recently vindicated,[44] Basil recognizes the charisms but is shy of sensible interior movements, reluctant to give large place to the wondrous or the unusual.[45] In this treatise directed to a monastic audience he does not have the distinction between the just (believers living in the world) and the perfect (those who have renounced everything) as one meets it in Origen and the Syrians, as we shall see. The monks, too, should remember the commandments, and all that Jesus Christ taught, and they should not use their charisms to cause wonder. Nor should they think that they enjoy special spiritual favors.[46] Very likely Basil is distancing himself from the enthusiastic monastic movement of his one time friend Eustathius of Sebaste, while at the same time honoring the rigor of his former friend's demands.[47]

With that caution in mind one asks whether the texts of Basil and Gregory show signs of being a formulation prompted by the abstract necessity of evaluating the charisms positively because they belong to the apostolic substance of faith. Athanasius is persuading a reluctant Dracontius to accept his election as bishop. Epiphanius is cataloging heresies. In his treatise *On the Holy Spirit* Basil is defending the way he prays the doxology, and, by indirection, the divinity of the Holy Spirit. In *On Baptism* he is attempting to guide the enthusiasm,

---

[43] Ibid., 29; SC 250:336.

[44] J. Ducatillon, Introduction, *Sur le Baptême*; SC 357:7-16.

[45] I, 2, 20; I, 3, 3; II, 8, 8; SC 357:169, 199, 265.

[46] Ibid. II, 8, 8; SC 357:263, 264.

[47] J. Gribomont, "Le Monachisme au IVe s. en Asie Mineure: de Grangres au Messalianisme," *Studia Patristica* 2 (1955) 400-15; Gribomont, "Saint Basile et le Monachisme Enthousiaste," *Irenikon* 53 (1980) 123-44.

which Eustathius has inspired, into the bosom of the church's living experience in harmony with gospel.[48] Gregory is giving a rather formal discourse on "this strange God," the Holy Spirit, in Constantinople which has been in the hands of the Arians for forty years.[49] Part of a series of five discourses, which earned him the title of "The Theologian," they were preached against the Arians, who denied the divinity of the Son and the Spirit. Though not the usual simple homilies, they were attended by the whole congregation and addressed to all.

Cyril is preparing catechumens for baptism, not an appropriate moment for theological speculation. Cyril is not prompted by the demands of giving balance to academic presentation. Quite the contrary, Cyril is the pragmatic pastor speaking to converts in immediate preparation for entrance into the awe inspiring mysteries. None seem primarily interested in defending the theoretical permanence of prophecy in the church, though that is by no means excluded. They are speaking of the life of the church, not of idealized forms.

Theological sources have different theological weights. Are the specific writings of Cyril, Basil, and Gregory, who relate the charisms to baptism, more casual, minor works? On the contrary, Cyril's CL, Basil's *On the Holy Spirit,* and Gregory Nazianzus' *Five Theological Orations* are major works of each author. If they are placed alongside other contributions to theological literature in that fertile fourth century, so full of writing of enduring value, they still emerge as major texts. Of the three, Cyril's carries the most theological weight for the question at hand. He is speaking to baptismal candidates, encouraging them to expect the heavenly charisms within the initiation rite, most especially prophecy.

Yet the case should not be overstated. Basil and Gregory may have preserved a relic of antiquity, when baptism and charism belonged together. However significant the testimonies of Cyril, Basil, and Gregory relating charisms to baptism, they seem to stand alone. Orthodoxy indeed continues the theoretical claim of the permanence of prophecy in the church, and searches

[48] Ducatillon, Introduction, SC 357:28.
[49] Gregory Nazianzus, fifth Theological Discourse, 1; SC 250;276.

valiantly for cases where charisms are exercised.[50] The monastic movements and Messalianism, which were arising just when the relation of charism to initiation was disappearing, continued to claim prophecy and prophetic charisms.[51]

If one grants that "the gift of the Holy Spirit" in the MC refers to the imparting of charisms, then one still needs to explain why there is still only this one shrouded mention. First, there is no essential necessity for the charisms to be in evidence in or immediately after the baptismal rite. So the bishop would not have commented on what was not yet manifested. Though possible, this does not seem altogether likely, given a number of baptisms, given the explicit exhortation to expect the "heavenly charisms." Secondly, the MC were Cyril's preaching notes on which he expanded; therefore, we do not have a complete text of what was preached.[52] Thirdly, at issue here may be the separate authorship of the two sets of lectures.

A long controversy over the authorship of the MC initiated by W. J. Swaan,[53] who thought the work should be attributed, with varying nuances, to Cyril's successor, John of Jerusalem, has found support among other scholars, W. Telfer,[54] E. Bihain,[55] G. Kretschmar,[56] A. A. Stephenson,[57] A. Renoux.[58] In 1960 F. L.

---

[50] Labriolle, La Crise Montaniste, 462.

[51] Messalianism, which began in Syria, claimed prophetic gifts. The earliest datable sources are about the 370s. Columba Stewart, " 'Working the Earth of the Heart'; The Language of Christian Experience in the Messalian Controversy, the Liber Graduum, the Writings of Pseudo-Macarius," (D.Phil diss., Oxford University, 1988). This valuable study will be published by Oxford University Press as Working the Earth of the Heart: the Messalian Controversy in History, Texts, and Language to 431. Theological Monograph Series (Oxford: Oxford University Press, 1991). I am indebted to Stewart for the references.

[52] Yarnold, "The Authorship of the Mystagogic Catecheses," 161.

[53] Swaan, "A Propos des 'Catéchèses Mystagogiques' Attribué à S.Cyrille de Jérusalem," Muséon 55 (1942) 1–43.

[54] Telfer, The Works of Cyril of Jerusalem, 39–43.

[55] Bihain, "Une Vie Armènienne de Saint Cyrille de Jérusalem," 340, note 73.

[56] Kretschmar, Studien zu Frühchristlichen Trinitätstheologie (Tübingen: Mohr/Siebeck, 1965) 166, note 2.

[57] Stephenson, The Works of Saint Cyril of Jerusalem, 2, 143–49.

[58] Renoux, "Les Catéchèses Mystagogiques dans l'organisation liturgique

Cross, and in 1966 A. Piédagnel did not believe the case against Cyril as the author was decisive.[59] Nor did J. Quasten, who suggested that possibly Cyril prepared and gave the *MC*, which were later revised by John of Jerusalem.[60] Were it ever demonstrated that the *MC* belong to John, that might suffice for the differences between the presentation of the charisms from the *CL* to the *MC*. In that case one would still want to know what prompted John to give only generic references to two complete lectures on an important biblical theme, the Holy Spirit and the charisms, a theme which had the stamp of apostolicity on them. In the *CL* Cyril had based his teaching concerning the charisms both on the scriptures and on the experience of the charisms in the diocese, the province of Palestine, and the universal church. Why had John suppressed more specific reference to what Cyril had received from the living tradition witnessed to by the universal church and rooted in the apostolic tradition? Why would John have curtailed so drastically the expansive treatment of the Spirit and the charisms which Cyril had given in chapters sixteen and seventeen?

Yarnold seems to have given sufficient evidence to establish a strong presumption in favor of Cyril.[61] The time span between the *CL* and the *MC* is thirty to forty years. Yarnold suggests that "the evolution of a single mind" over three of four decades is sufficient cause in itself to account for the changes.[62] Yarnold's arguments seem impelling.

Fourth, the attitude in Jerusalem toward the charisms may have changed in the span of thirty or forty years, perhaps because of the opposition to Montanism.

Apart from Cyril's situation, a number of historical developments forced prophecy, as it had been understood up to the mid-fourth century, from the church's life, so that, as Ash com-

hierosolymitaine du IVe et du Ve siècle," *Museon* 78 (1965) 355-59.

[59] Cross, *St. Cyril of Jerusalem's Lectures*, xxxviii, xxxix; Piédagnel, Introduction, Cyrille de Jerusalem, *Catéchèses Mystagogiques*; SC 126:33-40. Piedagnel reviews the history of the debate.

[60] Quasten, *Patrology*, 3:366.

[61] Yarnold, "The Authorship of the Mystagogic Catecheses," 143-61. See also F. Young, *From Nicaea to Chalcedon* (Philadelphia: Fortress, 1983) 128-30.

[62] Yarnold, "The Authorship of the Mystagogic Catecheses," 143-61.

ments, it "practically disappears in the third century and beyond,"[63] or as Botte puts it, "the question of charisms had practically no interest in the fourth century."[64] Given this judgment is it surprising to find any evidence at all of prophecy and the prophetic gifts in the church's celebration of Christian initiation in the fourth century, those rites which make the church to be church.

In summation, the differences between the *CL* and the *MC* may be due (1) to a time lag between the Easter Vigil and the first manifestations of the charisms; or (2) to the *CL* being the full text of what was preached, the *MC* sermon notes; or (3) to separate authorship.

Yarnold seems to have established a presumption that Cyril is the author of the *MC*. The Cyril of the *MC* is as much interested in the Spirit as the Cyril of the *CL*. In the *MC* he keeps the christological and pneumatological moments in tension, salvation beginning with Jesus who was anointed by the Holy Spirit as he came up from the waters of baptism. Cyril enunciates the principle that what the Spirit touches, the Spirit changes. However, in the *MC* Cyril gives diminished space to the charisms, limiting them to the phrase "the gift of the Spirit." Though, in my view, the charisms are present in the *MC*, and therefore present within the context of initiation, the capsulized formulation is problematic. Such abbreviated forms, however, can be found already in the *CL*, and do not necessarily signal a reduced value attached to charisms. Other witnesses, Athanasius and Ephiphanius, testify to the conviction that the prophetic gifts belong to the life of the church and are still part of the church's experience. Basil and Gregory Nazianzus put the charisms in a baptismal context. Though in both cases the references are made in major works, they are lonely and isolated witnesses which may be recording a vanishing tradition.

The disappearance of the charisms from the central tradition, and especially from the rites of initiation, may be a reaction to Montanism. The New Prophecy had promoted the charisms. In

[63] Ash, "The Decline of Ecstatic Prophecy," 249.
[64] Botte, "Le traité des charismes dans les *Constitutions Apostoliques*," *Studia Patristica* 12 (1975) 83.

fact Epiphanius recorded that it was the promotion of the charisms which was the most characteristic feature of Montanism.[65] This may have prompted Cyril to veil his references to the charisms in the *MC*. One could argue that what Cyril spoke of expansively in the *CL* in 348 he spoke of generically in the *MC* in the 80s because of Montanism. That still leaves unexplained why Montanism, which had been in existence for about two hundred years, was so impelling at a later date that Cyril took refuge in biblical shorthand. Why did Montanism not prompt discretion in 348? Can any light be shed on what was happening in that span of three or four decades which could account for such a drastic change, even in one person, from open and specific promotion of the charisms to the veiled indirect references? What changes were taking place in Jerusalem during the fourth century? We need to look at the history of Jerusalem in some detail to find a possible answer to this question.

[65] Epiphanius, *Panarion*, 2:1, 48; PG 41:856.

Chapter Eighteen

Cyril of Jerusalem: "We Can Also See and Feel"— The Transformation of Jerusalem

We have seen that Cyril might indeed have written of the charisms in the *MC* using a stock biblical phrase, a kind of scriptural shorthand, like "the gift of the Spirit." Some might not be convinced that "the gift of the Spirit" always and everywhere designates both the imparting of the Spirit and the charisms.

Those who hold these views can point to the very great disparity between the forceful, specific, expansive exposition in two complete catecheses (16 and 17) in the *CL*, and, on the other hand, the stripped, spare, scrimpy handling of the content of those two chapters, not in one sentence, but in one phrase. How could an issue of such importance to Cyril as the charisms be so muted in the *MC*, hardly a grace note. If "the gift of the Spirit" in Cyril does not designate the charisms, then we need another answer than that given above to what happened to them between the *CL* and the *MC*. Were there any changes in the character of Jerusalem which might account for this change? If there were any changes, what effect would they have on the way the charisms were related to the rites of initiation? An unassailable answer cannot be given. What can be attempted is an informed conjecture.

As a city Jerusalem had rich memories, but access was somewhat impeded, which may be one of the reasons David chose this easily fortified position as the location of his capitol. Isolated and up a mountain, it was away from the coastal road along which the trade flowed back and forth to the two poles of the Fertile Crescent, namely, Egypt, Libya, and the Pentapolis on the one side, and Mesopotamia on the other. A four year siege by Titus resulted in the extermination or removal of much of the Jewish population and the destruction of the city in A.D. 70. In 135 Emperor Hadrian crushed the Jewish Bar Cochba revolt against Roman rule, and the city was largely destroyed again. Hadrian rebuilt it, renamed it Aelia Capitolina, and turned it into a Gentile city complete with a Roman forum, which covered the two most important Holy Places, namely, Calvary and the Holy Sepulcher. No Jew was allowed to live or even enter the city (a ban which Constantine relaxed enough to allow them entrance one day a week to weep for their tragic history).[1] The diminished population deprived the city of much of its economic base. After 135 there was a small, purely Gentile church in Jerusalem, but the city remained mostly pagan and without great socio-political significance, even though Christians recognized it as the mother of all churches.[2] In 190 Bishop Narcissus of Jerusalem conjointly with the bishop of Caesarea presided over a regional council situated somewhere in Palestine, not necessarily in Jerusalem.[3] Still it was left in subjection to Caesarea. When the hierarchical structure of the whole church was developed in the second century the pagan Aelia Capitolina still lacked socio-political importance, which was largely determinative of ecclesiastical rank. In these terms Aelia could not stand alongside Rome, Alexandria, and Antioch as a co-equal. Nor even as a near equal.

In 346, when Cyril would have been about 31, Jerusalem was significant enough so that Maximus of Jerusalem could convene a regional council of Palestinian bishops favorable to Athanasius

---

[1] Barnes, *Constantine and Eusebius*, 252.

[2] *See* editorial comment of A. Piédagnel in SC 126:147, note 1. Stephenson would ascribe a more important place to Jerusalem, calling it "a second sun in Palestine." Introduction, *The Works of Saint Cyril of Jerusalem*, 12–21.

[3] Eusebius, *EH*, 5:23, 1: SC 41:66.

and in opposition to Acacius of Caesarea, Jerusalem's metropolitan, who inclined to the Arian position.[4] No date can be fixed for the beginning of the custom of the bishop of Jerusalem ordaining the Palestinian bishops, which was a metropolitan right, and therefore belonged to the bishop of Caesarea. By the beginning of the eighth decade the custom was in place.[5]

Of the main factors which changed this isolated, struggling town into the great center of religious consciousness, I will look at four: the construction of the churches in Jerusalem and vicinity by Constantine and his family, the liturgical development in Jerusalem, the new wave of pilgrim traffic, and, in a more modest way, the writings on Palestine of Eusebius of Caesarea (c. 260–c. 340).

Aelia Capitolina Glitters with Gold

During the years after the founding of Aelia Capitolina some memory of the holy places must have been kept alive by the Gentile Christian church. Even before the fourth century Jerusalem was visited by distinguished visitors.[6] Among them were Melito of Sardis (d. 190), who came less as a pilgrim and more to establish the canon of the Old Testament in those places "where these things were preached and done."[7] Alexander of Cappadocia (c. 212) was more properly a pilgrim, coming "to pray and to visit the (holy) places."[8] Very likely Origen, studying the scriptures in Caesarea, went to the Jerusalem area "in search of the traces of Jesus and his disciples and the prophets," more particularly, to verify a place name.[9] Bishop Firmilianus (d. 268), on a trip to Caesarea to sit at the feet of Origen, "took the occasion to visit the holy places."[10] Lastly

[4] Socrates, *Ecclesiastical History*, 2:24; PG 67:261, 264.

[5] Honigmann, "Juvenal of Jerusalem," 216.

[6] H. Windisch, "Die ältesten christlichen Palästinapilger," *Zeitschrift des Deutschen Palästina-Vereins*, 48 (1925) 145–58.

[7] Eusebius, *EH*, 4:26, 13, 14; SC 31:211. *See* A. E. Harvey, "Melito and Jerusalem," *JTS* New Series 17 (1966) 401–4.

[8] Eusebius, *EH*, 6:11, 2; SC 41:100, 101.

[9] Origen, *On John*, 6:204 (1:28); SC 157:286; Jerome, *On Famous Men*, 54; PL 23:664. Windisch, "Die ältesten christlichen Palästinapilger," 152.

[10] Jerome, *On Famous Men*, 54: PL 23:665.

came Pionius (d. 250), a contemporary of Origen.[11] As early as 320 Eusebius wrote of pilgrims from various parts of the empire coming to see Jerusalem and the Mount of Olives.[12] The Bordeaux Pilgrim (333–34) came, following an already formed pilgrim route leading from Bordeaux to Jerusalem.[13] The Holy Sepulcher was in the process of being built when the pilgrim from Gaul was there. Constantine had never visited Palestine as a Christian (he seems to have passed through as a young soldier in 296), but said of his death bed baptism, "I had thought to do this in the waters of the river Jordan," a wish left unfulfilled.[14]

The changing character of Jerusalem was in part due to the building activities of Constantine, Helena, and Eutropia. Very likely Constantine not only built the Holy Sepulcher, but himself conceived the plan as a "mystery-site connected with the death of Christ."[15] Helen's churches in Bethlehem and the Mount of Olives, and the basilica at Mamre erected by Eutropia, Constantine's mother-in-law, gave added splendor to Jerusalem and environs.[16] Given the age this was a truly "massive building program."[17]

The Sepulcher, begun about 326–27 was completed about 335 and its dedication is tied to the Council of Tyre/Jerusalem (335). To bring peace to the church torn with strife over Athanasius, Constantine called the Council of Tyre, which the emperor then translated to Jerusalem for the dedication.[18] "A troop of bishops," possibly as many as 110, were present for the dedication.[19] As part of the ceremonies Eusebius delivered what has been called an oration, but was less a speech and more an

---

[11] *The Martyrdom of Pionius the Presbyter and his Companions*, 4; *The Acts of the Christian Martyrs*, ed. H. Musurillo (Oxford: Clarendon, 1972) 140.

[12] Eusebius, *Demonstration of the Gospel*, 6:18; PG 22:457.

[13] *The Journey of the Bordeaux Pilgrim*; CSEL 39:1–33.

[14] Eusebius, *Life of Constantine*, 62: PG 20:1216.

[15] Yarnold, "Baptism and the Pagan Mysteries in the Fourth Century," *HeyJ* 13 (1972) 265.

[16] E. D. Hunt, *Holy Land Pilgrimage in the Later Roman Empire* A.D. 312–460 (Oxford: Clarendon, 1982) 28–49.

[17] L. M. Barth, "Jerusalem," *Theologische Realenzyklopädie*, 16:613.

[18] Barnes, *Constantine and Eusebius*, 235, 238.

[19] E. Bishop, "Liturgical Comments and Memoranda," *JTS* 13 (1912) 36, 37; Barnes, *Constantine and Eusebius*, 238.

apologetic treatise, praising Constantine for the construction of the Sepulcher.[20] Eusebius described the Sepulcher's interior as "being overlaid throughout with the purest gold," which "causes the entire building to glitter as it were with rays of light."[21] Splendor was not wanting. The dedication was part of the celebrations of Constantine's thirtieth year as emperor.

The Sepulcher's most prized relic was what Christians thought to be the true cross. Helen is credited with the finding of the cross of Jesus, but this link seems to be legendary as it is neither mentioned in Eusebius' *Life of Constantine*, nor in Eusebius' oration given at the dedication, nor in the account of the Pilgrim from Bordeaux. Nonetheless the report that the cross had been found spread widely in the last half of the fourth century and is attested by Cyril's *Letter to Constantius*, without attribution to Helen.[22] Regardless of whether or how it was found, it fired the imagination of Christendom and gave Jerusalem new possibilities of going beyond hearing the scriptures in the celebration of the mysteries. Cyril's dependence on the scriptures is not in doubt. He intended to limit himself to the proclaimed scriptures.[23] But now Jerusalem was in a new situation. With dazzling basilicas, with the wood of the cross, Cyril could boast "others only hear, but we can also see and feel."[24] In a brief space, almost in one breath, Cyril mentions "the holy cross, seen among us even to this day," Gethsemane, the Sepulcher, the Mount of Olives, Jordan, the sea of Tiberias.[25] Sixty-seven times Cyril calls attention to specific places in which the mysteries of Jesus were enacted.[26] Now began a new age when droves of pilgrims came to hear the word of God, see the hill on which Jesus was crucified, touch the tomb from which he rose.

Cyril's interest in the purely religious and liturgical sig-

---

[20] Bishop, "Liturgical Comments," 38; L. Duchesne, *The Early History of the Christian Church*, 3 vols. (New York: Longmans, Green, 1922) 2:139-44.

[21] Eusebius, *Life of Constantine*, 3:36; PG 20:1096.

[22] Cyril, *Letter to Constantius*, 3; PG 33:1167. Hunt, *Holy Land Pilgrimage*, 20–49.

[23] CL 16:2; CAO 2:206.

[24] CL 13:22; CAO 2:80.

[25] CL 10:19; CAO 1:284-86.

[26] John F. Baldovin, *Liturgy in Ancient Jerusalem* (Bramcote: Grove, 1989) 15.

nificance of the relic of the cross did not mean that he was unaware of the political possibilities it offered. G. Kretschmar thinks that the political exploitation of the relic of the cross as a protection for the Emperor and the Empire goes back to Cyril.[27] Together with H. Busse, Kretschmar holds that Constantine's Holy Sepulcher was understood as the equivalent of the temple of Solomon, having similar political functions. As the temple was the cultic center of ancient Israel, so the Holy Sepulcher was for the empire and Christendom.[28] This position is taken in spite of Cyril's apparent disinterest in the parallel between temple and Sepulcher.[29] However Egeria was aware of the biblical basis of this Jerusalem tradition.[30] If the Sepulcher is the cultic center of the empire, then no one can be surprised that Cyril, through his liturgical genius, could change Jerusalem from not being a source to the city which determined the liturgies of East and West in the latter part of the fourth and for the fifth centuries.[31] The influence of Jerusalem was "permanent."[32]

Aelia Capitolina Becomes the Holy City

Cyril was creating a new Jerusalem liturgy. By these very acts Cyril was contributing to changing the character of Jerusalem. Before the last decades of the fourth and the beginning of the fifth century Jerusalem had never been a liturgical source of the first order.[33] As we have seen, Jerusalem was situated on the

[27] "Festkalender und Memorialstätten Jerusalems in altkirchlicher Zeit," *Jerusalemer Heiligtumstraditionen in Altkirchlicher und Frühislamischer Zeit*, H. Busse and G. Kretschmar (Wiesbaden: Harrassowitz, 1987) 78.

[28] H. Busse, "Temple, Grabeskirche und Haran as-sarif: Drei Heiligtümer und ihre gegenseitigen Beziehungen in Legende und Wirlichkeit," ibid., 106.

[29] J. Wilkinson, "Jewish Influences on The Early Christian Rite of Jerusalem," *Museon* 92 (1979) 358.

[30] *Egeria's Travels* 48; SC 296:316. *See* M. Black, "The Festival of *Encaenia Ecclesiae* in the Ancient Church with Special References to Palestine and Syria," *JEH* 5 (1954) 78–85.

[31] H. Wegman, *Christian Worship in East and West* (New York: Pueblo, 1976) 76.

[32] Baldovin, *Liturgy in Ancient Jerusalem*, 5.

[33] Zerfass, *Die Schriftlesung im Kathedraloffizium Jerusalems*, 2; G. Kretschmar, "Die Geschichte des Taufgottesdienstes in der alten Kirche," *Leiturgia* (Kassel: Stauda, 1970) 198.

boundary between two spheres of influence, Alexandria and Antioch. Jerusalem's jurisdictional dependence on Caesarea, and through it to Antioch, was not a favorable climate for liturgical independence. The process of asserting its own jurisdictional independence, of breaking free of Caesarea and Antioch, began during Cyril's life. Among the first acts of independence was the creation of new liturgical forms responding, as Cyril says, to the demands of "those mysteries first instituted here in Jerusalem."[34] Should such a city be subject to Caesarea?

Liturgical development, however, began well before Cyril's day. A century before there was a Paschal celebration in Jerusalem. The fifth canon of Nicaea recognized the forty days before Easter as having a distinctive character.[35] The catechumenate may have started in Egypt when Bishop Demetrius put Origen in charge of candidates for baptism. If one can judge from Eusebius, at the beginning of the fourth century the population of Jerusalem already believed it had a glorious tradition of some antiquity.[36] As Jerusalem entered the fourth century it was not with a thread-bare history.

Cyril enhanced and developed that tradition with considerable creativity. A comparative study shows that Cyril's Holy Week and Easter cycle formed the model for future developments in both East and West. He gave the broad outlines of how the divine office was to be celebrated publicly. He developed the proper of the seasons as well as of the saints. More than to any other single individual the eucharistic doctrine of transubstantiation is traceable to Cyril.[37] In the churches of Jerusalem one meets for the first time with liturgical vestments, the carrying of candles, the use of incense at the gospel, the *lavabo*, the placing of the Lord's Prayer after the canon or anaphora. For better or worse he turned the liturgy away from an eschatological interpretation of redemption, that is, oriented toward Parousia. In its place he proposed an historical understanding, centered on

[34] *CL* 18:33; *CAO* 2:336.
[35] Mansi, 2:679.
[36] *EH* 5:23; *SC* 41:66.
[37] *MC* 4:2; *SC* 126:136.

the events of Jesus' life.[38] This major shift left its imprint on the fourth century as none other had.[39]

In large part we still live with Cyril's liturgical shift from eschatology to history. Only with great difficulty can we imagine the significance of the turn from the dynamic of salvation history moving toward a cosmic transformative event in the Parousia, and the turn to communion in the anointing of Jesus at his baptism, going down into the death of Christ, and ascending with the Risen Christ. Though both ways of knowing the mystery of Jesus Christ represent profound intuitions, though neither is to be dismissed as the lesser, the change meant that the celebration of the liturgy would never be the same.

Only in the age of Constantine did Aelia Capitolina become the Holy City,[40] or, as Eusebius put it, "the new Jerusalem."[41] The building of the Holy Sepulcher as "a pilgrim church," notes Edmund Bishop, is "a new creation," an epoch-making event in the history of the church, a point of departure for a new religious movement.[42] For us pilgrimages are so much a part of our religious consciousness that it is difficult to imagine the impact a Jerusalem pilgrimage church had on Christian piety. A new, indeed unprecedented, movement was now in motion. No longer isolated visits of single pilgrims or groups, but a stream of pilgrims coming to experience the mysteries of Christ on the holy ground where Jesus poured out his blood, to touch the stones of Calvary, to see the cross.

By his liturgical creativity Cyril had upped the voltage. In the last two decades of the century, that is, in the last years of

[38] The *caveat* of J. F. Baldovin should be noted: "Many authors have too quickly accepted historicization as the unique motive in the development of Jerusalem's worship." *The Urban Character of Christian Worship* (Rome: Oriental Institute, 1987) 87–90.

[39] Dix, *Shape of the Liturgy*, 350, 351. A. Schmemann, while admitting "the profound change" which took place in the fourth century, also asserts that the change was not without continuity with the past. *Introduction to Liturgical Theology* (London: Faith, 1966) 76, 77. *See* the critique of Dix in J. F. Baldovin, *The Urban Character of Christian Worship*, 102–4.

[40] Kretschmar, "Die Frühe Geschichte der Jerusalemer Liturgie," 22–46; Zerfass, *Schriftlesung Jerusalems*, 2.

[41] Eusebius, *The Life of Constantine*, 3:33; PG 20:1093.

[42] Bishop, "Liturgical Comments and Memoranda," 36, 37.

Cyril's life, the new liturgical practices of Jerusalem swept "like a flood all over Christendom."[43] Even Rome, slow to act, slow to innovate, usually needing two or three generations to accept ritual changes, was affected by Jerusalem's pervasive influence.[44] Egeria, a relentless gatherer of liturgical detail, is one example of how the pilgrims recorded every bow, numbered every candle, remembered every procession of the Jerusalem liturgies to serve as a model for their churches back home. In the 80s and 90s a whole generation grew up with a new Christian consciousness, a new way of knowing the mysteries of Jesus, in which Jerusalem was the ideal church representing correct liturgical celebration.[45] To celebrate the liturgical rites as in Jerusalem was the unwritten law.[46]

The Armenian Ritual and The Old Armenian Lectionary are products of Jerusalem's emerging liturgical imperialism. Despite the difference in the titles, both are lectionaries representing two stages in an on-going evolution. They reflect the liturgy of Jerusalem at the beginning of the fifth century. A. Renoux has established that The Old Armenian Lectionary was originally a Greek text used in Jerusalem. So the Armenian church preserved the tradition that its own liturgical lectionaries originated in Jerusalem from the time of James, its first bishop; James initiated the liturgical tradition, while Cyril completed it.[47] With powerful, colorful, reverent rites, carrying such a pedigree, the readings and liturgical rites were eminently exportable. What church could resist?

Not all bishops welcomed dictation in matters liturgical. An exasperated Augustine, responding in about 400 to the case of a returned pilgrim transformed into an over-eager rubricist, expresses a *caveat*. Augustine insists that even if in a place of pil-

---

[43] Dix, Shape of the Liturgy, 353.

[44] Ibid.

[45] Ibid.

[46] But Jerusalem had what no other city could claim, the actual sites, which presented some problems for those cities which wanted to imitate them. Hunt, Holy Land Pilgrimage, 107–27.

[47] Renoux "Liturgie Hiérosolymitaine et Vieux Lectionnaire Arménien," La Codex Arménien Jérusalem 121 (Turnhout: Brepols, 1969); PO 35:19–22; 29; Renoux, "Les catéchèses mystagogiques dans l'organisation liturgique hierosolymitaine du IVᵉ et du Vᵉ siècle," 355–59; Wilkinson, Egeria, 253, 254.

grimage (possibly Jerusalem) the rites are different from those observed at home, the pilgrim, on returning home, must not press with "aggressive obstinacy," that the local rites be changed to conform.[48] Liturgical rites are not eternal verities, handed down by the new Jerusalem. More than one right way to celebrate the mysteries exists.

Quarrels: Pilgrim Beware!

Tensions existed not only when pilgrims returned home to hound their bishops into conforming the liturgy of the local church to that of the mother of all churches, Jerusalem; the very practice of making a pilgrimage to Jerusalem came under attack.

When Maximus of Jerusalem died, Cyril succeeded him in 348. Soon he was quarreling with Acacius of Caesarea, to whom he owed his election. Acacius could not abide Cyril's claim that Jerusalem, as the mother church, indeed as the see with the greatest claim to being apostolic, had the right to metropolitan status. This was Cyril's interpretation of the seventh canon of Nicaea, which accorded to Jerusalem some place of honor, but left it in subjection to Caesarea.[49] The restive Cyril read into the seventh canon more than the council legislated, but his efforts were part of the dynamic which would change the character of Jerusalem.

Within two years of Cyril becoming bishop, Basil came to Jerusalem (c. 351). His purpose was to visit the monks and ascetics of the infant monastic movement and so learn the secret of their sanctity. This was not a pilgrimage in the usual sense; Basil showed himself singularly uninterested in the holy places. In a letter written in 375 to his some-time friend, Eustathius of Sebaste, he mentioned Alexandria, the rest of Egypt, Palestine, Coele-Syria, and Mesopotamia. Jerusalem was not explicitly mentioned.[50]

Thirty years after Basil's visit, his brother, Gregory of Nyssa, came. Jerome and Socrates say that Gregory had studied in Caesarea in Palestine, which was subject jurisdictionally to An-

[48] Augustine, *Letter*, 54; CSEL 34:161.

[49] Sozomen, *Ecclesiastical History* 4:25; PG 67:1196-200.

[50] Basil, *Letter* 223:2; *Saint Basil: the Letters*, ed. R. J. Deferrari (Cambridge: Harvard University, 1953) 292, 294.

tioch.[51] He might have heard Cyril of Jerusalem give the sixth and seventh *Catechetical Lectures;* similarities between these catecheses and Gregory's 28th *Oration* suggest this possibility.[52] This time he came on a mission from the civil rulers to Arabia (c. 380), which brought him through Palestine. He says specifically that he conferred "with the heads of the holy Jerusalem churches."[53] This visit would have been made during the last seven years of Cyril's life. The bishop whom Gregory visited may have been Cyril, though he did not specify.

Pilgrimage had now become a fashion and Gregory protested against the new devotion. Jerusalem did not edify. In fact it scandalized. With some scorn Gregory remarked that "if divine grace was so much more abundant in Jerusalem than elsewhere, sin would not be so much the fashion among those who live there."[54] Among the commandments given by the Lord, suggested Gregory, one looks in vain to find one commanding a pilgrimage to Jerusalem.[55] His visit to Jerusalem had neither increased nor diminished his faith. On his return he was accused of making a pilgrimage. Not so, said Gregory. That was not a pilgrimage. That was a trip. One should not imagine "that the Holy Spirit is in abundance in Jerusalem, but unable to travel as far as us."[56] Dissuade persons from making a pilgrimage to Jerusalem, Gregory counseled.[57]

Others looked on matters differently. The scholar Rufinus came and, together with Melania, founded a double monastery on the Mount of Olives about 381. A historian and translator, Rufinus was also busy quarreling with the acerbic Jerome living several miles away. The noise of their disagreements was published to the far corners of the scandalized church. Jerome had

[51] Socrates, *Ecclesiastical History* 4:26; PG 67:529; Jerome, *On Famous Men* 113; PL 23:745.

[52] Paragraphs 15 and 16 of Gregory's *Oration* 28 are similar to Cyril's 6th CL; paragraphs 22 through 30 bear many resemblances to Cyril's 9th CL. P. Gallay, *Grégoire de Nazianze, Discours 27–31;* SC 250:135 note 3; 145 note 3.

[53] Gregory, *Letter,* 2; *Gregorii Nysseni Opera,* 10 vols.; ed. W. Jaeger (Leiden: Brill, 1959) part 2, 8, 17 (hereafter cited as *GNO*).

[54] Ibid.; *GNO 8/2,* 15.

[55] Ibid.; *GNO 8/2,* 14.

[56] Ibid.; *GNO 8/2,* 15.

[57] Ibid.; *GNO 8/2,* 18, 19.

visited Jerusalem in 374 and then came to live down the road from Cyril in Bethlehem in 386. Cyril probably died in 387, so the two lived in close proximity for a year, long enough for Jerome to add Cyril's name to a rather extensive list of people he held in low regard.[58] To entice to Bethlehem his Roman friends, Paula and Eustochium, Jerome wrote of the universal character of Jerusalem's appeal in 392 or 393, that is five or six years after Cyril's death: "Here one can see the most important people from everywhere. . . . The one who is best known in Gaul is here. The person from Britain, far from the world we know (is here). . . . What shall we say of the Armenians, Persians, the people from India, Ethiopia and Egypt (so fertile in monks), Pontus, Cappadocia, Coele-Syria, Mesopotamia, and all the crowds from the east."[59] Here is the picture of a Jerusalem visited not by a few pilgrims, but by large numbers from distant lands. Jerome, however, wanted to place pilgrimages in perspective. "Faith is not deficient because you have not seen Jerusalem. . . . A great host of monks from Egypt, Mesopotamia, Pontus, Cappadocia, and Armenia, though they made no pilgrimage to Jerusalem, the door of heaven is still open (to them)."[60] John Chrysostom (c. 347–407), a younger contemporary of Cyril who spoke from the vantage point of Antioch, joined his cautionary voice, saying that pilgrimages could be a peril for the unwary.[61]

The Lady from Spain and the Deluge of Pilgrims

The pilgrim who left the most detailed account of her visit to Jerusalem was a nun, probably from Spain, named Egeria, who came late in the fourth century (381–84). Cyril was still alive. Her account allows us to see the considerable liturgical development which had taken place during these years from the writing of the CL (between 348–50) to the composition of the MC (between 383–86), and up to the dates of her pilgrimage in Jeru-

---

[58] J. N. D. Kelly, *Jerome* (New York: Harper & Row, 1975) 195.
[59] Jerome, *Letter*, 46:10; CSEL 54:338, 340.
[60] Jerome, *Letter*, 58:3; CSEL 54:531.
[61] John Chrysostom, *To the People of Antioch*, 3:2; PG 49:49.

salem.[62] Though we have no direct evidence that Cyril was the source of this astonishing liturgical flowering, his role as bishop makes him the logical person. Evidently between his thirtieth and seventieth year he was experimenting with liturgical forms.[63] The path of this development in the second half of the fourth century can be broadly traced by five documents: *CL, MC, Egeria's Travels, The Armenian Ritual,* and *The Old Armenian Lectionary.*

Egeria wrote of the crowds who came to Jerusalem to celebrate the annual eight day feast of the Dedication of Golgotha. Among the pilgrims are monks and ascetics from Mesopotamia, Syria, Egypt, Thebaid, and from every region and province. "Not one of them fails to make for Jerusalem to share the celebrations of this solemn feast. There are also lay men and women from every province gathering in Jerusalem at this time for the holy day."[64] She remarks the contrast between the small number of bishops that exist in the world and the large number of bishops present during these festival days, "no less than forty or fifty in Jerusalem at this time, accompanied by many of their clergy."[65]

The brilliance of the churches, the splendor of the ornaments, the grandeur of the liturgies attracted pilgrims in large numbers. Referring very likely to the celebrations during the octave of Epiphany, Egeria enthuses:

"On this day in this church (Great Church on Golgotha), and at the Anastasis and the Cross and Bethlehem, the decorations really are too marvelous for words. All you can see is gold and jewels and silk; the hangings are entirely silk with gold stripes, the curtains the same, and everything they use for services at the festival is made of gold and jewels. You simply cannot imagine the number, and the sheer weight of the candles and the tapers and lamps and everything else they use for the ser-

[62] P. Devos, "La date du voyage d'Egérie," *AnBoll* 85 (1967) 163–94. On the difficulties of reconciling Egeria's account of the Jerusalem catechesis with the readings for Cyril's *CL, see* Stephenson, "The Lenten Catechetical Syllabus," 103–16.
[63] Wilkinson, Introduction, *Egeria's Travels,* ed. J. Wilkinson (London: SPCK, 1971) 84. The translations of the texts come from this edition.
[64] *Egeria* 49:1; SC 296:318.
[65] Ibid.

vices. They are beyond description, so magnificent is the building itself. It was built by Constantine, and under the supervision of his mother it was decorated with gold, mosaic, and precious marble, as much as his empire could provide, and this not only at the Great Church, but at the Anastasis and the Cross, and the other Jerusalem holy places as well."[66]

Egeria refers to the Holy Week procession to Gethsemane with hundreds of candles, and a later gathering to venerate "the holy wood of the cross."[67] Passing by a table on which is a gold and silver box containing the holy wood of the cross, the faithful "stoop down, touch the holy wood first with their forehead and then with their eyes, and then kiss it, but no one puts out his hand to touch it."[68]

Jerusalem's attractions were many; not just glittering churches and the solemn rites. Within this exterior glory Jerusalem offered the opportunity of reliving the mysteries of Christ's life, death, and resurrection in symbol where he experienced them in reality. When they spoke of celebrating "the mysteries" they meant the participation, sharing, having communion in the whole spectrum of Christ's life: birth, baptism, public life, death, resurrection, and the sending of the Spirit at Pentecost. Communion in the mysteries was more than mime. Pilgrims were invited to experience the power of God from within the mysteries. The depth of the experience in this holy place, presented in liturgies which arose out of the demands of specific events in Jesus' life, tied to specific locales, was an occasion which could hardly fail to move the devout. Very likely Cyril had no intention of attracting pilgrims to Jerusalem; a local pastor uses what he finds at hand to celebrate the mysteries. In Jerusalem what a wealth of mysteries there were! The growth of the pilgrim traffic was assured.

How deeply the people were moved by the whole rite of initiation in such a setting is indicated by the burst of applause which greeted the bishop when the initiation rites were over, when the discipline of the secret was lifted, and the newly bap-

---

[66] Ibid., 25:8, 9; SC 296:252.
[67] Ibid., 37:1; SC 296:284.
[68] Ibid., 37:3; SC 296:286.

tized were exposed to the wealth of the mysteries. Referring precisely to this moment Egeria wrote: "The bishop relates what has been done, and interprets it (the mystagogy or explanation of the rites of initiation), and, as he does so, the applause is so loud that it can be heard outside the church. Indeed the way he expounds the mysteries and interprets them cannot fail to move his hearers."[69] Jerusalem had become a major pilgrimage city with visitors from distant lands drawn by the sites associated with Old Testament patriarchs and prophets, by the stones over which Jesus had walked and died, drawn by the glory of the basilicas. Even though Gregory scolded, Jerome cautioned, and Chrysostom warned, after Egeria's departure in 384 the great theologians were "unable to stop the deluge of pilgrims."[70]

One further factor contributed to the changed character of Jerusalem, namely, Eusebius, the man and his books. Apart from the imperial family, no other person did so much to make the Holy Land known.[71] *On the Place-Names in Holy Scripture* (commonly known as the *Onomasticon*), written in the 290s as an exegetical tool, is part of a larger work; it contains a book by book alphabetical index of biblical sites with geographical and historical descriptions, with special attention to Judaea.[72] Significant for our purposes, it gives the plan for the temple, the topography of Jerusalem, a description of ancient Judaea and the twelve tribes. Much of the last three items has been lost. That the *Onomasticon* was twice translated into Latin is an indication of the need it filled.[73] Praise for the book came from both East and West. Even today it presents "the most important source for the topography of the Holy Land."[74] The *Onomasticon* was available for at least fifty years before Cyril became a bishop and, therefore, years before the deluge of pilgrims began. Though intended as a scriptural tool, it was evidently used

[69] Ibid., 47:2; SC 296:314.
[70] Groh, "The *Onomasticon* of Eusebius, 23.
[71] A. E. Harvey, "Melito and Jerusalem," 403; Wilkinson, *Egeria's Travels*, 12.
[72] Barnes, *Eusebius and Constantine*, 106–11.
[73] J. Ziegler, "Die *Peregrinatio Aetheriae* und das *Onomastikon* des Eusebius," *Biblica* 12, (1931) 83, 84.
[74] Quasten, *Patrology*, 3:336.

as a pilgrim's guide. Egeria carried a Latin translation of the *Onomasticon* on her three-year pilgrimage to Jerusalem.[75] Now lost are Eusebius' description of ancient Judaea and its twelve tribes, plans for both the Temple and Jerusalem. Eusebius' work presented to the Christian world the prospect of *seeing* the actual places referred to in the scriptures, a powerful magnet.[76] Of lesser importance, but enhancing the attractions of Palestine, is Eusebius' *The Martyrs of Palestine*, an eye witness account of the martyrdoms, written about 311.[77]

How would one summarize this sprawling history? Clearly, the history of Jerusalem did not start in the fourth century. Nonetheless its character was transformed during that century principally through the building activities of Constantine and the imperial family, the writings of Eusebius, and the elevation of Cyril as bishop of Jerusalem. What Constantine did in stone, Eusebius did in text, Cyril in rite.

Jerusalem, an isolated backwater town, had its roots in the pre-Nicene church, in the apostolic memories of Pentecost, which were not easily dismissed as the mindless pursuit of thrills. Standing in the room where the apostles were said to have gathered when a mighty wind filled the house, imposed the necessity of distinctions. Prophetic charisms were not absolutely and under any circumstances simply Montanist excesses, not inevitably charismatic chaos. The author of Acts recorded the memories of the day fire fell from heaven, transforming the apostles and Mary. Here in Jerusalem, in the theater where the drama of salvation had found its stage, the remembrance of that first Pentecostal baptism in the Holy Spirit was honored.

[75] Ziegler, "Die *Peregrinatio Aetheriae,*" 83, 84. Note that Ziegler dates Egeria's pilgrimage as at least as late as 390, because he judges that she used a Latin translation made by Jerome. But what Jerome translated was a similar biblical index by Origen, which is extant, i.e., *Liber Interpretationis Hebraicorvm Nominvm* CChr 72:59-161. Wutz and Hanson deny Origen ever compiled an Onomasticon. *See* F. Wutz, *Onomastica Sacra* (Texte und Untersuchungen 41:1-2) (Leipzig: Hinrischs'sche Buchhandlung, 1914, 1915); R. P. C. Hanson, "Interpretations of Hebrew Names in Origen," *VC* 10 (1956) 120. Barnes contends that Origen did make such a compilation. *Eusebius and Constantine,* 109, 110.

[76] Hunt, *Holy Land Pilgrimage,* 99–106.

[77] PG 20:1457-520. Barnes, *Eusebius and Constantine,* 278.

During Cyril's leadership the whole year became a succession of mysteries of Christ to be celebrated in the splendor of the glittering basilicas, with vestments, candles, and incense. The news of these glories and the new way of knowing spread. All of this set in motion a new movement, indeed, a flood, of pilgrims in whose traffic were found simple people, learned bickering monastics, great lords, powerful bishops. All of these, together with the whole spectrum of the laity, were drawn by the holiness of Jerusalem, by the possibility of a new way of belonging to the history of Jesus, of a new entry into the mysteries of his death and resurrection. In Jerusalem they celebrated in symbol what Jesus had experienced in reality. After Constantine and Cyril came the deluge.

When in the middle of the fourth century Cyril preached about the charisms, he was laying claim to the pre-Nicene church, to the antiquity Irenaeus represented. If he accepted from the apostolic kerygmatic tradition the list of scriptural readings, and the themes for the Lenten catecheses, would he not have accepted the teaching on the charisms from the same source?

The bishop of Jerusalem prepared catechumens who were "soon to be baptized in the Holy Spirit," by explicitly exhorting them to approach the mysteries in awe, to expect the charisms, especially prophecy.

What the church of Jerusalem in the late 340s thought of the charisms is not a matter of conjecture. The charisms in general, and the prophecy in particular, belonged to the process of being baptized in the Holy Spirit, and to the endowment of the ordinary Christian community. Cyril had the conviction that the reception of the charisms signified that the apostles at Pentecost and the candidates of Cyril's day were "fully baptized," "baptized without anything lacking," a point on which he insisted. The texts are clear. The prophetic charisms must have had some role in the life of the church. Though we have no evidence what that was, we do know that in the CL from the late 340s the prophetic charisms are within the rites of initiation.

In the 380s Jerusalem was no longer a small provincial town, but a great religious center, standing in the forefront of Christian consciousness. In fact a transformation, a great leap forward, had changed Jerusalem from not being a liturgical source to the city which determined the liturgy in both East and West.

When Jerusalem ceased being an isolated, insignificant city, when Aelia Capitolina gave way to the Holy City, pilgrim bishops in numbers also came bringing their old antagonisms against the prophetic charisms. For them the charisms would be incipient enthusiasm, whose name was Montanism. They had seen their authority challenged, their priests in pursuit of enthusiasm, their flocks divided. Can the apostolic memories of Pentecost survive suspicion, sometimes justified?

Whether or not the text of the *MC* is a preacher's outline, there may be no change from the content of the *CL*. In an atmosphere suspicious of prophetic charisms, what could Cyril salvage from the kerygmatic tradition in which the charisms had their rightful place? He had given generous place to the charisms in the *CL* of 348. Possibly all he could save in the *MC* of the 380s was the generic reference to "the gift of the Spirit."

Whether or not Cyril's reason for choosing the generalizing phrase "the gift of the Spirit" in the *MC* was to protect the charisms from those who identified charism with Montanism, cannot be determined. Possibly Cyril was carrying on a rear guard defense of the charisms. Not surprisingly the prophetic charisms were everywhere in decline or already extinct. Jerusalem's increased contact with a whole spectrum of Christians, bishops, priests, monks, laity, who came to the Holy City to experience the communion in the mystery of Christ, may have imposed their suspicions on the Jerusalem church. If this is true, it may have become difficult to promote the charisms at the heart of the church's life, namely, initiation. Even the proximity to the place where the Pentecostal fire fell upon the church may not have been sufficient to save the charisms in the rites of the extremely important initiatory liturgy. Against the suspicion of Montanism the recollection of the first Pentecost may have been seen as a dangerous memory.

The use of biblical shorthand in the *MC* may be a defense of the charisms, or symptomatic of charisms' diminishing role in the life of the church. Both are possible explanations. In any case Cyril is still insisting, in the *MC*, as he had done in the *CL*, that the charisms belong within the rites of initiation.

We have no texts from Jerusalem posterior to the *CL* and the *MC* which deal with the charisms in relation to initiation. Some light on what was happening in Jerusalem might be found in a document from Antioch dating from the 380s (therefore during the last years of Cyril's life), namely, the *Apostolic Constitutions*. Though the *Apostolic Constitutions* are not precisely from Chrysostom's church, they are from his general area, at a time when he was already famous in Antioch as a great exegetical preacher and a homilist preparing catechumens for the Easter celebration. A look at this document can be a bridge to what John Chrysostom has to say about the charisms.

Chapter Nineteen

Apostolic Constitutions: Standardizing the Charisms

We are still trying to understand why there was a change in the way Cyril presents the charisms in 348 and the 380s. How another contemporary document handles charisms could help us understand the reduced role the charisms seem to have in the *MC*.

The *Apostolic Constitutions* (hereafter *AC*), dates from about 380, therefore in the last eight years of Cyril's life.[1] It has literary traits one meets frequently in the early centuries, namely, treating of a variety of ecclesial institutions (ecclesiastical hierarchy, widows, orphans, schisms, eucharist, ordinations), drawing from a number of earlier traditions or documents, and claiming an authority it cannot validate.[2] An anonymous compiler, together with his atelier of personnel very competent in the theological sciences, working in Antioch or its environs (but not in the same church as John Chrysostom), transformed a variety of documents into a creative whole. Among the sources used are the *Didascalia* (early third century), the *Didache* (parts of which antedate some books of the Bible, with the date of composition around 90), and the *Apostolic Tradition* attributed to

[1] M. Metzger, Introduction, *Les Constitutions Apostoliques*; SC 320:58-62.
[2] Ibid., SC 320:13.

Hippolytus (early third century), together with other elements of diverse parentage.[3] A literary or desk liturgy, in contrast to a living liturgy, it was not actually in use. The compiler preferred biblical to philosophical terms. Like both the CL and the MC, the compiler directed his text to the community, not to theologians.[4]

The AC is a constitutional document, concerned mainly with order and discipline. Such literature filled a "legislative void" before the emergence of Byzantine canon law.[5] To give the appearance of apostolicity, it presents itself as coming from the assembly of the apostles in Jerusalem.[6] False apostolic credentials should not be evaluated negatively; in the early centuries such apostolic attribution was widely practiced without a suggestion of diminished virtue.

The compiler provides a pastoral caution: "All those who prophesy are not pious, and all those who chase demons are not saints."[7] Because prophets and exorcists, along with other charismatic persons, act in unacceptable ways, something must be done to preserve tranquility and good order. The AC standardizes, that is, attempts to level, to control ministries and free charisms (not imparted during ordination) by conforming them to set patterns.

Standardizing already had a long history; the line of development is clear. In Paul apostles, prophets, teachers may be itinerant (1 Cor 12:28; Eph 4:11). The Didache went to great length to regulate these three functions. For instance, in the Didache prophets are called high priests.[8] In AC prophets are replaced with priests; priesthood co-opts prophecy.[9] Though the AC

---

[3] Ibid., SC 320:14, 38, 54, 61; 329:13, 14. J. Magne believes that one can retrieve the lost tract of Hippolytus' on the charisms embedded in AC 8. *Tradition Apostolique sur les Charismes et Diataxeis des Saints Apôtres* (Paris: Institut d'Etudes Semitiques de College de France, 1975) 87–104. M. Metzger presents strong arguments against the attribution of the *Apostolic Tradition* to Hippolytus in "Nouvelles perspectives pour la pretendue *Tradition Apostolique,*" *Ecclesia Orans* 5 (1988) 241–59.

[4] Metzger, Introduction, SC 329:11, 13.

[5] Ibid., SC 320:48.

[6] AC 1:1; SC 320:103.

[7] AC 8:2, 1; SC 336:135.

[8] Didache, 10:7; SC 248:182.

[9] AC 7:26, 6; SC 336:56.

gives greater place to virgins than to confessors and exorcists, it also wants to limit the importance of confessors, exorcists, and wonderworkers.[10] At the ordination of a priest the bishop prays that the ordinand will be filled with "therapeutic energies," an appropriation of powers belonging to the exorcist.[11]

While the *Apostolic Tradition* admits confessors of the faith to the presbyterate (not to the episcopate) without ordination,[12] the *AC* requires it for confessors becoming deacon, priest, or bishop.[13] Only the barest traces of the apostles, prophets, and teachers are found in the *AC*.[14] In principle, prophecy is still a real possibility, but the compiler gives it scant attention.[15] As models of prophetic vocation the compiler proposes women: Mary, the mother of Jesus, Elizabeth, Ann, and the daughters of Philip.[16] This may be an expression of control; women, as we shall see, were greatly impeded.

While not a despiser of prophecy, the compiler seems not to have a first hand experience of it, as his allusions to prophets indicates.[17] We may have here an example of a document with a false window: the compiler may be including prophets because he knows that without them something of the apostolic substance is missing. But prophets are placed in restraints.

The compiler does not want to exclude the possibility that free charisms can emerge. At the beginning of chapter 8 on church order, the compiler quotes in full the long ending of Mark (16:9-19), mentioning "the signs" which will accompany proclamation, among them exorcism, tongues, and healing. Unlike Cyril, the prophetic charisms are not linked to initiation, though he gives three accounts of the baptismal liturgy.[18] The confessor and the exorcist seem to experience some effusion of the Spirit.[19] Healing is less problematic than prophecy. The

[10] Metzger, Introduction, SC 329:58, 60.

[11] *AC* 8:16, 5; SC 336:218.

[12] Hippolytus, *Apostolic Tradition*, 9:1; SC 11bis:64.

[13] *AC* 8:23, 3; SC 336:224, 226.

[14] Metzger, Introduction, SC 329:57.

[15] *AC* 8:2, 10; SC 336:138. *See* Metzger, Introduction, SC 329:57, 58.

[16] *AC* 8:2, 10; SC 336:138.

[17] Metzger, Introduction, SC 329:57, 58.

[18] *AC* 3:16-18; SC 329:154-61; *AC* 7:22; 39-45; SC 336:46-48, 92-108.

[19] *AC* 8:23, 2; 26, 2; SC 336:224, 226, 228.

compiler recognizes that for healing, as for other free charisms, "God manifests and reveals it so that it is visible to all."[20]

Standardizing free charisms by giving privileged place to ordained ministers is one tactic of control. Another is the centralization of power in the hands of the bishop and the ordained clergy. Ignatius of Antioch has already moved in this direction,[21] a development which the AC reinforces. The insistent calls to obedience in the AC are an example.[22] Widows have the heaviest burden of obedience. Indeed, in the AC the list of those to whom the widows owe obedience is daunting: "The widows must be serious, obedient to the bishops, priests, deacons, to deaconesses, deferent, full of respect and fear, not authoritarian, undertaking nothing without the consent of the deacon. . . ."[23] Virgins and widows are compared to an altar, fixed in one place, not leaving their houses.[24]

The whole church order converges on the bishop, to whom a variety of titles are given: Father, Lord, Master, Levitical Priest, Director, King, Mediator, Agent of the Word, Ambassador, Witness, Pontiff, Teacher, President, Prophet, Medical Doctor.[25] Finally, the bishop is "the mouth of God," 'to be venerated as one of the gods.'[26] The bishop appropriates the charisms of prophet, teacher, and healer. Like the charism of the apostles, the episcopacy is itself a charism.[27]

The AC shows tendencies similar to the MC. In the MC Cyril acknowledges the presence of the charisms in a generic phrase, "the gift of the Spirit," which remains in an initiation context. The AC does not despise the prophetic charisms and intends to retain them, though in a greatly diminished role. The compiler standardizes the charisms, hedges them, institutionalizes them by appropriation, by over control. First the ordained clergy ab-

[20] AC 8:26, 2; SC 336:228.
[21] Ignatius, Eph. 2:1; Magn. 6:2; 7:1; 12:2; Tral. 7:1, 2; SC 10:58, 84, 90, 100.
[22] AC 2:26, 6; 2:28, 9; 2:30-32; 2:35, 4. SC 320:238, 248, 248-252, 258. AC 3:6, 1, 3; 3:8, 1; SC 329:132, 140.
[23] AC 3:8, 1; SC 329:140.
[24] AC 3:6, 4; SC 329:132, 134; AC 2:26, 8; SC 320:241.
[25] AC 2:20, 1; 2:25, 7; 26:3-4; 28, 8-9; 29; 41, 5; 3:3, 2; SC 320:196, 230, 236, 246, 248, 272, 274; SC 329:124.
[26] AC 2:28, 9; SC 320:248.
[27] AC 8:1, 21; SC 336:134.

sorb some of the charisms; then ordination is given precedence. This process ends up with neutered charisms, that is, charisms without their distinctive character, having little specificity.

A certain eminence rightly belongs to the bishop, as long as the tension between institution and charism is not extinguished. Controls were recognized as necessary as early as St. Paul (1 Cor 14). Not only free charisms need control, but also ecclesiastical offices. The temptation in standardizing, which is an expression of control, is to restrict the free charisms to the point of suffocation, a danger Irenaeus remarks in the second century, as we have seen.

Everyone understood that those with free charisms belonged to the church; no one thought that they stood outside even when they made prophetic protests against abuses in the church. They also belonged to the structural church in some loose fashion. The compiler, however, domesticates the charisms by incorporating them into the structures of authority, with clearly delineated limits. The charisms become identified in a new way with the institutional life to which they were supposed to give a prophetic witness. No longer is there tension between institution and charism.

Regulation did not always mean that charisms were little esteemed; the *AC* does honor them even when making it difficult for them to survive. Control, sometimes over control, could mean that the charisms would suffocate.

In summary, Jerusalem had some relation to Antioch through Caesarea, Jerusalem being jurisdictionally subject to the latter, which in turn was subject to Antioch. We have looked for clues to the events in Jerusalem by looking at a document originating either in Antioch or its environs, dated the last years of Cyril's life. I have tried to show that the compiler esteems the free charisms. But I have presented no evidence at all that Antioch ever had the imparting of the prophetic charisms as a conscious element of Christian initiation. In Jerusalem the Cyril of both the *CL* and the *MC* knows that they belong there, though Cyril speaks of the charisms with more restraint in the latter than in the former.

The compiler's *AC* and Cyril's *MC* may be moving in the same direction. If increased contact with the universal church, through the flood of pilgrims, forced Jerusalem in the 380s to adopt the suspicious attitudes of the universal church toward the charisms, and therefore to conform to the practice of not promoting them in the rites of initiation, why not Antioch? As a political, military, and trade center Antioch was the more cosmopolitan city, even after the deluge of pilgrims flooded Jerusalem. If the standardized charisms are part of Antioch's well ordered church, the rites of initiation would certainly reflect it. The name the "baptism in the Holy Spirit" could have been retained even while the prophetic charisms within the rites were no longer expected or encouraged. Antioch had no geographical Pentecost site to remind it of the day tongues of fire fell and rested on the church.

Like Cyril, the compiler calls the rites of initiation the "baptism in the Holy Spirit," linking it explicitly to an anointing.[28] Both the Cyril of the *CL* and the compiler esteem the charisms, both share the supposition that prophecy is a possibility for the church. Cyril, however, is more positive in his expectations, and in the exhortations he gives the faithful to be open to this charism.

The older Cyril of the *MC* may still maintain positive attitudes toward the charisms (especially prophecy), still call initiation baptism in the Holy Spirit. All this may be contained in the biblical shorthand "gift of the Spirit," if the *MC* are the preacher's notes, not his full text. On the other hand, the *MC* may be a rather exact record of what Cyril said. Then "gift of the Spirit," though yet positive in content and including the prophetic charisms, would indicate a significant shift in the direction of the *AC*. Jerusalem and Antioch then give the charisms a reduced role in the 380s. Cyril of the *MC* generalizes, the compiler standardizes.

Though we have not studied it, the increasing practice of infant baptism must have had an effect on how initiation was presented and received. As in Tertullian, Origen, and Hilary, so also in Cyril, one finds the elements in the rites of Christian initiation which the contemporary charismatic renewal identifies

[28] *AC* 8:16, 4; SC 329:156.

as belonging to the baptism in the Spirit: either imposition of hands or anointing, praying for the descent of the Spirit, expectation that the charisms will be manifested. Two contemporaries of Cyril, Basil of Caesarea and Gregory Nazianzus, place the charisms in relation to baptism. Further, Cyril recognizes the importance of laying on of hands in the tradition. In the *CL* he identifies this gesture as imparting the Spirit; in the *MC* imparting of the Spirit was tied to the anointing, following the Eastern tradition.

Cyril makes no attempt to give a complete list of the charisms, but he believes that all the charisms, in some generic sense, are present in the churches. Cyril neither gave special attention to tongues, nor avoided biblical texts where it is found. It was included in Paul's list in 1 Corinthians 12 which Cyril quoted at the very end of the whole catechetical series, just before the great Easter celebration of initiation.[29] Prophecy, on the contrary, he singled out as a charism of which he wished God would make the candidates worthy. In any case, the candidates were to enter into the mysteries expecting and open to "the heavenly charisms."

How will John Chrysostom proclaim the scriptures and prepare the catechumens for their baptism? Are there any traces of the prophetic charisms in relation to Christian initiation? Since the *AC* come from the general area of Antioch, but not from the church of Chrysostom, and is dated about 380, about six years before Chrysostom was ordained a priest in Antioch, will there be any links between the *AC*, on the one hand, and, on the other, his exegetical homilies and baptismal catecheses?

[29] *CL* 18:27; *CAO* 2:330.

Chapter Twenty

John Chrysostom: From Jordan to Calvary

To understand the relation of the baptism in the Spirit to Christian initiation it is important to ask other questions than just whether the liturgical presider at initiation mentions the charisms and exhorts the baptismal candidates to be open to them. Also significant is the larger character of the baptismal rite. Is something happening to the rites themselves, historically making it more difficult to think of the baptism in the Holy Spirit as integral to initiation? Or is there a shift in the theological matrix of initiation, a reshuffling of theological suppositions? Would such a shift in any way blur those elements of the baptism in the Holy Spirit, which at this time, and, perhaps historically up to this moment, were considered integral to initiation?

We have looked at Tertullian, Origen, Hilary, Cyril of Jerusalem, and *The Apostolic Constitutions* in a rather restricted perspective. In the next two chapters we turn to John Chrysostom. My purpose is to look at Chrysostom's understanding of charisms in a broader framework. Principally I want to see how Chrysostom is part of a development which had its roots in the Syriac rite, but then, ostensibly, moved away from the Syriac understanding of baptism. To see the developing pattern some

reference must be made to other fourth century authors, principally Didymus the Blind, Cyril of Jerusalem, Ambrose, and
Theodore of Mopsuestia. Besides Antioch two other cities have
a significant role in this unfolding liturgical and theological history, Jerusalem and Alexandria. I focus on the shift of the major
paradigm for Christian initiation from Jesus' baptism in the
Jordan to Jesus' death and resurrection. Why was the authority
of Jesus' baptism in relation to Christian baptism diminished?
What trinitarian model of the relation of christology to pneumatology was linked to the baptism of Jesus? Do these shifts have
any significance in our attempt to locate the baptism in the
Holy Spirit as integral to Christian initiation?

Antioch: The Beautiful City of the Greeks

As indicated in a previous chapter, Antioch was a major Greek
city in a Syrian area. How Greek it was can be seen from the
case of Chrysostom. He was born there about 347, grew up and
was educated there, and after ordination to the priesthood in
386 exercised his ministry there until he was made patriarch of
Constantinople in 398. Chrysostom was steeped in the Greek
culture of late antiquity as experienced at Antioch, and though
he distanced himself more from Greek classical literature than
Basil, he never escaped his rhetorical and classical training. In
spite of the heavy Greek presence in Antioch many who lived
there understood very little Greek. Chrysostom always
preached in Greek. In those fifty-one years he never learned
Syriac, which he considered a barbarian tongue.[1]

Like Jerusalem, Antioch was a boundary city where Greek
and Syriac culture met. Beyond the gates of the city the language was Syriac. Of all Libanius' students of Greek rhetoric
Chrysostom was the most eloquent. In 392, while still a priest
and six years before he became patriarch of Constantinople,
Chrysostom merited to be included in Jerome's exclusive club of
illustrious men.[2]

The liturgical language of the earliest community in Jerusalem
and the Judaeo-Christian communities in Palestine was very

[1] Bardy, Question des Langues, 19.
[2] Jerome, On Famous Men, 129; PG 23:713. Young, From Nicaea to Chalcedon, 146.

likely Syro-Aramaic. But from the beginning the liturgical language of the Antioch community was Greek. Since liturgical families at this time were determined more by patriarchal jurisdiction than language, this meant that other churches subject to its jurisdiction, such as Syriac speaking Mopsuestia (modern Misis in southern Turkey) and Edessa, carried on the liturgical traditions of Antioch which came to be called the West Syriac rite.[3] For example, the important baptismal and eucharistic liturgies of Theodore of Mopsuestia in Syria are, despite some differences, substantially those of Chrysostom's Greek rites in Antioch.[4] Liturgically both Antioch and Jerusalem belonged to the same Syriac family. Chrysostom's baptismal homilies are, indeed, one of the sources of Syriac rites.[5] This background is important for the understanding of the context out of which Chrysostom speaks, of his relation to Cyril, and crucial for the links between Chrysostom and the non-Greek Syriac liturgies.

In Antioch John Chrysostom emerged as a great preacher and ecclesiastic. He held the office of preparing the catechumens for baptism until the time he was a bishop and became the patriarch of Constantinople. Only two of the baptismal catecheses of Chrysostom delivered to the catechumens were known up until 1909. These two lectures were delivered in 388, therefore, while he was still a priest in Antioch.[6] In 1909 a second series of four catecheses were discovered by A. Papadopoulos-Kerameus and were printed by the University of Petersburg in an obscure series.[7] These four catecheses seem to have been delivered at Antioch, also in the Lent of 388. Again in 1955 a third series of eight homilies was discovered by A. Wenger in the monastery

[3] F. Reine, *The Eucharistic Doctrine and Liturgy of the Mystagogical Catecheses of Theodore of Mopsuestia* (Washington: Catholic University of America, 1942) 3, 4; J. Jungmann, *The Early Liturgy* (Notre Dame: University of Notre Dame, 1959) 200–05.

[4] A. Mingana, *Commentary of Theodore of Mopsuestia on the Lord's Prayer and on the Sacraments of Baptism and Eucharist* (Cambridge: Heffer, 1933) x–xi; Reine, *Theodore of Mopsuestia*, 1–5.

[5] L. Duchesne, *Christian Worship: Its Origin and Evolution* (London: SPCK, 1904) 55, 56; F. E. Brightman, *Liturgies Eastern and Western* (Oxford: Clarendon, 1896) 1:xvii–lxiii.

[6] *Montfaucon Baptismal Catecheses*, PG 49:223-40 (hereafter cited as *MBC*).

[7] A. Papadopoulos-Kerameus, *Varia Graeca Sacra* (St. Petersburg: University of St. Petersburg, 1909) xx–xxv and 154–83 (hereafter cited as *PKBC*).

of Stavronikita on Mount Athos. These, too, seem to have been delivered in Antioch shortly after 388.[8] Because there is some duplication, the total number of catechetical lectures comes to twelve.[9] All were delivered in Antioch before Chrysostom was a bishop, all around the year 388.

Like Cyril's *CL*, these homilies are specifically directed to the catechumens in preparation for the rites of initiation in the Easter Vigil. However, they have a slightly different character from Cyril's series of instructions. They were delivered to the whole of the assembly, not just to catechumens, as was the case for Cyril and also for Theodore of Mopsuestia. The discipline of the secret, which was in force for Cyril, was greatly relaxed for Chrysostom's congregation. His people heard him freely commenting on the meaning of the liturgical rites of initiation, which Cyril saved for the post- Easter *MC*. Further, the number of the pre-baptismal instructions is greatly reduced. Cyril of Jerusalem gave one Proto-catechesis, eighteen catechetical lectures; Theodore of Mopsuestia gave fourteen baptismal catecheses, while the Papadopoulos-Kerameus series of Chrysostom is complete with only four. This more modest number needs to be kept in mind. We do not have an exact account of all those who catechized the candidates whom Chrysostom was preparing for baptism. He mentioned "your excellent teachers," indicating that Bishop Flavian of Antioch and other traveling bishops, always numerous in a metropolitan capital such as Antioch, had also given instructions.[10] Any judgment as to what was taught, or not taught, has to be aware of the reduced number of instructions. Besides Chrysostom other instructors may have covered topics of which we have no record, and on which Chrysostom had not spoken.

[8] *Huit Catéchèses Baptismales,* ed. A. Wenger (Paris: du Cerf, 1970); SC 50bis (hereafter cited as *SBC*). The dating of the three baptismal series is discussed by Wenger, SC 50bis:63-65.

[9] All twelve are found in *St. John Chrysostom: Baptismal Instructions,* ed. P. W. Harkins (Westminster: Newman, 1963). The English translations come from this text.

[10] *SBC* 8:1; SC 50bis:247. The English translation of Chrysostom's sermons is a modification, except where indicated, of that found in vols. 10, 12, 13 of the *Nicene and Post-Nicene Fathers* (First Series) (New York: The Christian Literature Company, 1888–1889). Hereafter the number of the book of the bible is the number of Chrysostom's homily, not the chapter of the biblical book.

Because of the relationship between charism and the baptism in the Holy Spirit it is important to understand the paradigms Chrysostom used for Christian initiation. More specifically we need to look at the role of anointing and the water-bath in the baptismal rite.

As a priest in Antioch, Chrysostom inherited the rites of initiation as found in the broad pattern of Syriac rites. The placing of the anointing before the water-bath was an ancient practice when Chrysostom appeared on the scene. Hippolytus of Rome, possibly belonging to one of the many groups of Oriental Christians settled in Rome and destined to become the first antipope, had such an anointing. But it was an exorcism. The anointing served as a cleansing preparatory to the water-bath.[11] Syria, however, had its own tradition, and some expressions of it were culturally isolated from Greek influences. The Syrian author, Aphrahat (active around 340), was ignorant of an event as significant as the Council of Nicaea (325).[12]

Through the work of A. Raes, B. Botte, S. Brock, and others, we have a clear outline of the history of baptism in Syria.[13] Unlike Hippolytus the pre-baptismal anointing in the Syrian tradition is not an exorcism, but is the locus for the imparting of the Spirit. In the Syriac rites (and the Armenian which are dependent on them) there was probably only one anointing, preceding the water-bath. Scholars diverge a little in how this Syriac tradition is presented. Sebastian Brock points to the integrity of the Syrian rites, with the gift of the Spirit imparted by the whole rite, within which anointing and the water-bath form a unity.[14] If the baptism is one integral celebration in sacred time,

---

[11] *Apostolic Tradition* 21; SC 11bis:80. Ysebaert, *Greek Baptismal Terminology: Its Origins and Early Development* (Nijmegen: Dekker & Van de Vegt, 1962) 262, 339–51.

[12] I. Ortiz de Urbina, *Patrologia Syriaca* (Rome: Oriental Institute, 1965) 49, 50.

[13] Raes, *Introductio in Liturgiam Orientalem* (Rome: Oriental Institute, 1947) 115–54; Botte, "Le Baptême dans l'Eglise Syrienne," *L'Orient Syrien* 1 (1956) 137–55; Brock, "Studies in the Early History of the Syrian Orthodox Baptismal Liturgy," *JTS* 23 (1972) 16–64.

[14] *The Holy Spirit in the Syrian Baptismal Tradition*, The Syrian Churches Series, ed. J. Velllian (1979) 9:37. *See also* Brock, "Baptismal Themes in the Writings of Jacob of Serugh," *Orientalia Christiana Analecta* 205 (1978) 325–47.

the imparting of the Spirit can be located at different moments in historical time. If one Syrian author says the bestowal of the Spirit is located in the water-bath, "this does not exclude the fact that it is just as much conferred by the anointing(s)."[15] At Antioch the original sequence in baptism, that is, anointing then water-bath, was modeled on Jewish initiation where the circumcision came first and then immersion. Brock holds that the determination of the imparting of the Spirit was determined by two choices: paradigm and imagery. From the beginning the paradigm at Antioch was the baptism of Jesus when he was anointed with the Spirit and proclaimed Son of God. Baptism is a birth, not a death event. Only toward the end of the fourth century did the death and resurrection of Jesus in Romans 6:3, 4 ("Do you not know that all of us who have been baptized into Christ Jesus were baptized into his death? We were buried therefore with him by baptism into death.") begin to catch the imagination at Antioch. "If baptism is a death and resurrection, then the gifts of the Spirit can hardly be conferred before it."[16] Pentecost cannot come before Calvary. The imparting of the Spirit is shifted away from the beginning of the rite to the water-bath, as in Chrysostom, or to a post-baptismal anointing. The introduction of the death paradigm leaves a vacuum where the pre-baptismal anointing had been, which was filled with new cathartic content. Only at this rather late date did people note that the Spirit comes down on Jesus only *after* he emerges from the water. The transfer of the pre-baptismal anointing to a post-baptismal one can now invoke this literalist reading of the gospel as in harmony with the new sequence of images.[17]

Gabriele Winkler, whose publications on Syriac materials I am summarizing here,[18] has devoted attention to the cleansing and ex-

[15] *The Holy Spirit in the Syrian Baptismal Tradition*, 37.
[16] Ibid., 38.
[17] Ibid.
[18] G. Winkler, "The History of the Syriac Pre-baptismal Anointing in the Light of the Earliest Armenian Sources," *Symposium Syriacum 1976* (Rome: Oriental Institute, 1978) 317–24; "The Original Meaning of the Pre-Baptismal Anointing and its Implications," *Worship* 52 (1978) 24–45; "Zu frühchristlichen Tauftradition in Syrien und Armenien unter Einbezug der Taufe Jesu," *Ostkirchliche Studien* 27 (1978) 281–306; *Das Armenische Initiationsrituale* (Rome: Oriental Institute, 1982); "A Remarkable Shift in the 4th Century

orcistic themes in relation to the imparting of the Spirit in the Armenian and Syrian baptismal liturgies. Winkler seems to tie the imparting of the Spirit to the early Syrian pre-baptismal anointing in a more focused way than Brock. In its early form it was the head which was anointed (later the whole body).[19] In this Syriac and Armenian tradition the pre-baptismal anointing (there was no post-baptismal anointing) constituted the dominant, indeed pivotal, element in the rite; this anointing was the central act of initiation because it was the symbol of imparting the Spirit.[20] The early pre-baptismal anointing found in the Syriac rites was a pneumatological event.

Winkler demonstrates that in the Armenian and Syriac tradition the manifestation of the Spirit at the baptism of Jesus was an article of the creed: "We believe also in the Holy Spirit . . . who descended on the Jordan to proclaim the One-Sent (Jesus)."[21] The baptism of Jesus was considered the prototype of the Spirit's creative power, the normative manifestation.[22] So much was this so that in the eucharistic prayer, the anaphora, the epiclesis (the calling down of the Spirit on the gifts) is cast in terms of the baptism of Jesus while omitting any mention of the Spirit's role in the incarnation.[23] The role of the Spirit in Jesus' baptism is the model for eucharistic change, rather than the role of the Spirit in the incarnation. If one is tracing the beginnings of Spirit-christology it will be found in the baptism of Jesus.[24]

What is significant in this creed is that the prototype of Christian baptism is the baptism of Jesus at the Jordan. The greatest

Creeds: An Analysis of the Armenian, Syriac, and Greek Evidence," *Studia Patristica* 17, part 3 (1982) 1396–401; "Ein bedeutsamer Zusammenhang zwischen der Erkenntnis und Ruhe in Mt 11:27-29 und dem Ruhen des Geistes auf Jesus am Jordan. Eine Analyse zur Geist-Christologie in Syrischen und Armenischen Quellen," *Museon* 96 (1983) 267–326.

[19] Acting on a clue from J. Mateos, Winkler established that the early pre-baptismal anointing was only of the head. "Zur frühchristlicen Tauftradition in Syrien und Armenien unter Einbezug der Taufe Jesu," *Ostkirchliche Studien* 27 (1978) 281–306.

[20] Winkler, "The Original Meaning," 43–45; Winkler, *Initiationsrituale*, 168–75.

[21] Quoted from Winkler, "A Remarkable Shift," 1397.

[22] Ibid., 1399.

[23] Ibid.

[24] Winkler, "Geist-Christologie in Syrischen und Armenischen Quellen," 325.

theological weight was attached to this mystery.[25] As Jesus received the Spirit at his baptism in the Jordan, we receive the Spirit at ours. At the Jordan the epiphany of the Spirit had as its function to identify and proclaim that Jesus is the one sent from the Father. This very ancient creed not only safeguards the pneumatological content of Christian baptism, but retains a trinitarian dynamic. The Father sends the Spirit in whom Jesus is announced as the Sent One.

Anointing and Imparting the Spirit

The general post-biblical tradition saw the closest relationship between the anointing and the imparting of the Spirit. One cannot identify any New Testament passage which unambiguously refers to an external anointing in Christian baptism, though the point has been disputed.[26] One text already discussed by George Montague is especially evocative and tempting: "God it is who confirms *(bebaiōn)* us with you in Jesus Christ, and has anointed *(chrisas)* us; he has sealed *(sphragisamenos)* us and given us an earnest *(arrabōna)* of the Spirit in out hearts" (2 Cor 1:21, 22). This passage contains three elements of initiation: confirm, anoint, seal. Similar anointing language can be found in John: "you have been anointed by the Holy One and you all know . . . The anointing which you have received from him abides in you" (1 John 2:20, 27). In Luke the identification of the descent of the Spirit with anointing is attributed to the Lord himself: "The Spirit of the Lord is upon me, because he has anointed me" (Luke 4:18).

The biblical background for this identification may well be the baptism of Jesus in the Jordan, when "God anointed Jesus of Nazareth with Holy Spirit and power" (Acts 10:38). At his baptism Jesus is filled with the Holy Spirit (Luke 3:22; 4:14), and in this power he undertakes his mission (Luke 4:14). As George Montague has shown, Luke takes over all the healings from

[25] Winkler, "A Remarkable Shift," 1398, 1399.
[26] G. R. Beasley-Murray, *Baptism in the New Testament* (Grand Rapids: Eerdmans, 1973) 233; T. W. Manson, "Entry into Membership of the Early Church," *JTS* 48 (1947) 25–33; Mitchell, *Baptismal Anointing*, 15–20. Mitchell gives a short review of the discussion.

Mark, adding three of his own. Very likely the synoptics place such emphasis on Jesus' miracles because they understood that he was anointed with the Spirit and power.[27] Links in the prototype of Christian baptism are forged between anointing and healings, miracles, and other "mighty works and wonders and signs (Acts 2:22)."[28]

While it is possible that the New Testament knew of an actual anointing in Christian baptism, the texts do not demand such an interpretation. However a look at the post-biblical development can hardly leave a doubt that these New Testament texts were used by the early church as a justification of baptismal anointings.[29]

The ancient Syriac tradition of one pre-baptismal anointing by which the imparting of the Spirit was expressed may have been shared with Cappadocia, Armenia and Alexandria.[30] Didymus the Blind gives evidence, saying that "we were sealed and baptized in the name of the Father, and of the Son, and of the Holy Spirit."[31] Bradshaw interprets "the seal" to be the pre-baptismal anointing.[32] Further, an Arabic document reporting the usage of the Coptic church in Alexandria, and recounting an incident dated by explicit reference to John Chrysostom, tells of a woman sailing from Antioch to Alexandria, whose child fell ill during the voyage. The mother, fearing the child would die without baptism, drew some of her own blood and signed the child (as one does with oil).[33] Bradshaw sees in this a testimony to a pre-baptismal anointing in Alexandria, an anointing which is not exorcistic.[34] Clearly, the evidence is not extensive.[35]

---

[27] Haenchen, *Acts of Apostles,* 353.

[28] Ibid., 352, 353.

[29] Mitchell, *Baptismal Anointing,* 15–20; Beasley-Murray, *Baptism,* 233.

[30] Kretschmar, "Die Geschichte des Taufgottesdienstes in der alten Kirche," 133–36; 210–13.

[31] Didymus the Blind, *On the Trinity,* 2:15; PG 39:720.

[32] Bradshaw, "Baptismal Practice in the Alexandrian Tradition, Eastern or Western?" *Essays in Early Eastern Initiation,* ed. P. Bradshaw (Nottigham: Grove, 1988) 12, 13.

[33] L. Villecourt, "Le Livre du Chrême," *Museon* 41 (1928) 58.

[34] Bradshaw, "Baptismal Practice in the Alexandrian Tradition, Eastern or Western?" 12.

[35] Kretschmar, "Die Geschichte des Taufgottesdienstes," 133–36.

Though the rite on which Cyril of Jerusalem comments is basically the ancient Syrian rite, this one anointing became two, one pre- and the other post-baptismal.[36] The first was preparatory. The whole body was anointed but it has the character of purgation/exorcism: the oil cleanses from the traces of sin and chases away the invisible powers of Satan.[37] The anointing which followed the water-bath was the one by which the "soul is sanctified by the Holy and life-giving Spirit."[38] The five senses were anointed.

At Antioch from the time of Bishop Theophilus (d. 180), the anointing seems identical with becoming a Christian: "We are actually called Christians just because we are anointed with the oil of God."[39] Chrysostom resisted Cyril's example of pre- and post-baptismal anointings. But he did not retain the Syriac tradition of only one anointing before the water-bath; he had two pre-baptismal anointings, and none afterward. Anointing here signifies becoming a lower case christ who is owned by the upper case Christ in preparation for the battle with Satan. The second anointing has the theme of union with Christ, but it also has a purgative function. The exorcism and purgation prepares one for the water-bath.[40] In Chrysostom the anointings are no longer a symbol of the imparting of the Spirit. Now the imparting of the Spirit is related to the water-bath combined with the imposition of the bishop's hand. As in Cyril the anointing is deprived of its pneumatological content. The two anointings are exorcistic and purgative.

The development of the catechumenate, together with its emphasis upon cleansing and the transfer from the kingdom of

[36] Ratcliff, "The Old Syrian Baptismal Tradition," 143. The whole of this volume is significant for our study of Syriac baptismal rites. *See also* A. Guillamont, "Poème de Narsaï sur le Baptéme," *L'Orient Syrien* 1 (1956) 189–207; H. Braun, "Entscheidende Motive in den Berichten über die Taufe Jesu von Markus bis Justin," *ZTK* 50 (1953) 39–43; V. Desprez, "Le Baptême chez le Pseudo-Macaire," *Ecclesia Orans* 5 (1988) 121–55.

[37] Cyril of Jerusalem, *MC* 2:3; SC 126:106, 108.

[38] Ibid., 3:3; SC 126:124.

[39] *To Autolycus* 1:12; *Theophilus of Antioch: Ad Autolycum*, ed. R. Grant (Oxford: Clarendon, 1970) 16.

[40] *SCL* 2:22; SC 50bis:145, 146. Riley, *Christian Initiation*, 199–202.

darkness to the kingdom of light, with its repeated purgations and exorcisms, made it unlikely to have a pre-baptismal anointing as the rite for imparting the Spirit.[41] Not until all the trappings of the kingdom of darkness had been removed could the gift of the Spirit, the gift without parallel of the kingdom of light, be imparted; the reception of so great a gift could only take place after a thorough scouring had taken place.[42] What had been a rite for imparting the Spirit became a purgation and exorcism. This is true of Cyril,[43] Theodore of Mopsuestia,[44] and Ambrose (c. 339–97).[45]

The displacement of the imparting of the Spirit by an exorcism, and this at the beginning of the rite of initiation, creates a totally different environment, and creates a wholly different dynamics for baptism. The exorcistic anointing did not stand alone. Those in the catechumenate received exorcisms,[46] sometimes daily.[47] The oil was exorcised.[48] Demons were chased from the baptismal water,[49] which, Winkler records with some impatience, had previously signified the Jordan.[50] Outside of the baptismal rites at a communal meal, bread given to the

[41] Winkler, *Das Armenische Initiationsrituale*, 419.

[42] Winkler, "The Original Meaning," 42, note 63.

[43] Cyril of Jerusalem, *MC* 2:3; SC 126:108.

[44] Theodore, *Baptismal Homily*, 3:8; Mingana, *Theodore of Mopsuestia on the Lord's Prayer, Baptism, and Eucharist*, 54. Theodore has a quite original view of the anointing as a garment of immortality in which the candidate is going to receive baptism. Riley counsels caution: "It should not be overlooked that this interpretation of the ceremony reduces itself fundamentally to the exorcistic-healing motif, which was more explicitly present in Cyril's reference to the "oil of exorcism." *Christian Initiation*, 203.

[45] Ambrose, *On the Sacraments*, 1:4; SC 25bis:62. Here again is the motif of an athlete training for combat with the Evil One, which begins with a renunciation of Satan.

[46] Cyril of Jerusalem, *Protocatechetics* 9; *CAO* 1, 12; Chrysostom, *SBC* 2:24; SC 50bis:147.

[47] Egeria, *Egeria's Travels*, 46; SC 296:306.

[48] Cyril of Jerusalem, *MC*: 2:3; SC 126: 106, 108; *See* extensive ibid., 108, note of A. Piédagnel.

[49] Ambrose, *On the Sacraments*, 1:5, 18; SC 25:60.

[50] Winkler, "The Original Meaning," 42. *See also* E. Bartsch, *Die Sachbeschwörungen der Römischen Liturgie* (Münster: Aschendorff, 1967) 66–79; F. J. Dölger, *Der Exorzismus im altchristlichen Taufritual* (Paderborn: Schöningh, 1909).

catechumens was exorcised.[51] The increased emphasis on purgation and exorcism was not at ease with having the baptism of Jesus for the prototype. For this reason an anointing imparting the Spirit was moved away from the beginning of the rite and inserted after the water-bath, as seen in Cyril of Jerusalem,[52] Theodore of Mopsuestia,[53] and Ambrose.[54] In Cyril and Theodore the place of the imparting of the Spirit is in the anointing which follows the water-bath; in Ambrose in the post-baptismal anointing and/or in a consignation (which may or may not have an anointing connected with it). All three have the anointing, not at the beginning of the rite, as was the case when the baptism of Jesus was the primary model, but more toward the end of the rite. Chrysostom has the laying on of hands combined with the water-bath as the rite for imparting the Spirit. He, too, postpones the imparting of the Spirit, moving it away from the beginning of the rite. The rite starts with purgations and exorcisms. The new dynamics set in motion by these changes gives the entire Christian initiation a more pronounced purgative, a less pneumatological character.[55]

A diagram may help in keeping track of this complicated history (see next page). The before and after refer to the place relative to the water-bath. We can see here the tendency to move the imparting of the Spirit away from the beginning of the rite, Chrysostom placing it in the water-bath, but the others postponing it to the post-baptismal anointing. Note how exorcisms are increasingly tied to the anointings.

In presenting the Syrian baptismal practice some significance is attached to imparting of the Spirit before the water-bath. This represents a christology which is dependent on pneumatology, as over against a pneumatology which is dependent on christology, when the imparting of the Spirit takes place after the

[51] Hippolytus, *Apostolic Tradition*, 26; SC 11bis:105.

[52] Cyril of Jerusalem, *MC* 3:3; SC 126:124.

[53] Theodore, *Baptismal Homily*, 3:27; Mingana, *Theodore of Mopsuestia on the Lord's Prayer, Baptism, and Eucharist*, 69.

[54] Ambrose, *On the Mysteries*, 42: SC 25bis:178; Ambrose, *On the Sacraments*, 3:8; SC 25bis:96.

[55] Winkler, "The Original Meaning," 42.

ANOINTING DIAGRAM

AUTHOR	NUMBER OF ANOINTINGS	PLACE	THEME
Hippolytus of Rome (c. 170–c. 236)	Three	Before and After	*Before:* exorcism *After/First:* thanksgiving. *Second:* imparting the Spirit.
Ancient Syriac	One	Before	Imparting the Spirit
Didymus the Blind (c. 313–98)	One (?)	Before (?)	Imparting the Spirit (?)
Alexandria (fourth century)	One (?)	Before (?)	Not exorcism (?)
Cyril of Jerusalem (c. 315–86)	Two	Before and After	*Before:* exorcism-healing readying for combat with Satan. *After:* imparting the Spirit; Christ anointed with the Spirit; Christian anointed with the Spirit.
Ambrose (c. 339–97)	Two	Before and After	*Before:* strengthening the athlete to enter the arena and meet the adversary. *After:* imparting the Spirit; Spirit as pledge and seal.
John Chrysostom (c. 347–407)	Two	Before	*First:* soldier/athlete training for battle against Satan. *Second:* union with Christ making one strong for the battle with Satan.
Theodore of Mopsuestia (c. 350–428)	Two	Before and After	*Before:* exorcism-healing. *After:* imparting of the Spirit; Christ anointed with the Spirit; the Christian anointed with the Spirit.

water-bath (which itself has christological content).[56] Care must be exercised in the interpretation of this sequence. The basis for the Syrian sequence was not primarily insight into the biblical order, but, as Brock has indicated, the adoption of the sequence in the Jewish initiation rite, namely, circumcision, then water-bath. Irrespective of the original reason for the sequence, *de facto* a theological trinitarian understanding of baptism (and the baptism in the Spirit) charism, and the Christian life was attached to the Syrian order. In contrast to the Syrian perspective, Cyril, Theodore, and Ambrose have the mission of the Spirit dependent on that of the Son. In all three the imparting of the Spirit takes place after the water-bath. Chrysostom also has the Christ moment precede the Spirit moment, but it is ritually expressed differently: the pre-baptismal anointings have a christological character but they are dominantly exorcisms and purgations. The Christ moment in the anointings precedes the Spirit moment in the water-bath. In his baptismal rite the Spirit is dependent on Christ.

Both models, Christ as dependent on the Spirit and the Spirit as dependent on Christ, are authentically trinitarian, but the dynamics are somewhat different and the consequences can be quite divergent.[57] In any trinitarian theology of salvation both need to be found. The "style" of trinitarian theology is determined by which exercises dominance. The baptism in the Holy Spirit as integral to Christian initiation can be sustained by either model. However, Christ dependent on the Spirit presents a more favorable theological climate for expressing the theological meaning of the baptism in the Holy Spirit. Jesus' baptism in the Jordan preceding his public life seems to be expressing this dependence of Christ on the Spirit, as does the role of the Spirit in the conception of Jesus (Luke 1:35). On the other hand, the dependence of the Spirit on Christ is seen in the risen

---

[56] J. Zizioulas elaborates two styles in the tradition: christology dependent on pneumatology, and the pneumatology dependent on christology. "Implications ecclésiologiques de deux types de pneumatologie," *Communio Sanctorum*, Mélanges offerts à Jean-Jacques von Allmen (Geneva: Labor et Fides, 1982) 141–54.

[57] Ibid.; J. Zizioulas, "Christ, the Spirit and the Church," *Being as Communion* (Crestwood: St. Vladimir, 1985) 123–42.

Christ sending the Spirit (John 20:19-23), and also in Peter's interpretation of the Pentecost event: "This Jesus God raised up, and of that we all are witnesses. Being therefore exalted at the right hand of God, and having received from the Father the promise of the Holy Spirit, he has poured out this which you see and hear" (Acts 2:32, 33).

Behold! A New Person Ascends from the Water

Chrysostom joins the communication of the Holy Spirit to the water-bath: "When you come to the sacred initiation, the eyes of the flesh see water; the eyes of faith behold the Spirit."[58] The water-bath alone does not impart the Spirit, but is joined to the imposition of hands. After the anointing-exorcism the catechumen descends into the water-bath. The bishop places his hand on the catechumen's head, pushing and making the candidate's head go down into the water. This act is considered an imposition of hand(s). With some frequency the anointing is combined with the imposition of hands, in some cases the laying on of hands is not mentioned, or only alluded to.[59] All of these constitute one composite gesture by which the descent of the Spirit is signified: "It is at this moment that, by means of the words and the hand of the priest [who is a bishop], the Spirit descends, and it is a different person who ascends [out of the water]."[60]

Chrysostom has in mind the baptism of Jesus in the Jordan: it appears as though John the Baptist with his hand upon the head of Jesus immerses him in the river. The emphasis is upon appearance, because Chrysostom believes that in reality it is the divine Word which leads Jesus into the streams of the Jordan and baptizes him. "The master's body was baptized by the Word, and by the voice of his Father from heaven which said: 'This is my beloved Son,' and by the manifestation of the Holy

---

[58] PKBC 3:12; Varia Graeca Sacra, 169.

[59] This combined gesture can also be found in Hippolytus, Apostolic Tradition, 21: SC 11bis:85. See the discussion of laying on of hands in combined gestures in Riley, Christian Initiation, 146, note 12; 354, note 30; 404, note 159. See the historical reflections of A. Piédagnel in SC 126:131, note 1.

[60] SBC 2:25; SC 50bis:147.

Spirit which descended upon him."[61] Chrysostom has not entirely abandoned the baptism of Jesus. Then Chrysostom joins the Jordan to the Pentecost experience, quoting John the Baptist: "after me comes one . . . who will baptize you in the Holy Spirit and fire" (Luke 3:16).

Apart from the trinitarian formulations this is the sole mention of the Spirit in the rite itself. In the catechetical instructions, in contrast to the liturgical rite, Chrysostom refers to the Spirit repeatedly: the transforming descent of the Spirit,[62] the working of the Spirit,[63] the manifestation of the Spirit,[64] the indwelling Spirit,[65] and the fruit of the Spirit.[66] All of this forms the larger context for the composite rite of imparting the Spirit.

What is the symbolic content of this descent into, and ascent out of the baptismal waters? We have seen that Cyril uses both the birth and the death and resurrection images. For Chrysostom the matter is clear: "baptism is a burial and resurrection."[67] On this theme Chrysostom is expansive, never tiring of searching out new facets.[68] This is not a totally new baptismal theme. Two early authors had incorporated the death and resurrection into their baptismal liturgies, namely, Melito of Sardis (d. 190)[69] and Tertullian.[70] Among Chrysostom's contemporaries who represent this Pauline liturgical anchorage in the death and resurrection are Ambrose in the West,[71] and Theodore of Mopsuestia in the East.[72]

[61] PKBC 3:13; Varia Graeca Sacra, 169, 170.

[62] SBC 5:19; SC 50bis:210.

[63] MBC 1:26; PG 49:228.

[64] SBC 4:17; SC 50bis:191.

[65] Ibid., 3:6; SC 50bis:154.

[66] Ibid., 1:33; SC 50bis:125. T. M. Finn, The Liturgy of Baptism in the Baptismal Instructions of St. John Chrysostom (Washington; Catholic University of America, 1967) 178.

[67] SBC 2:11; SC 50bis:139.

[68] PKBC 2:4; Varia Graeca Sacra, 158.

[69] Melito, On the Passover, 1-14; 31-33; SC 123:60-67; 77.

[70] Tertullian, On Baptism, 19:1; SC 35:93.

[71] Ambrose, On the Sacraments, 2:16, 20; SC 25bis:67, 68, 71; On the Mysteries 21; SC 25bis:166.

[72] Theodore, Baptismal Homilies, 1:6, 7; 3:5, 6, 25; Les Homilies Catéchétiques de Théodore de Mopsuestia (Studi e Testi, 145), ed. R. Tonneau and R. Devreesse (Vatican City: Vatican Library, 1949) 331, 333, 411, 413, 415, 453, 455.

A broader acceptance of the death and resurrection as a prototype of Christian baptism came about partly as a result of a rediscovery and reappropriation of the Pauline letters in the fourth century.[73] To this can be added Cyril of Jerusalem's new exploitation of the sites of Jesus' passion and resurrection in his catecheses, which turned the liturgy from an eschatological orientation to a historical. In Chrysostom some attention to the baptism exists alongside his major paradigm, the death and resurrection. Symbols can be multiple and can occupy the same space.

The change is from, on the one hand, the conferral of the Spirit at the pre-baptismal anointing, tied to the Jordan event, to, on the other hand, the imposition of the hand in the very act of baptizing as a going down into the death of Jesus. Is this move from pre-baptismal anointing to water-bath, to a post-baptismal anointing as the locus for imparting the Spirit, a damaging concession? Is it a partial alienation of the primary content of baptism? So G. Winkler has argued.[74] The problem was not primarily a ritual one. What changed was the understanding of Christian baptism as an icon of Jesus' baptism. A passion for purgation called for ritual expression.[75] The cleansings and exorcisms preempted the anointing before the immersion.[76]

As exorcistic and purgative themes moved to the fore of Christian consciousness, the baptism of Jesus at the Jordan receded from Christian awareness. Now it was more difficult to retain Jesus' baptism as the paradigm because of the ease with which going down into the water was identified with going down into the death of Jesus. Gradually baptism as an icon of Jesus' death and resurrection came to dominate. The shift in paradigms of baptism, as Winkler notes, was the catalyst for revision of the rite of baptism. If Dix and Mason are right in saying that the baptism of Jesus may have been the church's first choice of a baptismal prototype,[77] and if the Syriac sources sup-

---

[73] Kretschmar, "Die Geschichte des Taufgottesdienstes," 148.

[74] Winkler, "The Original Meaning," 42.

[75] Ibid.

[76] Ibid., 42–45.

[77] G. Dix, *The Theology of Confirmation in Relation to Baptism* (London: Dacre, 1946) 15; Manson, "Entry into Membership," 26.

port such a contention (as it seems they do),[78] then the loss is very great.

No illusions should be entertained as to what was lost. In John 3:5 ("unless one is born of water and the Spirit, he cannot enter the kingdom of God") this birth theme is not related exegetically to Jesus' own baptism. In the Fourth Gospel the baptism of Jesus is only reported through the mouth of John the Baptist and water is not mentioned. Nonetheless being born of water and the Spirit is linked with the Jordan in the Syrian tradition, making the baptism of Jesus a birth event.[79] We have already seen the baptism at the Jordan presented as a birth event in Hilary of Poitiers and the *Didascalia*.

To move away from the Jordan event as a primary prototype is to intervene in the baptismal dynamics at the interior of its meaning. Now purgation and the death and resurrection determine the rite. This, claims Winkler, is a move to a Pauline mystique of dying.[80]

If the cathartic, exorcistic concerns dominate, then the pre-baptismal anointing can scarcely be maintained as the locus of imparting the Spirit. Chrysostom will be able to designate the water-bath, with the imposition of the bishop's hand in the acting of immersion, as the place where the Spirit is conferred. However, the dynamic is already in motion for the transfer of the ritual expression of the imparting of the Spirit to yet a later rite, the post-baptismal anointing. Already in Cyril of Jerusalem this has happened.

One cannot deduce that this shift was prompted by the desire to diminish the role of the Spirit in order to exalt that of Christ. But the baptism of Jesus as a symbol of Christian baptism has been compromised. Because the prototype has been changed, the Spirit's role in baptism has been diminished. If it is true that the central reality of baptism is the imparting of the Spirit,[81] this is

[78] W. Nauck, *Die Tradition und der Charakter des ersten Johannesbriefes* (Tübingen: Mohr, 1957) 147–82.

[79] Winkler, "Zur frühchristlichen Tauftradition."

[80] Ibid., 44, note 66; Quite rightly the dying of Jesus is given prominence in typifying Paul's theology, but a fairer characterization of Paul would speak of a mystique of dying *and* rising.

[81] U. Wilckens, *Der Brief an die Römer* (Zürich: Benziger, 1980) 131; R. Schnackenburg, "Die johanneische Gemeinde und ihre Geisterfahrung," *Die Kirche des Anfangs*, ed. R. Schnackenburg, J. Ernst, and J. Wanke (Frie-

more appropriately symbolized by the baptism of Jesus than by his death and resurrection. The accounts of Jesus' baptism in the four Gospels are about more than just the Jordan event. They are also about Christian baptism.

In terms of the biblical witness of Romans 6, the death and resurrection of Jesus has some baptismal claims which need to be acknowledged. Beyond those claims, death is a heavier universal experience, more threatening, rooted deep in the archaeology of dread, more primary in human consciousness, tapping unconscious forces of great power. In symbol, drama, and imagination, its relentless crudity makes the baptism of Jesus, important as it is, to seem almost decorative. The shift, then, from Jordan to Calvary is not all loss. To move toward death and resurrection does not exclude the Spirit. The same Paul who says that we have been "baptized into his death" (Rom 6:3) also says "by one Spirit we are all baptized into one body" (1 Cor 12:13).

The symbolic weight of death helps answer another question. If the pre-baptismal anointing in relation to the water-bath carried the baptism of Jesus as a major paradigm, why could not the anointing after the water-bath fulfill the same function? Was the shift from the beginning of the rite to a later position all that crippling? But the issue is not simply that the location of the anointing has been changed, from before the water-bath to after it. The issue is the character, the primary meaning, of Christian baptism has been changed from a birth to a death event.[82] The matter must not be judged simply on the basis of having an anointing, whether before or after the water-bath, as the ritual gesture for imparting the Spirit. If one has changed the environment, the whole symbolic universe, from birth to death, retaining the post-baptismal anointing as the gesture of imparting the Spirit will not make it all come out the same.

Further, when the overpowering death and resurrection paradigm is used, and is rather immediately followed by the less dramatic birth image of the baptism of Jesus, the latter can easily pass unnoticed. At least in the West this is what seems to have hap-

burg: Herder, 1978) 28; D. J. Lull, *The Spirit in Galatia: Paul's Interpretation of Pneuma as Divine Power* (Chico: Scholars Press, 1980) 53.

[82] Winkler, "The Original Meaning," 42–45.

pened. For instance, one can point out Western texts which mention the Johannine theme of baptism as being born of water and the Spirit. Ambrose has it after the immersion, around the end of the fourth century.[83] The *Gelasian Sacramentary*, the first sacramentary of the Roman church composed by Roman presbyters in the mid eighth-century, mentions it after the water-bath.[84] The reformed rites after Vatican II (1976) retain it in relation to the post-baptismal anointing.[85] So ritually it is present. But in all three cases being born of water and the Spirit has been overpowered by the death and resurrection, which writes the script for the drama, defines the stage, controls the dynamics in which the anointing of the catechumen, symbol of Jesus anointing at the Jordan's birth event, is placed. Besides the question of environment, the mere mention of a birth paradigm in a text will have little impact if the catechesis supporting it is wanting.

Because these shifts were already accomplished facts by the later quarter of the fourth century, Kretschmar views Cyril as an end of an age, the term of a long development: the demise of the baptism of Jesus as the primary model and the strengthening of the death of Jesus as the dominant paradigm.[86] Because of the changed nature of Jerusalem sketched in an earlier chapter, Cyril's liturgical practice became normative for East and West.

John Chrysostom belongs to the same closure, to the same move away from the Jordan toward Calvary, a decisive move which will still leaves some references to the baptism of Jesus in his own catechesis and in the pre-baptismal anointings of later liturgies which have their origin in Antioch.[87]

Besides the paradigm shift another factor was operative in the broader theological climate, namely, adoptionism, which brought

---

[83] Ambrose, *On the Sacraments*, 2:24; SC 25bis:88.

[84] *Liber sacramentorum Romanae ecclesiae ordinis anni circuli* (Rome: Herder, 1960) 74.

[85] *The Rites of the Catholic Church* (New York: Pueblo, 1976) 148. I am indebted to Aelred Tiegels for these references.

[86] Kretschmar, "Recent Research on Christian Initiation," *Studia Liturgica* 12 (1977) 92.

[87] Brock, "Studies in the Early History of the Syrian Orthodox Baptismal Liturgy," 29.

the baptism of Jesus into ill repute, as Winkler and others have pointed out. The adoptionists used the baptism of Jesus to promote a "low christology," that is, to teach that Jesus was a mere man when the Spirit descended on him at his baptism, so that he worked miracles, but did not become divine. Other subordinationists held that he became divine at his baptism, still others, at his resurrection. The baptism of Jesus, therefore, became identified with a denial that Jesus was divine from the first moment of his existence. This contributed to the abandonment of the baptism of Jesus as a paradigm for Christian baptism.[88]

In Antioch the baptism of Jesus would have been especially problematic. Two adoptionist bishops, Theophilus (late second century) and Serapion (d. 211) sat on the episcopal throne. Then about 260 Paul of Samosata became bishop of Antioch. His teaching on the person of Christ was condemned at two, possibly three, synods at Antioch. Paul held a variant of adoptionism, dynamic monarchianism, as it is sometimes called. So three successive bishops of Antioch had represented a form of adoptionism.[89] The bishops of the region gathered in Antioch to depose Paul for his teaching in 268. Chrysostom, as a priest of Antioch, would have been especially sensitive to the historic doctrinal implications of the baptism of Jesus. For this reason he may have been shy of giving it an important place in his catecheses and liturgy.

To sum up, Chrysostom, like Cyril, is working within a tradition which is essentially Syrian. In the oldest strata of the Syrian biblical understanding the baptism of Jesus was so central to the Christian life that it was an article of the creed. The baptism of Jesus is the model for Christian baptism. As Jesus went down into the water, was anointed with the Spirit at his baptism, and was declared the Beloved Son, so those wishing to become Christians go down into the waters, are anointed, receive the Spirit at theirs, and become adopted sons and daughters.

When exorcisms and purgative themes came to dominate the catechumenate, and attention was focused on the death and resurrection, the pre-baptismal anointing lost its character as a

---

[88] Winkler, "A Remarkable Shift," 1399.

[89] J. N. D. Kelly, *Early Christian Doctrines* (New York: Harper & Row, 1978) 115–19.

Spirit moment. Purgation and exorcism were its principal functions. Indeed exorcistic elements were multiplied. This represents a new understanding of baptism, introduces a new dynamic. Also it prompted a change in the rite. In Cyril and Theodore the pre-baptismal anointing was transferred to a post-baptismal anointing, in Ambrose to the consignation after the water-bath and anointing; in Chrysostom to the water-bath combined with a species of laying on of the hand. In all four it meant the demise of a trinitarian model within initiation in which Christ is "dependent" on the Spirit.

Jesus' baptism in the Jordan is a sign of that dependence. Among the charisms he receives at baptism to fulfill his mission is healing, one of the prophetic charisms. Not only healing, but all the miracles of his ministry flow from his baptism in the Jordan.

No reason exists why a post-baptismal anointing, or the water–bath, cannot also anchor initiation in the baptism of Jesus. However, it seems that the interest in exorcisms and in the death and resurrection of Jesus loosened the relation of the baptism of Jesus to Christian baptism. Also the baptism of Jesus, linked to a rite placed after the water-bath, has great difficulty remaining a major paradigm when it is forced to exist in the symbolic universe created and defined by the death of Jesus. Death swallows up birth. To avoid all ambiguity, the issue is not the want of all mention of the baptism of Jesus as a birth event. Rather, the issue is whether the baptism of Jesus can survive as a role model of real significance, when preceded by the death of Jesus, whose power creates and controls the symbolic cosmos. Even less chance of survival as a major image exists, if the baptism of Jesus as a birth event is given no place of importance in the catechesis. The use of the baptism of Jesus to promote the "low christology" of adoptionism also contributed to the demise of the Jordan event as a major paradigm.

The Spirit sent by the Father at the Jordan event has a function beyond that of singling Jesus out of the crowd as the long-awaited messiah. Such a function, vital though it is, can only be a foreshortened one because it is too limited, too exterior. The baptism of Jesus re-establishes his identity, defines his ministry.

To mourn the loss of the trinitarian model of Christ's dependence on the Spirit is not to dismiss the trinitarian model in which the Spirit is dependent on Christ as unimportant. Within any trinitarian vision the two views must be kept in tension. But the loss of the baptism of Jesus as a major paradigm at the heart of initiation will make it more difficult to recognize baptism in the Spirit as integral to Christian initiation.

Chapter Twenty-one

John Chrysostom:
Then and Now—
A Study in Zeal and Apathy

Vocabulary betrays vision. In this chapter I ask the meaning of
a terminological shift from *charisma* to *dōrea* in two different
kinds of preaching, expository and baptismal catechesis. What
can that shift tell us about the experience of Chrysostom's congregation, indeed, of Chrysostom himself? Chrysostom wrestled,
not always successfully, with the question of apostolicity and its
normative claim. Here I focus more closely on the role of the
charisms in initiation during the apostolic age as understood by
Chrysostom. Once established I discuss how he thought the
church of his day measured up to that apostolic ideal. How
would he handle any discrepancy between the New Testament
paradigm and the ecclesial reality of his day? What aspects of
the apostolic paradigm does Chrysostom lift up as still operative
in the church? Finally, is Chrysostom's solution to the disparity
between apostolic paradigm and ecclesial reality credible?

Present or Charism?

We have seen that *charisma* in the New Testament and in post-
biblical usage has a spectrum of meanings. One use of *charisma*
in Paul is to designate a free gift of the Spirit, or a ministry

freely bestowed by the Spirit for the upbuilding of the body. *Dōrea* does not appear in the synoptics but otherwise it is used of the gift which God gives to humankind, in John 4:10 for Christ himself, and in Acts 2:38 for the Spirit given in baptism. In Romans 5:15, 16 Paul uses both *dōrea* and *charisma* almost in the same breath: he describes justification as grace (*charis*), gift (*dōrea*), donation (*dōraema*), and charism (*charisma*).[1] *Dōrea* can refer to a present, the gift of the Spirit in baptism, baptismal chrismation, baptism itself, or Christ's teaching.[2] Sometimes it is used as a synonym for *charisma*. For instance Cyril, in his last *CL*, shortly after citing Paul's list of charisms in 1 Corinthians 12:28, says: "the real and true life, then, is the Father, who through the Son in the Holy Spirit pours forth upon all as from a heavenly fountain his heavenly gifts (*dōrea*)."[3] In the same *CL* he later says: I exhort "all of you to prepare your souls for the reception of the heavenly gifts (*charismata*)."[4] Examples could be multiplied. Nonetheless in its most characteristic use *dōrea* is not a synonym for *charisma*, and means present.

The baptismal catecheses have a special character and may have a special vocabulary. Cyril of Jerusalem's admonition at the beginning of his own series of baptismal catecheses is valid for Chrysostom: "Do not confuse pre-baptismal instructions with ordinary sermons."[5] A curious anomaly presents itself when one compares Chrysostom's baptismal homilies with his ordinary sermons. Chrysostom has three sets of baptismal catecheses all delivered around 388 in Antioch to the same general audience. To limit oneself for the moment to the Stavronikita series, Chrysostom always refers to a gift as *dōrea* (once as *dōron*) a sum total of forty-two times. *Charisma* does not occur. In the other baptismal homilies he does not refer to gifts received in baptism as *charismata*. Chrysostom does not suggest in these baptismal homilies that the prophetic charisms

---

[1] "In some texts, the Vulgate uses *donum* (Rom 5:15; 11:29; 1 Cor 7:7), which makes *charisma* equivalent to *dōrea* (John 4:10; Acts 2:38; Rom 5:15)." A. Vanhoye, "The Biblical Question of 'Charisms' after Vatican II," 441.

[2] Lampe, *Lexicon*, 395.

[3] *CL* 18:29; *CAO* 2:332.

[4] *CL* 18:32; *CAO* 2:335.

[5] *CL*, Protocatechesis 11; *CAO* 1:14.

are available or expected. When speaking of the gifts which await the candidates as they enter the church he refers to them as *dōrea*. "Therefore, when you are about to be led into the church at the ninth hour, recall the great number of your virtuous deeds and count those gifts (*dōreas*) which await you."[6] It is not a case of Chrysostom using *dōrea* to refer to the same reality as *charisma*. Rather, he uses *dōrea* to designate more general graces, other than the prophetic charisms, received in baptism, or to baptism itself.[7]

To his ordinary sermons delivered to the general congregation belong his homilies on Romans, a series of thirty-two homilies, which he began shortly after Easter 392;[8] a series of forty-four homilies on 1 Corinthians, which he gave in the Fall and Winter of 392–93;[9] and the twenty-four homilies on Ephesians, given during the last years of his priesthood in Antioch in the years 396–97.[10] All of these were preached in Antioch before he became a bishop, all in the years 392–97, all to the same general congregation. In these sermons Chrysostom refers to a gift as *charisma*. Further, after he became patriarch of Constantinople he preached fifty-five sermons on the Acts of the Apostles. Though Luke does not use the word *charisma*, nor is it used in any other gospel, Chrysostom does in exegeting pertinent passages of Luke's gospel.[11]

What is significant here is not that Chrysostom uses *dōrea* in those cases where Paul would have used *charisma*. Since the one can be used as a synonym for the other this would not be unusual. What is significant is the general consistency with which Chrysostom uses *dōrea* in the baptismal catecheses directed

---

[6] *PKBC* 3:20; *Varia Graeca Sacra*, 171.

[7] *SBC* 1:15, 18, 25, 26, 33; 2:1; 3:6; 4:2; 5:18; 6:23; SC 50bis:116, 118, 121, 121, 125, 133, 153, 183, 209, 226.

[8] Chrysostom, *On Romans*, 22; PG 60:601-10. Dating is according to M. von Bonsdorff, *Zur Predigttätigkeit des Johannes Chrysostomus* (Helsingfors: Mercators, 1922) 32–40.

[9] Chrysostom, *On 1 Corinthians*, 29–35; PG 61:239-306; Bonsdorff, *Zur Predigttätigkeit*, 40–45.

[10] Chrysostom, *On Ephesians*, 11; PG 62:81-85; Bonsdorff, *Zur Predigttätigkeit*, 64–71.

[11] Chrysostom, *On Acts*, 18; 40: PG 60:144; 284. Twice in the last citation.

specifically to candidates for baptism, and the same consistency with which he uses *charisma* in the more scriptural homilies intended for more general audiences.

How does one account for this different usage in the two groups of homilies? One possible explanation is that unlike Cyril, Chrysostom did not think that the prophetic charisms were real possibilities for the life of the local church. Neither Chrysostom nor his congregation had any direct experience of the prophetic charisms. He stands in contrast to Tertullian, Origen, Hilary, Cyril, who had such experience. Such a supposition seems to be supported by the lack of an appeal, in either the lectures preparatory to baptism at the Easter vigil, or in the biblical homilies, to the church's broader experience of the charisms, such as is found in Cyril's *CL*.

Chrysostom's handling of 1 Corinthians, Romans, and Ephesians is lively, full of forceful images, and suited to the intelligence of his hearers. Though he speaks of charism in these texts as *charisma*, he nevertheless gives the impression of a lecturer commenting on a historical text which is alien to the lives of his people.

One might appeal to a text from Chrysostom's homilies *On Matthew* which one could interpret as an outpouring of the charisms, more specifically the prophetic gifts. When explaining the meaning of "He will baptize you in the Holy Spirit" he mentions nine graces received in initiation: "forgiveness of sins, remission of punishment, justification, holiness, redemption, filiation, fraternity, sharing in the inheritance, abundant outpouring of the Holy Spirit."[12] The expression "abundant outpouring of the Holy Spirit" might have been an expression for the generous bestowal of charisms, including the prophetic, had Chrysostom given any sign that the prophetic charisms were real possibilities for the life of the church in other passages. His use of *dōrea* instead of *charisma* in his baptismal catecheses, his lack of any direct reference to the prophetic charisms in the life of the congregation he was addressing in his biblical homilies does not support the interpretation of this passage as a reference to a generous outpouring of prophetic charisms in his own church.

[12] Chrysostom, *On Matthew*, 11; PG 57:197.

Chrysostom admits that the matter of the charisms in 1 Corinthians 12 is "very obscure."[13] The reason, he said, is the want of experience in the church of his own day: "many of the wonders which then used to take place have now ceased."[14] Because the spectrum of charisms identified in 1 Corinthians are not actualities in the life of the church, there is no contemporary reference which might illumine the text.

What, in fact, was the experience of the apostolic church in Chrysostom's view? According to him "whoever was baptized at once spoke in tongues, and not only in tongues, but many also prophesied; some performed many other wonderful works."[15] To give this much prominence to the absolute immediacy with which the prophetic charisms were manifested in the very rite itself is very likely an exaggerated interpretation of the Pauline text. Nonetheless Chrysostom maintains that the imparting of the Spirit was tied to laying on of hands and baptism.[16] Those who were converted from paganism "at once received the Spirit at their baptism."[17] Here Chrysostom is probably referring to text in Acts 10:47 in which receiving the Spirit is understood to be a duplicate of the Pentecost event. Chrysostom is clear that "all" (*hapantōn*) who were baptized in the apostolic age received "certain excellent charisms," among them prophecy, wisdom, healing, raising the dead, and the charism of prayer.[18] Charisms were not restricted to a certain group or special individuals.[19] Here Chrysostom is one with Tertullian and Cyril.

Because the Spirit was not visible, God provided sensible proof of power in the charisms. Chrysostom thought of tongues as real languages, a topic to which he returned.[20] The apostles first received the gift of tongues, so the believers continued to

---

[13] Chrysostom, *On 1 Corinthians,* 29; PG 61:239.
[14] Chrysostom, *On Romans,* 14; PG 60:533.
[15] Chrysostom, *On 1 Corinthians,* 29; PG 61:239.
[16] Chrysostom, *On Pentecost,* 1; PG 50:459; *On 1 Corinthians,* 29; PG 61:239.
[17] Chrysostom, *On Romans,* 14; PG 60:533.
[18] Ibid.
[19] Ibid.
[20] Chrysostom, *On 1 Corinthians,* 29; PG 61:239; 35; PG 61:295, 300, 310.

receive it at initiation, in addition to other charisms. Some had more charisms, some less. The gift of prophecy was given to many.[21] Indeed, prophecy was much more in evidence in the early community than in the Israelites of the Old Testament: "This grace was poured out abundantly, and every church had many who prophesied."[22] The charisms were called "spiritual signs because they were the work of the Spirit alone; humans contributed nothing to the working of such wonders."[23]

Two things flow from this formulation. First, Chrysostom thinks of the charisms as divine gifts, not just enhanced human powers. Though he does not expect prophecy or tongues, he still teaches that if you pray for a charism, "you will surely receive it."[24] Secondly, the proper environment for the appearance of the gifts is the public celebration of the rites of initiation. The charisms are not matters of private piety. The apostolic liturgical assembly was one of the contexts for the exercising of the charism. During the liturgies "they used to compose psalms charismatically, by means of a charism."[25]

As Paul before him, Chrysostom struggles with the gift of tongues. The preacher reminds his congregation that the gift of tongues is "excellent, indeed, necessary" (*kalon men gar kai anagkaion to charisma*) in the way that a finger is necessary; but only as long as it remains joined to the other members.[26] The "necessity" is quite diminished. Like Paul he thinks it reprehensible that the Corinthians of the apostolic age were "wild about tongues," seeking glory while only receiving the reputation of insanity.[27] Yet neither Paul nor Chrysostom want to hold this gift in disdain. Tongues were divisive only because those who sought them did so for reasons of vanity.

Chrysostom has a long section on love as the more excellent way which is given, not to one who has this charism or that, but to all. Love is the universal gift, the charism, according to

[21] Ibid., 35; PG 61:301.
[22] Ibid., 32; PG 61:265.
[23] Ibid., 29; PG 61:241.
[24] Ibid., 35; PG 61:299, 300.
[25] Ibid., 36; PG 61:310.
[26] Ibid., 35; PG 61:298.
[27] Ibid., 36; PG 61:309.

him, which binds together the other charisms.[28] Here he does not seem to go far enough in distinguishing the charisms from the gift of love. Paul not only distinguishes the charisms and love (*agape*), but may be placing them in antithetical relationship.[29] Paul never calls *agape* a charism. Love in 1 Corinthians seems to be of an entirely different, more primary, order of religious reality. Love is not a charism, but a way. Love is the primal matrix of the charisms.

In spite of the difficulties in the Corinthian community caused by those who exalted the gift of tongues, Chrysostom idealizes the church of the apostolic age: "The church in those days was a heaven. The Spirit governed all things, moving and inspiring each of the rulers."[30]

The Church Now: Impotent and Full of Tokens

In the apostolic days the charisms were implicit in ecclesial life, "but now no longer."[31] In fact the "charisms are long gone."[32] Nostalgia typifies Chrysostom's look backward to the apostolic community. Chrysostom laments that the glory of those apostolic days, when all was heavenly, is past. He longs for the age when the congregation answered the celebrant at the eucharistic mysteries with the response "and with your Spirit" because they were genuinely "moved by the Spirit."[33] Continuing his nostalgia for the purity and probity of that far off apostolic age, he complains: "The present church is like a woman who has fallen from her former prosperous days. In many respects she retains only the symbols of that ancient prosperity. She displays, in fact, the repositories and the caskets of her gold ornaments, but she is, in fact, deprived of her wealth. The present church represents such a woman."[34] Lest his lament over the sad state of the church be misunder-

---

[28] Ibid., 22; PG 61:267, 268.
[29] J. D. G. Dunn, *Jesus and the Spirit* (Philadelphia: Westminster, 1975) 294.
[30] Chrysostom, *On 1 Corinthians*, 36; PG 61:267, 268.
[31] Ibid., 29; PG 61:239.
[32] Chrysostom, *On 2 Thessalonians*, 4; PG 62:485.
[33] Chrysostom, *On 1 Corinthians*, 36; PG 61:312.
[34] Ibid., 36; PG 61:312, 313.

stood, Chrysostom hastens to add, somewhat inconsequentially, that if it were a matter only of the charisms (here he includes consecrated widows and virgins among the charisms) it would be nothing astounding. What matters is that the church is void of "life and virtue . . . . Only the tokens (*symbola*) of the charisms remain of those ancient times."[35]

In the apostolic age there was an experiential dimension to initiation. To be baptized into one body, whether Jew or Greek, bond or free, is the work of the Spirit. To all and each the Spirit gives charisms, by which the body attains a greater perfection of unity. Jews and Greeks all experience the same initiatory mysteries, all eat at the same table, all were given the same Spirit to drink. When Paul says that both Jews and Greeks were made to drink of the same Spirit, Chrysostom believes he was referring to "that visitation (*epiphoitēsis*) of the Spirit which takes place in us after baptism and before the mysteries (eucharist)."[36] The "visitation of the Spirit" is the descent of the transforming Spirit. Very likely *epiphoitēsis* is the translation of a technical term of Syriac speaking churches, *magen*, meaning the *epiclēsis*.[37] Here "visitation" can mean simply the coming of the Spirit,[38] the cause of prophetic utterance, and re-

---

[35] Ibid.

[36] Ibid., 30; PG 61:251. Chrysostom is a little ambiguous about locating the imparting of the Spirit. He speaks of the imparting of the Spirit in the water-bath, but here after the water-bath and before the eucharist. Sebastian Brock addresses this problem, saying that the early authors agree that the candidates for baptism receive the Holy Spirit, but that sources, even from the same author, are far from united. "The gift of the Spirit is essentially conferred by the rite *as a whole*, and within the rite the anointing and the baptism in water form an inseparable unity. . . . Christian baptism is a single unit, as it were, in sacred time, (and) its salvific effect can be localized simultaneously at different points in historical time; in other words, if a writer states that the gift of the Spirit is conferred by the water, this does not exclude the fact that it is just as much conferred by the anointing(s)." *The Holy Spirit in the Syrian Baptismal Tradition*, 37.

[37] B. D. Spinka, "The Consecratory Epiklesis in the Anaphora of St. James," *Studia Liturgica* 11 (1976) 34; S. Brock, "Passover, Annunciation and Epiclesis: Some Remarks on the Term *Aggen* in the Syriac Versions of LK. 1:35," *NovT* 24 (1982) 232, 233.

[38] AC 8:26, 2; SC 336:228.

newal.[39] Chrysostom does not further specify, except to describe it as "drinking the Spirit."[40] His language seems experiential.

To be carefully noted is the locus of this visitation, namely, within the rites of initiation, more precisely after the water-bath and before the eucharist. The setting is the liturgical celebration of Christian initiation at the same place in the rite which Tertullian had designated as the proper moment in which to pray for the charisms, namely, after the water-bath and before the eucharist. Tertullian seems not to separate the laying on of hands, "inviting and welcoming the Holy Spirit," and the explicit repeated request for the charisms when the neophytes are coming up from the water-bath and entering the eucharistic room.[41] Chrysostom also does not separate, on the one hand, the bestowal of the Spirit, which takes place in the water, as the bishop lays his hand on the candidate, pushing it under the water, and on the other, the visitation of the Spirit, which takes place after the water-bath and before the eucharisitc celebration. Given Chrysostom's understanding that the prophetic charisms have ceased, could it be that he has kept an archaic expression for the imparting of the charisms, and retained it in the very place within the rites which it had in former times, and this even though the prophetic charisms are no longer part of the church's experience? One wonders.

Chrysostom's list of nine effects of baptism has been mentioned. Charisms are not included. No suggestion is found that the gifts of 1 Corinthians 12 are matters of expectation. This want of any awareness that the charisms are available to the community seems to be confirmed by Chrysostom's use of *dōrea* instead of *charisma* in instructing the catechumens on what is to be expected in baptism.

Strategic Retreats and Strained Adjustments

How does Chrysostom handle the discrepancy between the power and glory of the apostolic age and the dull impotence of

[39] Didymus the Blind, *On the Trinity*, 2:6; PG 39:533.
[40] Chrysostom, *On 1 Corinthians*, 30; PG 61:251. *See also* SBC 2:25: SC 50bis:147.
[41] *OB* 8; SC 35:76.

the present? He is much exercised that the lack of the prophetic charisms could be interpreted to mean that the church has been released from the imperatives of the apostolic paradigm. Such a situation could spell disaster. No church can exist if the apostolic community is not "the goal and measure of the Christian life."[42] Without the call to the apostolic life—as the following of the apostles—the church ceases to exist. Because the prophetic charisms were obviously built into the structures of ecclesial life in the apostolic age, strenuous effort must be made to demonstrate the apostolic character of the church of Chrysostom's day by claiming the presence of the same charisms. To make the adjustments obviously called for, without severing the links to the apostolic ideal, Chrysostom employs a number of adjustments, and builds some hedges against a future reckoning.

First, he internalizes the charisms. In a Pentecost sermon Chrysostom declares that the absence of the prophetic charisms does not mean that the charismatic dimension is absolutely absent from the church. What formerly was wondrous and externally visible is now accomplished in an unseen manner. Without the unusual manifestations of healings, prophecies, and tongues, all perceivable to the senses, we still retain the forgiveness of sins in baptism, which can be grasped only by faith.[43]

Chrysostom also spiritualizes the charism as a way of accounting for their absence. Protesting that the charisms as signs are not the exclusive privilege of the apostolic era, he contends that they continue in a changed, spiritualized form.[44] If you as a Christian turn from cruelty toward others to alms giving, you have cured the withered hand, which is an exercise of the charism of healing. If you keep your eyes off the prostitute, you have opened the eyes of the blind. If you march yourself, not to the theaters, but to church, you have cured the lame. If anyone asks where the miracles and the wonders of the apostolic age are to be found today, you point to these acts. Obviously Chrysostom's presentation of the charisms in this context is attenuated to the point of non-existence. The rhetoric is not convincing.

[42] A. M. Ritter, *Charisma im Verständnis des Joannes Chrysostomos und seiner Zeit* (Gottingen: Vandenhoeck & Ruprecht, 1972) 34.

[43] Chrysostom, *On Pentecost*, 1; PG 50:459.

[44] Chrysostom, *On Matthew*, 32; PG 57:387.

In the apostolic age the wonders performed were not meant to strengthen the faith of believers. They were directed to unbelievers, as a demonstration of the power of the gospel.[45] Chrysostom contends that the absence of the prophetic charisms must not be attributed to God's low esteem of signs and wonders. Quite the contrary: God esteems us more because we do not need them. Now that we are mature we believe without the signs, as becomes adults.[46]

Chrysostom is not impressed with arguments about the relative importance of some charisms over others. "In fact, I do not make much account of the difference between the charisms."[47] What is significant is that every charism, whether at the top of the hierarchy of charisms or at the bottom, is a demonstration of the Spirit; each builds up the church.[48]

While the charisms should be esteemed, they belong to a second order of religious reality (*kai tou biou deutera esti ta charismata*).[49] This is demonstrated in the way that the charisms are ordered to proclamation and evangelization. The Corinthian church was structured with apostles, prophets, and teachers coming first. Following them come the more unusual, and in some cases, miraculous charisms.[50] As Ritter points out, Chrysostom's understanding of the charisms is functional.[51] Charisms are goal-oriented. They do not find their justification in themselves: "If, for instance . . . one raises the dead, but no one profits from it (*sic*), no one is edified, then the charism is in vain. If this (edification) is the purpose of charism, and if it is possible to effect it (edification) in another way, that is, without a charism, then do not boast that you have the signs. If the charisms are absent, do not complain."[52] Here we see a functionalism which is well grounded in the biblical text. However, it is radicalized in a way which seems to go beyond the Pauline perspective.

[45] Chrysostom, *On Pentecost*, 1; PG 50:459.
[46] Ibid.
[47] Ibid., 36; PG 61:310.
[48] Chrysostom, *On 1 Corinthians*, 29; PG 61:244.
[49] Ibid., 32; PG 61:270.
[50] Ibid., 19; PG 61:245.
[51] Ritter, *Charisma*, 32.
[52] Chrysostom, *On 1 Corinthians*, 36; PG 61:310.

Chrysostom's refusal to restrict charism to the prophetic charisms, and his refusal to bind them in an exclusive way to the apostolic age gives him an exit when confronted with the question of the continuing presence of the charisms. He can point to the Pauline charisms of helpers and administrators.[53] These, too, belong to that church which is entirely ministerial. Chrysostom's understanding of "the word of knowledge" as a grasp of the faith which each believer possesses, makes this charism present in all Christians.[54] The charism of prayer is still an actuality in the church.[55] The charisms live on in the church in consecrated virginity, almsgiving, and the care of the sick. The apostolic concept of office, too, is seen under the rubric of charism, which continues in the church. Because we have toiled long and labored much does not mean that we thereby demonstrate the apostolic character of our ministry. By no means: the apostolic office is ours because it has been given as a charism.[56] All the fruits which flow from the exercise of office come from the power of the gospel given to us in the charisms.[57] The whole ecclesial reality, with its roots in the apostolic life, attains goals which are beyond human striving. In the power of the Spirit the charisms are made manifest.[58]

Communion in the Awe-Inspiring Mysteries

Tertullian exhorted the candidates to pray for the charisms after the water-bath and before the entrance into the eucharistic space. Cyril, as we have seen, had more than one explicit reference in his *Catechetical Lectures* to the expectation of the charisms in relation to the rites of initiation. Just before the beginning of the rites of initiation he expressed a desire that the catechumens would be found worthy to receive the charism of prophecy. No such expectation is to be found in Chrysostom, nor in Ambrose, nor Theodore of Mopsuestia. Theodore escapes

---

[53] Ibid., 32; PG 61:266.
[54] Ibid., 29; PG 61:245.
[55] Chrysostom, *On Romans*, 14; PG 60:533, 534.
[56] Ibid., 1; PG 60:397, 398.
[57] Ibid.
[58] Chrysostom, *On 1 Corinthians*, 32; PG 61:265, 266.

the necessity of constructing elaborate justification for the absence of the prophetic charisms by embracing a dispensationalism limiting these charisms to the apostolic age. He claims that prophecies and tongues, along with "knowing in part," are superfluous "now that the faith has spread all over the world."[59] Consequently they have ceased. We, however, are more blessed, because we have faith, hope, and charity.[60]

What Chrysostom does share with Tertullian, Hilary, and Cyril is the conviction that the church is communion. For Chrysostom the baptismal celebration is "the communion in the mysteries."[61] He describes the great communal joy with which those emerging from the water were received: "As soon as they come forth from the sacred waters, all who are present embrace them, greet them, kiss them, rejoice with them, and congratulate them, because those who were heretofore slaves and captives have suddenly become free men and sons and have been invited to the royal table."[62] The eucharistic table, that is the celebration of the mysteries, is referred to in a tone of great reverence, variously as "the sacred table,"[63] "the royal table,"[64] "the mystical table filled with good things beyond number."[65] What is offered to those just washed in the sacred bath is "the awesome cup which is filled with abundant power, more precious than any other creature; the initiated know the strength of this cup, and after a short while you, too (as you come up fresh from the sacred waters), will know it."[66]

One celebrates the mysteries with wonder and risk. Only in holy fear has one "communion (koinōnia) in the mysteries."[67] Chrysostom upbraided the young who give themselves up to

---

[59] K. Staab, *Pauluskommentare aus der Griechischen Kirche* (Münster: Aschendorff, 1984) 191, 192.

[60] Ibid.

[61] Chrysostom, *On the Unknowability of God*, 4:1; SC 28bis:258; PKBC 2:11; *Varia Graeca Sacra*, 159.

[62] SBC 2:27; SC 50bis:148.

[63] PKBC 3:32; *Varia Graeca Sacra*, 175.

[64] SBC 3:6; SC 50bis:185.

[65] Ibid., 6:24: SC 50bis:227.

[66] MBC 1:3; PG 49:224. Finn, *The Liturgy of Baptism*, 200.

[67] Chrysostom, *On 1 Corinthians*, 37; PG 61:318.

disordered passions, those who neglect prisoners, widows, and orphans. By such moral laxity they demonstrate that they have forgotten "the fearful and ineffable communion in the divine mysteries."[68] The "communion of the mysteries" is where Chrysostom believes the prophetic charisms were imparted in the apostolic community.[69] The communion manifested in the whole initiatory celebration is not allowed to remain at that sacral level. "For communion [in apostolic days] was not only in prayers, nor in doctrine alone, but also in things regarding the social order (politeia)."[70] An over-spiritualized communion, all caught up in God but leaving the human realities of poverty and hunger untouched, was not what Chrysostom meant by full communion.

Is Chrysostom's Doctrine Believable?

If one approaches Chrysostom's teaching on the prophetic charisms, which have been historically problematic, then a distorted picture can result. To single out the prophetic charism (chiefly tongues, prophecy, and healing) means that the argument is immediately caught up in the contrast between the glorious apostolic "then" and the dull "now." The tension between these two poles can result in a negative evaluation of the charisms which is not reflective of Chrysostom's true mind. Chrysostom does not have an enthusiastic conception of the charisms, that is, he does not reduce charism simply to the prophetic, miraculous, and the wondrous. He clearly wishes to see the charisms as vital to the life of the church, indeed, as belonging to its structure.

One would not be true to his thought by presenting his doctrine of the charism as a seamless garment. This arises partly out of the character of his presentations. He left behind more than any other Greek Father, a corpus so extensive (eighteen volumes in Migne) that only the dauntless venture to master his thought. For this reason he is often passed over by researchers. However, it is not just the extent of his writings which defies

[68] SBC 6:1; SC 50bis:216.
[69] Chrysostom, On 2 Corinthians, 30; PG 61:608.
[70] Chrysostom, On Acts, 7; PG 60:63.

systematization. Quite simply, he was not a systematician. He wrote little and preached much, his sermons being taken down by stenographers. Some of the transcripts he corrected, others he did not. As is likely in the case of a preacher who is preaching a biblical text verse by verse, he preached without much attention to the demands of over-all coherence.[71]

Another factor, more intrinsic to his theological position, is the general inability, by no means limited to Chrysostom, to give a consistent, coherent doctrine of charisms, once the theologian is forced into an unwanted but *de facto* exclusion of part of the full spectrum of charisms. Chrysostom does not want the absence of some charisms to dispense the church of his day from accepting the apostolic church as the only paradigm, as constitutive. If Chrysostom exalts the apostolic church as "heavenly," and sees the full spectrum of the charisms present there, the justifying reasons for the tokenism of the church of his day is much more difficult to sustain. Chrysostom is juggling with colored balls, all of which he is not able to keep in the air at the same time. Two are especially difficult to keep in proper relationship, namely, the apostolic church with the full spectrum of the charisms, and the contemporary church with a segment missing. Like so many he accepts the experience of the contemporary church in which the prophetic charisms had no part. Then he finds himself at a loss to assert the full apostolic reality of the fourth century church in a believable way. His only recourse is a partial retreat, embarrassed shifts, and clumsy adjustments.

Chrysostom holds that all the charisms belong to the apostolic life of the church. Nonetheless, he maintains the charisms are not absolutely necessary. The goal of building up the church can be achieved without them. Some of the charisms evident in the apostolic church continue in a different, more spiritualized form. The changed nature of the charisms arise from the changed situation. In the apostolic era they were directed to the task of evangelizing unbelievers. Among those who are already believers they do not have that function. Besides, today the faith of believers is more mature, not needing the support of at-

[71] Young, *From Nicaea to Chalcedon*, 143–59.

tention grabbing, unusual gifts. God esteems us more, not less, because we believe without the buttress of the wondrous.

The argument here is not without theological rationale, but it is tortuous. No one would want, I think, to suggest that if the charism which Paul placed as the lowest of the gifts, tongues, were absent, the church would immediately be unmade. One can change the question. If the church were without the prophetic gifts, would the church be unmade, rendered a non-church? This is obviously more difficult to answer. The church is "built upon the foundation of the apostles and prophets, Jesus Christ himself being the chief cornerstone" (Eph 2:20). The foundation is made up of Jesus Christ and two charisms, apostleship and prophecy. The charisms belong to the structure of ecclesial reality.[72] "The church is determined in its most intimate essence by the charisms."[73] "Prophecy," Karl Rahner says, "is to be a permanent endowment of the church and a proof of her supernatural mission."[74] One cannot relegate the prophetic charism to the apostolic age as if they were to be transient adornments, though, as Rahner remarked, "the social and psychological forms of the prophetic charisma and its mode of influencing church history may alter with time."[75]

To recapitulate, Chrysostom may be signaling that the prophetic charisms are no longer real possibilities for the life of the church when he consistently chooses *dōrea* instead of *charisma* in speaking to the baptismal candidates about the gifts they will receive in initiation. What is significant is not that Chrysostom uses it at all, but that in speaking to the catechumens he consistently uses *dōrea*, instead of *charisma*. No illusions should be entertained about the meaning of this choice. The change is more than terminological. Chrysostom understands the prophetic charisms, by whatever name, as no longer integral to Christian initiation, no longer an expected dimension of the ordinary life of the normal Christian community.

---

[72] G. Hasenhüttl, *Charisma: Ordnungsprinzip der Kirche* (Freiburg, Herder, 1969) 235.
[73] Ibid.
[74] Rahner, *Visions and Prophecies* (New York: Herder and Herder, 1963) 102.
[75] Ibid., 28.

Chrysostom states that in the earliest antiquity Christian initiation included a prayer for the coming of the Spirit (in the water-bath) with the laying on of the hand, and, finally, the manifestation of the charisms, including the prophetic charisms of prophecy, tongues, wisdom, healing, raising the dead. These were regularly manifested at initiation in apostolic times. Because of this regular occurrence, Chrysostom knows that the prophetic charisms in the apostolic age must have been expected. For him they were divine gifts, not human talents upgraded and embellished.

The church of his day is like a woman who wants to display her jewels, but when she opens the coffer it is empty. The church of tokens looks back to the apostolic age, when all was "heavenly." Persons, endowed with wondrous charisms, were truly guided by the Spirit. This endowment took place during the public celebration of the rites of initiation. Public liturgy rather than private piety was the context for the reception of the charisms in the apostolic age.

Are there any links between Chrysostom and the *AC*? Links in the sense of dependence may be too strong. Both engage in a process of standardizing, that is, conforming the charisms to set patterns. The *AC* does this in more structural terms, i.e., the bishop takes over the charisms of prophet, teacher, and healer. Chrysostom spiritualizes the charisms, i.e., if you turn from cruelty to almsgiving, you have cured a withered hand and exercised the charism of healing.

All the elements which the modern charismatic renewal understands as belonging to the baptism in the Holy Spirit are present in the apostolic paradigm of initiation as understood by Chrysostom. They were present, not in some non-specific way, but as integral to the rites of initiation in the apostolic church, rites which make the church.

Chapter Twenty-two

Philoxenus:
"Our Baptism *is* the Holy Spirit"

If one has tasted the Greek and Latin sources one has done
well. But what if there were a Semitic form of the gospel,
whose religious and cultural integrity was fully intact, through
which the good news was first preached in Aramaic? What if
we knew almost nothing of this non-Western, non-European
tradition?[1] How serious would our ignorance be?

Sebastian Brock and Arthur Vööbus, among others, have
pointed to a Semitic stream alongside of Greek and Latin Christianity. This tradition was Palestinian and Aramaic in its origins. What is especially significant is that originally the gospel
was preached to the Syriac speaking people in Aramaic.[2] What
language Jesus spoke has never been definitively established,[3]

---

[1] S. Brock, *The Syriac Fathers on Prayer and the Spiritual Life* (Kalamazoo:
Cistercian Publications, 1987) xi.

[2] Brock, "The Syrian Tradition," *The Study of Spirituality,* eds. C. Jones,
G. Wainwright, E. Yarnold (Oxford: Oxford University, 1986) 199–215; *The
Holy Spirit in the Syrian Baptismal Tradition* (Poona: no publisher given, 1979)
1; *Spirituality in the Syriac Tradition* (Kerala: St. Ephrem Ecumenical Re-
search Institute, 1989) 1–4; "Early Syriac Asceticism," *Syriac Perspectives on
Late Antiquity* (London: Variorum, 1984) 1:1-19; Vööbus, *The History of
Asceticism in the Syrian Orient,* CSCO 184, 197.

[3] C. Rabin, "Hebrew and Aramaic in the First Century," *Jewish People*

though the supposition is that, as a Galilean rabbi, he very likely spoke Hebrew and the Galilean dialect of Aramaic. Behind the Greek gospels are the teaching and sayings of Jesus in the Palestinian Aramaic tradition.[4]

Aramaic is often thought of as the language of Jesus, having little impact beyond the confines of Palestine. The contrary is true. From the sixth to the third centuries of the pre-Christian era, Aramaic was one of the great languages of the East. From the Euphrates to the Nile it was the international language of government, culture, and commerce, even in countries where there was no native Aramaic culture. Possibly during or after the Babylonian exile it became the language of the Jews. As a result of the conquests of Alexander the Great, Greek attained a dominance throughout the civilized world. Nonetheless Aramaic was not displaced among the Jews of Palestine and Babylon or among the Semitic peoples in Syria and Mesopotamia. Greek was studied and used also in these areas, but Syriac was still the dominant written and spoken language. In the first century both Greek and Syriac flourished in places like Jerusalem and Antioch.[5] In Antioch itself the dominant language was Greek.

Two persons, one speaking the Galilean Aramaic, the other Syriac, would be able to understand each other.[6] Syriac is a dialect of Aramaic, or, more precisely, is Late Aramaic. The affinity of Syriac to Aramaic is not just a dry bone scholars like to worry. Through the Syriac sources one is put in contact with the thought forms, the speech patterns, the religious vocabulary, the images, and the literary genres of Jesus.

No suggestion is made that the Syrian regions received a written form of the gospels in Palestinian Aramaic. On the contrary, the Syriac New Testament is based on the Greek. Apart from the scriptures, however, "the earliest Syriac authors—Aphrahat, Ephrem, and the liturgical poets—are purely Semitic and owe little or nothing at all to the influence of Greek cul-

in the First Century, 2 vols.; eds. S. Safrai, M. Stern (Philadelphia: Fortress, 1976) 2:1033.

    [4] M. Black, *An Aramaic Approach to the Gospels and Acts* (Oxford: Clarendon, 1967) 16.

    [5] Ibid., 15.

    [6] Brock, *The Syriac Fathers on Prayer and the Spiritual Life*, x.

ture."[7] Ephrem (c. 306–73) was the first to write a biblical commentary in the language of Jesus, though in a different dialect. The exegetical style of interpretation in Aphrahat (early fourth century) and Ephrem "bear an outspoken Jewish mark."[8]

Even as late as the fourth century the Syriac church remained spiritually in touch with the synagogue culture.[9] Jewish Christianity was not a relic. Jerome traveled to Aleppo to visit the Jewish Christian community, and he became acquainted there with the Aramaic Gospel.[10] Jerome spent two or three years in the Syrian desert where he must have picked up a smattering of Syriac.[11] Both in the Syrian desert and in Caesarea he made the acquaintance of this Semitic Christianity and its Syriac scriptures.[12]

Aphrahat seems to have been isolated enough as to be unaware of both Arianism and the Council of Nicaea (325), though he was still writing in 345. Ephrem probably knew little or no Greek. While he did not completely reject Greek culture, he did say "Happy the man who has not tasted of the Greek poison."[13] More specifically, the poison was pagan Greek influence on theology. Though there had been a rupture between church and synagogue, nonetheless the Syriac church "remained very close to the parent Synagogue."[14] This real linguistic and cultural isolation should not be exaggerated however. From the time of Ephrem no great divide separated the Semitic exposition of Christianity from that of Christians writing in Greek and Latin.[15] There had been a variety of contacts, commercial and cultural. Edessa was the center of Syriac-speaking Christianity

---

[7] Brock, *The Holy Spirit in the Syrian Baptismal Tradition*, 1; *The Luminous Eye: The Spiritual Vision of St. Ephrem* (Rome: Centre for Indian and Inter-Religious Studies, 1985) 128.

[8] Vööbus, *History of Asceticism*, CSCO 184:8.

[9] R. Murray, *Symbols of Church and Kingdom: A Study in Early Syriac Tradition* (Cambridge: Cambridge University, 1975) 18.

[10] G. Quispel, *Makarius: Das Thomasevangelium und das Lied von der Perle* (Leiden: Brill, 1967) 13.

[11] Kelly, *Jerome*, 46–49.

[12] *On Famous Men*, 3; PL 23:644, 645.

[13] *Hymns on Faith*, 2:24; Brock, "From Antagonism to Assimilation: Syriac Attitudes to Greek Learning," *Syriac Perspectives on Late Antiquity*, 5:19.

[14] Murray, *Symbols of Church and Kingdom*, 18.

[15] Brock, *Luminous Eye*, 129.

and the home of both the Old Syriac New Testament (the earliest Syriac translation probably around 300) and the Peshitta (the early fifth-century official Syriac translation of the New Testament). The philosophers taught Greek thought in Syriac dress, and religious artists used Greek forms in the graphic and literary arts. In Edessa Syriac traditions were clothed in Greek disguise.[16]

Brock divides the process of the hellenization of Syriac culture into three periods.[17] Aphrahat and Ephrem, both fourth-century writers, belong to the first period. Both represent a Christian culture which is still Semitic in its vision and style, Ephrem alone showing the beginnings of some borrowings. The liturgical poets, such as Jacob of Serugh (c. 451–521), have remained largely unhellenized. After this beginning the process gains momentum in the fifth and sixth centuries, which mark the second phase. Philoxenus of Mabbug (c. 440–523), though chronologically of the same period as Jacob of Serugh, is in the process of making a distinctive synthesis, using both Greek and Syriac sources. The third phase is in the seventh century, when hellenization attained its high point.

After looking at Philoxenus' education, his place in a process of hellenization, his commitment to the ascetic/monastic movement, I want to show how Jesus' baptismal experience becomes the paradigm for those who strive for the perfection of the Christian life. In this optic I will examine Philoxenus' understanding of how faith tends to sensation, which prompts him to conclude that sacramental baptism is not enough. To demonstrate that baptism demands completion I will look at Philoxenus' image of growth (fetus) and the species of symbolic logic he uses (three births, two baptisms).

Is Virginity Holiness?

Philoxenus came from a Christian Aramaic family. His education would have included the study of the Old and New Testament and the Syriac masters. As Vööbus indicates, the focus of

[16] H. J. W. Drijvers, "East of Antioch: Forces and Structures in the Development of Early Syriac Theology," *East of Antioch* (London: Variorum, 1984) 1:3.

[17] Brock, "From Antagonism to Assimilation: Syriac Attitudes to Greek Learning," 5:18, 19.

Philoxenus' studies were on biblical interpretation, using literary, philological, lexical, and historical tools.[18] Significantly Philoxenus was entering the School of the Persians about the time of the death of Hiba, whose Syrian epithet is "The Translator," a reference to a movement promoting translation of Greek authors into Syriac. Hiba's name is associated with the translation, among others, of Theodore of Mopsuestia, whose writings became textbooks for students of exegesis, considered as models of biblical interpretation.[19] This contact with Theodore has some significance for his teaching on the charisms.

Given this background it is not surprising that this Syriac speaking Persian would apologize for Ephrem's imprecise Syriac terms, saying "our Syriac tongue is not accustomed to use the precise terms which the Greeks use. . . . "[20] Because of "the many mistakes" which Philoxenus perceives in the early translations from Greek to Syriac, he proposes that a new translation of the Bible be made.[21] In his other writings also Philoxenus shows a clear preference for Greek precision over Syriac symbolism, a shift away from the integrity of Syriac language and culture, toward all things Greek.

Philoxenus was educated in the teachings of the theological school of Edessa and attached himself to the monophysite party in opposition to the Antiochian christology, thus isolating himself from a great number of his contemporaries. At an early age he joined the ascetic movement, becoming a hermit. In 485 he became bishop of Mabbug, which, under his leadership became a stronghold of monophysite christology. His books, written in Syriac, gave the nascent monophysite church its christological rationale. His other major preoccupation was the ascetic/monastic movement. In the *Discourses*, which is our principal source here, Philoxenus is addressing a monastic audience. Though sometimes called homilies, he nevertheless intends the monks to read them.[22]

[18] *The History of the School of Nisibis*, CSCO 266:14.

[19] Ibid., 17.

[20] Philoxenus, *Letter to the Monks of Senoun*, CSCO 232:42.

[21] *Commentary on the Prologue of John*, CSCO 381:52, 53 (hereafter FL and FM for fragments of Luke and Matthew respectively, FCML for the CSCO edition). Brock, "Syriac Attitudes to Greek Learning," 5:20.

[22] E. Lemoine, Introduction Generale, Philoxène de Mabboug, *Homélies*; SC 44:12.

The Syrian ascetic movement was an indigenous manifestation, independent of the early monastic movement in Egypt. Possibly Syrian monasticism traces its history back to the beginnings of Christianity.[23] Some evidence exists that Syrian monasticism was only "a continuation (though subject to certain exaggerations) of discipleship, taken literally by some as an imitation of the poor, homeless, celibate Jesus."[24] Syrian culture gave Syrian monasticism its own distinctive character. In a more pronounced way than its Egyptian counterpart, Syrian monasticism was open to religious experience.

St. Simeon Stylites (c. 390–459), who isolated himself on the top of a pillar, characterizes the style of Syrian monastic mortification and individualism.[25] Egyptian monasticism was more cenobitic, while the solitary spiritual athlete typifies the Syrian movement. This religious bravado expressed itself in a rigorist attitude toward marriage, attitudes which were very widespread in a number of the early Christian communities, especially in Syria and Mesopotamia.[26] Such were the Encratites, who carried the ascetic doctrine to the extreme, ending in heresy. In some cases they forbad wine, flesh meat, and marriage. Tatian (c. 160), a pupil of Justin Martyr, with a mind of his own, held that marriage was fornication, relating it to Satan.[27] None of this extreme asceticism is found in the fourth-century writers such as Aphrahat and Ephrem. They did not condemn marriage; they enthused about virginity. Indeed in Aphrahat "virginity" is nearly synonymous with holiness.[28]

"In the Jordan He Laid Down the Boundary"

Philoxenus comes out of the tradition of Aphrahat and Ephrem. His theological stance is greatly influenced by his zeal for the ascetic movement. For him married persons in the world can be justified, but "it is not possible for them to arrive at perfection,

[23] Brock, "Early Syrian Asceticism," 1:3.
[24] R. Murray, "The Features of Earliest Christian Asceticism," *Christian Spirituality*, ed. P. Brooks (London: SCM, 1975) 66.
[25] Vööbus, *History of Asceticism*, CSCO 197:315.
[26] Brock, "Early Syrian Asceticism," 1:6.
[27] Clement of Alexandria, *Stromata*, 3:12; PG 8:1131.
[28] Brock, "Early Syrian Asceticism," 1:10, 11.

the world itself being an obstacle to perfection.''[29] As for
Aphrahat and Ephrem so for Philoxenus the ascetic movement
constituted a major pillar of the church. The weight of its presence in the communities was dominant, profoundly influencing
the value system of other Christians.[30] How could it not be, if
living in the world was an obstacle to perfection, rendering
great holiness impossible?

Those ordinary Christians leading ordinary lives, Philoxenus
teaches, belong to the Old Testament righteousness, while
those who wish to be perfect withdraw from the world and live
as ascetics. The Jordan experience is the boundary between the
two: "Our Lord himself in his own person depicted and
showed us the end of the path (Old Testament) and its beginning (New Testament). In the Jordan he laid down the boundary between them. For he ended that path, which was after the
law, in which he was journeying because he kept the law, and
from it (the Jordan) he began the path, which he showed in his
own person, as it were, teaching those who loved perfection.''[31]
The mystery of Jesus' baptism marks the frontier and points the
way. Through his own baptism Jesus demonstrates "the spiritual and perfect conversation (way of life).''[32] Jesus lives under
the law until his baptism.[33] In the Jordan Jesus is "formed of
Fire and Spirit of baptism.''[34] The baptism of Jesus is "a place
of crossing from one world to the other, from the carnal world
to the spiritual world.''[35]

After his baptism Jesus went into the wilderness, "without
followers . . . without beloved friends . . . without riches,
without possessions . . . being accompanied (only) by the

[29] *Discourse 8; The Discourses of Philoxenus*, 2 vols. (E. A. W. Budge, London: Asher, 1894) 2:21 (hereafter cited as *DB*). The English translation in
the text has been modified to conform to contemporary usage.

[30] J. Neusner, *Aphrahat and Judaism: The Christian-Jewish Argument in
Fourth Century Iran* (Leiden: Brill, 1971) 3.

[31] *Discourse 9:274; DB* 2:262.

[32] Ibid., 9:275; *DB* 2:263.

[33] Philoxenus, *Commentary on the Prologue of John 2; Commentaire du prologue johannique*, CSCO 381:3 (hereafter cited as *CPJE* and *CPJ* respectively).

[34] *Discourse 9:261: DB* 2:251.

[35] Ibid., 9:274; *DB* 2:263.

Spirit."[36] When Jesus lives with the Spirit as his only wealth, he signs the demand for "absolute poverty."[37] The masters of wealth must know that they must leave all "to go forth to the saints (who have done the same), to run to the solitary dwellers (the monks)."[38] Beyond marking the border between the two covenants, the baptism of Jesus involves believers in a cosmic transformation. Until the baptism of Jesus the whole of creation groaned in travail, straining toward the baptism of Jesus, from which dates the renewal of all things visible and invisible.[39] The baptism of Jesus effects joy and "an amazing change."[40] "This is the mystery which was fulfilled in the baptism of our Saviour, which (baptism) indeed the Father ratified by his voice and the Spirit by his descent."[41] The Jordan event is unmistakably the place of a trinitarian manifestation which defines Christian initiation. Our baptism is Jesus' baptism, because after his own baptism "immediately he gave it to us."[42]

Faith Tends to Sensation

Philoxenus is fully a man of his tradition. Before him Aphrahat had written of the search for God grounded in faith.[43] In Philoxenus faith is more than firmly held belief. Normally, faith tends to what he calls "sensation." Faith is the germ developing and growing into the higher knowledge of the mystery.[44] Each Christian "receives faith through (Christian) initiation and the Holy Spirit through baptism."[45] The spiritual sensation given at baptism,[46] grows and develops after baptism as one struggles "to put on the new person . . . by the true ex-

---

[36] Ibid., 9:275; DB 2:263.
[37] Ibid., 9:317: DB 2:303.
[38] Ibid., 8:248; DB 2:238.
[39] Philoxenus, FL 53; FCML:CSCO 393:70.
[40] Ibid.
[41] Ibid.
[42] FM 13; FCML:CSCO 393:17.
[43] Demonstration 1; SC 349:207-34.
[44] André de Halleux, Philoxène de Mabbog: Sa Vie, Ses Écrits, Sa Theologie (Louvain: Catholic University, 1963) 328.
[45] CPJ 65; CPJE 161; CSCO 381:161.
[46] Ibid.

perience of the knowledge of the Spirit."[47] The sensation given in initiation only becomes experience through the ascetic discipline. Christ lives in the Christian only if the believer dies to every bodily sensation. If the Christian dies, then the believer will be able "to see, hear, taste, touch in a sense (more) interior than the body (can). . . . In fact the sensing of all the (mysteries) proper to the new person is far from the sensing of the old (person), who does not know what these mysteries are."[48]

Baptism is not Enough

Philoxenus understands initiation as "the womb of baptism," which still leaves a person in the world as in a womb.[49] A child in the mother's womb is still in darkness. The world as a womb is a place of limit. No matter how much the child grows, the measure of growth is limited by the capacity of the mother's womb. The baptized person is, indeed, a righteous person. However that righteousness cannot grow, cannot blossom, limited as the person is by the capacity of womb world. As long as the new Christian lives in the womb of the world the believer "cannot become complete in the perfection of the Spirit."[50]

"As the child casts off the womb" of its physical mother, so the believer must cast off the world entirely.[51] Once freed from the constrictions of the womb world, the baptized will receive "fresh increase" leading to "spirituality and perfection."[52] In a word, the new Christian must make a decision to leave the limit situation of the world for the limitless life in the Spirit. To pass from limit to unlimit is a matter of growth, of gradual putting off the old self. One can be baptized without renouncing the old for the new, slavery for freedom, corporality for spirituality. "Mere baptism," "through the hearing of faith," gives one entrance to this intermediate stage. At baptism the new life is ours, as freedom and spirituality, but only "by the hearing of

---

[47] *Discourse* 9:267; *DB* 2:256.
[48] *CPJ* 67; *CPJE* 167; *CSCO* 381:167.
[49] *Discourse* 2:29; *DB* 2:26.
[50] Ibid., 9:263; *DB* 2:252, 253.
[51] Ibid., 9:263; *DB* 2:254.
[52] Ibid., 9:263; *DB* 2:253.

faith."[53] At this point "they are all strangers to our perception," which is to say, we have yet to experience the new life by our own labor and weariness. Still before us is the need to make these ours by experience.[54]

To move through that gradual maturation from faith to sensing and experiencing is not to leave behind the realm of faith however; "the whole world of the spirit is perceived by faith."[55] Though throwing off the world by "our work and our fatigue" is central to the growth process by which we arrive at sensing and experiencing,[56] we enter and complete the task only by grace: "Our Lord, in giving us the grace to sense it (the world of the Spirit) first gives us the faith by which we sense it (the world of the Spirit)."[57] Faith gives a kind of vision: "For the body sees bread, wine, oil, and water. But faith compels sight to see spiritually what the body cannot see. In other words, instead of bread we eat the body, and instead of wine we drink the blood, instead of water we see the baptism of the Spirit, and instead of oil the power of Christ."[58] In summing up, Philoxenus says "the whole world of the spirit is perceived by faith, and it is faith which sees, and faith which senses."[59] The one who responds to this grace by weariness and labor "shall enter the mysteries of the Spirit."[60]

From Fetus to Full Humanity

To picture this journey from baptismal birth to baptismal sensation Philoxenus often returns to the image of the fetus. What passes through the birth canal, emerging from the mother, is still considered a fetus until freed of the afterbirth and umbilical cord. He thinks of the fetus first within the womb, then the fetus outside of the womb but still in the afterbirth and attached

---

[53] Ibid., 9:267; DB 2:257.
[54] Ibid.
[55] Ibid., 2:35; DB 2:32.
[56] Ibid., 9:267; DB 2:256.
[57] Ibid., 2:36; DB 2:33.
[58] Ibid., 3:56; DB 2:53.
[59] Ibid., 2:35; DB 2:32.
[60] Ibid., 9:288; DB 2:276.

by the umbilical cord, and finally the infant entirely free from the mother. As far as the constitution of the fetus, the essential humanity is present and some measure of growth is possible within the limits of the mother's womb. Only when the fetus leaves the limit place of the womb, and is freed of the afterbirth and umbilical cord, can it grow to full stature.[61]

The baptismal events are built on this paradigm. "The spiritual fetus is conceived by baptism, with all its spiritual members and senses. . . . Just as the natural fetus grows to the measure determined by the womb, so the spiritual fetus grows in the world after being born of baptism, until arriving at that measure which is defined for children . . . the person of the Spirit cannot come to full spiritual perfection, to the full stature of humanity, as long as the person remains in the world as a womb. One must be born again, leave the world completely as the fetus leaves the womb (completely). Then the new born receives a fresh growth which will bring it to spiritual perfection."[62]

The reality, growing and maturing, is given in baptism, as, in the physical world, the nature capable of growth is given in the womb.[63] Even when the natural child has been born and begins to grow, it knows nothing of the physical world. It neither thinks, nor speaks, and is wholly dependent on its parents. So in the spiritual world "the womb gave us birth (that is, in the baptism in which the Spirit is mixed), and we are born in faith."[64] The spiritual infant born in the bowels of baptism cannot depart from the God who gave it birth. Rather, like a newborn infant it hears God's words, receiving them without question, behaving only as God commands.[65] Because it receives this nurture from the hand of God the baptized person "grows in the things which are proper to the order of its birth . . . continues gaining a pure mind according to the measure of its growth into stature."[66]

---

[61] Ibid., 9:260,261; DB 2:249-51.
[62] Ibid., 9:263; DB 2:252, 253.
[63] FL 54; FCML 71; CSCO 393:71.
[64] Discourse 2:29; DB 2:25, 26.
[65] Ibid., 2:28,29; DB 2:25, 26.
[66] FM 12; FCML 15; CSCO 393:15.

In yet a more forceful way Philoxenus insists that experience and knowing do not come first. Rather first you receive, and then you experience and know: "The boast of the arrogant is puffed up, saying he will not believe without first knowing, will not profess without first touching, and will not affirm without having seen. But here the customary practice of restraint in the matters of initiation into the church first invites everyone to believe, and (invites everyone) to ask for baptism, and (invites everyone) to keep the commandments, and to purify one's intellect, becoming an adult according to Christ. And only afterwards such a one will know the power of the words confided to the faith, (only afterwards) receiving the spiritual vision, (only afterwards) also feeling the mystery hidden in each of those words."[67]

What is given at baptism is unfolded and actualized in a long process of maturation, a conception which, as we shall see, Philoxenus shares with other Syrian authors, John of Apamea and Joseph Hazzaya.

From Non-Sensing to Sensing

To receive baptism is no guarantee that the mystery, namely, "what was set within baptism, fire, and the Spirit," has been fully appropriated.[68] Philoxenus is even more specific: "It is evident that not all who are now worthy of this mystery sense it through baptism; not all of those who at that time (as infants at baptism) to whom it (the mystery) was transmitted and flowed, (sensed it at baptism)."[69] Experience is actualized sensing. Sensation becomes experience only if there is a disciplined response from the believer.

As we have seen, Philoxenus believed that up to the time of Jesus' baptism he lived under the Law. The Jordan is the boundary. Jesus became "a spiritual man, fulfilling the commandments of perfection, free and teaching with authority" in

[67] CPJE 65; CPJ 161; CSCO 381:161.
[68] FM 12; FCML 13; CSCO 393:12, 13.
[69] FL 54; FCML:CSCO 393:71. For the Greek and Syriac background of "sensation," see Stewart, "Working the Earth of the Heart," 151–62; 195–208. The theme of sensation and experience runs through Stewart's thesis.

the waters of the Jordan.[70] The history Adam began Jesus finishes. Justice lived in Adam because he was created according to the image and likeness of God. Adam "sensed," experienced the justice of God; but then he lost the sensation. Some who lived after Adam but before Christ were justified by their works and faith. Philoxenus singles out Seth, Enoch, Noah, Shem, Abraham, Isaac, and Jacob. These "sensed (the justice) after the sensation had perished from Adam; (they sensed the justice) because of their works and faith."[71]

Up to the moment that Jesus entered the Jordan only a few sensed the image of God of which Adam had lost the sensation. By his baptism Jesus crossed the Jordan boundary. After Jesus gave his baptism to us, all the baptized possess the image of God. Only those sense it "who through labors and sundering cast off from themselves the old persons and live in the way of life of the new person."[72] Formerly the spiritual riches flowed through the Jewish nation, though, in fact, "not through the whole of it," but only through those who "handed it on and transmitted it (e.g. Abraham to Isaac)."[73]

Now we are in a wholly new situation. Today "through baptism (the spiritual wealth) has been given freely to all," though only those sense it who exercise ascetic discipline and faith.[74] Therefore the one baptized in infancy does not inherit the sensing of the newness of life.[75] Or to state it in a more Philoxean mode, the baptized infant inherits the capacity of sensation, but not the actualized sensing.

The Symbolic Logic of Three Births, Two Baptisms

In a species of symbolic logic Philoxenus has created a chain of three births and two baptisms. The first birth constitutes the logic and dynamics for the second and third, the latter two be-

[70] *Discourse against Habib* 9:98 as quoted in de Halleux, *Philoxène*, 453, footnote 25.
[71] *FL* 54, FCML:CSCO 393:71.
[72] Ibid.
[73] Ibid.
[74] Ibid.
[75] *Discourse* 1:24; *DB* 2:21.

ing of an entirely different order of reality. The first baptism actualized in experience becomes the second baptism.

First Birth	Second Birth	Third Birth
(natural birth from womb of the mother)	(first baptism; from the womb of baptism into the womb of the world; sacramental baptism)	(second baptism; out of the womb of the world into the fullness of the Spirit by self-emptying and the ascetic life)

The first birth is the natural birth, when the fetus emerges from the womb of its mother. The second birth takes place at sacramental baptism, when the infant becomes a child of God. The third birth occurs "when someone is born of their own will out of the bodily way of life into the spiritual, where self-emptying of everything is the womb that gives this birth."[76]

Significant here is the logic which binds the second and third births. What is given in the second matures under ascetic discipline until it blossoms in the third birth. The reality given to infants in sacramental baptism is actualized in a new way, so the second and third births are organically linked. The third birth adds experience to the second birth. Quite concretely Philoxenus describes the third birth as the full realized, actualized awareness of our former birth, sacramental baptism in infancy. When we journey from the second to the third birth we begin a journey into a limitless place. No matter how long the road, no matter how often we travel from place to place in this eternal spaciousness, no matter how deep we penetrate, no matter how high we ascend, we are in a country without borders. The world of the Spirit is beyond boundaries, beyond limit.[77]

"You have two baptisms. One is the baptism of grace which arises from the water; the other is the baptism of your own free

[76] Ibid., 9:342; DB 2:327.
[77] Ibid., 9:343; DB 2:327, 328.

will.''[78] This expression of Philoxenus can be deceptive. He is not suggesting that the devout effect the third birth solely through their human effort. Such would be contrary both to the larger Syriac tradition and to Philoxenus' own teaching. The grace of the second baptism is not just the naked human will. The discipline of emptying the self turned in on itself is one with the whole process of unfolding the grace of baptism. The act of the free will is the human yes, the mature yes, the graced yes to the invitation of the self-emptying of Christ into whose death and resurrection one is baptized. Further, Aphrahat and Ephrem could speak for the whole tradition of the role of faith in all Christian acting. Aphrahat devotes his first *Demonstration* to an extended teaching on faith, through which all good works are performed.[79] Ephrem has his *Hymns on Faith.*[80]

Further, a certain Patricius writes to Philoxenus wanting to avoid the fatigue and stress of the good works which the ascetic discipline demands. In a word, Patricius is looking for a short-cut to contemplation, and seeks Philoxenus' approval. Philoxenus will have none of this. He writes a long reply denying that one can attain contemplation without the labor of asceticism. With his letter to Patricius Philoxenus sends ''a short treatise on faith.''[81]

The Wiles of the Spirit who Lures

Philoxenus does not deny that even fallen reason can of itself attain some knowledge of God.[82] He hands on the tradition of Ephrem and the earliest Syriac authors who evaluate positively God's gifts of free will and choice.[83] Using the rhetoric of wonder, Ephrem says: ''This is the graciousness of God: although without any trouble God had the possibility of forcing us to be

---

[78] Ibid., 9:276; DB 2:265.

[79] SC 349:207-34.

[80] CSCO 212, 213.

[81] *Letter to Patricius*, 133; Patrologia Orientalis 30:873 (hereafter cited as *LP* and PO respectively). Very likely this treatise on faith is the second and third of the thirteen *Discourses*. No other writing on faith has come down to us. Note 32 of R. Lavenant PO30:873. Both Aphrahat and Philoxenus are concerned about right faith, but that is not the only aspect which interests them.

[82] CSCO 212, 213.

[83] Brock, *Spirituality in the Syriac Tradition*, 74

beautiful (good), God used all possible means that we would form our beauty by our own will, with the colors we collected with our freedom. Had God dressed us up in beauty, we would have been like a picture that another person formed and spruced up with that person's own colors, (not our own)."[84] When Philoxenus speaks of the will of the baptized person remaining free, he is speaking out of the central Syriac consciousness: "Free will is not under any compulsion. I did not say that the Spirit compels our soul to do good. (The Spirit) only entices and lures it."[85]

"Come to Me by My Road"

Philoxenus' anthropology is not ours. His theology is worked out in the larger symbolic field of the Exodus passage through the Red Sea to the desert. His teaching on the passing from the second birth (first baptism) by grace to the third birth (second baptism) by free will is in the service of the ascetic movement. He unflinchingly proposes the Christian ideal of the solitary monk in the wilderness. Perfection is attained only by those who undergo the full Exodus experience.

Philoxenus notes that during the actual crossing of the Red Sea the Hebrews were filled with fear and trembling because of the pursuing Egyptians, and the terror of the walls of water. The Israelites had forsaken all their possessions, left Egypt, passed through the terror of the waters of the Red Sea, and marched on through the desert. Now they are in a new order of history. Consequently "they received another rule, and were accounted worthy of other food . . . and they received heavenly revelations, and were accounted worthy of spiritual visions."[86] In the desert they lived under a different rule. "New waters were made to gush forth to supply them with drink, and other commandments and laws were delivered to them to keep."[87]

The different rule, other food, new waters, are all signs of that second baptism tied to the third birth. "The Hebrews did

[84] *Hymns on Faith* 31:5; CSCO 165:86
[85] *On the Indwelling of the Holy Spirit*; Brock, *The Syriac Fathers on Prayer and the Spiritual Life*, 16.
[86] *Discourse* 9:276; DB 2:264.
[87] Ibid., 9:277; DB 2:265.

not immediately receive joy when they left Egypt."[88] Likewise, those who are sacramentally baptized "do not immediately receive joy," nor are they immediately "worthy to taste the spiritual delights."[89]

Only after the Hebrews had observed the discipline God had given them "did they receive heavenly revelations, were found worthy of spiritual visions," only then were they given "participation in spiritual powers," only then was healing manifested among them.[90] For the Christian, therefore, only after the second baptism, which in reality is the first baptism actualized in a new way, is the believer brought "into the new world of the conversation of the Spirit."[91] Now one is worthy to enter "into the mysteries of the Spirit."[92] Only now does the believer come to experience a kind of joy "which never comes to the senses of the body."[93] In a formulation which evokes Hilary of Poitiers' "intense joy," Philoxenus stumbles over himself in trying to express the spiritual exultation the second baptism brings: "You will only know that you experience happiness, but what that happiness is you will not be able to express."[94]

Philoxenus also uses John the Baptist to draw his readers to the second baptism. John received the Holy Spirit while he was still in the womb of his mother, preparing him for the period after birth when he would "receive visions and revelations."[95] The symbolic structure which implies the reception of the charisms within the baptismal rite is clearly stated.

Jesus repeats the Exodus. At the beginning of the ninth *Discourse* Philoxenus points out that "immediately after baptism Jesus went forth" to the place of "absolute poverty," that is, to the desert.[96] Empty and barren, the desert is still "the world of the Spirit."[97]

[88] Ibid., 9:277; DB 2:266.
[89] Ibid.
[90] Ibid., 9:277; DB 2:265.
[91] Ibid., 9:287; DB 2:275.
[92] Ibid., 9:288; DB 2:276.
[93] Ibid., 9:289; DB 2:277.
[94] Ibid.
[95] Ibid., 9;301,302; DB 2:288.
[96] Ibid., 9:257; DB 2:247, 248. Philoxenus returns to the theme of absolute poverty often in the ninth *Discourse*: 292, 317, 330, 341; DB 2:280, 303, 315, 326.

Any one who wishes to attain the third birth must do what the Israelites, John the Baptist, and Jesus did, namely, renounce all of their possessions, whether few or many. Philoxenus puts on Jesus' lips the words "whoever wants to be my disciple must inherit poverty from me."[98] In absolute poverty one submits "to the rule of the country," that is, the rule of the Spirit.[99]

The Exodus passing through the Red Sea and Jesus passing through the waters of the Jordan symbolize the second birth (and first baptism). Then the entry of the Israelites into the desert and Jesus into the wasteland symbolize the third birth (and second baptism). The force of Philoxenus' argument seems to imply the charisms. What is implicit here becomes explicit, as we shall see, in his *Letter to Patricius*.

"The True Experience of the Knowledge of the Spirit"

Philoxenus has a high view of baptism. If there is a universal horizon within which every response to the gospel is placed, it is faith and baptism. In briefest terms "our baptism *is* the Holy Spirit."[100] This high view belongs to the second birth. Yet he has an even higher view of the third birth, which is the second baptism. All the potentialities of the second birth are exploited and realized in the third birth. The capacity for "sensing" present in the second birth becomes experience in the third. While the Spirit is given in the second birth, only in the third does one have "the true experience of the knowledge of the Spirit."[101] Only in the third birth does one "enter into the mysteries of the Spirit."[102] At the gate to this passage one finds the solitary monk, who has had the Exodus experience, who has imitated John the Baptist, who has heard the words of Christ, "Come to me by my road." The solitary ascetic has followed Christ from his baptism to the desert, accompanied only by the Holy Spirit.[103]

[97] Ibid., 9:259; DB 2:248.

[98] Ibid., 9:313; DB 2:300.

[99] Ibid., 9:275; DB 2:264.

[100] On the Indwelling of the Holy Spirit; Brock, *The Syriac Fathers on Prayer and the Spiritual Life*, 112.

[101] *Discourse* 9:267; DB 2:256.

[102] Ibid., 9:288; DB 2:276.

[103] Ibid., 9:272; DB 2:260.

As one looks back at Philoxenus' teaching, is there anything noteworthy when placed side by side with other contemporary theologies? What about "Messalianism"? The title is taken from the Syriac word for "those who pray." Messalianism needs to be carefully distinguished from Montanism, though both are expressions of enthusiastic Christianity. The difference between them is large. Montanism had clearly recognizable churches, complete with structures of ministry, rites of initiation, and other ecclesiastical instruments of normal church life. The so-called "Messalians" had none of these. As Columba Stewart has suggested, the people tagged with this label seemed to have had some kind of communal life, greatly esteemed pneumatic experience, and were perceived as resistant to episcopal authority.[104] Ephrem appears to be the first to note them in a hymn composed between 363-73, labelling them "extravagant."[105] Two local synods leveled canonical condemnations, the city of Side in Pamphylia about 388, and in Antioch about 390. The years of their greatest impact were from 420-40.[106] The Council of Ephesus (431) also thought them of sufficient importance to merit a condemnation.[107] Three authors included them in their collections of heresies, each giving a list of their offensive teachings: Theodoret of Cyrrhus (c. 393-c. 466) in his *Compendium of Heretical Fables*,[108] and also in the *Ecclesiastical History*;[109] Timothy of Constantinople (d. 517) in *On Those Who Return to the Church from Heresy*,[110] and John Damascene (c. 657-c. 749) in *On Heresies*.[111]

There is much duplication in these lists. Among the Messalian tenets are: "Satan and the Holy Spirit co-dwell in a person" (John Damascene);[112] "no benefit for the worthy follows from

[104] Stewart, "Working the Earth of the Heart," 272.

[105] Ephrem, *Hymns against Heresies* 22:4; CSCO 170:78.

[106] A. Guillaumont, "Messaliens," *Dictionnaire de Spiritualité*, 10:1074-83.

[107] "Definition against the impious Messalians or Euchites," Tanner, 1:66, 67.

[108] 4:11; PG 82:429-32.

[109] 4:9; PG 82:1141-45.

[110] PG 86: 45-52.

[111] 80; PG 723-37. These lists should be used critically, e.g., are they first hand reports or based on hearsay.

[112] Ibid. PG 94:729.

holy baptism" (Theodoret);[113] "the believers do not receive the immortal and divine garment through baptism, but through prayer" (John Damascene);[114] "they perceptibly receive the entry of the Holy Spirit and have manifest sensation in the soul of the entry of the Spirit" (John Damascene);[115] "the soul feels such communion with the heavenly bridegroom as a woman feels in being with a man" (Timothy of Constantinople);[116] "they call the fantasies of their dreams prophecies" (Theodoret);[117] "some . . . never share in the mysteries (most likely the Eucharist) unless they feel the coming of the Spirit perceptibly occuring at that time" (John Damascene);[118] "not in the church's baptism, nor by the ordinations of clerics, do the baptized fully receive the Holy Spirit. . . . It is proclaimed that the sensation of the Spirit is given to them through praying with them" (John Damascene).[119]

The label "Messalian" could be applied to various groups which esteemed religious experience, but might be in wide disagreement on the significance of sacraments, the structures of ministry, and ecclesiastical authority. Messalianism was a current/tendency/attitude, that is, unstructured, non-formal, independent. Frequently it was associated with monastics. It had a spiritual vocabulary, an idiom of experience, which sounded unusual but strangely attractive to Greek ears, although the idiom was at home in Syriac culture. Syriac is a Semitic language, given more to the symbolics of poetry than to the precision of philosophy.[120] In the turbulent period after the Council of Nicaea (325) and into the fifth century, there was a desperate, often quarrelsome, search for a vocabulary to handle the christological and trinitarian mysteries. The poetry of symbolic language could be seen by those unfamiliar with its modalities as dangerous, even heretical. With the increasing contact be-

---

[113] *Ecclesiastical History* 4:10; PG 82:114, 115.
[114] *On Heresies* 80:6; PG 94:729.
[115] Ibid.
[116] *On those who Return to the Church from Heresy* 4; PG 86:48.
[117] *Ecclesiastical History* 4:10; PG 82:1144.
[118] *On Heresies* 80; PG 94:733.
[119] Ibid.; PG 94:733. C. Stewart translated the texts.
[120] Stewart, "Working the Earth of the Heart," 271–79.

tween Greek and Syriac cultures (there had long been a degree of communication), and the consequent Hellenization of Syriac patterns of life, the possibility of friction grew. The unfamiliarity of Greek Christianity with the modalities of the Syriac idiom gave rise to misunderstandings. The danger was even greater when some saw any openness to religious experience as a denigration of sacraments and hierarchy.[121]

A wide spectrum of ecclesiastics and monastics, both orthodox and heretical, shared a well developed pneumatology; the same persons thought it proper that the experiential have some role in the Christian life. To suggest that every use of "sensation" or "experience" or "charism" is suspect is to miss the character of Syrian Christianity. If the lists, composed by the victorious opponents of the Messalians, have any authority there must have been real doctrinal errors, as occurs in movements. What generally distinguishes those accused of Messalianism from orthodox Syrian believers is the Messalian tendency to up the pneumatic and experiential voltage to the point where authentic elements of the gospel no longer stand in a balanced relationship to the whole.[122]

Philoxenus is an opponent of Messalianism, clearly naming it a heresy.[123] He and, as we shall see, the other Syrian authors reviewed in the next chapter write from within the geographical areas where Messalianism is present. The high point of Messalian influence is from 420–40; Philoxenus would have been born at the end of that period (c. 440). Messalianism remained a force up to the seventh century. If Philoxenus uses a vocabulary of experience, if he implies the prophetic charisms, and if in one instance, as I will show, he attributes the charism of healing to ascetics, and if the other Syrians also use the idiom of experience and promote the charisms, they do so in spite of the reported Messalian excesses. Even though the idiom of experience is used by the Messalians, and even though they exercise the prophetic charisms, the broad central Syrian tradition will not be intimidated. The Syrians understand that the

---

[121] Ibid.

[122] Desprez, "Le Baptême chez le Pseudo-Macaire," 128.

[123] LP, 108; PO 30:851. Philoxenus identifies Adelphus (perhaps his identification of Pseudo-Macarius) as the "founder" of Messalianism.

charisms and some measure of the experiential are authentic elements of the Christian life. No reports of unusual experiences among the Messalians, and no misuse of the charisms by enthusiastic monastics are going to deprive the great church of its inheritance.

In summary, we have seen how basic the ascetic movement is to Philoxenus' doctrine of perfection, the full Christian life. Jesus crossed the Jordan and went into the desert without friends or possessions, accompanied only by the Holy Spirit. As soon as Jesus had experienced baptism he gave it to us for our baptism. In baptism we receive sensation, a perception of God, which is not yet experience. But the Jordan is a boundary experience. To imitate this model one has to inherit Jesus' poverty, that is, abandon the world. The excesses of the Messalians do not move Philoxenus to reject the experiential and charismatic dimensions of the Christian life. By ascetic discipline sensation in the context of faith becomes experience, the first baptism becomes the second. The believer attains full maturity by moving through the process of three births.

Is there anything retrievable from this monastic aristocracy, from this elitist view of the Christian life? What about the married or unmarried Christian living in the world? What further evidence is there of the charisms in relation to initiation in Philoxenus and other Syriac writers? To these questions I now turn.

Chapter Twenty-three

Philoxenus and the Syrians: The Monasticized Charisms

John Chrysostom taught that in apostolic times each person received a charism at initiation. Regretfully, he continued, the church of his day is a church of tokens, a sign of which is the absence of the prophetic charisms. Chrysostom gave this teaching during his years in Antioch, the Greek city in Syria. Would the surrounding Syriac cities (Mabbug, Apamea, Cyrrhus) reflect the same awareness of the apostolic tradition? Would the Syrians speak of the charisms as "long gone," as only a historical memory? In this chapter I will look closer at the charisms in relation to the ascetic/monastic movement. Do the Syrians place the charisms in relation to initiation? What other mystery of Christ's life do they place in relation to baptism which stamps initiation with a charismatic character? What valuable, permanent contribution do they make to the theology of Christian initiation? Is there anything here retrievable for the Christian living in the world?

Dear Patricius: Charisms Belong to Real Monks

Philoxenus sends a letter to Patricius in response to a question about possible shortcuts to contemplation. Patricius wishes to avoid the *praxis*, the struggle of following the radical commandments of the gospel, the weary exercise of the virtues, in a word, to avoid fussy asceticism.[1] Philoxenus' letter to Patricius contains the only passage where he writes directly on the charisms of 1 Corinthians 12.

Philoxenus has been recounting the marvels which Jesus performed, among them healing the sick. "In the book of his (Jesus') gospel we find a goodly number of other analogous acts, both for the remission of sins and for the health of the body. In those days it was so, but today it no longer happens in that way. He no longer forgives sins just in any manner whatsoever, nor does he heal everyone who comes. In what concerns sins, as I just said, (they are forgiven) by means of a long and extended penitence. As for healing of the body, he (Jesus) scarcely gives such power to the just, or not at all, except by means of the rules of life, works, and practice during many years, together with complete death to the world."[2]

Philoxenus recognizes that the charism of healing is given only to those who lead the ascetic life, that is those who have entirely renounced the world. He uses a distinction between the just and the perfect, probably inherited from the *Liber Graduum*, an anonymous Syrian collection of thirty sermons from the fourth century, Semitic in character, with little evidence of Hellenistic influence. The *Liber Graduum* describes progress toward mature Christian stature in steps or degrees, therefore the title "The Book of Steps," or "The Book of Ascents." There is a "visible (sacramental) baptism" in which the initial incomplete indwelling of the Spirit is imparted. The Christian, living according to the gospel and aided by the incomplete indwelling of the Spirit, moves up from justice or righteousness to perfection.[3] Progressively the indwelling Spirit takes fuller and more complete possession. Perfection is attained by the ascetic discipline, and complete renunciation of the world. This perfection is manifested in an invisible (second) baptism, which

---

[1] I. Hausherr, "Contemplation et sainteté: un remarquable mise au point par Philoxène de Mabboug," *Revue d'Ascétique et de Mystique* 14 (1933) 177, 178.

[2] Philoxenus, LP 118; PO 30:861.

[3] *Liber Graduum*, Sermon 3:11; 7:11; 13:1-3; 15:19, 20; 28:2-5; but especially 14:1-4; Patrologia Syriaca 3:67-70; 146, 147; 306-14; 383-86; 387-94; 323-34. Stewart, "Working the Earth of the Heart," 114-20.

is nonetheless dependent on the visible baptism. "Without this
visible baptism no one is baptized with fire and the Spirit."[4] Using
elements from the *Liber Graduum* Philoxenus teaches that justice or

[4] *Liber Graduum*, Sermon 12:4; Patrologia Syriaca 3:295. The charisms in
the *Liber Graduum* and their relation to Philoxenus, to John of Apamea,
and the other Syrians need further study. The Pseudo-Macarian Homilies
are another corpus which should be studied for the manner in which they
relate charisms to baptism. Though written in Greek they were probably
composed in Syria/Mesopotamia, and, like the *Liber Graduum*, have a pneumatic orientation. In *Homily* 45:7; PG 34:792 the author speaks of an effusion of the Spirit and the charisms. "He distinguishes between the
reception and the enjoyment of the pledge of the Spirit, which corresponds to the distinction which the *Liber Graduum* proposes between the
reception of the pledge and the reception of the Paraclete." A. Guillaumont, "Les 'Arrhes de l'Esprit' dans le Livre des Degrés," *Mémorial Mgr.
Gabriel Khouri-Sarkis* (Louvain: Imprimerie Orientalist, no date) 113. The text
of Pseudo-Marcarius reads: "If a virgin in our country receives some
pledges, and after the pledges numerous gifts (from the groom), and even
if she has full power over the inheritance, but has not yet come to carnal
union, she will not belong fully to the man whose name she carries. So
also the soul which remains a virgin for Christ, even if she receives
pledges through baptism—since baptism represents the perfect pledges of
the inheritance still to be received—and immediately after baptism is the
beneficiary of numerous gifts, (such as) word (of wisdom or knowledge),
interpretation (of tongues), healing, or some other charism, but is not favored with the union with the incorruptible spouse, she will not fully belong to him (spouse). In a word, it is not by the presence of charisms that
one recognizes the ointment of gladness and the marriage robes, but by
filial adoption itself, where one finds constant charity. If, then, you have
the pledge of baptism, you possess the perfect talent, but if you have not
yet made it (the baptism) worth its value, you remain imperfect. . . . So
the charisms are given in view of a service, according to the distribution
wished by God, for those who are still infants and imperfect (while it is
charity which makes them perfect)." *Homily* 28:3, 1-4; SC 275:337, 338.
Charisms here are related to baptism. But they are also not seen as signs
of perfection. Rather they belong to the "way station," to the beginning,
still imperfect, state. H. Dörries, *Die Theologie des Makarios/Symeon* (Göttingen: Vandenhoeck & Ruprecht, 1978) 291, 292, 370, 430. Though Pseudo-
Macarius had a great impact in subsequent history, Philoxenus thought
that he was "the inventor of the heresy" of Messalianism. LP 108; PO
30:851. Contemporary scholars have cast doubt on the justice of labeling
Pseudo-Macarius a Messalian. J. Stiglmayr, "Pseudomakarius und die Af-
termystik der Messalianer," *Zeitschrift für Katholische Theologie* 49 (1925)
244–60; W. Jaeger, *Two Rediscovered Works of Ancient Christian Literature:
Gregory of Nyssa and Macarius* (Lieden: Brill, 1954) 224–30; Quasten,

righteousness is the work of first baptism, and perfection the work of second baptism. For him the charisms belong to second baptism.

Philoxenus continues his answer to Patricius:

"We do not complain against his (Jesus') will because of that, nor do we take him to court. Why is that up to that time these events occurred, but now no longer? Among the first believers, as soon as they were baptized they received the Spirit through baptism. The operation of the Spirit appeared in them by all kinds of wonders. Not only through those (charisms) which they perform for the benefit of others, but also by those (charisms) which manifest themselves in their own persons. The one immediately spoke in new tongues, the other prophesied, the other revealed the thoughts of others, as St. Paul said: 'There is a diversity of powers, and gifts, and operations, but one it is which operates in each.' And: 'To the one is given a word of wisdom in the Spirit, to the other, a word of knowledge in the same Spirit, to another the discernment of spirits, and to another the diversity of tongues. . . . ' All this happened among the first believers when they were baptized."[5]

Philoxenus believes that in the apostolic era the prophetic charisms manifested themselves in all the believers at their initiation. This constitutes the apostolic model. He notes the discrepancy between the apostolic church and the church he knows. The difference is a matter of regret, but he is not going to bring God to court for swindling.

"Now again, the Holy Spirit is given by baptism to those who are baptized and they really receive it (the Spirit), like the first believers. However in none of them, does it (the Spirit) manifest its (the Spirit's) work visibly. Even though it (the Spirit) is in them, it (the Spirit) remains hidden there. Unless one leaves the world to enter into the way of the rules of the spiritual life, observing all the commandments Jesus has given, walking with wisdom and perseverance in the narrow way of the Gospel, the work of the Spirit received in baptism does not reveal itself."[6]

Patrology, 3:164, 165, 273, 273; Stewart, "Working the Earth of the Heart," 271–79.

[5] LP 119; PO 30:860.
[6] LP 120; PO 30:861, 863.

Though all Christians receive the Spirit at baptism, the Spirit does not come to visibility in the prophetic charisms in everyone. The charisms are visibly manifested in those who completely abandon the world, and follow the ascetical rules, and persevere in the wisdom of the gospel. No short-cuts to Christian maturity exist. Vain is the expectation that the prophetic charisms will be given without years of struggle with one's passions. This is a highly "monastic" view of the following of Jesus, restricting charisms to a group within the church, excluding Christians who marry, who do not renounce and leave the world. Charisms, like contemplation, belong at the end of years of ascetic discipline. The charisms have been monasticized.

"The difference between what happened among the first believers, and that which happens now in us, is total. Whether it is a question of the forgiveness of sins, or the healing of the body, whether it be the various charisms which manifest themselves in the baptized, or is some spiritual contemplation received by the intelligence of those who received the Holy Spirit, (the difference is total). The cause and the distinctive diversity of these facts appear evident to those who are instructed in this matter, even if, seeing the limits of this exposé, we do not have place here to indicate its causes."[7]

A vast difference exists between the Christians of the apostolic age and Philoxenus' time. In the apostolic age the charisms were given to all; in his age they are given only to ascetics. In this framework the charisms belong to the few rather than to the many. Paul would hardly recognize his teaching on the charisms, which belong to the normal, everyday life of the ordinary Christian community. Philoxenus places a high value on the charisms, explicitly says they are given to the ascetics. However he mistakes their true function.

Philoxenus states explicitly in his *Letter to Patricius* what is only implicit in his *Discourses*. Why? Possibly because of the authority of John Chrysostom and Theodore of Mopsuestia, who both held that the prophetic charisms had ceased. His *Letter to Patricius* is written to a specific person and therefore

[7] Ibid.

more private than the *Discourses* directed to the larger public. If Philoxenus is more restrained in the latter it is scarcely in doubt that he implied the charisms.

"Fire and Spirit are in Our Baptism"

Would the Syriac teaching on baptism, whether in relation to the ascetic movement, or in a more general way, make it a likely place to locate the charisms? Such a likelihood exists when Pentecost is linked to baptism. Sebastian Brock points out the Pentecostal character of baptism in the Syrian tradition. He demonstrates that the influence of the event of Pentecost was not narrowly limited to baptism.[8] Ephrem (c. 306–73), a witness to a Syrian tradition largely intact from Greek influences, has a series of mysteries determined by Pentecostal imagery: Annunciation, the Baptism of Jesus, and the Eucharist:

"Fire and Spirit are in the womb of her who bore You,
Fire and Spirit are in the river in which you (Christ) were baptized.
Fire and Spirit are in our baptism,
    and in the Bread and Cup is Fire and the Holy Spirit."[9]

Jacob of Serugh (c. 451–521), whose life is almost coterminous with Philoxenus', also brings together fire and water. With the earlier Syrian tradition, which is evident already in Ignatius of Antioch,[10] Christ's entry into the Jordan effects all baptismal waters.[11] "(Christ), the coal of fire (Isa 6:6), went down to wash in (Jordan's) streams, and the flames of its sanctifying power poured forth."[12] Christian initiation is a baptism "in the fire and the Spirit" (Matt 3:11; Luke 3:16).

In addressing the Upper Room where the disciples were gathered waiting for the promise of the Father, Jacob of Serugh says: "In you was accomplished that promise of baptism, for in

[8] "Baptismal Themes in the Writings of Jacob of Serugh," *Orientalia Christiana Analecta* 205 (1978) 334.

[9] *Hymns on Faith* 10:17; CSCO 155:35, 36.

[10] Ignatius of Antioch, *To the Ephesians*, 18:2; SC 10:74. Brock, "Baptismal Themes in the Writings of Jacob of Serugh," 326.

[11] Ibid.

[12] Jacobus Sarugensis, *Homiliae Selectae Mar-Jacobi Sarugensis*, 5 vols.; ed. P. Bedjan (Paris: Harrassowitz, 1905) 1:183 (hereafter cited as *HSMS*).

you were all the disciples baptized with Holy Spirit and fire.''[13]
The Upper Room is identified as the place in which the Spirit
was poured forth like a mighty river, thus indicating the relation between Pentecost and baptism; the rhetoric of abundance
and power found in the account of Acts 2:1-4 makes it evident
that "baptism is also a Pentecost, a charismatic event."[14]

Given the general charismatic nature of the ascetic movement,
given the dominant baptismal consciousness in Syrian thinkers,
it is appropriate that they would exploit the baptismal and
charismatic possibilities of the mystery of Pentecost. One finds
in Ephrem, an important early witness, and in Jacob of Serugh,
a noted contemporary of Philoxenus, the catechesis on baptism
as a Pentecostal event. No one would be surprised if Philoxenus
and others either implied that the prophetic charisms were imparted in relation to initiation, or stated it explicitly.

John of Apamea: Wondrous Gifts at Second Baptism

John of Apamea, sometimes called John the Solitary (first half
of fifth century with the literary career between 430–50), has an
identity shrouded in mystery. Three persons bear that name.[15]
Nothing is known of his life, except that he was of sufficient
fame for the ascetic Thomasios to travel some days journey
from Palestine to sit at his feet in Apamea, a city on the
Orontes river in Syria.[16]

John, too, is addressing ascetics. He, too, explains why Jesus'
teaching and miracles began after his baptism. Just as Jesus
works no miracles before the Jordan event, so "no knowledge
of the divine mysteries is manifested in a person before coming
to receive baptism."[17] John then explains that there are two

[13] Ibid., 2:679.

[14] Brock, *The Holy Spirit in the Syrian Baptismal Tradition*, 134.

[15] Though placed here after Philoxenus, he chronologically belongs to the
period slightly before Philoxenus. John's literary career was between 430
and 450, while Philoxenus was probably born about 440, becoming bishop
of Mabbug in 485. The priority of John seems to have been established by
W. Strothmann, *Johannes von Apamea* (New York: de Guyter, 1972) 62, 91.
Philoxenus, however, places John among the heretics because of unacceptable elements in his eschatology. Ibid. 88–91.

[16] John of Apamea, *Dialogues and Treatises* 1:1; SC 311:47.

[17] Ibid. 10:117; SC 311:149.

baptisms: "By baptism I do not mean the visible baptism, but (also) that which takes us completely out of communion with this world. Just as after his baptism, our Lord manifested his power by signs and wonders, so once a person perfectly possesses in oneself the power of holy baptism, the glory of the soul appears, as it is adorned with all of the divine gifts."[18] Anyone who wishes to know the heavenly mysteries must go beyond the visible sacramental baptism. As in Philoxenus, the second baptism, an actualization of the first, is tied to the renunciation of this world. At this second baptism the divine gifts, given in the first baptism, become manifest.[19]

John, therefore, makes a comparison between, on the one hand, the occurrence of miracles in Jesus' life after his baptism, and on the other hand, the appearance of divine gifts in the life of the one who has practiced the ascetic discipline after the invisible and second baptism. This seems to imply that the manifested divine gifts also have a wondrous character. John does speak of the charisms of prophecy, healing, miracles.[20] For him all graces and charisms, indeed the whole of salvation, is contained in baptism.[21] In baptism one receives the pledge, the first payment, of what will blossom forth into visibility only later. Like Philoxenus, John uses the image of the fetus in the womb of the mother; in John it occurs about a dozen times.[22] What is given in "visible" baptism (the fetus), that is, sacramental initiation, unfolds in a growth process.

Theodoret: The Chronicler of the Charisms

Theodoret of Cyrrhus (c. 393–c. 466), is a native of Antioch, and educated in the monastic schools of that city. In 423 he was consecrated bishop of Cyrrhus, a small village near Antioch. The-

---

[18] Ibid.

[19] Brock, *The Syriac Fathers on Prayer and the Spiritual Life,* 79.

[20] *Dialogue on the Soul and the Passions* 9,10; Jean le Solitaire, *Dialogue sur l'Ame et les Passions des Hommes,* ed. I. Hausherr (Rome: Oriental Institute, 1939) 34, 35.

[21] Strothmann, *Johannes von Apamea,* 77; Brock, *The Syriac Fathers on Prayer and the Spiritual Life,* 79.

[22] Lavenant, Introduction, *Jean d'Apamée, Dialogues et Traités;* SC 311:21, footnote 5.

odoret is a man of great learning and vigor. More than any other eastern author his competence extends across the whole spectrum of the sacred disciplines.[23] He belongs to an earlier generation, but he is identified with the party Philoxenus opposed.

Because Theodoret was born and educated in Antioch, he would most likely have known of the teaching of John Chrysostom on the charisms. As I have indicated, Chrysostom probably preached his homilies on Acts and Romans in Antioch. Without ambiguity Chrysostom taught that the bestowal of the charisms within the rite of initiation is the apostolic paradigm. Theodoret could have known the teaching of Theodore of Mopsuestia on the prophetic charisms in a fragment of his commentary on 1 Corinthians: "After the faith had been spread over the whole earth, prophecies, tongues, and 'knowing in part,' as superfluous things, cease. Then there remain these three necessary things, of which he rightly says that charity is the greatest."[24] If Theodoret and others are going to take a positive position on the charisms they will have to do so in opposition to these two authorities of considerable weight.

Theodoret's *History of the Monks in Syria*, written about 444, recounts the lives of twenty-eight men and three women, most of them living near Antioch.[25] Though he did incorporate some legendary material, he is careful in his use of sources. In fact he goes out of his way to assure his readers: "I have seen with my own eyes some of the events which I am going to relate. But all that I have not seen, I have learned from those who have seen these persons." (*sic*).[26] Obviously aware that a certain distrust in hagiography exists, he protests that the witnesses he cites are as trustworthy as Luke and Mark, who also did not see the events they narrate.[27] This does not exclude Theodoret's use of a theological framework known to hagiographical authors, namely, using the gospel miracles to demonstrate that

[23] Quasten, *Patrology*, 3:538.
[24] Staab, *Pauluskommentare aus der Griechischen Kirche*, 191, 192. I owe the translation to Francis Sullivan.
[25] Quasten, *Patrology*, 3:550.
[26] *History of the Monks in Syria*, Prologue 11; SC 234:143 (hereafter cited as HMS).
[27] Ibid.

God still acts in his saints, that holy men and women exercise powers beyond human nature.[28] The ascetics imitate the lives of the prophets and the apostles. Nothing surprising, then, so goes the assumption, that a similarity exists between the events in the lives of the prophets and apostles and those in the ascetics.[29] In both East and West the wondrous was tied to the holy person, but are no longer realities in the life of the church. Theodoret reports relatively few miracles when compared to analogous works; out of the seventy ascetics he links miracles only to twenty.[30] He identifies nine of the ascetics as exercising the charism of healing.[31]

In the prologue to his history Theodoret places the list of charisms of 1 Corinthians 12.[32] He cites this passage because it structures his whole narration. In describing his method of handling seventy ascetics, Theodoret says: "We will write their eulogy, but not a collective eulogy, for they have received different charisms from God."[33] For this reason he writes individually of each monk.

He places the imparting of the charisms within the rites of initiation. First, he wants to be sure that the reader of his history will not be turned away by the greatness of the charisms given to the ascetics. The measure of their rich endowment is not that of the reader. "They should know that God is accustomed to measure the charisms of the Holy Spirit by the souls of the saints; God gives the greatest (charisms) to the greatest saints."[34] The presence of the greater charism is a sign of greater holiness, a view which would be difficult to defend but would become widespread in subsequent centuries.

[28] P. Canivet, Le Monachisme Syrien selon Théodoret de Cyr (Paris: Beauchesne, 1977) 118, 121.

[29] Ibid. 118.

[30] Ibid. 119.

[31] HMS 2:18; 8:11; 9:5; 11:4; 13:13; 14:3; 16:2; 22:4; 26:16; SC 234:237, 239; 397; 415-23; 459; 497, 499. SC 257:13; 29; 129; 195.

[32] HMS, Prologue, 8; SC 234:138. Here Theodoret omits "discernment of Spirits," but includes this charism in his commentary on 1 Corinthians. SC 234:139, footnote 1.

[33] HMS Prologue, 8; SC 234:139.

[34] HMS Prologue, 10; SC 234:140.

Then Theodoret turns his attention to those not yet initiated. "We need to say these things for the sake of those who have not been initiated to the things of God."[35] Those who have not experienced Christian initiation cannot know about the charisms and how they are distributed. But it is another matter for those already Christians. "Those who are initiated to the mysteries of the Spirit know the generosity of the Spirit, and know what miracles (the Spirit) works in a person, through a person."[36] The liberal outpouring of the charisms seems to be a reference to the Pentecost event of Acts 2. But in the present age, unlike the apostolic age, the Spirit imparts those charisms, which are higher on the hierarchy of gifts, to the greater saints. Theodoret seems to tie charisms to holiness in a way alien to St. Paul. The charisms do, however, have a role beyond demonstrating that God still acts in history in his saints. "By the grandeur of their prodigies they draw unbelievers to the knowledge of God."[37] The abundant outpouring of gifts may be a Pentecost theme linking charisms to initiation and evangelization.

Theodoret would agree with Chrysostom that the charisms are no longer given to all the baptized. On other hand Theodoret would not agree with Theodore of Mopsuestia's dispensationalism, in virtue of which the prophetic charisms are now superfluous. Theodoret gives them a baptismal framework. The charisms demonstrate the holiness of the saint, but they are also in the service of evangelization; they elicit faith from the unbeliever.

Severus of Antioch: Abundance and Initiation

Severus of Antioch (c. 465–538) does not touch on the Pentecost/baptism relationship, but he gives confirmatory evidence of the charisms being bestowed after one is exercised in the ascetic discipline. He is perhaps the most learned of the monophysites. He was born in Pisidia, the mountainous region of Asia Minor, off the main trade routes, of a fiercely independent people. Baptized at the age of about twenty-three, he later became a monk, and a passionate monophysite. In 512 he became Patriarch of Antioch, due in part to the theological victory of the

[35] Ibid.
[36] Ibid.
[37] Ibid.

party to which Philoxenus belonged. Severus and Philoxenus never became friends. Such a friendship would be an improbability between a Greek speaking Pisidian and a Syriac speaking Persian, the former having the benefits of a classical literary and juristic education in the universities of Alexandria and Berytus, the latter educated in the more fervent, unsophisticated schools of Edessa.[38]

By no means did Severus have the charisms as a major preoccupation, but when he did come to speak of specific ones they are the word of wisdom, the word of knowledge, healing, miracles, and prophecy.[39] Like his contemporary and neighbor, Philoxenus, Severus understands that God imparts charisms only after one "has been exercised in the discipline of divine wisdom," that is, one who has made progress "in virtue and contemplation (theoria)."[40] Nothing in the text suggests that Severus expected the charisms apart from the ascetic discipline. This seems to be verified when Severus was preaching a festal sermon in honor of Basil and Gregory Nazianzus. Severus mentions their monastic vocation.[41] "Besides the (charism) of the word of wisdom, the word of knowledge," they also received "all those magnificent charisms of the Spirit."[42] Both were "dispensers of the mysteries of the Spirit," probably a reference to their presiding at the eucharist or at Christian initiation.

In a fragment preserved in the British Museum, Severus is commenting on Romans 8:26: "We mortals do not know how to pray as we ought, but the Spirit intercedes for us with sighs too deep for words. The Spirit who searches the hearts knows the mind of the Spirit because the Spirit intercedes for the saints according to his will." In reference to this text Severus asks: "What do these words mean? The auditor should know that numerous charisms were bestowed on believers at that (apostolic) time, and those who were baptized by the apostles also received various favors."[43] Severus believes that the

[38] de Halleux, Philoxène de Mabbog, 76.
[39] Homily 37, On the Martyr Leontus; PO 36:567; Homily 9, On Basil and Gregory; PO 38:341.
[40] Homily 98, On the Prophecy of Isaiah quoted by Matthew 3:17; PO 25:160.
[41] Homily 9, On Basil and Gregory; PO 25:341.
[42] Ibid.
[43] Severus, On Prayer, 25; PO 38:447.

charisms were imparted to adult Christians at initiation and that the outpouring was abundant. Though not given to each believer at baptism now, the charisms are to be found among "the spiritual persons," those who follow the discipline of asceticism. The charisms are part of the holy person syndrome.

Joseph Hazzaya: The Mysticism of Experience and Intellect

Joseph Hazzaya (born c. 710–13), one of the great Syrian mystics, living some two hundred and seventy years after Philoxenus, fuses two mystical streams which at times appear in opposition, namely, the mysticism of experience and the mysticism of the intellect.[44] He is a theoretician of the spiritual life, a great light in the Syrian heaven. His stature is due to the way he systematizes and analyzes the pursuit of God, taking his own personal experience as the point of departure.[45] That experience was in a monastic mode. Born of Zoroastrian parents, he became a captive, was sold first to the Arabs, and later to Christians. Impressed by the example of local monks, he sought baptism. After being freed by his Christian owner, he became a monk. If Abdisho of Nisibis (d. 1318) is correct, Joseph, besides his dedication to both the eremitical and cenobitic life, wrote 1900 treatises, some of which he published under the name of his own brother Abdisho, also a monk.[46]

Joseph understands the action of the Holy Spirit to be a sensible movement, or more precisely, "an inflamed motion."[47] Joseph was one with Philoxenus in viewing the whole of life in the Spirit as an unfolding of baptismal graces,[48] as did others in the seventh and eighth centuries.[49] The almost compulsive return to baptism is seen in Joseph's text combining the complete abandonment of the world, the ascetic life, the charisms of tears

---

[44] A. Guillaumont, "Sources de la doctrine de Joseph Hazzaya," *L'Orient Syrien* 3 (1958) 24.

[45] R. Beulay, "Joseph Hazzaya," *Dictionnaire de Spiritualité* 8, 1349; Brock, *The Syriac Fathers on Prayer*, 314, 315.

[46] Addai Scher, "Joseph Hazzaya," *Revista degli Studi Orientali* 3 (1910) 45.

[47] A. Mingana, *Early Christian Mystics* (Cambridge: Heffner, 1934) 262; Guillaumont, "Sources de la doctrine de Joseph Hazzaya," 19.

[48] Beulay, "Joseph Hazzaya," 1345.

[49] Brock, *Spirituality in the Syriac Tradition*, 75.

and tongues ("a flowing of spiritual speech"), and word of knowledge. In this text Joseph identifies the third birth in the same way as Philoxenus, taking place after the practice of asceticism. Both Joseph and Philoxenus are addressing a monastic audience, most of whom had been baptized as infants. The text from Joseph Hazzaya is long, but because of its importance, most of it is given here:

"The first sign of the effective working of the Spirit is when the love of God burns in the heart of a person like fire. From this, revulsion for, and complete renunciation of the world are born; at the same time, love of solitude and the ascetic life—which is the mother and educator of all virtues—are also born.

"The second sign through which you will feel that the Spirit received from baptism is working in you, my brother, consists in true humility being born in your soul. I am not alluding to the humility of the body, but to the true humility of the soul, which induces a person to consider himself dust and ashes, a worm and no man (Ps 22:6), notwithstanding the great and wonderful things done to him by the Spirit who dwells in him. . . .

"The third sign of the working of the Spirit within you consists in the kindness which represents within you the image of God, through which, when your thoughts extend to all people, tears flow from your eyes like fountains of water, as if all people were dwelling in your heart, and you affectionately embrace them and kiss them, while you pour your kindness on all. When you remember them, your heart is kindled with the power of the working of the Spirit within you as with fire. . . .

"The fourth sign from which you will know that the Spirit is working within you consists in true love, which does not leave in your thought any remembrance apart from the remembrance of God alone, which is the spiritual key through which the inner door of the heart is opened. . . .

"The fifth sign of the working within you of the Spirit, which you received in baptism, consists in the illuminated vision of your mind, a vision which is seen in the firmament of your heart like the sapphire sky. It is this vision which receives the light of the Holy Trinity, and it is this sign that leads you to the vision of the material natures (that is, the physical world), from which you then rise further to the knowledge of intelligible natures (that is, the spiritual world). . . .From this glorious and holy vision you will fall into a state of wonder at that extensive world, the benefits of which are ineffable. From this state of wonder you will derive a flow of spiritual speech (that is, the charism of tongues), and a knowledge of both worlds (word of knowledge), of the one that has passed, and the one that shall pass; and you will gain a consciousness of the mysteries to come. This will be accompanied by a holy scent and taste, the fair sounds of the spiritual intelligences, joy, jubilation, exultation, praise, glorification, songs, hymns and odes of magnification. . . .

The above are the signs by whose presence within you, you will realize that the Holy Spirit, which you received from holy baptism, is working within you."[50]

Three times in these passages Joseph refers to the Spirit given in baptism, a trait he shares with Philoxenus.[51] To place the charisms within a baptismal framework may be an expression of the great importance the Syrians attributed to the mystery of Jesus' baptism. Earlier I noted that the Syrians and Armenians honored the baptism of Jesus as an article of the creed.[52] To this, one can add the creed of Aphrahat (early fourth century) containing the phrase "one believes in the mystery of baptism," adding, "such is the faith of the church."[53] Philoxenus' and Joseph's baptismal consciousness is, therefore, not idiosyncratic.

In summary, both John of Apamea and Theodoret note the baptismal context of the charisms, John mentioning prophecy, healing, and miracles, Theodoret writing of the generosity with which the charisms are poured out. The latter uses the charisms to structure his history of Syrian monks, and both he and Severus tie charisms to holiness and living the ascetic ideal. Severus also recognizes, with John Chrysostom, that the imparting of the charisms within Christian initiation is the apostolic paradigm. Joseph Hazzaya, who speaks out of his own

---

[50] Mingana, *Early Christian Mystics*, 165–67.
[51] E. Lemoine, "Introduction Generale," Philoxène de Mabboug, *Homélies*; SC 44:12.
[52] Winkler, "A Remarkable Shift in the 4th Century Creeds," 1399.
[53] *Demonstrations* 1:19; SC 349:233.

personal experience, sees the whole of life in the Spirit as an unfolding of baptismal graces, which is also explicit in Philoxenus and John of Apamea. Joseph Hazzaya insistently returns to baptism when speaking of abandonment of the world and the charisms of tears, tongues, and word of knowledge.

The only time Philoxenus writes specifically on the charisms of 1 Corinthians is in response to a question about the relationship of ascetic discipline to contemplation, both monastic issues. He acknowledges that the prophetic charisms are manifested in the lives of those who die to the world. In this view charisms are for the few and are linked to monastic holiness. In brief, the charisms are monasticized. Whether or not it was monasticism which prompted Syrian authors to look at the relation of Pentecost to baptism, it enhanced the tradition's ability to keep the charisms alive. Philoxenus writes of the joy that cannot be named. This exaltation occurs at the later experiential appropriation of infant baptism. Indeed, that baptismal moment is caught up in the rush of a lofty doxological rhapsody. One hears echoes of Hilary's experience of "intense joy."

André de Halleux sums up Philoxenus' teaching that the baptized person has "yet 'to actualize' what the person has become 'in power' by faith and the sacrament, this is to say that (after infant baptism) there remains the experience of the ontological transformation. . . . "[54] In more Philoxean terms "one ought to pass from the un-sensed renewal by baptism and the Spirit to an experience of the mysteries."[55] Here, then, Philoxenus, together with John of Apamea, Theodoret, Severus, and Joseph Hazzaya, join the earlier witness of Augustine and the much later testimony of Symeon the New Theologian in speaking of the grace of baptism received as an infant, actualized as an adult.

Writing in a summary way Sebastian Brock contends that "what Philoxenus is saying here is something of great value. He is looking at the relationship between the personal experience of Pentecost, of the coming of the Holy Spirit upon an individual, and the actual rite of baptism, in a context where, because of the practice of infant baptism, the two events may

[54] de Halleux, *Philoxène de Mabbog*, 395.
[55] Ibid. 136.

be separated by many years of time. Philoxenus' point is that the rite itself confers the gift of the Spirit, but that, since giving also involves receiving, a conscious act of the will, accepting the gift, is required on the part of the recipient if he is to experience properly the benefits that result from the gift. This acceptance involves the self-emptying that Christ himself underwent (Phil 2:7): only once the ego has been stripped away can the gift of the Spirit be fully experienced. The 'two baptisms' are thus but two aspects of the one sacrament, the first seen from the point of view of the Giver, the second, from that of the receiver.''[56]

Brock recapitulates the broader Syriac material: ''The Syriac fathers are well aware that the pentecostal effects of baptism do not necessarily manifest themselves at baptism itself, but may be delayed until later: the 'pledge of the Spirit,' the potential, however, is already present as a result of baptism.''[57] Brock contends that from the end of the fifth century onwards Philoxenus and other Syriac authors focus more on how the pledge given in infant baptism might become full reality years afterwards. A problem remains. Philoxenus, John of Apamea, and Theodoret have developed their doctrine of two baptisms (in reality the second a later reappropriation of the first) as part of a monastic theology which fails to give due dignity to the married and unmarried state lived in the world, a common failure for centuries. Can nothing be retrieved?

While not accepting the view that people in the married state cannot attain perfection, we can affirm other important elements in the Syrian tradition as significant for any state, married or celibate. Philoxenus in particular and the Syrians in general represent the same situation in which we find ourselves, namely, a population which was baptized as infants. What was possible for the Syrians is possible for us, namely, the actualization in adult life of a baptism received in infancy. They understood the permanent meaning of baptism as an enduring source of the Christian life. Life in Christ through the Spirit is a growth process seen in the three births, two bap-

---

[56] *The Holy Spirit in the Syrian Baptismal Tradition,* 138, 139.
[57] Ibid. 137.

tisms. The fetus has to exit from the baptismal womb but also from the womb of the world. This renunciation of the world is effected by emptying that self which is turned in on itself, stripping the self. The experience, deeply personal, as one actualizes the gift of the Spirit, is joy, jubilation, exultation, praise, as Joseph Hazzaya witnesses. Or it is a happiness so great and so interior that one cannot name it, as Philoxenus would say. As in apostolic times, Philoxenus and Severus remind us, numerous charisms were imparted at baptism. The Syrians acknowledge the word of wisdom, the word of knowledge, healings, miracles, discernment, and tongues. According to Theodoret those who have been initiated into the mysteries of the Spirit at baptism are not surprised by this abundance. All of this is an unfolding of the baptismal reality, a gradual growth into the maturity to which the Spirit lures us. In spite of the authority of John Chrysostom (the prophetic charisms are long gone) and of Theodore of Mopsuestia (the prophecies and tongues ceased when the faith had spread all over the world) the Syrians insist on the relevance of the charisms. The evidence is not extensive, but it is there, and is set in a baptismal context.

The Oxford scholar Brock concludes that in the Syriac authors baptism is not a one time event. "Baptism is seen as just the beginning which opens up all sorts of new possibilities, provided the baptized person responds with openness to the presence of the indwelling Spirit."[58]

[58] Brock, *Spirituality in the Syriac Tradition,* 74, 77.

Chapter Twenty-four

Conclusion:
Spirit Baptism and Initiation
in the Early Post-Biblical Tradition

1. The Paradigm Shift and its Significance

To become a Christian one becomes a member of the body of
Christ, enters into the local communion. The original locus of
communion is the life held in common by the Father, Son, and
Spirit into which the believer enters on receiving the Holy Spirit
at initiation. The church is, in fact, a communion in the Spirit.
When the communion gathers to share the gospel, to eat
together the bread which it breaks, to drink together the cup, it
has fellowship in the mysteries of Jesus, until the final, ultimate
gathering into an eternal communion.

Entrance into this earthly communion is an act of God made
in the communion's sacramental celebration of initiation. The
initiative at every stage in the life of the communion remains
with God. To enter the communion catechumens do not remain
passive. They respond, they posit acts, they pray, they bring
and share earth's gifts, water and bread. What they bring to the
process of initiation is caught up in God's act, in one inter-
locked reality of divine initiative and human making. This
sacramental mode of entering the communion uses two primary
paradigms to lay bare the realities: the baptism of Jesus and his

death and resurrection. As baptismal paradigms, both of these mysteries are of great antiquity. Some have suggested that the baptism of Jesus was the Christian community's first choice of an initiatory paradigm, but the origins are obscure. We do know that being born of water and the Spirit was linked to the Jordan event, that the baptism of Jesus was an article of the creed in Syria, which was used in the baptismal celebration. What is undoubted is a tendency to move away from the baptism of Jesus to the death and resurrection of Jesus. Though he did not initiate this move, Cyril was largely responsible for its adoption by the churches of East and West. By the fourth century the death and resurrection came to dominate, even though the baptism of Jesus was never totally abandoned.

What is lost if the baptism of Jesus is neglected? Jesus' baptism in the Jordan is his baptism in the Spirit. There he is declared Son of God. By a claim he himself made, at the Jordan he is anointed with the Holy Spirit and given charisms to fulfill his messianic ministry. According to Hilary and the *Didascalia*, Jesus' baptism in the Jordan is a birth event, possibly inspired by John 3:5 ("unless one is born of water and the Spirit, one cannot enter the reign of God"). Like the Annunciation, the Jordan event is an act of identification but not simply by external signs, "the Spirit as a dove coming down and remaining upon him." The Spirit remaining, resting on him, is the power of God in which he lives, prays, and ministers. The Spirit belongs to the interior substance of Jesus' identity.

The baptism of Jesus orders, structures, Christian baptism. As Philoxenus says: after Jesus' baptism "immediately he gave it to us." If Jesus' baptism is the definition of Christian baptism, then to downgrade his baptism, to obscure its memory, is to imperil an aspect of Christian baptism. If the baptism of Jesus as a birth event in the Spirit, as Hilary and the *Didascalia* pointed out, is blurred, then the specific birth in the Spirit character of Christian baptism is imperiled. Then Christian initiation as the locus of imparting the Spirit, whereby we become daughters and sons of God, adopted but real, is diminished. Then living in the memory of that experienced presence which calls us to praise, then being equipped with the power of God in the charisms to serve the community, is attenuated.

The new appreciation of the Pauline letters, the emergence of cathartic and exorcistic themes, the transformation of Jerusalem as a major place of pilgrimage, Cyril's interest in exploiting the places of Christ's death and resurrection for liturgical purposes, the suspicions which the adoptionists brought upon the baptism of Jesus, the growing practice of infant baptism, all conspired to withdraw the attention from the Jordan event and concentrate it on the death and resurrection of Jesus. As a model, the death and resurrection of Jesus is more primary in human consciousness, invested with greater power, because death is the threat of unknown pain, and, in purely human terms, the menace of ultimate nothingness. Nonetheless the downgrading of the baptism of Jesus, a foundational mystery mentioned in all four gospels, is a significant loss. Some way of compensating within the rites of initiation needs to be found.

There is a further consideration. If the church is faithful to the two paradigms, it has still fallen short of the true richness of the mystery. Pentecost in our writers never attained the stature of Jesus' baptism, or the death and resurrection of Jesus. But it is a second order model in Hilary and among the Syrians. For Cyril, at least, the Pentecost paradigm is not minor, perhaps because of the geographical proximity to the place of the Pentecost outpouring. Cyril understands Luke's account of Pentecost to be truly baptismal. In catechizing candidates he three times returns to the baptismal meaning of Pentecost for the apostles and Mary: they were "completely baptized," "baptized without anything being wanting," "baptized in all fullness." Cyril understood Pentecost to belong to a baptismal catechetical tradition of some antiquity. The imparting of the charisms could not be separated from a Pentecost catechesis.

The baptismal catechesis needs to be faithful to the three paradigms: baptism of Jesus, death and resurrection, and the Pentecost event. Only when all these facets are present does the church truly symbolize the mystery of Christian baptism.

2. Charisms and the Rites of Initiation

In the rites of initiation, Tertullian, Hilary, and possibly Cyril, have both the imposition of hands and anointing. If one includes Chrysostom, there was in all four authors, a calling down of the Spirit. No initiatory rite, East or West, could claim baptism without it. Whether using the death and resurrection or the baptism of Jesus, Tertullian, Hilary, Cyril, Basil, Gregory Nazianzus, John of Apamea, Philoxenus, Theodoret, Severus, and Joseph Hazzaya, in varying ways situate the imparting of the Spirit and the reception of the charisms within the rites of initiation. John Chrysostom (and possibly Severus) no longer has any experience of the prophetic charisms as belonging to the ordinary everyday life of the normal Christian community. Consequently he does not have any actual experience of them within the rites of initiation. Nonetheless, with great clarity Philoxenus and Severus recognize that the reception of the prophetic charisms was part of the apostolic paradigm of Christian initiation. In the apostolic community, Chrysostom teaches, every baptized person received a charism. In every community the prophetic charisms of tongues, wisdom, healing were found. Prophets were numerous.

For Tertullian this generous outpouring constitutes that special part of the children's inheritance which the father bestows with loving generosity. Tertullian, who was recording the liturgical practice of North Africa rather than propounding an ideal way of celebrating initiation, recommends insistent prayer for the charisms within the rite itself. Origen speaks in more formal terms, stating that baptism is "the principle and source of the divine charisms." He is more preoccupied with the higher, intellectual charisms, word of wisdom, word of knowledge, faith, and prophecy. Under the image of the Holy Spirit as the River of God, Hilary writes of the community being "inundated with the gifts of the Spirit." Tertullian and Theodoret speak of the generous outpouring of charisms in relation to Christian initiation. Hilary, Cyril, and John of Apamea mention prophecy among the charisms received. Both John of Apamea and Philoxenus mention healing, while the former mentions miracles, and, in a global way, "all the divine gifts." Joseph Hazzaya refers to tongues and the word of knowledge.

In the last catechesis before the baptismal liturgy begins, Cyril twice singles out prophecy as a charism of which he hopes the catechumens will be found worthy. In his two catecheses (16 and 17) on the Holy Spirit Cyril recounts the Pentecost experience of Acts 2, with its imparting of the Spirit and outpouring of charisms, as the moment when the apostles were completely baptized. With the reference to the charisms of chastity, virginity, almsgiving, poverty, and exorcism, Cyril appeals to the experience of the diocese, the province, the Roman Empire, indeed, the whole world. He makes appeal to the experience of "all the laity." The Spirit comes down as rain, effecting wisdom in one, prophecy in another, martyrdom in yet another.

Hilary stands out from the others. Because the manifestation of the Spirit is a demonstration of power, believers have "absolute knowledge" of the charisms. Not for adornment are they given. Charisms are profitable. Use them!

More dramatic is Hilary's appeal to experience, namely, his own baptism. In bold, sentient language he writes of experiencing "intense joy" when the neophytes "feel the first stirrings of the Holy Spirit within." This movement of the Spirit within is expressed in charisms of knowledge, prophecy, wisdom, exorcism. He uses the same image of rain as does Cyril. But in Hilary the gentle rains become small streams which join to become a torrent.

Philoxenus and Joseph Hazzaya also speak in bold experiential language. The Bishop of Mabbug writes of the faith which tends to sensation, of the sensation given at first baptism becoming experience in the second. By living the gospel as a response to God's initiative the Spirit imparts spiritual senses. One can see, taste, and touch the mysteries of the Spirit, bringing joy no words can name. The mystical writer Joseph Hazzaya speaks of the burning fire within, the abundance of tears, the gift of tongues, and the delight of the spiritual senses, especially abundant joy.

Philoxenus mentions healing, but in spite of his teaching on baptism, in spite of his expansive doctrine of faith passing through sensation to experience, he is reticent about naming the other charisms. The force of his argument leads up to the other prophetic charisms; but then he stops. He clearly implies charisms other than healing. He does not address the issue of Messalianism. The Messalian presence in Syria, including Antioch, may account for his more guarded stance. In any case, given the teaching on the charisms in other Syriac witnesses, his teaching on the three births and two baptisms seems to be missing an element: the prophetic charisms.

Justin Martyr, Origen, Cyril of Jerusalem, the *Apostolic Constitutions*, and Didymus the Blind all name Christian initiation "Baptism in the Holy Spirit." No claim is made here that all the relevant early post-biblical texts have been identified.

No claim is made here that all the relevant early post-biblical texts have been identified.

3. Assessing the Effects of Montanism and Messalianism

How much Tertullian was aware of Montanism when he wrote *On Baptism* is not known, though we do know that there is no evidence of Montanism in this specific tract. Hilary is aware of Montanism; indeed, he traveled extensively in Asia Minor where we know some Montanist churches were still flourishing. Not one to be easily intimidated, Hilary wrote openly and extensively on the charisms during his exile in Asia Minor, therefore in proximity to those existing Montanist communities. One looks in vain for any pastoral caveat, any timely admonition about the perils of religious experience. After he returned to Poitiers from his exile in Asia Minor, in the full maturity of his last years, he wrote vividly of the experience of his own initiation. Integral to his experience of initiation were the charisms of word of knowledge, prophecy, wisdom, healing, and exorcism.

Cyril mentions the Montanists in the *CL* composed possibly while still a priest, or at least during his young years as bishop. That knowledge did not dissuade him from expounding the charismatic succession from Moses to which the church belongs. Where Cyril is expansive on the charisms in the *CL*, he is lapidary, concise in the *MC*. This may fully account for the biblical shorthand, "gift of the Spirit," for the reception of the Spirit and the charisms, which he uses in the *MC*. Or it may be that Cyril was forced by the new Jerusalem, now visited by hordes of pilgrims, among them many bishops, to conform to the suspicions in which the rest of the church held the prophetic charisms, because of Montanism. Whichever way the evidence is read, Cyril understands that the prophetic charisms belong to Christian initiation both in the *CL* and the *MC*.

However much the prophetic charisms were suspect elsewhere, in Jerusalem they were held in honor. The immediacy of
the place where fire fell from heaven that first Pentecost would
act as a reminder that the prophetic charisms were not necessarily mindless enthusiasm. Irenaeus, whom Cyril had read,
would have warned him against those who, out of fear of
abuses, banish prophecy itself from the church.

The period when the Messalians had their greatest impact
was between 420–40, with Philoxenus being born about 440. In
spite of the reported excesses of the Messalians, in spite of the
condemnations of two synods and the Council of Ephesus,
Philoxenus and the other Syrians were unwilling to surrender
the experiential elements in their tradition, unwilling to ban the
charisms. On the contrary, with proper reservations, they invited others to share in the piety which has some place for experience. This they could do with assurance because they
shared with the whole of Syrian Christianity a developed pneumatology, an opennenss to the charisms. The tradition which
esteemed the baptism of Jesus as so central to the identity of
Jesus and to the nature of the Christian life as to find a place of
honor in the creeds used in the liturgies would not be easily intimidated by the reported pneumatic excesses of some. A central mystery of Jesus and the empowerment there signed is the
common property of all. Such cannot be jettisoned as peripheral
or alien.

4. The Syrians and the Second Baptism

John of Apamea, Philoxenus, Severus, Joseph Hazzaya, and
quite likely Theodoret, think within a two-baptism framework,
the second, received later in life, actualizing the first, received
in infancy. The two-baptism schema must be interpreted with
some care. This does not appear to be an early form of the second blessing theology found in the Holiness and Pentecostal
movements. For the Syrians the second baptism is not a new
grace, not a second blessing in the usual sense, but the unfolding, the full flowering of the reality given in first baptism. However, the two-baptism framework is based on the distinction
between the just (believers who live in the world) and the per-

fect (who renounce everything, including marriage), a doctrine of some tenacity, but no longer acceptable in the church.

The Syrians write in a church practicing infant baptism. In it the Spirit and the whole baptismal reality, including the charisms, is imparted. Also in infant baptism one receives the sensation, or sensing, of the divine Spirit within. Though present, the sensation, paradoxically, is not felt until one has observed the discipline of the ascetic life (prayer, vigils, fasting, silence). At the second baptism the charisms become visible and sensation becomes experience. In varying degrees the other Syrians share this monasticized view of the charisms and the full baptismal reality.

The Syrian authors have retained the apostolic paradigm, acknowledged by Cyril and Chrysostom. However, they restrict the second baptism to those following the ascetic life. Neither Tertullian, nor Hilary, nor Cyril, restrict the experiential dimensions and the charisms in this way (though Cyril's catechumens are a select group).

Is it possible that the Syrians inherited from antiquity, from apostolic times, a charismatic element belonging to the integrity of Christian initiation, which was appropriated by the ascetics as theirs? The supposition, which cannot be satisfactorily demonstrated, goes like this. In the Syrian church there were, as I mentioned earlier, rigorist attitudes toward marriage. A. Vööbus has shown that in early Syrian communities these rigorist attitudes were used to make celibacy a requirement for baptism.[1] By the time of Aphrahat (early fourth century), and Ephrem (c. 306–73), these attitudes toward marriage were a matter of history. Would it not be likely that the ascetics, having to yield their exclusive right to sacramental baptism, retreated to a second line of defense, and established their claim at another level of the initiation experience. The exclusive claim to first baptism was shifted to second baptism. In this reading, what was common to the church as a whole became the preserve of a few. The ascetics built a monastic wall around the actualizing of infant baptism.

[1] *Celibacy, A Requirement for Admission to Baptism in the Early Syrian Church* (Stockholm: Estonian Theological Society in Exile, 1951). Vööbus includes a helpful bibliography.

Origen is an earlier witness to this tendency to sequester the charisms. Though the charisms are given in baptism, which is their principle and source, the exercise of the more intellectual charisms seems restricted to the spiritual Christians, those who demonstrate their earnestness by embracing the ascetic discipline.

5. The Authority of These Witnesses

Most of the authors examined are not engaged in impulse writing, that is, in recording an accidental, vagrant thought when occupied with another theme. Some give evidence of planning to write about the charisms. Tertullian is commenting on the actual liturgical practice long in use in North Africa. An important part of Hilary's teaching on charisms is found in his *On the Trinity*, for which he made a detailed outline before commencing to write. Cyril is following an inherited reading list of some antiquity, giving specific themes for the baptismal catecheses. John Chrysostom is commenting on the text of 1 Corinthians. Only with difficulty could one separate John of Apamea's teaching on the two baptisms from the prophetic charisms. Theodoret uses the charisms to structure his monastic history.

I have examined Tertullian, representing the Latin tradition of North Africa; Origen, speaking out of his catechetical experience in Alexandria and expressing the Greek mind in the city of the empire which was second in size and importance only to Rome; Hilary, who embraces both the Latin culture of Poitiers in Gaul and the Greek wisdom of Asia Minor; and the Greek speaking Cyril, who has his roots in the pre-Nicene church of Jerusalem, the heir of the Syriac rites of the mother church. Basil and Gregory of Nazianzus, representing Greek culture in Cappadocia, and John Chrysostom and Severus in the Greek/Syriac boundary city of Antioch in Syria, in varying ways witness to the baptismal context of the charisms. John of Apamea, Philoxenus of Mabbug, Theodoret of Cyrrhus (the latter writing in Greek but on a Syrian theme), and Joseph Hazzaya near Mount Qardu (in contemporary northern Iraq) speak for the Syriac sources, testifying to a later experiential appropriation of the graces of baptism conferred in infancy. All of them testify that the charisms were sought, or expected, and received within the rites of initiation or in relation to them. The witnesses extend from the end of the second century into the eighth. Geographically they almost ring the Mediterranean seaboard. Hilary, Cyril, John Chrysostom, Basil, and Gregory Nazianzus are all Doctors of the Church, a title given to those who are outstanding in identifying the faith and practice of the church.

6. The Focus of this Study

I have concentrated on the prophetic charisms because of the evidence in Luke of the relation of these charisms to the baptism in the Spirit. Also, that is the way the baptism in the Spirit has been identified in the Classical Pentecostal/charismatic movements. But the prophetic charisms do not exhaust the Christian life. Other important charisms are also imparted during initiation. A church made up of only those possessing prophetic charisms would be a noisy church. Such a church would have little claim to apostolicity.

Some of the texts we have examined are not liturgical in character, but theological, even devotional. These texts place the prophetic charisms within the rite of initiation, even though they do not specify ritual elements.

I have been looking for three elements in the authors studied: (1) a sign of the prayer for the descent of the Spirit, usually the imposition of hands, but also anointing, (2) praying for the descent of the Spirit, (3) an expectation that the charisms will be manifested, and/or the actual manifestation. These three elements are not the baptism in the Spirit itself, but are signs usually associated with the baptism in the Holy Spirit. The baptism in the Spirit is the whole rite of initiation. In various ways and in varying degrees the elements which are associated with the baptism in the Holy Spirit in a patterned way in the Pentecostal/charismatic movements are integral to Christian initiation in the authors studied.

In more specific terms what does "integral" mean in this context? Some technical, philosophical terms are in order. If a baby girl is born without a right arm, her essential humanity is intact. That is, what constitutes human nature is all there. No one would refuse to call this baby a human being. But there is something missing, her right arm, not a minor appendage. In technical terms we say that the right arm is a property of her humanity. A property does not belong to the essence but flows from that essence. The right arm does not belong to the essence of humanity (otherwise the baby would cease to be a human being), but it flows from that essence and belongs to the wholeness of being human.

Baptism in the Spirit, as the awakening of the full life of the Spirit with the charisms (including the prophetic), does not belong to the essence of Christian initiation. Otherwise there would have been few authentic (valid) baptisms since the early centuries. The essence of Christian initiation has remained intact. Every authentic initiation confers the Holy Spirit. But Christian initiation has been missing a property, which flows from its essence, namely, what today is called the baptism in the Holy Spirit, the full flowering of the sacramental grace. Like the missing right arm, the baptism in the Holy Spirit is not a minor appendage. It belongs to the wholeness of Christian initiation.

Chapter Twenty-five

General Conclusions:
Where We Were and Where We Are

1. *Christian initiation, modeled on the baptism of Jesus or on his death and*
   resurrection, involved essentially the gift of the Holy Spirit.

In the synoptics, Jesus' being anointed with the Holy Spirit
from the moment of his baptism sets the pattern for Christian
initiation, which is essentially a "baptism in the Holy Spirit."
The Spirit descends on Jesus upon or after his coming out of
the water, not during his submersion in it. This sequence is
noted by all the synoptics. On the one hand this indicates that
the Spirit comes on Jesus as a sovereign intervention of God (the
heavens are opened) and not just because Jesus received the
baptism of John. On the other hand, the descent of the Spirit is
immediate (even Luke considers it part of the baptism story).
Consequently, when Jesus' Jordan baptism becomes the icon for
Christian initiation (Christian baptism being modeled on Jesus'
baptism rather than John's baptism), the gift of the Spirit must
be integral to the initiation rite. The post-biblical theology, especially in the East, would distinguish two moments but it considered them inseparable—immersion into the water (seen as a
union with Christ) and gift of the Spirit.

It is the gift of the Spirit which is the diagnostic mark of being a Christian, for one cannot belong to Christ without the Spirit of Christ (Rom 8:9; Acts 19:1-7). And this Spirit is normally received at the moment of baptism (1 Cor 12:13), which John describes as a new birth of water and Spirit (John 3:5). In Paul, too, baptism involves essentially the gift of the Spirit (1 Cor 12:13), but the sacrament is also modeled on the death and resurrection of Jesus (Rom 6:25), a model that in the later church became the dominant one. Although Paul does not allude to the baptism of Jesus except possibly in 2 Corinthians 1:21-22, he understands the resurrection of Jesus to be his empowerment as the last Adam to be source of the Spirit for the church (1 Cor 15:45; Rom 8:11). Hence the sacramental immersion into the paschal mystery was also for Paul the gift of the Holy Spirit (1 Cor 6:15-20). In the subsequent history of the church, the primary effect of this immersion into the paschal mystery, namely, the gift of the Holy Spirit, became obscured.

How the church historically ritualized the imparting of the Spirit in the celebration of Christian initiation varied even when the primary paradigm is unmistakably the paschal mystery. In Hilary and Cyril it is in the post-baptismal anointing; in Chrysostom it is the water-bath with the laying on of the hand of the bishop.[1] These are ritual variables, the imparting of the Spirit is the constant.

Mysteries other than the death and resurrection or the Jordan event enter into the identity of Jesus as related to the Spirit. Matthew and Luke are concerned to show that the relation of Jesus and the Spirit begins long before the Jordan. From the moment of Jesus' conception, the Spirit is active in constituting who Jesus is and, in an ongoing way, gives structure, profile, and finality to Jesus' personhood. The act of the Spirit here cannot be exterior to Jesus' identity. Constitutive of who Jesus is, the act of the Spirit reveals that mutuality between the Spirit and Jesus which is grounded in the mission of each from the Father.

[1] In Tertullian the water–bath is not related to death and resurrection themes but rather to the primeval waters on which the Spirit came down and remained. For Tertullian the Spirit is imparted by the laying on of hands.

The anointing with the Spirit at the Jordan has exterior aspects to it which the annunciation did not have, namely the descent of the Spirit in the form of a dove coming upon Jesus and "remaining upon him" (John 1:32-33) and the Father's voice. These external manifestations to the reader, if not to the gathered crowd, are important functions. As interpreted by Luke, the Spirit here defines Jesus' public messianic character as one coming from the Father (Luke 4:18; Acts 2:22). But the externality of this dimension does not exhaust the meaning. Rather the anointing with the Spirit at the Jordan touches Jesus at the deepest interior of his personal identity. At the baptism of Jesus, the Spirit also identifies the specific character of what Jesus comes to do. Jesus himself is witnessing to his own baptism when he proclaims that the Spirit is upon him to proclaim the good news to the poor, to set the captives free, to give sight to the blind. The prophetic charisms of healing and miracles are integral to Jesus' baptism. The baptism of Jesus announces the charismatic character of Jesus' own ministry.

Tertullian, Origen, Hilary, Cyril, Chrysostom, and Philoxenus all saw the importance of the baptism of Jesus for Christian initiation. Hilary believed that the baptism of Jesus structured or ordered Christian baptism. In a similar vein Cyril handed on the Syriac tradition that Christian baptism is an icon of Jesus' baptism in the Jordan. Though not the first to use the Pauline theme of Jesus' death and resurrection to interpret Christian baptism, Cyril was largely responsible for its adoption. Chrysostom, too, wanted to retain the baptism of Jesus as one of the models for Christian baptism, though he did not exploit it as a context for the charisms. Hilary, Cyril, and Chrysostom all retain the death and resurrection as the dominant paradigm. Philoxenus sees the baptism of Jesus as the boundary which Jesus crosses, as a mystery Jesus fulfills only to give it to us. At some point in liturgical history, the significance of the baptism of Jesus, once an article of the Creed, was diminished. The East was more successful in retaining it as a meaningful paradigm. The Syriac tradition, as developed by John of Apamea, Philoxenus, Jacob of Serugh, Theodoret, Severus of Antioch, and Joseph Hazzaya, considered Jesus' baptism the paradigm not only for Christian initiation but also for the full development of the Christian life. The West was never quite sure of the theological content of Jesus' baptism, nor what to do with it.

The loss of this tradition, though understandable in the light of the reaction to adoptionism, has been an impoverishment. The displacement of the baptism of Jesus as a significant prototype and the removal of Jesus' baptism from the creed are events the importance of which can hardly be exaggerated. Such a change at the very center of the rites of Christian initiation, rites which defined the church and constituted her inner life, cannot but have a profound effect on worship, theology, and the Christian life. To regain the primitive emphasis on Jesus' baptism, the solution would not be to discard the death-resurrection as a model. Such a rejection would have enormous effects of possibly catastrophic proportions. What is regrettable is that no way was found to incorporate the baptism of Jesus into the rite of initiation as a major paradigm. If our interpretation of Mark 10:38-39 is correct, the description there of the passion as a baptism intentionally connects Calvary with the Jordan event. As the death-resurrection model became dominant that early Markan connection to Jesus' baptism faded from view.

Thus the restoration of the baptism of Jesus to its rightful place alongside the death-resurrection must not be looked upon as a denigration of the importance of the cross. What one gives to the baptism of Jesus is not to be taken away from the death and resurrection. For the baptism not only inaugurates Jesus' Spirit-filled mission but is itself a forecast of the passion through which the Spirit will pass to the church (see also Luke 12:49-50). However, the ritual act itself gives a different accent. Jesus' baptism in the Jordan is a going down into the water; ideally our baptism is by immersion. From a ritual perspective, therefore, the resemblance of Christian baptism to the baptism of Jesus is clearer than it is to his death and resurrection.

Though John does not expressly connect the passion to Jesus' baptism, which he does not even relate (he hands down a report from John the Baptist), he clearly connects the cross with the gift of the Spirit. The Spirit is given, proleptically, in Jesus' last breath (John 19:30) or flows from his pierced side (John 7:39; 19:34). The Spirit thus links Calvary and Pentecost: "For there was no Spirit, because Jesus had not yet been glorified" (John

7:39). The cross releases the fullness of the Spirit. "The Spirit of Jesus which departs at the cross in death is the same Spirit which brings life at Pentecost."[2] For Ignatius of Antioch, Jesus' baptism and passion sanctified the baptismal waters (*Eph* 18:1).

In the post-biblical period the Johannine theme of being born of water and the Spirit became associated with the baptism of Jesus, which, as we see in Hilary, is itself a birth event. But the mere mention of the Johannine theme of being born of water and the Spirit will not solve the problem. It did not solve it in the past. In both ancient baptismal texts, Ambrose from the fourth century, and the *Gelasian Sacramentary* (around 750), and in modern ones such as *Roman Ritual* (1976), baptism as a birth event is mentioned, using Johannine language. But no explicit link is made to the baptism of Jesus. Again, the mere mention of any theme whatever does not assure its viability, if there is no accompanying conviction of its importance demonstrated in a substantive catechesis.

The neglect of Jesus' baptism in favor of the tradition of being born of water and the Spirit, makes the recognition of the baptism in the Spirit more difficult. Jesus' baptism is his baptism in the Holy Spirit. The Jordan event stands guard over the baptism in the Spirit.

The Jordan event likewise has great meaning for ecclesiology. If one narrows the mysteries of Jesus which define Christian baptism, one has also narrowed the vision of what the church is. The church is the communion in the mysteries of Christ, including not only his death, resurrection, and ascension but also his baptism. To become a Christian is to become a member of that community which has communion in these mysteries. Whether one speaks of the church as a communion or as the body of Christ, access to the mysteries is socially controlled, that is, there are no free standing Christians. There are only Christians in community. In this perspective one receives the charisms because at initiation one has been taken up into the communion. The charisms are ministries in the communion, to the communion and to the world. The charisms are therefore

---

[2] Burge, *Anointed Community*, 95, 100.

primarily directed to the building up of the body, to the growth of the communion.

Two questions can be asked. Is it a matter of coincidence that the relation of the charisms to Christian initiation seems to be lost about the same time that the death and resurrection of Jesus assumed a new dominance in the baptismal liturgies? Historically is there a demonstrable relation between the church's acceptance of the prophetic charisms and the viability of the baptism of Jesus as a major paradigm for Christian initiation? To answer these questions much more research needs to be done.

2. Two Equal Missions?

In maintaining that the primary effect of integral Christian initiation is the imparting of the Spirit, it might appear that our attempt has been to replace a deficient pneumatology with an inflated doctrine of the Spirit and the charisms. Or we are downgrading the role of Christ to upgrade the role of the Spirit. This we do not believe is the case. However much one has reason to speak of the neglect of the Spirit, neither the New Testament nor the theological tradition makes the Holy Spirit the central content of the gospel or the principal focus of theological reflection. The center of the good news in Paul is Jesus Christ, crucified and risen from the dead. Both Jesus and the Spirit occupy the center but in different ways. In oversimplified terms Jesus is at the center as the "what" of the gospel, the Spirit as the "how."[3]

The relation of the Spirit to Christ is seen in the way being "in Christ" is related to being "in the Spirit." This relationship is clearest in Paul, for whom being "in the Spirit" and being "in Christ" express the same reality from different viewpoints. "Being in the Spirit" becomes the proclamation of "being in Christ," both as the crucified and risen one. Later liturgical formulations use the expression "through Christ in the Spirit."

The Father sends two on a mission of salvation, the Son and the Spirit. The Son is sent in the power of the Spirit, and the

[3] McDonnell, "A Trinitarian Theology of the Holy Spirit," TS 46 (1985) 191–227.

Spirit is sent through the risen Christ. These two missions must be equal, that is, of the same theological weight. Equal but not the same. If the two missions are not equal, then the doctrine of the trinity collapses. The one God in three persons cannot support two unequal missions.

Who can doubt that pragmatically in our theologies, worship, and prayer they are often not given equal status? To the Son is ascribed a major mission, to the Spirit a junior size mission, which in fact involves an unacceptable subordination. There is, of course, an acceptable, indeed necessary, nonontological subordination: "the Father is greater than I" (John 14:28). But the mission of the Spirit, in practice, seems hardly to equal the mission of the Son. In some circles there is even a supposition that what is given to the Spirit is taken away from the Son.

To assert the equality of the two missions does not compromise the deeply personal (not private) commitment to the Lord Jesus. Such a commitment, sometimes absent in born Catholics, belongs to the retrieval of the full reality of Christian initiation. Precisely the power of the Spirit brings about such a life-changing commitment to Jesus who is Lord. No reception or exercise of the charisms can usurp the primacy of the personal and communal relationship to the Lordship of Jesus, which communion in the baptism of Jesus and the paschal mysteries is meant to bring about.

3. The Spirit and the Charisms

Various effects are attributed in the tradition to the gift of the Spirit: regeneration and life, sonship, freedom, inheritance, the fruits of love, joy, peace—to mention only a few. While sanctification and personal transformation clearly enjoy a privileged place, love, being clearly of a superior order (1 Cor 13), what appears to us the least exploited in the church today is the empowering by the Holy Spirit associated unambiguously in the early tradition with Christian initiation. This is not to say that the charisms were the central reality, but clearly they were considered an integral element of that central reality which was the gift of the Spirit. This charismatic empowering is implicit already in the New Testament in the modeling of Christian initiation upon Jesus' baptism, which was an anointing for the ministry of the kingdom. It becomes explicit in Acts, in Paul, and increasingly so in Tertullian, Origen, Hilary, and Cyril. Paul's exhortation to seek the spiritual gifts (1 Cor 14:1) is picked up by Tertullian and Cyril in their baptismal exhortations to seek and expect the charisms, and in Hilary's urging the faithful to *use* them. Cyril, referring to the apostles at the Pentecost event, which included the imparting of the charisms, gives a three-fold variation: the apostles were "completely baptized by the Spirit," "baptized without anything wanting," "baptized in all fullness."

While Paul in 1 Corinthians sees the spectrum of charisms as structuring the community, Basil and Egyptian monasticism are admittedly reserved toward the prophetic charisms. Basil, for instance, does not promote the prophetic charisms in the way Paul did. Tertullian, Hilary, Cyril, and the Syrians, however, are more open and affirming of the range of charisms.

For John of Apamea one must "perfectly possess in oneself the power of holy baptism," then one will be "adorned with all the divine gifts." Further, he places this empowerment through the actualized baptism in contrast to Jesus' life before the Jordan experience. Just as Jesus manifested himself in "signs and wonders" only after his baptism, so the charisms manifest themselves only after one has perfectly possessed the power of baptism. Theodoret calls on those who have already been initiated into "the mysteries of the Spirit" to witness to "the generosity of the Spirit" in the demonstration of power.

The charisms involved a wide range of gifts—Irenaeus said they were too numerous to list. Most highly prized were the prophetic gifts. Whether tongues be included as one of the prophetic gifts is an academic distinction. In Acts 2, Peter identifies tongues as part of prophecy; in 1 Corinthians 14, Paul distinguishes them from prophecy, though he considers interpreted tongues virtually equivalent to prophecy, indicating their close connection. The evidence from the first four centuries indicates that as late as the mid-fourth century the gift of prophecy was expected and sought at baptism.

There were other less spectacular charisms, of course, like "administration" and "assistance." Today these "service charisms" are more readily accepted in the church, but often more as "jobs to be done" than as Spirit-anointed ministries proceeding from a genuine gift of the Holy Spirit. The charisms are not "things," nor are they to be identified with merely human talents, though these may be informed by the charisms. They are movements of the Holy Spirit. The one who exercises them properly yields to the Holy Spirit and thus serves the growth of charity both in self and others.

4. The Baptism in the Holy Spirit as an Experience

"Long before the Spirit was a theme of doctrine, He was a fact in the experience of the community."[4] If by experience we mean not mere feelings but an effect that transforms and empowers lives, then clearly the earliest Christian initiation was an experience. As evidence of the coming of the Holy Spirit Luke not only notes tongues and prophecy but joy as well, a joy that Hilary describes as intense. Philoxenus also has a pronounced experiential language. Although receiving baptism is no guarantee that one has experienced "fire and Spirit," this gift is "set within baptism," wherein one received "the sensation" of justification, which one later experiences when one responds to God's initiative by following Jesus. When the first baptism is actualized by living the gospel, then sensation becomes experience, a joy beyond words. In this profound reappropriation of infant baptism one has "the true experience of the knowledge of the Spirit." "An inflamed motion," a sensible movement, is how Joseph Hazzaya perceives the action of the Spirit. He appeals to his own experience. The fire of the Spirit within gives rise to "joy, jubilation, exultation, praise, glorification, songs, hymns, and odes." Paul, too, often associates the Spirit with joy, and he lists nine fruits of the Spirit, including joy and peace, which could hardly have been present without manifesting themselves experientially (Gal 5:22). Furthermore he appealed to his readers' experience of the Spirit as proof of the superiority of the gospel to the law (Gal 3:1-5).

In a more general context and without reference to the charisms, Rudolf Schnackenburg remarks:

---

[4] Schweizer, *TDNT* 6:396.

". . . the Spirit for the Johannine community was an experienced reality. . . . This must mean a 'regular' inner experience of the Spirit, a conscious awareness of its presence.
Paul witnesses to the same reality, but in a different way in
Galatians 4:6 and Romans 8:14-16. The modern critical reserve
concerning such an experience of the Spirit should not obscure
the fact that early Christianity was convinced of it. On the contrary the witness of Paul, as of Johannine Christianity, asks us a
question. In this matter have we not become blind and poor?"[5]

Hilary clearly assumes an experiential dimension when he
speaks of the "intense joy" at the "first stirrings of the Holy
Spirit," which he associates with baptism. In the Syrian monastic tradition Philoxenus actually constructs a model of spiritual
"sensation," to which the development of the life in the Spirit
should lead.

Doubtless such experiences differed from person to person as
much as the charisms did, dramatic in some, less so in others,
and open to subsequent manifestations. There is no reason why
catechumens today should not be encouraged to have such an
expectation as long as it is made clear that the experience is
gift, that the Spirit follows its own timetable, that the intensity
of the experience is not a gauge of the certitude of salvation,
and that a gradually developing experience may be just as valuable as an initial "peak" experience.

5. Baptism in the Holy Spirit initiates a progressive development.

It is evident in Paul that the Spirit works a progressive transformation of the Christian into the image of Christ (2 Cor 3:18).
And in Titus 3:5, the term "renewal by the Holy Spirit" likewise indicates an ongoing process. For Origen, the baptism,
which is the principle and source of the charisms, is joined to
the ascetic surrender, placing one in that gradual ascent to perfection and to the Father. Hilary, too, speaks of the gifts entering like gentle rain and "little by little they bear fruit." While
the Syriac Philoxenus gives perhaps undue privilege to the

[5] "Die johanneische Gemeinde und ihre Geisterfahrung," *Die Kirche des
Anfangs*, ed. R. Schnackenburg, J. Ernst, and J. Wanke (Freiburg: Herder,
1978) 286.

ascetic form of spiritual growth, it is clear that he does not believe the full grace of baptism is exploited in the "first baptism," but that it calls for a progression, a journey into the
unlimited space of the Spirit. Several consequences follow from
this fact: (1) The rhythm of spiritual growth may differ from
person to person; (2) it may at times be dramatic, at other times
slow and hardly perceptible; (3) for one already under the influence of the Holy Spirit a "new departure" may happen at
any time, and experience shows that for one baptized in infancy, being prayed over for the release of the Holy Spirit is
often just such an occasion; (4) a periodic renewal of the original grace of the Holy Spirit is certainly possible (a model for
this is the "second Pentecost" in Acts 4:23-31); (5) the Spirit can
come to visibility in a charism at a later time in answer to
"seeking prayer" (1 Cor 14:1).

It does not follow from this that the Christian life is a a progress from peak experience to peak experience or is dominated
by unusual experiences. On the contrary, life is lived mostly in
the valleys. Often in the desert. Even such an outstanding man
of the Spirit as Isaiah, whose prophetic ministry spanned more
than forty years under three different kings, may have lived his
entire life off the single inaugural vision.[6]

To accept and welcome religious experience within the rites of
initiation, or in relation to them, is one thing; the passion for
spiritual elevations is another. The pursuit of religious experience is the shortest path to illusion. Feelings and sentiments
always need careful discernment.

6. The Syrians and the "More" of Jesus

Philoxenus has a monastic imperialism which defines the Christian life through the optic of absolute poverty, the spiritual athlete alone in the desert. In this perspective married or single life
lived in the world cannot attain perfection because the world itself is an obstacle. Those married and single may be God's children, and may attain salvation, but perfection will evade them.
No one will be surprised that much of Philoxenus' teaching on the
two baptisms is found in Discourse 9, on the topic of poverty.

[6] See S. Terrien, The Elusive Presence (New York: Harper & Row, 1978)
250.

Our criticism of Philoxenus and the other Syrians should not make us insensitive to the problem they were facing, namely, the reconciliation, on the one hand, of the universal call to great holiness ("You must be perfect as your heavenly Father is perfect," Matt 5:48), and, on the other hand, the words of Jesus to the rich young man which imply a life-style apparently not elsewhere expected of every disciple ("If you would be perfect, go, sell what you possess and give to the poor, and you will have treasure in heaven; and come, follow me," Matt 19:21). Jesus here uses the category of "more."

Vatican II was still struggling to reconcile the universal call with the "more." It stated that Jesus directed his challenge to be perfect as the Father is perfect to all, "regardless of their situation."[7] The council expanded: "All the faithful of Christ, whatever their condition or rank, are called to the fullness of the Christian life and the perfection of charity."[8] And further: "There is one holiness cultivated by all who are led by the Spirit of God."[9] The married and single are called to the same high holiness as priests and religious.

Yet the council felt compelled to honor Jesus' category of "more" used when addressing the rich young man. Those who today hear these words of Jesus as addressed to them and respond with a "yes," do so in order "to draw *more* abundant fruit" from their baptism; they "consecrate themselves *more* closely to the service of God. . . . This consecration will be the *more* perfect in as much as by *firmer* and *more* stable bonds Christ is *more clearly* seen to be united to his bride the church by an indissoluble bond."[10]

The tension between the two gospel perspectives with which the Syrians struggled still remains after Vatican II. One would still quarrel with Philoxenus' solution, but we honor his dilemma. We should also esteem the particular insight of the Syrians, that is, persons baptized in infancy may actualize the

---

[7] ". . . cuiuscumque conditionis praedicavit." *Constitution on the Church* 40; Tanner, 2:880.

[8] ". . . omnes christifideles cuiuscumque status vel ordinis ad vitae christianae plenitudinem et caritatis perfectionem vocari." Ibid.

[9] *Constitution on the Church* 41; Tanner, 2:881.

[10] Ibid., 44; Tanner, 2:885. Emphasis added.

full richness of baptismal grace only years later. The position in which the Syrians found themselves is the same as ours, a population baptized in infancy. The Syrians can be helpful in understanding how baptism in the Holy Spirit is integral to Christian initiation.

Beyond honoring Philoxenus' dilemma, we value the truth which he and the other Syrians spoke. The Oxford scholar Sebastian Brock contends that "the Syriac fathers found no difficulty in identifying Christian baptism with 'baptism in the Holy Spirit and in fire' . . . baptism is also a charismatic event."[11] The Syriac fathers "are well aware that the pentecostal effects of baptism do not necessarily manifest themselves at baptism itself, but may be delayed until later: the 'pledge of the Spirit,' the potential, however, is already present as a result of baptism. . . . What Philoxenus is saying here is something of great value. He is looking at the relationship between the personal experience of Pentecost, of the coming of the Holy Spirit upon an individual, and the actual rite of baptism, in a context where, because of the practice of infant baptism, the two events may be separated by many years of time. Philoxenus' point is that the rite itself confers the gift of the Spirit, but that, since giving also involves receiving, a conscious act of the will, accepting the gift is required on the part of the recipient, if he is to experience properly the benefits that result from the gift. This acceptance involves the self-emptying that Christ himself underwent (Phil 2:7): only once the ego has been stripped away can the gift of the Spirt be fully experienced. The 'two baptisms' are thus but two aspects of the one sacrament, the first seen from the point of view of the Giver, the second, from that of the receiver."[12]

Earlier, Origen had linked the ascetic self-emptying with baptism, to the point that without this moral discipline, one has not been properly baptized.

Baptism is not a one time event. Rather, Brock concludes, "baptism is seen as just the beginning which opens up all sorts

---

[11] *The Holy Spirit in the Syrian Baptismal Tradition,* 134.
[12] Ibid., 137–39.

of new possibilities, provided the baptized person responds with openness to the presence of the indwelling Spirit."[13]

7. Breakup of the Link between Christian Initiation and the Charisms

We are not writing a history of how charisms were severed from initiation; but we do want to make a few comments. The reasons for that severance are multiple. Among them was the acceptance of infant baptism as a norm. In a church which has infant baptism, there is more chance of the charism imparted at baptism going unused. Another reason was the growth of Montanism. The general acceptability of the charisms in the life of the early church was one of the reasons why Montanism spread so easily. Among its adherents were some of the most serious-minded persons. But the excesses, either real or implied, brought disrepute on the Montanists. By proximity, the prophetic charisms themselves became suspect, as they came to be identified by many with Montanism. Thus they could no longer be promoted within the context of Christian initiation, as they had been in the Catholic Tertullian, Origen, Hilary, Basil, Gregory Nazianzus, and Cyril, or as a reappropriation of initiation in Philoxenus, John of Apamea, Theodoret, Severus, and Joseph Hazzaya.

But the tradition in which the charisms were part of Christian initiation left some footprints. For Chrysostom the prophetic charisms were no longer a part of the living experience of the church. In this respect Chrysostom recognized that the church of his day was a church of tokens. In fact, Chrysostom still recognized that in the apostolic age the paradigm for Christian initiation included the manifestation of the charisms. Such an admission on the part of Chrysostom involved him in strategic retreats and strained adjustments. In order to keep the apostolic substance he felt compelled to see the charisms actualized in the church of his time. To accomplish this he internalized and spiritualized some of the charisms. Indeed, he gave them a new morphology. Of the gift of tongues with unutterable groanings, Chrysostom said that this is what the deacon does in the liturgy when he intercedes for the people. If one gives alms, one is ex-

[13] Brock, *Spirituality in the Syriac Tradition*, 74, 774.

ercising the gift of healing. If one marches oneself not to theaters but to church, one has cured the lame. Paul's doctrine is hardly recognizable here.

Theodoret and Severus also record the apostolic paradigm. Both of them believe numerous charisms were imparted at initiation in the age of the apostles. Is it an historical accident that the tradition which gave the most prominent place to the baptism of Jesus (even as an article of the creed in Syrian liturgies) was the tradition retaining the charisms within the rites of initiation the longest?

The Syrian monastic tradition clung to the charisms as founded in initiation, but it was as a rock in the midst of a torrent that was flowing past it. Even in that tradition the charisms were actualized only in a few, as a sign of holiness. The greater the charism, the greater the holiness. The stage was set for the prevailing assumption of later centuries that the prophetic charisms were not given to the entire church, but were extraordinary gifts marking the sanctity of individuals.

Our reference to the decline of the prophetic charisms has been chiefly from the liturgical point of view, i.e., how the charisms gradually disappeared from the catechesis and practice of Christian initiation. But there were other factors in this decline, and among them it is common to list as chief the closure of the canon, leading to a dispensationalist view,[14] the solidification of hierarchical power,[15] or, as D. E. Aune has expressed it, "the earlier role of the prophets as articulators of the norms, values, and decisions of the invisible head of the church was taken over by the visible figures of the teacher, preacher, theologian, and church leader."[16] The last stage of the redaction of the *Didache* (15:1-2) indicates that the bishops and the deacons perform the task of the prophets.[17]

[14] This was Harnack's view, which, according to J. L. Ash ["The Decline of Ecstatic Prophecy in the Early Church," *TS* 37 (1976) 227-28] is echoed in other studies by J. N. D. Kelly, A. Ehrhardt, H. Chadwick, and J. Pelikan.

[15] G. Friedrich, *TDNT* 6:828-61; E. Käsemann, "An Apologia for Primitive Christian Eschatology" in *Essays on New Testament Themes* (London: SCM, 1964) 188; J. L. Ash, "The Decline of Ecstatic Prophecy," 227-52.

[16] Aune, *Prophecy*, 338.

[17] "Appoint for yourselves, then, bishops and deacons who are worthy of the Lord—men who are unassuming and not greedy, who are honest

This development does not, of course, exclude the possibility, even the likelihood, that those chosen and appointed to these offices were those in whom prophetic gifts had in some way been manifested. This can be detected already in New Testament times in the transition from the charism to the more institutionalized office of prophet. But it becomes clear in Ignatius of Antioch, a bishop who considered himself to have the gift of prophecy and actually exercised it in a dispute with a troublesome element of the church in Philadelphia.[18] Polycarp and Melito of Sardis, both respected bishops, were considered to have been prophets.[19]

Thus it would be an over-simplification of the process to say that bishops were struggling to assert their power over the manifestation of prophecy in the community. Such was not the case in the earlier period at least. Rather, as other authors have pointed out, the primary cause of the decline of the prophetic gifts was the struggle for orthodoxy and only consequentially to the clarification of hierarchical power in order to deal with false prophecy and teaching.[20] In the late fourth century the *AC* conforms charisms to set institutional patterns and exalts, almost

and have been proved. For they also are performing for you the task of the prophets and teachers." *Didache* 15:1. Cf. R. A. Kraft, *The Apostolic Fathers: The Didache and Barnabas* (New York: T. Nelson & Sons, 1965) 64, 67, 1974; J. P. Audet, *La Didache. Instructions des apôtres* (Paris: Gabalda, 1958) 200–206.

[18] *Phd.* 7:1-2. W. R. Schoedel [*Ignatius of Antioch: A Commentary on the Letters of Ignatius of Antioch* (Philadelphia: Fortress, 1985) 195] calls him "the charismatic bishop." Although Ignatius in the passage cited uses the gift of prophecy to urge submission to the "bishops and the presbytery and the deacons," it does not follow that Ignatius was in conflict with the prophetic office as such but only with such members of the community as were proclaiming an interpretation of the Old Testament at variance with his own (Schoedel, 205). The fact, however, that Ignatius appeals to his prophetic utterance rather than merely to his authority as bishop indicates the high regard prophecy still retained at the beginning of the second century. While in Ignatius' mind authentic prophecy supports the unity of the church founded in the bishop, there is still the commonly shared conviction that speech directly inspired by the Holy Spirit has a divine authority.

[19] Ash, "The Decline of Ecstatic Prophecy," 227–52, esp. 234–35.

[20] von Campenhausen, *Ecclesiastical Authority and Spiritual Power*, 178–212; D. Hill, *New Testament Prophecy*, 191.

divinizes, the role of the bishop. The *AC* removes the tension between institution and charism.

A final word should be said about tongues in the post-biblical literature. Two elements are noticeable. On the one hand, while there continues to be an emphasis on the prophetic gifts, tongues is rarely mentioned among them. And on the other hand, when tongues *is* mentioned, the authors seem to understand the gift as the actual speaking of foreign languages (e.g. Chrysostom). This understanding of tongues seems to have derived from a literal reading of Luke's Pentecost account in Acts 2; but it misunderstands Paul's treatment of the gift as non-rational or pre-conceptual prayer or speech.[21] More research needs to be done in this area, but a plausible hypothesis is that since tongues as foreign languages was rarely if ever experienced by the post-biblical writers, they simply avoided mentioning it. But as "pre-conceptual" prayer or speech it survived in what Augustine describes as *jubilation*:

"Words cannot express the things that are sung by the heart. Take the case of people singing while harvesting in the fields or in the vineyards or when any other strenuous work is in progress. Although they begin by giving expression to their happiness in sung words, yet shortly there is a change. As if so happy that words can no longer express what they feel, they discard the restricting syllables. They burst into a simple sound of joy, of jubilation. Such a cry of joy is a sound signifying that the heart is bringing to birth what it cannot utter in words. Now who is more worthy of such a cry of jubilation than God himself, whom all words fail to describe? If words will not serve, and yet you must not remain silent, what else can you do but cry out for joy? Your heart must rejoice beyond words, soaring into an immensity of gladness, unrestrained by syllabic bonds."[22]

8. History, Geography, and Languages of the Spirit

Looking at the exegesis of the New Testament texts we have presented, one might object that their interpretation is disputed.

[21] George T. Montague, "Baptism in the Spirit and Speaking in Tongues: A Biblical Appraisal," *Theology Digest* 21 (1973) 342–60.
[22] Ps. 32, *Sermo*, 1, 7–8; CCL 38, 253–54.

We think, on the contrary, that the exegesis is well-founded.
But if there remains dispute about the meaning of some of the
texts, there can be no dispute about Cyril. In speaking of the
Pentecost experience in the context of Christian initiation, which
included the charisms, he three times dwells on the fullness of
this baptism. He has a broad view of the charisms. For him the
charisms belong to the integrity of initiation. Creative in matters
liturgical but not in theological reflection, Cyril himself claims
that he is setting forth nothing innovative but only what is
found in the scriptures. He appeals to the history of the Spirit
from Moses to Pentecost and beyond. He appeals to geography
by citing the universal experience of believers everywhere in the
Roman Empire.

Long before Cyril the prophetic charisms were an undoubted
fact of Christian life, as seen in Ignatius of Antioch, the *Didache*,
Pastor Hermas, Apollinarius, Eusebius, and especially Irenaeus.[23]
However, our concern here is not the charisms in general but
the prophetic charisms in relation to rites of initiation. By the
fourth century the prophetic charisms were in decline. Nonetheless, with Cyril stand witnesses from Tertullian to Joseph
Hazzaya who testify that initiation is the primary locus of imparting the charisms.

In varying degrees these ancient Christian writers also witness
to the expectation that the charisms will manifest themselves in
the initiatory rites, or, for those who were baptized as infants,
that the charisms will be manifest at a later date through a
process of actualizing baptism. They testify to the historical
span, geographical extension, and linguistic differentiation of
theologies, liturgies, and cultures, which place the charisms
within, or in reference to, initiation: Tertullian in North Africa
at Carthage (c. 198),[24] Hilary in Gaul at Poitiers (c. 350), Cyril in
Palestine at Jerusalem (c. 364); Basil in Capadocia at Caesarea
(366 and 374–75); Gregory Nazianzus at Constantinople (380); in
Syria there is Philoxenus at Mabbug (end of the fifth and beginning of the sixth century), John the Solitary at Apamea (430–50);

[23] J. R. McRay, "*Charismata* in the Second Century," *Studia Patristica* 13,
part 1 (1975) 232–37.
[24] The dates given here refer to the approximate dates of the relevant
texts.

Theodoret at Cyrrhus (c. 444); and Joseph Hazzaya (eighth century) at Qardu (in contemporary Iraq). John Chrysostom (c. 392 –93) and Severus of Antioch (end of the fifth and beginning of the sixth centuries) recall the apostolic paradigm, that is, that the prophetic charisms are imparted during initiation. Almost the whole of the Mediterranean seaboard bears witness, representing Latin, Greek, and Syriac cultures.

The witnesses are not minor personalities. Tertullian, quite apart from his later association with Montanism, is perhaps the greatest theologian of the West, Augustine excepted. Origen is a towering genius, one of the great thinkers in the whole history of the church. Hilary, Cyril, Chrysostom, Basil, and Gregory are all Doctors of the Church, a title given to those who have a weightier role in identifying the faith and experience of the church. Philoxenus is a major figure in the Syrian church.

9. If Integral, Then Normative

Our reading of the biblical texts and of the witness of the ancient Christian authors has led us to the conviction that what we commonly call the baptism in the Holy Spirit is integral to Christian initiation, to those sacraments (baptism, confirmation, and eucharist) which are constitutive of the church. Without suggesting that were tongues to cease the Christian community would be unchurched, we believe with Apollinarius that the prophetic gifts must continue until the final coming. In some way the charisms, including the prophetic ones, structure the church. If the church is built upon the apostles and the prophets (Eph 2:20), the charisms are in some way essential. One cannot suppose that to suppress, denigrate or "abolish" the charisms would leave the church unchanged. They belong to the baptism in the Spirit, which is integral to Christian initiation.

This is not a sectarian view. Edward Schillebeeckx frequently returns to the baptism in the Spirit in relation to what constitutes the church, to what church does.[25] The baptism in the Spirit for him was accompanied by manifestation of the pro-

[25] Schillebeeckx, *The Church with a Human Face* (New York: Crossroads, 1987) 34, 35, 122, 123.

phetic gifts.[26] The spread of the church and formation of new Christian communities were based on the baptism in the Holy Spirit and the charisms there manifested. "All who received Christian baptism formed one prophetic, pneumatic people of God."[27] Later, when the ministry in the church began to have a more structured and hierarchical form, the baptism in the Holy Spirit remained "the matrix of ministry."[28] In Schillebeeckx's usage, the baptism in the Holy Spirit is another name for Christian initiation. Though linked to initiation the modalities of the charisms may differ. Rahner and Vorgrimler state: "The forms taken by charismata . . . cannot be foreseen, precisely because they belong by their very nature to the saving history of the Church; and therefore they must be constantly rediscovered and accepted."[29]

The baptism in the Holy Spirit with its imparting of the charisms, including the prophetic, is normative. This raises a further question: normative for each individual, or normative for the community?

In some streams of Classical Pentecostalism, tongues is "the initial evidence" that one has received the baptism in the Holy Spirit.[30] In this view the normative character of the baptism in the Holy Spirit is tied to the individual believer. If one has not spoken in tongues, one has not received the baptism in the Holy Spirit.

We read the New Testament and post-biblical evidence differently. To us it seems clear that the biblical evidence gives a privileged place to the prophetic charisms. The patristic evidence continues to give a place of privilege to these charisms (prophecy, word of wisdom, word of knowledge, healings). We interpret the evidence to mean that the baptism in the Holy Spirit

---

[26] Ibid., 37, 73, 83, 122.

[27] Ibid., 36.

[28] Ibid., 120.

[29] *Dictionary of Theology*, 2nd edition (New York: Crossroads, 1981) 64.

[30] W. J. Hollenweger, *The Pentecostals: The Charismatic Movement in the Churches* (Minneapolis: Augsburg, 1972) 33, 33; 330–347; B. C. Aker, "Initial Evidence, A Biblical Perspective," *Dictionary of Pentecostal and Charismatic Movements*, eds. S. M. Burgess, G. B. McGee, P. Alexander (Grand Rapids: Zondervan, 1988) 455–59; G. B. McGee, *Initial Evidence* (Peabody: Hendrickson, 1991).

with the prophetic gifts is normative for the local community. This means that in the normal, healthy, well-operating community, one would expect to find the larger spectrum of the charisms, because they belong to the equipment of the community for attainment of its goals. Indeed, the charisms structure the community.[31] The church is a web of mutual supporting ministries, some prophetic (tongues, prophecy, word of wisdom, word of knowledge, healings), some non-prophetic (helpers and administrators, 1 Cor 12:28). Not every member of the communion has to have a prophetic charism, tongues for instance. However, because of the privileged place tongues has in the biblical evidence, and because of its humble rank in the list of charisms, one would not be surprised to find many persons in the community with it. Some who have been fully initiated have the service charisms, but they belong to the community where the larger spectrum of the charisms, including the prophetic, are operative. That they have been fully baptized in the Spirit must not be held in doubt. While all are encouraged to aspire to the prophetic gifts (1 Cor 14:1), normativity is tied directly and immediately to the community, not to the individual.

If the baptism in the Holy Spirit is integral to Christian initiation, to the constitutive sacraments, then it belongs not to private piety but to public liturgy, to the official worship of the church. Therefore the baptism in the Spirit is not special grace for some but common grace for all.

Though their importance needs to be stressed in an age of neglect, the charisms were never meant to claim the center of attention. Tertullian, Hilary, and Cyril would at least have thought it most strange to seek the baptism in the Spirit merely in order to receive a charism. That would indicate that the seeker has not understood the prebaptismal instructions. The rites of initiation are the introduction into the body of Christ, the sacraments by which one has communion in the mysteries of Christ's death and resurrection, thus becoming a part of a worshipping, evangelizing community. The charisms are empowerments which equip one in a church which is wholly

[31] G. Hansenhüttl, *Charisma: Ordnungsprinzip der Kirche* (Freiburg: Herder, 1969) 235–239; 354–359.

ministerial, a church which is a web of mutually supporting ministries. Though given to individuals, they are primarily enrichments for the church and the world.

To insist on the charisms is not to suggest, therefore, that they dominate Christian consciousness. They need not be front, center, and noisy. The operative word is "normal." A church preoccupied with charisms would have small claim to be embodying the norm. The charisms are rather a premise to the day-to-day life of the normal healthy communion.

When one insists on the whole spectrum of charisms as real possibilities for the life of the church, is one thereby dispensing with the need for institutional forms? In the rather extensive literature on charism and institution it has become a dictum that institution without charism is death, while charism without institution is chaos. If the church were to attempt to live solely off the charismatic, it would be delivered to sectarian enthusiasm and fragmentation. Charisms and institution, when kept in mutuality, reciprocally discipline and support one another. Even the New Testament book most explicit about the prophetic charisms, the Acts of the Apostles, quite clearly emphasizes that all charismatic ministry must be done in communion with the Twelve and the mother community of Jerusalem.[32]

If the baptism in the Spirit is integral to Christian initiation, it is also integral to the paradigm for social transformation. Initiation equips one to do what Jesus did: to preach the good news to the poor, to proclaim liberty to the captives, to restore sight to the blind, to let the oppressed go free (Luke 4:18). This program demands liberation and justice for the poor, dignity and equality for women, a living wage for those who labor, sharing of talents and resources of wealthy nations with developing countries. The whole vast program for social justice and social transformation finds its source where the word of God is proclaimed, communion in the mysteries of Christ is celebrated, and the Spirit and the charisms are imparted, that is, in Christian initiation. The demand of initiation is integral renewal, integral conversion, in which the interior transformation is made visible outwardly in social patterns and institutions. There must

---

[32] *See* our comments above on Philip's evangelization of Samaria.

be no privatized, overspiritualized, foreshortened, truncated vision of what God wants for the church and world. A purely interior renewal is too timid for the God of Pentecost.

If the baptism in the Spirit belongs to those sacraments which
are constitutive of the deepest nature of the church, if the baptism in the Spirit belongs to public liturgy, if it belongs to initiation as the matrix of all ministries to the church and world,
then the baptism in the Spirit is normative.

10. *The Baptism in the Holy Spirit and the Charismatic Renewal*

Undoubtedly the contemporary interest in the topic of this book
has been aroused by the phenomenon of the charismatic movement in the Christian churches, and this in turn owes a debt to
Classical Pentecostalism.

Pope Paul VI called the charismatic renewal "a chance for the
church and the world." Pope John Paul II described the charismatic renewal as "a bold statement of what the Spirit is saying
to the churches." The respected Catholic theologian Yves Congar has written that the charismatic renewal "is a grace that
God has given to the times we are living in."[33] These judg-
ments are confirmed by the admirable fruits of the baptism in
the Holy Spirit observable in transformed lives, a new hunger
for the word of God, a new love of prayer, a new generosity in
the service of others, a rediscovery of Christian community,
and evangelism.

Within some groups in the movement, of course, problem
areas have at times been identified: fundamentalism, over-
control, pietism which fosters pure interiority without social
awareness, the pursuit of the unusual. But the discrepancy between good fruits and weaknesses is not the sole preserve of
the charismatic renewal. It is shared by all renewal movements,
indeed by all who hear the word of God and have communion
in the mysteries of Christ.

This book has not been about the charismatic renewal. It is
about the baptism in the Holy Spirit. If that distinction is not
kept in mind then a false equation emerges. When a crude
identification is made between the baptism in the Spirit and the

---

[33] Congar, *I Believe in the Holy Spirit*, 2:158.

charismatic renewal, then the baptism in the Spirit is too easily identified with particular forms of community (prayer groups, covenant communities) or with a particular manner of praying or with a special way of prophesying. The divine reality and the mysteries in which one is given communion through the baptism in the Holy Spirit can be brought to expression in many different forms, some undoubtedly still to evolve. If one embraces the baptism in the Holy Spirit, one need not embrace the charismatic renewal. The two are separable.

The purpose of our study has not been to defend or champion the charismatic renewal. Rather, the charismatic renewal has been the occasion for our researching our roots to see what the baptism in the Holy Spirit meant to the early church. What we have found there indeed presents, we believe, a major challenge to the church today. The energizing power of the Holy Spirit, manifesting itself in a variety of charisms, is not religious fluff. Nor is it—as viewed by many today—an optional spirituality in the church such as, among Catholics, the devotion to the Sacred Heart or the stations of the cross. The baptism in the Holy Spirit does not belong to private piety, but, as we have demonstrated, to the public official liturgy of the church. It is the spirituality of the church. By that account it is not—let it be said clearly—the property of the charismatic renewal. The unique gift which the charismatic renewal brings to the church is the awareness of the baptism in the Holy Spirit. This is all the more reason why the baptism in the Holy Spirit is not to be identified with any group or movement. Because it belongs to the church as an integral element of Christian initiation, it must be taken with ultimate seriousness. Indeed, the baptism in the Spirit is normative.

11. *Is the Baptism in the Holy Spirit a Sacramental Grace or a Grace of Prayer?*

It should be obvious from our study that the New Testament church and the major streams of the church's tradition for the first four centuries considered Christian initiation itself to be the "baptism in the Holy Spirit," with all that meant of conferring the fullness of the Spirit, including charisms. In attempting to correlate the contemporary experience of the "baptism in the

Spirit" with traditional Catholic categories, some have proposed that it is an awakening or a coming into consciousness of the original baptismal gift and therefore essentially a sacramental grace. Others have simply associated it with a gift of prayer. Some have used the categories of the missions or sendings of the divine persons as expounded by Thomas Aquinas, without any sacramental reference.[34]

The Thomistic view of a new sending of the Holy Spirit cannot be impugned theologically. However, once the relation of charism to initiation disappeared from the tradition, Aquinas would quite naturally look to the theology of the mission of the Spirit to explain the presence of the prophets in the church. Had Aquinas known of the tradition of the first centuries, going back a thousand years to Tertullian and Origen, and eight hundred seventy-five years to Hilary, Cyril, and John Chrysostom, and from five to eight hundred years to the Syrians, he would not have set aside without comment a theological position of such antiquity proposed by persons of such stature. He would have been even less inclined to discard, without comment, a theological position representative of the geographical areas of Carthage in North Africa, Alexandria in Egypt, Poitiers in Gaul, Jerusalem in Palestine, and Antioch, Apamea, Mabbug, and Cyrrhus in Syria, representing Latin, Greek, and Syriac cultures.

The advantage of the sacramental view is the clarity with which the prophetic charisms, bestowed in Christian initiation, belong to those constitutive, church making sacraments. Prophecy and the other prophetic charisms are much less likely to be seen as appendages or decorations. Rather, they belong in some structural way. Further, if the baptism in the Spirit, including the prophetic gifts, is integral to Christian initiation, then, as we have said, the baptism in the Spirit no longer belongs to private piety but to public liturgy. Then the baptism in the Spirit is normative. The theology of missions as applied to charisms does not seem to carry these imperatives.

---

[34] Thomas Aquinas, *Summa Theologiae* I, 43, 6, ad 2um. *See* F. A. Sullivan, *Charisms and Charismatic Renewal* (Ann Arbor: Servant Books, 1982) 70–75; Sullivan, "The Catholic Charismatic Renewal," *Dictionary of Pentecostal and Charismatic Movements,*" 118, 119.

The sacramental approach draws on the tradition of Augustine in the West and, in the East, on the Syrian ascetic tradition, and especially on Symeon the New Theologian. Both Augustine and Symeon wrote of the reactualizing of a previous sacramental grace. They would have support in 2 Timothy 1:6: "I remind you to rekindle the gift of God that is within you through the laying on of my hands."

The imparting of the charisms within Christian initiation constitutes a pattern. The Spirit is not, however, imprisoned in the divinely willed sacraments. The Spirit is free to bestow graces and charisms as the Spirit wills. Historically, it is our suspicion that the reason many Catholics looked for a sacramental explanation was their sense that the new experience was a discovery of a heritage somehow connected with their baptism. Some of the Catholics involved from the earliest hours of the renewal were theologians and liturgists aware of the church's rich biblical and liturgical tradition. The choice of this theological route was doubtless reinforced by the fact that the term "*baptism* in the Holy Spirit" was already widely used in the Pentecostal/charismatic circles at the very beginning of the Catholic charismatic renewal. The terminology could easily suggest that there is a second baptism, and therefore a second sacrament whose effect is to convey the Spirit which was not conveyed in water–baptism. Catholics wanted to avoid this conclusion and yet do justice both to the newness of the grace received and to the full meaning of their original baptism. John of Apamea and Philoxenus do write of two "baptisms," but the second is only a later appropriation of the first, and therefore is only a new face of infant baptism. Both authors are explicit in their doctrine of two "baptisms," but the tradition is common to the Syrians.

The practical consequences which we suggest as a result of this study have nothing to do with changing the practice of the laying on of hands for the gift of the Spirit as is presently done in the charismatic renewal. Nor is this study, or any other, likely to dislodge the term "baptism in the Holy Spirit" or its relationship to the laying on of hands. Whether the release of the Spirit is due to an awakening of sacramental grace or merely the fruit of prayer, the important thing is that it *happen*. The consequences of our study are telling, however, for how the church should regard the baptism of adults, both in preparatory catechesis and in actual celebration of the sacrament. If early church practice, witnessed both by scripture and tradition, is normative, then the baptism in the Holy Spirit with the full expectation of charisms, should be the effect and the expectation of every adult baptism. For a church which has infant baptism, the baptism in the Spirit is a new actualization, a new level of one's awareness and experience, as a responsible person, of what was received at baptism through the sovereign act of Jesus who is the Baptizer.

12. Some Pastoral Orientations

If the neglected element in the tradition of initiation is the Holy Spirit and the charisms, then the most logical pastoral strategy would be to attempt to incorporate the experience of the "baptism in the Holy Spirit" into contemporary church life, particularly in the process of initiation. We do not consider ourselves equipped, however, to give specific pastoral advice on incorporating the full baptismal reality into parish life. The theological principles seem clear, the pastoral application problematic. What we offer here are tentative, rather generic suggestions which need to be tested.

(a) *Equivalence?* When looking for strategies to activate the pneumatic dimension of Christian initiation, a more general question occurs at the beginning: Is the baptism in the Holy Spirit as experienced in the charismatic renewal today equivalent to the baptism in the Holy Spirit as described in the New Testament and the post-biblical tradition we have examined? While we would hesitate to claim an exact equation between the two, if we go by the descriptions used throughout the documents here examined, the number of parallels is impressive. What the church of today appears widely to share with Chrysostom is his assumption that the prophetic charisms are not to be taken seriously as actual possibilities for the church. Yet what the church today seems not to share with Chrysostom is his anxiety that such a situation of tokenism does not in fact correspond to the apostolic paradigm. Without destroying the important and necessary structures of the church, some way needs to be found to exercise the spontaneous charisms. Perhaps the prayer meeting is the solution, though some liturgies might provide place at times for exercising the prophetic and healing charisms. However, no one should assume that the only places for exercising the charisms are the prayer meetings or liturgies. They have place also outside of sacred situations.

(b) *Charisms and "normal" parish life.* Only with great caution and in union with the bishop should a prayer group's exercise of the spontaneous charisms be introduced into the structures of an already existing parish. Obviously parishes can only be led, not forced. For most parishes the best that can be done is the gradual development of awareness of the biblical and historical teaching through preaching, baptismal preparation, Lenten series, the catechumenate, or as part of the Rite of Christian Initiation of Adults. The future forms are then left open. The founding of a new parish might provide an easier occasion for incorporation of the charisms. We know, in fact, that this has been done successfully in a number of cases.

In this connection, however, a caution is appropriate in the other direction. Those outside the charismatic renewal may be inclined to pass over the less rational gifts of tongues and prophecy in favor of the more "manageable" ones. While tongues is not the only sign of receiving the Spirit, and not even all charismatics speak or pray in tongues, those who do testify that the moment of their yielding to tongues was a real breakthrough, a new departure in their Christian life, the door to other charisms, the gate to other levels of life in God. Similarly, the gift of prophecy is not primarily a gift of foretelling the future (it was not even so in the Old Testament), but simply a hearing of the word of God in a meaningful way, as God's light on the present, so that it can be shared for the upbuilding of the community. Like any gift, it can be misused. But, as the adage has it, "abuse does not invalidate use." Long ago, Irenaeus (and Paul before him) said that the fear that prophecy will be misused is no reason to extinguish the gift in the church.

(c) *Awakening the charisms.* Christians who have been baptized (and confirmed) but who have not been aware that the charisms

Where We Were and Where We Are 377

are implicit in their baptismal gift, should be encouraged to discover them. The usual way, after adequate preparation, is through the laying on of hands with a prayer for the release of the Spirit. The Spirit that came upon the disciples at Pentecost came again in response to the prayer of the community (Acts 4:23-31), giving them a new empowering. Though 2 Timothy 1:6-7 refers to the grace of "ordination," it can also serve as a model for "fanning into flame" the dormant gift of the Holy Spirit.

(d) *Confirmation*. In conferences and workshops we have held since the first edition of our work, one question habitually surfaces: What light does our study shed on the sacrament of confirmation and in particular on the present pastoral question about the age of confirmation? There are four points we would like to make:

1) *Baptism and Confirmation*. In the early church there was the closest relationship between the confirming anointing or laying on of hands, sign of the Spirit, and the water-bath (both were given in the same rite in adult baptisms, and this practice has continued today in the Eastern churches, even for infant baptism). That relationship should not be obscured by the catechesis and pastoral practice of the sacrament. The link with baptism should be emphasized. This is important both for continuity with the biblical model and for communion with the Eastern churches.

2) *Role of the Bishop*. The church's concern, manifested already in Acts 8, to understand the gift of the Spirit in terms of *koinonia* or *communio* makes reasonable the church's desire to manifest the mystery of unity by involving the bishop of the local communion at some point in the sacraments of initiation. Traditionally, this has been done at confirmation, following the practice of the early church in which the bishop anointed and/or laid on hands on those newly baptized. The biblical evidence, however, is not compelling that the gift of the Spirit is available *only* through the laying on of apostolic hands. (In current pastoral practice, the norm is that the baptizing minister, whether priest or bishop, should also confirm the adult candidate.)

3) *Pre-confirmation catechesis*. When separated from baptism, confirmation should be prepared by a catechesis that not only

assures an adequate knowledge of the Catholic faith but also awakens the desire and expectation of the transforming power of the Holy Spirit and the reception of the charisms. This transformation moves in the direction of a closer conformity with Christ (2 Cor 3:18), which involves greater holiness and some participation in his ministry through the charisms. The orientation of the sacrament toward ministry to the communion and beyond should be emphasized.

4) *Post-confirmation catechesis.* The major pastoral issue is what to do with the large number of Christians in whom the sacrament of confirmation (and baptism, for that matter), already received, has not taken visible effect. This fuels the argument for making confirmation a rite to be given at the threshold of adulthood. Experience shows, however, that a particular chronological age is no assurance that the effects of the sacrament will be immediately seen. Consequently, if the transforming power of the Holy Spirit has not been evident, some kind of structure needs to be devised to help the "sacramentalized but not evangelized" Christians to appropriate the grace of the sacrament. Obviously, the first strategy is to proclaim the gospel afresh in such a way as to stir up a longing for the full life of the Spirit, sanctifying, relational, and charismatic. Once the desire is there, and the expectation, the prayer of other Christians with the laying on of hands ("baptism in the Holy Spirit") has been shown to be effective and transforming among millions of Christians. Because the sacraments of initiation already signified what is being petitioned here, it is our view that the laying on of hands signifies an awakening of the grace of baptism/confirmation.

(e) *The RCIA and the Liturgical Year.* In the Rite for Christian Initiation of Adults (RCIA) the Roman Catholic church has recovered the catechumenate so important to Christian initiation in the first centuries (see, for instance, Tertullian, Origen, and Cyril), and the fruits are already being felt. The present program envisions a lengthy catechumenate culminating in the reception (and baptism/confirmation) of the adult candidate at the Easter Vigil. Within the rite as it presently stands, there are points where a catechesis on the Holy Spirit and the charisms

Where We Were and Where We Are 379

would be appropriate.[35] However, a more leisurely and appropriate time might well be the season between Easter and Pentecost. After the "high" of the Easter initiation, there is often (according to the testimony of many involved in RCIA ministry), a "let down" time, and the orientation to ministry is often little more than inviting the newly initiated to sign up for some ministry in the parish. This would seem, however, to be the ideal time to begin a series of instructions (the "Life in the Spirit" seminar would be one example) preparing the baptized to appropriate fully their "patrimony" (to use Tertullian's expression) already received in baptism but yet to be fully manifested. This could culminate on the feast of Pentecost by their being prayed over for the full release of the Holy Spirit, of which the paradigm is Acts 2. The readings during this season are particularly appropriate, for they detail the activity of the Holy Spirit in the church after the resurrection with wonderful examples of what the baptized has a right to expect — living in the power of the Holy Spirit with (to borrow from Tertullian again) "the abundance of charisms." The movement toward ministry, then, is not just "signing up for something," but rather a genuine movement of the Holy Spirit, a gift to be sought and discerned by the individual and the community, which impels to the divine activity of building up the church, the communion.

(f) *Charisms and Holiness.* Our tracking of the charisms in relation to personal holiness suggests a corrective of a misunderstanding common in the last centuries. In the New Testament and early post-biblical period, no necessary connection can be observed between the charisms and personal holiness or maturity in the Christian life. On the contrary, although Paul does speak of a wisdom of which only the mature are capable, the charisms seem to be given with a certain abandon, like the sower casting seed at random. So much so that Paul, Matthew, and

[35] For example, #36, where the inquirers are asked to allow their hearts to be "opened by the Holy Spirit"; #75, 2, "following supernatural inspiration" in their deeds; #75, 4, "spreading the gospel and building the church"; #154, 168, 175 in the exorcisms the presider prays they will open themselves to Christ and be given the Holy Spirit.

other writers have to urge the importance of love, righteousness, good works, and other marks of the ethical life upon the charismatically endowed neophytes.

While Origen speaks of baptism as the "principle and source" of the charisms, and probably expected some charisms to be manifested early, he extends Paul's distinction between the immature and the mature in wisdom (1 Cor 2:6; 31-3) to include not only the word of wisdom but also knowledge and faith, thus implying that some charisms, if not all, come to full operation only in those who enter the way of discipline. This goes beyond Paul, who finds the Corinthian community, otherwise immature in many ways, to "abound in every gift," especially in the gifts of word and knowledge (1 Cor 1:4-7). Origen is thinking especially of the intellectual gifts of Scriptural interpretation. Paul would probably agree that the wise *use* of the charisms demands discipline and maturity, but he does not limit the divine liberality to the "perfect" in the way Origen does. With the Syrians, the charisms became monasticized. They are for the ascetics and only for the "perfect" ones.

This ascetical understanding became the dominant one for centuries following. Though not limited to monastics, the charisms were thought to belong to consummate holiness, even becoming a necessary sign for the canonization of saints. This limitation does not correspond to the apostolic model, in which the charisms are given at initiation, and maturity appears to be the goal of a journey which only begins with initiation.

Whichever model is operative, it engenders a corresponding expectation with profound consequences for the church, especially in the area of evangelization. If Christians must wait until they are "perfect" before expecting and exercising the charisms, then they will tend to remain in privatized, domesticated spirituality (individually or collectively). If, on the other hand, Christians expect and seek endowment with the charisms, even the prophetic ones, from the beginning — the apostolic model — then the empowerment for building the church and for evangelizing the world have a much greater chance of engendering the kind of growth we see in the early church — and, we might add, in those churches today that promote the charisms. The question of maturity must not be neglected, but if maturity is made a condition for receiving the charisms, the power of Pentecost will rarely be evident.

(g) *Baptism in the Spirit and Movements.* The imparting of the charisms within initiation constitutes a pattern. The Spirit, however, is free to bestow gifts and charisms as the Spirit wills.

By accepting the baptism in the Holy Spirit, one does not thereby join a movement. The baptism in the Holy Spirit is captive to no camp, whether liberal or conservative. Nor is it identified with any one movement or with one style of prayer, worship, or community. On the contrary, we believe that baptism in the Holy Spirit belongs to the Christian inheritance of all those sacramentally initiated into the church.

General Index

Abbreviations, vii–x

Abdisho of Nisibis, 333

Adam, Karl, 123

Adoptionism, 278–79

Aelia Capitolina, 235–40, 250

Alexandria, significance in early Christian church, 193–94, 205

Ambrose, 138, 156, 269, 270; and anointing, 271; and baptism, 278

Anointing, 26, 48, 74, 98, 98n, 107, 270–71; in Chrysostom, 263, 266, 268, 271, 277; in Cyril, 210, 217, 221; in Hilary, 173, 188–89

Antioch, and Chrysostom, 260–61; in Cyril, 257; in early Christian church, 195–97, 205

Aphrahat, 300–01, 302, 304, 306, 313, 313n, 335, 346

Apocatastasis, 135–36

Apostolic Constitutions (AC), 196, 251, 252–58, 298

Apostolic paradigm, in Chrysostom, 282–87, 291–92, 296

Apostolic Tradition, of Hippolytus, 107, 252–53, 254

Aquinas, Thomas, and baptism in the Spirit, 374

Aramaic language, significance of, 299–300

Armenian Lectionary, Old, 241, 245

Augustine of Hippo, 106, 106n, 165, 241–42; and infant baptism, 94–95; on Tertullian, 106, 107, 129, 131, 132

Aune, D. E., 364; on prophecy, 51n

Baptism, Christian, 19, 20, 21, 22, 24, 27–28, 33, 48, 73, 265–66; in Cyril, 210; gentile-Christian understanding of, 32–33; Jewish-Christian understanding of, 32–33; in Origen, 139–40 in Syrian rites, 263–64, 272; in Philoxenus, 307–10, 312, 316

Baptism in the Spirit, 348–49; and charismatic renewal, 372–73; as experience, 358–59; as integral to Christian initiation, 39,

368-69, 373, 374; as normative, 373; pastoral orientations for, 376-77; and progression of grace, 359-60; as sacramental, 95-97, 374-75

Baptism of Jesus, 263-66, 273, 275-77, 279, 335, 350-51, 353, 354; as baptismal paradigm, 7, 26, 340; as birth event, 60, 65, 280; and charisms, 352; and the church, 21; in Cyril, 210, 215; in Hilary, 173-76; in Luke, 24-25, 24n, 28; and manifestation of the Spirit, 7, 17, 19, 25, 25n, 28; in Mark, 6-7, 6n; as paradigm in rite of initiation, 352-53; and his passion, 10-11; in Philoxenus, 305-06, 310-11

Baptismal homilies of Chrysostom, 261-62, 283-84

Barrett, C. K., 3n, 87

Basil of Caesarea, 225-26, 227, 228, 242, 258, 332, 342, 347-48; on Origen's work, 141, 153

"Born again" event, 69

Brock, Sebastian, 263-64, 265, 289n, 299, 302, 326, 336-38, 362

Brown, S., 28, 35n

Bruner, F. D., 3n, 39

Bultmann, R., 39

Catechetical Lectures (CL) of Cyril, 191-92, 193, 207-08, 219-20, 223, 230, 231, 233, 243, 244, 249, 250, 256, 257, 344

Catechumens, catechumenate, 106-07, 339; in Cyril, 192, 219, 227, 239; in Chrysostom, 262; in Origen, 147

Catholic charismatic renewal, 16n, 94, 98n, 372-73

Charisma, 111, 113, 143; in Chrysostom, 282-85

Charismatic gifts of the Spirit, 51, 71, 73, 74, 76-79, 81, 85, 87, 88-90, 98

Charismatic grace, in Ephesians, 81-82, 90

Charismatic ministry of Jesus, 13, 14, 16, 17, 26, 74

Charisms, 111, 112, 115, 323n, 324, 325; in Apostolic Constitutions, 255-56; in Basil and Gregory Nazianzus, 227; in Cyril, 199-200, 202, 206, 212, 213-15, 217, 222, 224, 249, 250, 369; in Eusebius, 203; in Hilary, 160, 161, 168, 172, 177-81, 185-88, 189, 369; and institution, 370; in Irenaeus, 202-03, 204; in John of Apamea, 328, 335; in 1 Peter, 64-65; in Philoxenus, 336; and rite of initiation, 88-89, 341-43; in Tertullian, 369; in Theodoret of Cyrrhus, 329-31, 335

Christian birth and growth, in Philoxenus, 312, 314, 316

Christian initiation, 7, 14, 24, 28-29, 30, 35, 38, 39, 40, 43, 44, 46-51, 55, 86, 99, 105, 176, 225, 246, 250, 257, 307, 326; in Chrysostom, 263, 270, 277; and gift of the Spirit, 34-35, 350-55; in Hilary, 182-86, 187

Chrysostom, John, 196, 217, 244, 259-98, 321, 325, 329, 331, 338, 342, 377; and anointing, 264, 266-68, 271; and baptism of Jesus, 263-66, 273, 352; baptismal homilies, 261-62, 283-84; and charisms, 363; credibility of his doctrine, 295-98; on death and resurrection of Jesus, 352; use of charisma in homilies, 283-85, 297

Church and charisms, 297

Church as communion, in Chrysostom, 294-95

Classical Pentecostals, xi, xii, 27, 27n, 31, 37, 44, 53, 54, 89

Communion, communion ecclesiology, 104–08, 106n, 114, 121

Communion/community, see *Koinonia*

Confirmation, sacrament of 31, 48, 90, 377

Congar, Yves, on charismatic renewal, 372

Constantine, 236–37, 248, 249

Conversion-initiation, as distinct from baptism in the Spirit, 53

Cornelius event, in Acts, 36–37

Crouzel, H., on source of charisms in Origen, 142–43

Cyprian, 112n, 156; influence on Hilary, 158, 159

Cyril of Jerusalem, 191–251, 262, 268, 270, 275, 341, 342, 343, 347; on anointing, 210, 217–18 280; on baptism of Jesus, 215, 352; on charisms, 206, 213–14, 220, 222, 258, 357, 367; on death and resurrection of Jesus, 340, 341, 352; on *dorea*, 283; and historical understanding of liturgy, 239–40; on Montanism, 344; as pragmatic pastor, 227; on principle of mystagogy, 220–21; on prophecy, 223–25, 258, 293

Damascene, John, and Messalianism, 317–18

de la Potterie, I., on anointing, 48

Death and resurrection of Jesus, as prototype of Christian baptism, 275–76, 277, 278, 340, 353

Didache, 106, 252, 253, 364, 367

Didascalia Apostolorum, 174n–75n, 252

Didymus the Blind, 170, 216, 267; and anointing, 271

Disciples, 29, 37–38, 40, 68–69

Dorea/gift, in Cyril, 200n, 283; in Chrysostom, 283–85, 297

Dove, as image of Spirit, 7

Dunn, J. D. G., 3n, 5n, 9–10n, 11n, 16n, 24n, 27, 27n, 28, 34, 42, 46, 52, 70, 71

Egeria, and liturgical development, 244–46, 247, 248

Encratites, 304

Ephrem, 209, 300–01, 302, 304, 313–14, 317, 326, 327, 346

Epiphanius, 133, 144, 145, 169–70, 224, 227, 232

Ervin, H. M., 43, 53, 54

Eucharist, eucharistic interpretation, 44, 45–46, 75, 94, 100; in Hilary 182, 187

Eucharistic celebration, 107, 110

Eusebius of Caesarea, 158, 160, 163–65, 170–71, 193, 201–03, 236–37, 239, 247, 248; and influence on Cyril, 201–03; on Tertullian, 117

Exodus experience, in Philoxenus, 314–15, 316

Exodus imagery in Paul's letters, 45

Exorcisms, 41, 236–37; role of Spirit in, 8–9, 13, 16–17, 25

Faith to sensation, in Philoxenus, 306–07, 308

Farmer, W. R., 13

Fetus in baptismal imagery of John of Apamea, 328; of Philoxenus, 308–09

Feuillet, A., 7n, 10n, 12n

Fire, image of, 4–5, 15, 23, 26

Graces received in initiation, in Chrysostom, 285, 290

Gregory Nazianzus, 226–27, 228, 258, 332, 342, 347, 348; on Origen, 136

Gregory of Nyssa, 242–43; on Origen, 136–37

Haenchen, E., 34–35n

Hazzaya, Joseph, 310, 333–35, 338, 342–43, 347; on charisms, 336; and work of the Spirit, 334–35

Healing, in Philoxenus, 322; and work of the Spirit, 9, 21, 26

Hilary of Poitiers, 14, 155–90, 342–43, 347; on baptism of Jesus, 340, 352; on charisms, 357; on death and resurrection of Jesus, 352; on Montanism, 344; and Tertullian, 129, 132

Hippolytus of Rome, 107, 118, 252–53, 254, 263; and anointing, 271

Hocken, Peter, 95n–96n

Holy Spirit, as effect of initiation, 37, 51; functions of, 51; in 1 Peter, 59–60; significance in New Testament, 355

Ignatius of Antioch, 28, 224, 365, 365n

Imparting of Spirit at baptism, in Chrysostom, 289, 289n, 290

Infant baptism, 108, 345, 363, 377

Irenaeus, 102, 120, 192, 226; on charisms, 204, 357; and Cyril, 192, 200–01, 202; influence on Hilary, 158, 159; on Tertullian, 120

Jacob of Serugh, 326

Jerome, 133, 301; and Cyril, 243–44; on Hilary of Poitiers, 155, 157–58, 162, 166; on Montanism, 170; on Origen, 134, 144–45; on Tertullian, 117, 127–32

Jerusalem, and early Christendom, 192–95, 205–06; early history of, 234–37, 241–44, 246, 249–50

Jesus as baptizer in the Spirit, 9, 16

John of Apamea, 310, 327–28, 310n, 342, 347; on baptism, 328; on charisms, 357; and fetus imagery, 328; and two-baptism doctrine, 345–46

John the Baptist, 4, 5, 15–16, 19, 23–24, 27, 28, 67, 273–74, 276; in Philoxenus, 315, 316

John Paul II, Pope, and Catholic charismatic renewal, 372

Jordan event, 340, 351, 354

Joy, 60–61

Judgment, 4–5, 16n

Justin Martyr, 102, 109n, 120, 128, 147, 204, 216, 304

Kirby, J. C., 80

Koinonia/communion/community, 40, 73, 74–76, 85, 97, 99–102, 114, 131, 182, 187, 188, 339

Kretschmar, G., 238; on Cyril, 278

Languages in early church, 299–300

Laying on of hands, 30, 33–39, 54, 73, 80, 86, 107, 110, 115, 377; in Chrysostom, 270, 273; in Cyril, 208–09, 217, 258; in Irenaeus, 202–03; in Hilary, 173

Liber Graduum, 322–23, 323n

Liturgical character of 1 Peter, 59–60

Liturgical development, in Cyril, 239–41

Messalianism, 229, 229n, 317–20, 345

Milk and honey, 62

Mohrmann, Christine, on Tertullian, 128, 130

Montanus/Montanism, 116–21, 122, 123, 125, 158, 165, 203–04, 224, 232, 250, 317, 344–45, 363; and Hilary, 167–71, 180

"More," as perfection beyond Jesus' universal call to holiness, 360–61

Mystagogical Catecheses (MC) of Cyril, 191–92, 219–20, 223, 229–30, 231, 244, 250, 255, 256, 257, 344

Neophytes/newly baptized, 108–15, 131, 220
New Prophecy, 116, 117–18, 123, 124, 169, 204, 231; *see* Montanus/Montanism
New understanding of baptism, in Chrysostom, 279–80
Nicaea, Council of, 193, 301, 318

On the Trinity, Hilary's, 156
On Baptism, Tertullian's, 107, 108, 112, 116, 122, 123–25, 128, 131
Origen, 133–54; on baptism, 139–40, 148–49; as catechist, 145–46; on *charisma*, 143; and charisms, 150–51, 160–63, 164; and influence on Hilary, 158, 160, 161–62

Pamphilius, on Origen, 133–34
Pantaenus, 146
Pastoral orientations, for baptism in the Spirit, 376–81
Patricius, in Philoxenus, 313, 313n, 321–26
Pentecost event, 27, 30, 36, 80, 341; in Cyril, 212, 216, 217, 223
Peter the Apostle, 36; as author of 1 Peter, 56–58
Philip's baptism of Ethiopian, 32–34
Philoxenus of Mabbug, 298–338, 342–43, 347, 360–61; on baptism of Jesus, 340, 352; on charisms, 324–26; and fetus imagery, 309–10; on healing, 322; on Messalianism, 319–20; and rite of baptism, 307–08, 362; and two-baptism doctrine, 337–38; and zeal for ascetic movement, 304–05

Prophecy, 18, 29, 30, 39, 40, 72, 73, 74, 79, 87, 88, 98, 120, 357; in *Apostolic Constitutions*, 253–54; in Chrysostom, 287; in Cyril, 220, 223–25, 249; in Eusebius, 203; in Hilary, 168; in Ignatius of Antioch, 365n; in Origen, 152–53
Prophetic charisms of the Spirit, 17, 26, 44, 88–89, 319–20, 324, 345; in Chrysostom, 285–88, 290, 291–93, 296–98; decline of, 363–64, 365, 366, 367

Q tradition, 4–6, 15, 16–17
Quasten, J., 122, 124, 128, 230
Quesnel, M., 3n, 27, 32–34, 38n, 46

Refoulé, R. F., on Tertullian, 122
Regeneration and renewal of the Spirit, 52, 73
Resurrection of Jesus, 50
Rite of Christian Initiation of Adults (RCIA), 90, 377, 379–80
Ritter, A. M., on charisms in Chrysostom, 291, 292
Rufinus, 243

Schillebeeckx, Edward, on baptism in the Spirit, 368–69
Scholarius, George, on Origen, 133–34
Schweizer, E., 3n, 87
Seed, as image for the Word, 61n
Sepulcher, Holy, 236, 237, 238, 240
Severus of Antioch, 331–33, 342, 347; and charisms, 332–33
Silvanus' role in authorship of 1 Peter, 57, 59
Social transformation and Christian initiation, 371
Spirit, and charisms, 357–58; gift of in Cyril, 222–23, 229, 233, 250; history of in Cyril, 211–12;

in Philoxenus, 324–25; in relation to Christ, 355–56

Spirit-baptism, in John, 66–72; in Mark, 6–9, 13, 14; in Matthew, 19–20, 21–22; in Paul's letters, 42–55

Stephenson, A. A., 192n; on gift of Spirit, 222, 234n

Stewart, Columba, on Messalians, 317

Sullivan, Francis, on theology of the baptism in the Spirit, 93, 93n, 94n

Syriac authors, 300–01; dialect, importance of, 300–01, 302; language, 218; tradition, and baptism of Jesus, 265–67, 352

Syrian ascetic movement/monasticism, 304–05

Tatian, 304

Tertullian, 24, 28, 48, 70, 98, 99, 104–32, 156, 176, 188, 199, 274, 341–42, 346, 351n; on charisms, 111–12, 293, 357; imparting of Spirit at baptism, 290; influence on Hilary, 158, 159

Theodore of Mopsuestia, 196, 261, 262, 269, 270, 274, 303, 325, 329, 331; and anointing, 271; on charisms, 293–94

Theodoret of Cyrrhus, 328–31, 336, 342–43, 347; and Messalianism, 317–18

Timothy of Constantinople, and Messalianism, 317–18

Tongues, as charismatic gift, 13, 29, 30, 39, 40, 79, 87, 98, 357; in Chrysostom, 286–87

Tract on the Psalms, Hilary's, 156–57, 160

Two-baptism doctrine, 345–46, 362

Upper Room, 327

Victor, Pope, and Montanism, 118–19

Vööbus, Arthur, 299, 302–03

Water-baptism, 7, 10n, 24, 26–29, 33, 43, 70, 86, 94

Water-bath, 52–53, 107, 110, 280; in Chrysostom, 263, 270, 273, 277; in Cyril, 209

Water of baptism, 62

Winkler, Gabriele, 264–65, 275–76, 279

Word, influence of in 1 Peter, 61, 65

Yarnold, E, 209, 230, 231

Index of Biblical References

Genesis

1:2	7n
2:7	68
6:3, 12	164n
8:8-12	7n

Numbers

11:25, 26	210
11:28	211
11:29	211

Job

9:31	10n
22:11	10n

Psalms

2:7	174, 174n
17:8f	164n
22:6	334
34:8	62
42:7-8	10n
64	160, 164, 187
64:9	181
64:9, 10	182

68	80
68:3	164n
68:18	81
69:2-3, 15	10n
80:10	161
83:3	164n

Sirach

1:26	151

Isaiah

4:4	5
6:6	326
11:1-3	161
11:2	173
27:8	5
29:18-21	16n
33:11	5
35:3-6	16n
42:1-2	16
43:2	10n
44:3	70
61:1	210

61:1f	164n
61:1-2	16n, 185
61:2	161

Jeremiah

| 4:11-12 | 5 |
| 31:33 | 75n |

Ezekiel

| 36:25-26 | 70 |
| 36:27 | 75, 75n |

Joel

| 2:28 | 185, 217 |

Amos

| 7:4 | 4 |

Jonah

| 2:3-6 | 10n |

Micah

| 1:2 | 164n |

Malachi

| 3:1-2 | 6 |
| 3:2, 19 | 4 |

Matthew

1:18, 29	19
1:23	21
3:7-10	15
3:11	4, 19, 20, 326
3:12	4, 15
3:13-15	16
3:15	20n
3:16	19
3:17	21, 174
4:1	20
5:20	21
5:48	361
7:22	18n
7:22-23	17
10:1	18, 21n, 74
10:5-8	74
10:8	18

10:41	17, 18
11:2-6	5, 16
12:15-21	16
12:18	21
12:22-30	16
12:28	16, 19, 74
12:30	19
12:31-32	16
12:32	19
15:32-39	173
16:18	18n
19:14	173
19:21	361
20:22-23	20n
20:23	12
23:34	18
24:11-12	18
28:19	4n, 19, 20, 29, 70
28:20	21

Mark

1:1	9
1:7	6
1:7-8	8
1:8	4
1:9-11	6, 10
1:10	19, 20
1:11	174
1:15	74
1:22	8
1:22-28	8
1:32-34	8
2:10	8
3:11	8, 9
3:14	9n, 13
3:14-15	9
3:22-30	8
3:29	13
4:1-34	61n
4:8	186
5:1-20	8
5:7	9
6:45–8:26	25
7:24-30	8
8:11	8
8:31	11

8:32-33	8-9
8:34	14
9:14-29	8
9:38	9n
9:38-40	19
10:2	8
10:38	11n, 43
10:38-39	7, 10, 14, 353
10:39	11, 12
10:45	11
12:15	8
14:36	10, 12
16:9-19	254
16:9-20	12–13, 73
16:16	13, 29
16:17-18	13

Luke

1:35	272
2:42	74
3:16	4, 20, 23, 187, 274, 326
3:17	4
3:21	24
3:21-22	41
3:22	20, 48, 174, 266
4:1	20
4:1-2	26
4:14	26, 266
4:16-19	185
4:17	210
4:18	48, 161, 174, 352, 371
4:18-19	25, 26
6:13	9n
7:18-23	5, 23
10:12	60
10:21	26, 33n
10:40	64
11:1-13	40
11:11-13	41
11:13	31, 40, 41
11:14-23	41
11:20	74
12:49-50	11n, 26, 353
12:50	43

13:10-17	25
14:1-6	25
17:11-19	25
24:49	25, 29, 30

John

1:32-33	352
1:32-34	66
1:33	4, 68n
3	209
3:5	28, 52, 71, 276, 340, 351
3:5-8	60, 68–71
3:22	67
3:22-26	6n, 70
3:34	69
4:1-2	70
4:2	6n, 67
4:7-15	67
4:10	67, 283, 283n
4:14	181
7:20	67
7:37-39	45, 67
7:39	6n, 67, 69, 181, 353, 354
8:48	67
8:49-53	67
10:20	67
12:31	67
13:27	67
14:12	71
14:16	212
14:26	68
14:28	141, 356
14:30	67
15:9	68
15:26	68
16:7	68
16:11	67
16:12-13	71
16:12-15	74
16:13	89
19:30	11, 67, 353
19:34	353
19:37	69
20:19-23	273

20:21	68
20:22	20, 68, 69
20:22-23	67
20:23	68
Acts	
1:2	34
1:2-5	98
1:4	29
1:5	19, 23, 24, 26, 30, 177, 216
1:8	34, 61, 187
1:15-26	35
2	26, 36, 61, 331, 342, 357
2:1-4	98, 327
2:1-11	40n
2:1-38	40
2:3	23
2:4	31
2:14-18	29
2:22	267, 352
2:22-24	99
2:28	217
2:32, 33	273
2:33	25, 25n, 81, 143
2:37	99
2:37-39	29
2:38	19, 24, 25, 30n, 31, 32, 39, 99, 222, 283, 283n
2:38-39	32
2:41	41n
2:42	35
2:42-44	40
2:44-46	99, 99n
3:21-22	41
4:23-31	31, 41, 360, 377
4:32-33	99
5:32	61
6:2	65
8:8	32n
8:9-19	31–35
8:9-25	35n
8:12	19, 34
8:14-17	31n, 98, 226

8:15-19	32
8:16	19, 24
8:17	40n
8:20	222
8:26-40	32, 33
8:38	41n
8:38-39	40
8:39	35n, 60
9:17	35
9:17-18	33, 37
10:38	10n, 25, 48, 161, 187, 210, 266
10:44	223
10:44-46	40n
10:44-47	98
10:44-48	32, 40, 226
10:44–11:18	36–37
10:45	19
10:46	37
10:47	98, 286
10:48	24, 32
11:15	223
11:16-17	36
11:17	223
11:23-24	33n
12:2	12
13:48	60
13:52	33n, 60
15	118, 132
15:11	36
16:15	40, 41n
16:33	40, 41n
16:34	60
18:8	40, 41n
18:24-28	38
18:25	134
19:1-6	24n
19:1-7	32, 33, 37–39, 39n, 98, 226, 351
19:5	19, 24, 40
19:6	39, 40n, 199
22:16	24, 33, 46
Romans	
1:4	45, 50n
3:2	64n

5:5	81	6:15-20	351
5:15	111, 198, 283, 283n	6:17	50
		7:7	111, 199, 283n
5:16	283	10:1-4	45
5:17	81	10:2	4n
5:20	81	10:4	44
6:1-5	49	10:16	75, 76
6:2	50n	10:16-17	101
6:3	12n, 264, 277	10:17	46
6:3-11	209	12	112, 143, 149, 154, 177, 178, 179, 184, 185, 186, 199, 211, 258, 286, 290, 322, 330
6:4	50n, 52, 264		
6:25	351		
8:9	38, 49, 351		
8:11	351		
8:14-16	359		
8:15	41	12–14	63, 77, 85
8:26	332	12:1-3	72
8:26-27	88	12:1-4	198
11:29	111, 283n	12:3	43
12:2	52	12:4	143, 154
12:3	78n	12:4, 5	149
12:3-8	199	12:4-10	199
12:6	64, 81, 111	12:7	46, 77–78
12:6-8	77, 198, 199	12:7-11	213
12:7	64	12:8	64, 151, 198
12:8	64	12:8-11	78, 78n
14:17	60	12:9	43, 151
15:13	60	12:10	64
15:26	75	12:11	46
		12:12	45
1 Corinthians		12:13	4n, 42, 47 50, 50n, 63, 277, 351
1:1-3	149		
1:4-7	47	12:14	45
1:5-7	77	12:28	78, 82n, 199, 253, 283
1:9	76		
1:13	19	12:31	79, 111
1:15	19	13	63, 79n, 356
2:1	77n	13:13	199
2:4	61	14	78n, 79n, 256, 357
2:8f	164n	14:1	79, 79n, 88, 89, 90, 357, 360
3:3, 4	150		
3:11	4n	14:2, 28	64
3:16	164n	14:14-16	79
4:1-2	63n	14:15	88
6:11	19, 33, 46–47, 60	14:26	79, 83
6:13-17	45	14:32	161

15:16	83
15:44-45	45
15:45	50, 50n, 351
15:53	164n
16:15	65

2 Corinthians

1:5	100
1:11	111, 198, 199
1:19	57
1:21-22	48–49, 266, 351
3:12-18	61
3:18	50n, 52, 53, 89, 359
4:6	52
8:3-5	101
8:4	74
9:13	75
11:8	64
13:13	19, 75
13:14	100

Galatians

3:1-5	47, 61, 358
3:2-5	77
3:4	47
3:5	47
3:27	45
4:6	41, 49n, 359
4:26	164n
5:22	51, 60, 89, 358
6:1	150
6:6	106

Ephesians

1:8	81
1:13	48
1:13-14	80n
2:4-6	80n
2:11-22	80n
2:20	119, 203, 297, 368
4:1-6	80
4:1-16	80, 88
4:5	63, 80
4:7	78n, 81, 82
4:7-16	80, 90

4:8	80
4:8-10	81
4:11	180, 253
4:11-16	82
4:12	65
4:16	63, 79n, 84
4:22-24	80n
4:23-24	52
4:30	80n
5:14	80n
5:26	80n

Philippians

1:5	75, 101
1:9	81
2:1	75, 100
2:7	337, 362
3:10	75, 100

Colossians

1:9	88
2:12	54
3:10	52
3:16	88

1 Thessalonians

1:1	57
1:5	61
1:6	60
1:10	60
3:12	81
4:8	53
5:19-20	77, 89

2 Thessalonians

1:1	57
1:10	77n
2:13	60

1 Timothy

1:18	88
3:15	164n
4:14	94

2 Timothy

| 1:6 | 94, 131, 375 |

1:6-7	378
1:8	77n
4:11	64

Titus

1:7	63n
3:4-7	51
3:5	62, 89, 359
3:5-7	60

Philemon

1-25	88–89
6	75

Hebrews

2:4	61, 64, 77
5:12	64n
6:1-5	53–55
6:2	40

James

1:18	61
5:14-15	88

1 Peter

1:1	56
1:2	60
1:3	60
1:3–4:11	59
1:3-5	60
1:4-5, 13	60
1:5, 7-9	62
1:6-7	60
1:8	60
1:11	61, 88
1:17	60
1:18-19	60
1:23	60
1:23-25	61
2:2	60, 62
2:2-3	88
2:5, 9	62
2:11–4:9	63
2:13-17	57
3:8	63
3:21	60, 62

4:7-9	63
4:8-11	63
4:10	199
4:10-11	88, 199
4:13	60
5:1	63
5:1-5a	65
5:5	63
5:5b	63
5:9	56
5:11	57
5:12	57

2 Peter

1:20	88
3:1	58

1 John

1:1-4	152
1:3	76
1–4	101, 101n
2:2	164n
2:20	48, 266
2:20-27	71
2:27	266
3:24	101, 101n

2 John

10	88

3 John

5–10	88

Jude

8–13	88
20	88

Revelation

2:7	72
2:11	72
2:17	72
2:19	65
2:29	72
3:6	72
3:13	72
3:22	72

19:10	72	22:17	72
21:6-7	72	22:18	88
22:1-2	72	22:18-19	72, 74
22:7	88		

"A careful and significant study . . ., succinct and pastorally suggestive . . . It offers building stones and encouragement to develop an ecclesiology of communion and, ultimately, a Spirit Christology and ecclesiology. . . . If baptism in the Spirit is truly integral to Christian initiation, this conclusion . . . attests that the charismatic is crucial to the survival and growth of the Church and its capacity to engage in transformative service for the sake of the world . . . [The authors] have impressively made their case."

Robert P. Imbelli in *Theological Studies*

" 'Thumbs up' to *Christian Initiation and Baptism in the Holy Spirit*. The book surveys scripture and the first eight centuries for evidence that far from being a private, born-again experience, baptism in the Spirit imparts the charisms of the Spirit to all initiated into the community through the sacraments of initiation."

James B. Dunning, President, North American Forum on the Catechumenate

"A research of exceptional quality." *Esprit et Vie*

"This volume challenges, in one way or another, nearly all the previous treatments of the subject. . . . Pentecostals and Charismatics alike would do well to read and reflect upon these important contributions to the subject, especially in view of the fact that they hold a key to the potential for Christian spiritual health as well as Christian unity."

Cecil M. Robeck, Jr. in *Pneuma: The Journal of the Society for Pentecostal Studies*